Understanding Disability

Ranu Uniyal · Fatima Rizvi
Editors

Understanding Disability

Interdisciplinary Critical Approaches

Springer

Editors
Ranu Uniyal
Department of English and Modern
European Languages
University of Lucknow
Lucknow, Uttar Pradesh, India

Fatima Rizvi
Department of English and Modern
European Languages
University of Lucknow
Lucknow, Uttar Pradesh, India

ISBN 978-981-99-4924-3 ISBN 978-981-99-4925-0 (eBook)
https://doi.org/10.1007/978-981-99-4925-0

This Springer imprint is published by the registered company Springer Nature Singapore Pte Ltd.
The registered company address is: 152 Beach Road, #21-01/04 Gateway East, Singapore 189721, Singapore

Paper in this product is recyclable.

Dedicated to all persons with special needs and all caregivers without whose attentiveness living could become a challenge

Foreword

This collection brings to the Indian academy the plethora of evidence and analysis existing throughout the world of disability as other, suitability for metaphorical story-telling, and the exclusion from spaces physical, emotional, and spiritual. Students under the mentoring and teaching of the disability studies environment will find this offering an invaluable resource for reading, reflection, research, and practice.

At the heart of disability studies is an academic discipline that examines the meaning, nature, and consequences of disability. Disability studies is established as a degree, certification, or at least taught as a course, in colleges and universities around the world. A long-held rationale for those of us that teach disability studies is that the material helps students to see the world from the perspective of those who experience disability rather than from an ableist perspective. Time and again we hear students who focus on disability studies as life changing and eye opening. Students often change majors as they assess their current career path as stemming from ableist traditions in foundation and expected practice. The personal impact of disability studies has been anecdotally well described as providing information and reflection for existential growth and practical action. Disability studies centres the understanding of disability as a political, cultural, and historical experience. It analyses how society teaches us to think about disability and ability, and how those thoughts turn into actions that so-often negatively impact the lives of disabled people. Many scholars identify as a disabled person, and many are non-disabled emerging professionals striving to know the actions of an ally and professional that makes a difference. After spending time studying disability culture, experiencing the disabled person's reality, or unveiling the meaning of their own experience, many of the scholars are ready and driven to change the world. After a longer period of research, disability studies as analytical framework scholars often take up the role and strategies of change agentry and practice.

This current and exhaustive collection of disability studies practice, theory, and research in India strives to expand and provide a foundation for communities of practice and environments of research. Understanding the nature of disability, its impacts, and the perceptions that surround it in our own hearts and minds yields great promise for moving towards a world that "works" for everyone. Indeed, this collection of diverse original writing allows us to look through many lenses in which disability as a concept is examined. It may lead the reader to important questions which are at the heart of the movement across India to create a society in which all people are seen and known for who they are, where difference is valued (normalized), and where all people's gifts are seen, are recognized, and are accepted with gratitude. The West has been, in some ways, mired in paradigms of fixing and eliminating disability and has been able to shake loose some of the most persistent stereotypes.

This text firmly roots issues associated with disability in the practices and traditions of India, allowing for what may be a fresh start in the uniqueness of the Indian experience, combined with the overarching universalities which impact all people in all places.

The divides between the perspectives of disability theory, practice, research, and personal connection are often wide, yet in this book, you will travel from one to the other, able to make connections and find points that touch each other in ways that expand our understanding.

Dr. Naval Pant's description of the unrelenting everyday person's naming of a school at the "*School for Mad Children*" echoes the devastating mindsets and stereotypes documented in the chapter on Social Role Valorization in the Indian context.

Our lens is further deepened by the past and the lookback on the past that was unearthed in Aahuti Dhandhukia's chapter on the treatment of disability in two films.

While Akshata Jaiprakash's paper may call into question whether disability is real, or if instead it resides in the gaze of the perceiver, there is no doubt left when studying the outcomes of the families studied in Terrell and Resnick's study on the very real distresses experienced by people with disability as well as those who love them.

We owe our gratitude to the co-editors for drawing together this collection. Dr. Ranu Uniyal has walked in all these worlds. As a poet, her words have woven a tapestry which feature the human experience—vast joys and wrenching hurts, often bumping up against one another in surprisingly uncomfortable ways.

As an activist, her courage in standing up against injustice and telling the truth when it needs to be told has made its mark within the field of disability within India. As a professor, I can only say she instigates curiosity, incites passion, and serves as a role model for new ways of being and thinking vis a vis oppressed and marginalized people in India.

As a mother of a young man with significant disabilities, she identifies closely with the experiences of difference and disability, and this has shaped her work and her life in ways that can both be seen and felt.

As a celebrated translator of powerful Urdu literature, co-editor Dr. Fatima Rizvi has applied her keen facility in the transitions within languages and literature towards a searching probe into the issues presented by disability within the culture. In fact, that curiosity and questioning is not simply intellectual inquiry but grounded in her friendships and close relationships with people experiencing significant impact of disability within their own lives.

At this very moment, we stand on the threshold of changing attitudes, led by people with lived experiences, and those who walk alongside them. I invite you to explore and discover the many threads that bind this collection and examination of disability together. In order to understand and see the transcendent truths in this body of work, one must use the head, the heart, and the hands. Thinking, feeling, and doing are our ways forward towards a world that does, indeed, work for everyone. Welcome to the challenge.

Thomas J. Neuville, Ph.D.
Professor of Disability Studies
and Educational Foundations
Millersville University
Millersville, PA, USA

Preface

'Disability' as a social phenomenon has emerged as a rapidly growing concept that is gaining widespread critical attention from a wide range of disciplinary backgrounds. The study of disability in India has long been dominated by policy studies. A primary focus of such research is on identifying problems related to disabled people and addressing these concerns through policy measures. Disability policy research has critically assessed disability governance in significant ways and enabled developments that benefit the lives of disabled people. Nevertheless, what remains under-researched within the Indian context is an investigation of the very concept of disability. Disability has, thus far, been treated as a self-evident category. Disability studies as a recently emerging field of academic inquiry has inaugurated research on disability that moves it away from the predominant problem-solution framework. Academic reflection on disability, in the Western context, has begun to shift focus from an individuated understanding of disability as located in a person, to an examination of processes that 'other' individuals ostensibly on the basis of their bodily and cognitive differences. This has required thinking of disability not merely as a problem that has to be solved through treatment or prevention but as a way of being that requires critical approaches of study. Disability studies as a field of academic inquiry is committed to the study of interrogating norms that consistently, yet variously produce body-minds of difference. Such a set of approaches has enabled thinking about the experience of living with disability not as if it were self-evident but as something that is always in the making, at the stage of 'becoming'. Researchers with and without disabilities have engaged with the subjectivity of being disabled and the structures that frame disability and normalcy. Disability studies focuses on the uplift of marginalized identities and emphasises the need of diverse representation in the cultural constructions of the society. Disability studies theorists try to construct cultural poetics by voicing the opinions of the disabled. How, if at all, do these advances benefit academic inquiry of disability in the non-Western contexts? Given that disability theorizing in the Western context is inextricably linked to the historical development of disability as a category within that realm, it becomes necessary to concentrate on conceptualizations of disablement within the Indian context in order to know disablement and our responses to it within specific socio-cultural and historico-political contours. Disability scholars researching the Indian contexts have long felt the need to break away from modes of theorizing that are Western in orientation. The time may have arrived to decolonize the study of disability and direct ourselves to investigations that would enable our understanding of local ways of knowing and going about body-minds of difference. It is time to think about disability not as an isolated category of difference but as one that is inevitably interlinked to differences on the basis of gender, caste, religion, class, sexuality and geography, both political as well as physical.

Human perceptions and critical perspectives are allied forces that may serve to highlight, enhance, and illuminate the living standards of the differently abled across the world. The literary community remains a potent medium for giving voice to a diverse range of critical perspectives that may operate across the usage, interpretation and reception of varied mediums of expression available to us in the contemporary times and bring the notion of a 'disabled body' as close as possible to the mainstream strata of the society. As a social stigma, the inclusion of the 'disabled' is restricted by society. Their contribution in the development of the society is often considered trivial and insignificant. The present critical volume aims at contributing to the knowledge system surrounding the discipline of 'disability studies' that remains an emerging area of study and addresses the issue of marginalization and stigmatization of disabled people. This book investigates disability or corporeal and cognitive differences in the Indian contexts by considering materially embodied experiences of disablement and its literary and cultural representation in narratives of bodily and cognitive difference. It seeks to explore local ways of knowing and talking about bodies/minds/body-minds and read disability's intersections with other categories of marginality or minority. Also within the perspective are ideas related to disability hierarchy in social stratification of different impairment groups, and some political contours of disability. The book seeks to raise and answer questions regarding notions of 'stigma' and 'normalcy', and study responses of disabled individuals in institutions or under specific controlled situations. It seeks to decode the use of diverse media technologies by both the disabled as well as the non-disabled theorists in the field of disability studies; the use of language in relation to disability and the social paradigm's operating across the research areas concerning disability studies.

Lucknow, India

Ranu Uniyal
Fatima Rizvi

Acknowledgements

The editors would like to thank the Indian Disability Studies Collective (IDSC), and PYSSUM (www.pyssum.org), an institute for people with intellectual and developmental disabilities in Lucknow, for co-hosting the inaugural disability conference "Deglobalizing Disability: Texts and Contexts" in October 2019, in collaboration with the Department of English and Modern European Languages, University of Lucknow, Lucknow. Several papers in this volume were presented at this conference. Many thanks are due to all our contributors without whose contributions it would not have been possible to bring out this volume. We have greatly benefited from Prof. Thomas Neuville's valuable comments and are grateful to him for reading the manuscript and writing the Foreword. We would like to express our gratitude to our Vice Chancellor Prof. Alok Kumar Rai for his enthusiasm and support. We would also like to express our especial thanks to Yusuf Ayaz for helping with the copy-editing. Our heartfelt thanks to Springer for accepting our proposal and encouraging us to give a shape to this book.

Contents

Editors and Contributors

About the Editors

Ranu Uniyal is a bilingual poet. She is Professor and Former Head Department of English and Modern European Languages, University of Lucknow. She has written four books of poetry—*Across the Divide* (2006), *December Poems* (2012), *The Day We Went Strawberry Picking In Scarborough* (2018) *and Saeeda Ke Ghar* (Hindi poems 2021). She was a Commonwealth Scholar at the University of Hull, UK. Her areas of interest are women and literature, postcolonial studies, and disability studies. She has published extensively in India and abroad. Her major publications include: *Women and Landscape: The Fiction of Margaret Drabble and Anita Desai* (2000), Women in Indian Writing: From Difference to Diversity (2009), coedited *Raja Rao's Kanthapura* (2007), *Reading Gandhi: Perspectives in the 21st Century* (2022), and *Mahatma Gandhi: Essays on Life and Literature* (2023). She coedited a special issue on South Asian Women's Writing ZAA quarterly of Language, Literature, and Culture, 2018. She also works for people with special needs in Lucknow (PYSSUM.org).

Fatima Rizvi is Professor in the Department of English and Modern European languages, University of Lucknow. Her areas of academic interest include colonial and postcolonial studies, translation studies, and Urdu studies. Her research papers have been published in journals of national and international repute and in anthologies of criticism. She translates Urdu and Hindi. She has published *Beyond the stars and Other Stories* (2021, Women Unlimited), a translation of Qurratulain Hyder's *Sitaron se Aage* (1947). She is a Meenakshi Mukherjee Memorial Prize and Jawad Memorial Prize awardee.

Contributors

Radhika Bali is Senior Research Fellow at the Department of English and Cultural Studies, Panjab University, Chandigarh, India. Her thesis is titled as *The Intersectionality of Disability and Gender: Deconstructing the Representation of the 'Mad Woman' in Select Novels from India.* She aspires to strengthen the fields of disability studies, mad studies, and feminist studies in the ensuing research. She has presented papers at the international conferences.

Arunabha Bose is Assistant Professor of English at Vivekananda College, University of Delhi, New Delhi. Arunabha Bose is Assistant Professor of English at Vivekananda College, University of Delhi. He previously taught at Shyam Lal College (M), University of Delhi till 2015. He has been associated with the UGC Postgraduate e-Pathshala Project since 2014 and has contributed on gender studies. He has lectured and presented papers at various international and national seminars including at Indian Institute of Advanced Studies, Shimla (2017). He has published extensively in international journals and books. His research publications are on Mahasweta Devi, Subaltern History, and Bengali Literature.

Percy Cardozo is a mental health professional with over 25 years of experience in child development, adolescent health, and education. She holds a Master's degree in Psychology and a Bachelor's in Education and works at a non-profit mental health research organization in Goa. With her experience in clinical work, she has provided counselling services to young people with psychosocial and learning problems. Percy believes that educational institutions play an important role in shaping the lives of young people and is passionate about creating nurturing, inclusive, and enabling learning environments. She has worked extensively with educational institutions in the state of Goa and across India and has pioneered and successfully led statewide disability advocacy campaigns for the empowerment of children and families. e-mail: percy.cardozo@sangath.in

Mitu De is Associate Professor, Gurudas College, Kolkata, West Bengal. She has worked for decades to uplift lives of people with autism and those of their families. She has been involved as key member of the leadership of Autism Society West Bengal, promoting inclusive practice and full lives. First introduced to Social Role Valorization in 2016, she has spearheaded the national SRV movement by co-creating the All-India SRV Alliance and has conducted many national-level training events. Her research, many publications, and passion centres on full lives for people with autism have featured SRV implementation as a core foundational strategy and are fuelled by her experience as a parent of a son with autism.

Aahuti D. Dhandhukia is a person with low vision due to albinism. She has been serving as Assistant Professor (English) at Government Engineering College, Bhavnagar, Gujarat, affiliated to Gujarat Technological University, Gujarat. She is perusing her Ph.D. in the area of "Literary Disability Studies" from the Department of English, M. K. Bhavnagar University, Bhavnagar, Gujarat. She obtained her M.A. from SNDT

Women's University, Mumbai. She also holds a Bachelor of Education. She has also served as Translator in Legislative and Parliamentary Affairs Department, Secretariat, Government of Gujarat. She has presented 13 papers in national/international conferences and has 7 publications to her credit. She has successfully completed a Winter School, a certificate course, two MOOC, two eFDP, and a workshop on disability studies. Disability studies, feminism, translation studies, and English language teaching are the areas of her interest.

Sumit Garg is Assistant Professor in English at Punjabi University College, Ghudda (Bathinda), Punjab. He is presently pursuing Ph.D. in the field of Literary Disability Studies from Department of English, Punjabi University, Patiala. He is M.A. in English and has qualified UGC-NET (English). He has published various research papers in UGC-CARE listed journals as well as double-blind peer review journals. e-mail: sumitgarg23@pbi.ac.in

S. Gokul is Senior Research Fellow at the English and Foreign Languages University, Hyderabad, India. He is also Associate Editor of an Online International Journal called *New Literaria* (ISSN 2582-7375), indexed by MLA and leading databases. His thesis is titled *Disability and Gender: Exploring the Intersectionality in Indian Disabled Women Life Narratives*. His areas of interest include disability and religion, disability and sexuality and South Asian marginalized women writings. He has published papers in Scopus and peer review journals.

Akshata Jaiprakash holds a Master's degree in English from St. Josephs' College, (Autonomous) Bengaluru. She has been teaching English at Undergraduate level from 2009, in Hyderabad and Bengaluru. She has done a course on learning disability from Spastic Society of Karnataka, Bengaluru. She is an active trustee member of Saadhya, a school for children with special needs, in Coimbatore. Her concern towards special children was stirred as a student, when she had taught dance for children with special needs. She is pursuing her Ph.D. at Kuvempu University, working on Disability and Children's Literature. She is Research Scholar, in the Department of English Studies and Research Centre, Kuvempu University, Shankarghatta, Karnataka.

Ankur Konar is Assistant Professor in English at Sir Rashbehari Ghosh Mahavidyalaya, University of Burdwan, West Bengal. He has authored *Cultural Poetics: Poetry, Society, Theory* (2012), *Kolkata and Narrative Geographies* (2019) and *The Kolkata Football: History and Representation* (2022) and has edited *Popular Narratives: Texts and Contexts* (2020).

Sushil Kumar is Associate Professor in English and Head, Guru Kashi Department of Languages, Punjabi University Guru Kashi Campus, Damdama Sahib, Talwandi Sabo. He has an experience of editing and translating many books such as *Notes from Underground* by Dostovesky, *Story of Tools* by Gordan Childe and having more than twelve years of research experience.

Pranita Lele is Adjunct Faculty at the Indian Institute of Chartered Accountants, Dubai Chapter. She has been an educationist for more than three decades in Bahrain and Dubai. She is a column writer for the prestigious national and international newspapers and magazines like *Khaleej Times*, *Gulf News*, *Business World* and is the editor of books- *Hey Ram to Jai Shree Ram* and *The Journey from Ayodhya to Ram Setu.*

Raymond Lemay has decades of experience supporting the development, dissemination, and application of Social Role Valorization (SRV) theory. He worked closely with Wolf Wolfensberger since the early days of Normalization and SRV as a graduate student at Syracuse University, then as Executive Director of child welfare organizations in Ontario, Canada. He has taught and written extensively on Social Role Valorization (SRV) theory, but also about resilience and organizational change. He is a founding member of the International SRV Association (ISRVA), as well as serving as a member of the North American SRV Council. e-mail: raylemay@rogers.com

Dipanwita Mondal is Assistant Professor in the Department of Comparative Indian Language and Literature at University of Calcutta, Kolkata, since 2015. She worked as Assistant Professor of English in Shirakole Mahavidyalaya, West Bengal, before joining University of Calcutta. She completed her B.A. in English from St. Xavier's College, Kolkata, in 2009, M.A. in English from Jadavpur University in 2011, M.Phil. in Comparative Literature from Jadavpur University in 2013, and Ph.D. in Comparative Literature from Jadavpur University in 2021. Her research area is translation theory and translates literary pieces some of which have been published. Her other interests include partition literature, comparative literature, comparative Indian literature, Indian English literature, disability studies, and Women's Writing.

Nicky Naincy is Assistant Professor in the Department of Applied Science and Humanities, Institute of Engineering and Technology, Lucknow (Uttar Pradesh). She has a Ph.D. from Zakir Husain centre for educational studies, Jawaharlal Nehru University, New Delhi. Her areas of interest are behavioural economics and educational economics. Her research papers have been published widely. She contributes regularly to editorial columns of various Hindi and English language newspapers.

Megha Negi is Assistant Professor in the Department of English, Lucknow Christian Degree College, Lucknow. She received her Ph.D. in English from the Department of English and Modern European Languages, University of Lucknow. Her area of research is about place and condition of Widows in Indian literature. Her work has been published in an edited book by AMU, entitled *Women of Marginalised Communities: Concerns about Exclusion.*

Elizabeth Neuville has rich experience spanning 35 years as a leader in inclusive practice across the world. She has worked extensively with the ideas of Normalization and Social Role Valorization and provides training and consultation internationally, with extensive experience in Central and Eastern Europe, and India. She is fully accredited by the North American Social Role Valorization Council as a senior trainer of SRV and co-founded the International SRV Association in 2015.

She is well known for her work supporting and leading SRV and person-centred practice initiatives across the USA and in India, Ireland, UK, France, Holland, Turkey, Azerbaijan, Romania, and the Republic of Moldova. Elizabeth studied under the mentorship of Dr. Wolf Wolfensberger, the developer and foremost proponent of Social Role Valorization, and has, in turn, mentored and supported a generation of people committed to personal human service to others. e-mail: Eneuville@khs.org

Richa Joshi Pandey is Assistant Professor at the Department of English, School of Languages, Doon University, Dehradun, India, where she has been working for the last eight years. She was awarded her Ph.D. degree in 2016 by HNBGU, Srinagar Garhwal, Uttarakhand. Her areas of interest include environmental humanities, medical humanities, Indian writing in English, literary theory and criticism as well as gender studies. She has published research papers and articles in journals of national and international repute and has organized and convened various national and international workshops, seminars, symposia, and conferences. She trained as a physiotherapist and worked at Nanavati Hospital, Mumbai, before completing her Masters and Ph.D. in English literature. She believes that diverse areas of scholarship and experiential training have helped her to be keenly receptive to people and their individual needs, desires, drives, and challenges. e-mail: richa.j.pandey@doonuniversity.ac.in

Naval Chandra Pant is Founder Director of PYSSUM (www.pyssum.org), an organization working for the Children and Adults with Special Needs in Lucknow. PYSSUM was founded in 2005 and focuses on inclusive education through early intervention, child development programme, vocational training and rehabilitation for special need children as well as adults along with the exclusive training for special educators, parents, and anyone working in the field of intellectual disabilities. He also conducts career orientation for students, motivational and quality enhancement training workshops for school teachers. His doctoral research is on educational philosophy. e-mail: navalpant@pyssum.org

Dr. Meenakshi Pawha retired as Professor from the Department of English and Modern European Languages, University of Lucknow. Her research interests include Indian drama, folk theatre, climate change, films studies, disability studies, translation studies, postcolonial literatures and English language teaching (ELT). A Mellon Fellow at Harvard University (2017) Fulbright Scholar at New York University (2006), Charles Wallace India Trust fellow at Cambridge University, she is the author of two books—*The Dramatic Art and Vision of Tom Stoppard* (2007) and *Alan Ayckbourn: Chasing the Comic Muse* (2007). Her translations of short stories and essays in literary criticism have been published in South Asian Review, Indian Literature and Hindi, Language, Discourse, Writing. Some of her forthcoming titles of her translations of Hindi plays are *Godse @Gandhi.com* (Vani Prakashan); *Yeh Aakash Mera Bhi Hai* and *Ek Bhikaran ki Maut*. Dr Pawha is a voracious reader, an avid traveller and cinephile. She is fond of listening to music in any form and is passionate about the rich cultural heritage of the performing arts and textiles of India.

Ega Peter is Senior Research Fellow at Vimala College (Autonomous), Thrissur, under the University of Calicut. She has worked as Assistant Professor at St. Mary's College, Thrissur, for three semesters. Her research interests include literary disability studies, narratology, and Indian English fiction. A postgraduate and an M.Phil. in English literature degree holder, she has been trying to understand the literary and cultural expressions of disability unique to her own culture and community.

Cecily Resnick holds a Ph.D. in Clinical Psychology and a Ph.D. in Biophysics. Currently, she is a practising psychologist. In the past, she has taught statistics, research methodology, and computer courses at the college level. e-mail: drresnick@cecilyresnick.com

Amrita Sharma is Assistant Professor in the Department of English at Sri Venkateswara College, University of Delhi, India. She is a Ph.D. in English from the University of Lucknow and has been a Fulbright Fellow at the Centre for the Study of Languages and Cultures, University of Notre Dame, USA. Her works have previously been published in several national and international journals. Her first collection of poems is titled The Skies: Poems and has been published as a part of 'The Hawakal Young Poets Series 2022.'

Anu Raj Singh is Assistant professor of psychology at Banasthali University, where she has been teaching and conducting research for over ten years. She earned her Ph.D. in Psychology from Banasthali University and done M.Phil. in Jawaharlal Nehru University, New Delhi. She has published numerous articles in prestigious academic journals on topics ranging from educational psychology to gender psychology. Dr. A. R. Singh is particularly known for her work in the area of Educational and gender psychology, with a focus on understanding the social and emotional development of children and adolescents. In addition to her research, she is a dedicated teacher who is passionate about inspiring the next generation of psychologists. She has taught courses on personality development, Indian psychology, and human values, among others. e-mail: anurajsingh@banasthali.in

Gaele Sobott is a writer and independent scholar from Darug land in Western Sydney, Australia. She has a Ph.D. in literature from the University of Hull, UK. She is the founding director of Outlandish Arts, a disabled-led arts company.

Saumya Srivastava has done her Ph.D. from the University of Lucknow, Lucknow, Uttar Pradesh, India. She has several publications to her credit. Her area of interest lies in contemporary literary theory, disability studies, and Indian writing in English. She is a creative writer and academician with five years of teaching experience at Amity University, Lucknow, as Assistant Professor.

Dana Elken Terrell LCSW, EAC has been practising Bowen family systems theory since 1979, and EMDR therapy 7 since 1997. She has been training EMDR therapists in her integrative Bowen and EMDR therapy since 2009 and was a presenter at the 2014 and 2017 EMDR International Association Conferences. She has written a self-help book about Bowen and EMDR called "When I Do Relationships SO RIGHT

How Do They Go SO WRONG." She lives, practices, researches her protocols, and writes in San Diego, CA, and gives workshops and presentations nationwide and internationally.

Jaya Upadhyay is Assistant Professor in the Department of Humanities and Liberal Arts, DIT University. She received her M.A. and Ph.D. in English from the University of Lucknow in 2012 and 2019, respectively. Her area of research is gender studies. Her studies have appeared in *Cinej: Cinema Journal*, a publication of the University of Pittsburgh. Her work has also been published by the Banaras Hindu University. She was awarded the Harrison Middleton University's "Fellowship in Ideas 2021." One of her poems, "A Clockwork Madness" was published in the University of Lucknow's *Rhetorica* journal, and she has also authored blogs for Harrison Middleton University, Arizona, USA.

Introduction

Disabled/

Dysfunctional/Disturbed/

Disaster/Disobedient/Disappointment//

Disfigured/Distress/Disrepute/ Disgust … the list is endless of what it means to be disabled.

As the *Stanford Encyclopedia of Philosophy* rightly points: "Ableism systematically interacts with other power structures that stigmatize to produce race, gender, sex, and disability. Ableism shapes our world and produces disability". As we inhabit a society that constantly rejects an equal space for persons with disability, we also continue in our efforts to shape a critical theoretical framework, a literary database and a social understanding that deconstructs this rejection. With many prominent sociologists laying the foundation of a theoretical base that attempts to understand the 'stigma' of a difference, the past few decades have witnessed the growth of a critically developed disability theory in different parts of the globe. While names like Lennard J. Davis, Rosemarie Garland-Thomson, Simi Linton, Tom Shakespeare, and many others stand out from the West, a significant amount of work is also developing within the Indian academia. Collectively, we strive to make a positive change.

This book on disability is a very personal project hoping to help us work in and for a community of people who are not looked at with respect and dignity. It brings together people from diverse backgrounds, academia, and disability activism to discuss and open a debate in an area of enquiry that has remained under the carpet for centuries. It is heartening to note that in the new millennium disability studies has emerged as an academic discipline with a firm desire to bring in a change in our minds and hearts. It is now being introduced in the undergraduate and postgraduate programmes and in higher education as a subject that will not only sensitize young minds but would lead to better opportunities for people with disability. Awareness of the conditions in which people with disability function in their everyday lives, the difficulties they face, and the humiliation they bear is necessary for us to see and feel if we wish to bring in a change in society. We hope to be able to provide material for our students and researchers that would give them a fresh perspective and enable them to look at the much-maligned world of disability with care and compassion. Our own understanding of the subject changed once we were introduced to the subject of SRV—social role valorization. SRV is a concept developed by Wolf Wolfensberger (it has been discussed at length in a paper by Elizabeth Neuville and others). Linked with the concept of SRV is the idea and practice of devaluation. In a so called "able" or "normal" society, many people who belong to the periphery face social devaluation. Devaluation of people on grounds of class, caste, colour, creed and country is a universal phenomenon. People with disability are at the worst end of the spectrum because they embody characteristics and conditions that lead to devaluation. This enhances their sense of wounding, puts them at risk of physical or mental assault. Deep wounds may never heal and leave them with permanent scars. It is important for each one of us to value human life or any life on this earth. We have tried to discuss and look at disability / impairment not merely as an impediment but have laid emphasis on lives that need to be valued, loved, integrated, and valorized. There is no reason why the disabled cannot play valued roles in society. Distinguished scholars from India and other parts of the globe have very generously sent us their contributions. It is fascinating to see disability studies evolve as an interdisciplinary charter of knowledge with a conflation of diverse practices. It draws from various knowledge systems. Multiple theoretical positions consider the diversity and differences linked with the representations of disability in literature, language, and life. Lived experiences are crucial to this project.

In the contemporary times, disability studies is an emerging and constantly evolving field of study. With academicians, social workers and disability rights activists from every part of the world paving a way towards greater awareness regarding 'disability' today, the project continues to grow. From providing a theoretical framework to study 'disability' in contrast to 'normalcy' in the society, scholars in this field have provided models and concepts to understand the subject. From the very basic example of the 'medical model' and the 'social model' of disability to more complex theories of 'embodiment' and 'othering' in context of disability, the various terms associated with persons with disability are now being dissected through diverse frames (Pant).

We hope the book will help us develop an understanding of the predicament and overcome prejudices against disability. Perceptions matter. In a people first approach, it is significant that one pays attention to the voice, desires and needs and aspirations of the people with disability. Disability is not a disease but a condition. It is not a problem to be fixed, nor is it a tragedy. It does not define our identity. It calls for a dialogue that would help us build strategies to change mindsets, remove physical and social barriers, challenge myths and stereotypes, create narratives of empathy and understanding, inclusion and acceptance. It seems a tall order, but to hope for good things of life is certainly possible. If for one vision is about shared energy, it is also about shared dreams for another and about shared efforts to all of us involved in this vision. The Old Testament has put it rightly "Without a vision, the people perish".

This collection brings together multiple perspectives that help us formulate a contextual framework thus enabling diverse ways of seeing disability.

The Essay: I can Hear her Breathing: Disabled writers writing disability discusses the social and justice models of disability that inform the way" (Sobott Gaele). The essay reminds us that the narrative of the disabled story of the past often reflects the disabled child as relentlessly cheery, which presents for non-disabled readers an untrue truth. The reader will be aware of the common practice of disability as metaphor, a useful concept to keep in mind as we move through our day unconsciously speaking and telling daily stories. The writing from the disabled experience, according to Gaele Sobott, is important to imagine other ways of being human that disrupt and transcend current limitations.

In the Pilot Research Study: Utilizing the EMDR Integrative Group Treatment Protocol Online to Help Parents with the Stresses of Having a Special Needs Child, it is suggested that studies have demonstrated that in fact, special needs children experience more trauma than their typical counterparts. An increasingly popular comparison to the symptoms of posttraumatic stress syndrome is drawn. The reader is asked to consider a possible reality that "Parents are often dismayed at having to be such strong self-advocates to professionals who serve them and their special needs child. Rather than experiencing a helpful, concerned, and cooperative relationship, parents sometimes experience the parent-professional relationship as conflictual and adversarial." (Petr, 250). (Terrell, Resnick & Cecily).

Social Role Valorization Theory in India: An Idea with Consequences and Neuville et al. reveals that essays throughout this collection frequently give evidence of the universal truths of the themes and concepts embedded in Social Role Valorisation. This essay provides the perspective of historical roots and uses the concept of the good things of life. "Such good things include a home, relationships, a decent reputation, belonging, a robust self-image, opportunities, a comfortable lifestyle, and these are near universal in terms of their values across peoples and across cultures." (Neuville, Cardozo, De, & Lemay) The authors discuss "The infliction wounds that set up entire classes of people, as well as individual persons, to experience very poor treatment at the hands of society" (Wolfensberger, 2013). (Neuville, Cardozo, De, & Lemay) An uncomfortable truth is discussed in the assessment that "unfortunately, many programmes intended to make life better for people with disabilities tend to focus on providing activities and keeping people busy" (Neuville, Cardozo, De, & Lemay).

"Hold Your Breath" is an essay that links education and religious practices. The essay posits that religious practice has deep roots in the human experience and much that comes from that experience can be merged with scientific theories for healthy living. Breath and the practice of mindfulness may be a path to knowledge of/participation in higher-order value systems that give meaning and direction to life, and provide community (Wolfensberger, 2013).

The paper "Hold Your Breath" values the religious sentiments of all parents and institutions but urges them to make a sincere effort to analyse the scientific basis of these traditions and rituals. (Pant) "Hold your breath" does not display a state of comfort" (Pant). But rather brings us to consider the scientific parallels in religious practice. Opening the door to a more inclusive and disability lead personal practice and participation in higher-order systems.

Disability in Literature, Film and Theatre reminds us, through the search for meaning in literature not to "abilify" a disabled persons worth in relationship or practice. In "The Mad Mother in the 1BHK—Hallowing and Harrowing Positions in Jerry Pinto's Em and the Big Hoom", Peter reports that "the medical sciences have done a huge disservice to the understanding of disability. By locating disability in the individual that views disability as pathology. The reader sees that although personal writings from disabled people give glimpses of valued roles of loyal friend, a faithful lover, and a firebrand of a young woman, in the end people, due to confinement in spaces, experience the role of "lessor-being".

(No) Shared Towers concludes with a Foucault quote that "It is nothing but the space that divides them, the void through which they exchange their threatening gestures and speeches (Foucault, "Nietzsche, Genealogy, History" 150). Throughout the essay the reader reflects on how assumptions underlying cultural ableism are not only particularly counterproductive to individuals but also tend to pathologize individuals through language by homogenizing, trivializing and stereotyping".

Disability, Sexuality, and Postcoloniality in Bengali Fiction by Arunabha Bose introduces the reader to the concept that the disabled body in fiction, by virtue of its "defects" or inadequacy is an aberrant distortion and deviation from the norm of the stable and normative body. The author discusses the birth of "normal" and "binary" by introducing us to "Tom Shakespeare who disputes the fixity and absoluteness of binary categories such as disabled/able-bodied and pathological/normal since disciplinary regimes through practices of manipulation and repression first produce "normal" bodies which they claim to govern."

In Stigmatizing the Other: Treatment of Disability in Franz Kafka's "The Metamorphosis" The Category of "othering" is explored in Upadhyay's article as they examine Kafka's The Metamorphosis, which stands alone as a depiction of what one must do when transformed into monstrous vermin, what it means to be human, and what happens when those around you stop regarding you as such. Personal identity and interpersonal identification are negotiated between people, produced, and maintained through difference, which has disastrous effects."

Notions of Normalcy and Changing Definitions: Defeating Stereotypes and Creating Acceptance of Disability by Akshata Jaiprakash does what every text on disability studies is obligated to explore the "Notions of Normalcy". Jaiprakash meets this obligation through a review of the literature in which we discover that disability is a social construct. Jaiprakash's work throws light on the notions of 'acceptance' of a person with disability by parents, family members, the society, and their consequences and the role of representation.

In Normalizing Disability: Discourses of the Decolonized Body, Mondal discusses the scope of critical disability studies as a field of study and challenges its significance in the postcolonial context. She speaks of the need of a "collective and corrective" approach that might lead us to a more inclusive study.

The use of disability to define groups of people considered weak or of less value has roots that span the history of humans. This according to Srivastava in "Disabled Identities and the Linguistic World" is identified in the writings and teachings of Aristotle. Women, considered disabled based on their gender, represent the depth of social devaluation faced by disabled people now and throughout history. The consideration of the metaphor of disabled through literature brings the reader understanding and is a source for reflection.

From Narrative Prosthesis to Disability Counternarrative: Reading Cognitive Difference in Aparna Sen's 15 Park Avenue Pawha discusses the role of cinema and other visual cultures in producing disability counternarratives and their potency at large.

It is both profound and sad that we must in the twenty-first century strive to gain insight into disabled people as human. Dhandhukia, in the essay, Changing Social Perspectives on Disability in Hindi Films Dosti and Barfi, explores the connection between the nurturing of such negative perceptions and film. One learns as the essay is absorbed that the close connection between literature and society has existed from the time of Plato. An additional complication is explained by Dhandhukia as emanating from the religions of India.

The Societal Gaze and Stigma: A Study of Mahesh Dattani's Tara and Disability and Gender Interface in Dattani's Tara explore if sex is natural and gender cultural, what do we have to learn from disability studies? These two papers, by Negi and Konar respectively, posit that disability studies is the most unified and concentrated expression of biological discrimination in our society that is basically guided by parochial ideologies. The parallels between sexism and ableism are observed and the reader is encouraged to analyse and become aware. Konar shows the reader that paradigms of disability cannot be formulated in an isolated critical juncture, disability studies, being heavily interdisciplinary and transdisciplinary in nature. The intersection of thought and cultural norms is a lens the reader can use to understand "Tara" and subsequently other literature. The reader is left to ponder literary characters as being "inextricably woven together to denote the critical rubrics of art, disability and gender and their feasible nexus in representing an Indian context" (Konar).

In People of Determination—Making Achievements, Overcoming Challenges. Lele opens with telling the reader that disability statistics can provide extensive information on the experience of persons with disabilities. Lele further raises the question regarding the label or term "disabled". A question of identity that many members of the disability rights community have resolved by making the word representative of power and autonomy. The reader is brought to consider the impact of the label "disabled" as brought on by the dominant ideology versus the use of the label by disabled people as a powerful ownership of language. But the essay goes beyond simple language and broadens the discussion to the impact of ancient texts and practice. The vast implications and ramifications emanating from issues of labelling and representation are investigated in depth.

In Disability and Institutional Failure: A Study of Good Kings, Bad Kings by Susan Nussbaum, Garg and Sushil offer another consideration of the term disability. They point out that the term itself has led to the proliferation of the medical model, among other models of misguided approaches. The reader is reminded of the thoughts of Tom Shakespeare, "Disability, as such, does not carry a single meaning as it is contested, multidimensional, complex, and "should be understood in terms of a continuum". The essay leads the reader to see social institutions as shaped by representative language as presented in the novel "Good Kings, Bad Kings. The conclusion of the essays bears the consideration of all aspiring and current scholars of disability studies. "Being trapped in one kind of institution or another is the fate of many of us…". On the basis of the novel Good Kings, Bad Kings, it can be said that as far as disability is concerned or the care of the persons with disabilities is concerned, the institutions like ILLC in the novel have failed miserably".

In Education and Labour Market for Persons with Disabilities in India. Naincy & Singh bring to the discussion that information regarding disabled peoples socio-economic and socio-demographic variables is not "sufficient to develop an inclusive policy". This deficit in data is linked to the growth of the medical model in India, according to Naincy & Singh. They assert, however, that circumstances have led to a more person friendly social model of disability. The circumstances of lack of data or incorrectly focused data requires, according to Naincy & Singh, theoretical and empirical investigation of discrimination in the labour market for disabled people to find out which particular construct has to be taken while formulating inclusive policies.

Honk Honk: Women, You Drive Crazy! Bali, seizes on the realities of what is called the bifurcated society of masculine and feminine narratives. Bali uses this perspective to introduce the nature of people to "live up to expectations". Value or marginalization, it is suggested, is created when people live up, or down, to their assigned roles. This historic consideration of gender roles is presented in the context of both disability and the underlying connection of women, in the past, being considered disabled. From that beginning Bali brings the reader to see the nature of intersectionality.

In Contesting Representation, Writing Self: A Critical Study of Disabled Life Narratives in A Bumblebee's Balcony and One Little Finger, Gokul presents the concept, history, and evolution of "life narratives" as a developing media moving from stories of expected roles of deviance to personal truths being openly told. The analysis further considers differences in personal narratives from rural vs urban experiences.

An in-depth consideration of the autobiography gives the reader a foundational understanding of narrative as a writing genre. The author concludes that first-person narratives have the power to break stereotypes and assumptions long held and nurtured by third-person narratives.

Shaping the Disability Discourse: From Theoretical Groundwork to Lived Experiences. Towards the end of the book, Amrita's paper presents an overview of the factors that have shaped the disability discourse and continue to do so. As the theoretical discussions on the wider subjects of 'stigma' and 'othering' have initially laid the foundation of disability studies, it is more specific and streamlined theoretical works and the lived experience narratives that remain central to shaping a new discipline devoted to the study of disability.

With its unique collection of essays, this book hopes to strengthen, stimulate, and strategize the existing corpus of disability studies.

Reference

Wolfensberger, W. (2013). *A brief introduction to social role valorization: A high-order concept for addressing the plight of societally devalued people, and for structuring human services* (4th ed.). Valor Press.

Part I
Disability and Empirical Experiences

Chapter 1
I Can Hear Her Breathing: Disabled Writers Writing Disability

Gaele Sobott

Abstract This paper explores some of the ways disabled writers in varied contexts challenge disablist narratives and expectations. It provides examples of disabled writers creating their own rules and writing paths, often shaped by their impairments and access requirements. The essay argues the importance for disabled writers to understand and harness their embodied experiences of life and how this manifests in their writing as disability aesthetics.

Keywords Disabled writers · Disrupting disableist narrative · Disability aesthetics · Embodied writing

> If someone does not empathise with a disabled subject and personhood, they will not be in a position to understand the intimate core of my disabled self.
>
> – Anita Ghai
>
> Another world is not only possible, she is on her way. On a quiet day, I can hear her breathing.
>
> – Arundhati Roy

The social and justice models of disability inform the way I move through my environment and almost everything I do, especially my writing and my reading. I am constantly aware of the need and my own desire to build a world where physical, attitudinal, communication, and socio-economic and political environments reflect experiences of impairment as an expected expression of human diversity. I choose to read writing that assists in creating a world that is enriched by such diversity, especially writing by disabled writers from varied contexts. I actively seek out writing by disabled writers of colour, writers whose reflections on life differ from dominant Western takes on disability, work translated into English. I have neither the time nor energy to read work that supports and perpetuates dominant views on disability or tries to make impairment and the resulting disability palatable to non-disabled audiences. Having said that it is sometimes best to read a book before dismissing it.

G. Sobott (✉)
Independent Scholar, Writer and Poet, Sydney, Australia
e-mail: gaelesobott@gmail.com

R. Uniyal and F. Rizvi (eds.), *Understanding Disability*,
https://doi.org/10.1007/978-981-99-4925-0_1

Australian, disabled writer, Amanda Tink recently published an essay in *Sydney Review of Books* called 'A History of Reading: Alan Marshall and Helen Keller.'[1] Alan Marshall's book, *I Can Jump Puddles*, was one of the few books available in Braille at Amanda's school. She didn't finish the book because she felt that, as much as Marshall may have been telling the truth about his childhood experiences, he was also lying by omission.

That his life as a child with polio during the 1920s, in fact any disabled child's life then or now, could not be that relentlessly cheery. If you go to the website of Marshall's publisher, Penguin, the blurb emphasizes that this is a story of a happy childhood in which, "despite his crippling poliomyelitis," Marshall plays, climbs, fights, swims, rides, and laughs.

Amanda recently decided to take another look at Marshall's writing and read *I Can Jump Puddles* in its entirety. She writes that Marshall does placate non-disabled audiences, but there's a lot more there, especially in the last fifth of the book where after a year of trying, he is portrayed as having triumphed over his impairment because he learns to ride a horse.

I moved my seat a little to the right in the saddle then thrust my left hand under the saddle flap beneath my leg. Here I could grasp the surcingle just where it entered the flap after crossing the saddle. I could bear down upon the inner saddle pad to counter a sway to the right or pull on the surcingle to counter a sway to the left.

For the first time I felt completely safe. I … urged Starlight into a canter. His swinging stride never moved me in the saddle. I sat relaxed and balanced, rising and falling with the movement of his body and experiencing a feeling of security and confidence.[2]

Amanda Tink points out that Marshall's breakthrough comes, not as retellers of his story would have it, 'despite' or when he 'overcomes' his impairment, but when he gives up on trying to ride horses in a standard way, and develops a method that utilizes his impairment as a resource. This worked for Marshall when riding a horse, and probably in a lot of other areas of his life, I believe utilizing our impairment as a resource works equally as well when applied to disabled writers writing disability.

What this means in our writing practice will vary considerably. It may vary according to our impairment and our particular social and cultural experiences of disablement. It may vary according to form or genre, for example, life-writing by disabled writers lends itself to writing directly about disability as context. Australian appearance activist, Carly Findlay's book, *Say Hello*, says in bold letters—'I am a proud disabled woman and I will speak about it. I will make you uncomfortable with my politics and my pride.'[3] Harriet McBryde Johnson, a writer and lawyer from Charleston in the USA, was active for more than twenty-five years in the struggle for social justice, especially disability rights. In her book, *Too Late to Die Young*, she says that one of the ways she has resisted formulaic narratives of disability is by telling stories, that don't aim to satisfy the general curiosity about what it's like to

[1] Tink (2019).

[2] As quoted by Tink (2019).

[3] Findlay (2019).

live in a withered body like mine or feed the public appetite for inspirational pap. Like all stories, they are most fundamentally a chance to ride around inside another head and be reminded that being who we are and where we are, and doing what we're doing, is not the only possibility.[4]

Fiction writers and poets too may deliberately write disability as content. In her book, *Sister Mine*, Nalo Hopkins tells the story of Makeda and Abby, conjoined twins born to a demigod father and a human mother. The twins are surgically separated leaving Abby with a permanent limp and depriving Makeda of the inherited ability to make magic. Abby retains this ability which 'takes the form of an unearthly skill with music and rhythm.'[5]

Interviewed by Sofia Samatar, Nalo Hopkins says of the book,

> I'm curious about the experiences of conjoined twins throughout history. I'm interested in the folklore and belief systems of the Caribbean, where I'm from. I'm interested in how siblings get set up to feel inadequate in the face of each other's accomplishments. I'm interested in the lives and loves of black people, especially the non-heteronormative ones.[6]

Gayle Kennedy is a proud Wongaibon woman from south-west NSW in Australia. In her book, *Me, Antman & Fleabag*, the main character is disabled, Antman is a cancer survivor and Fleabag, the dog has a physical impairment. Gayle writes about disability within the context of First Peoples' ongoing pain and intergenerational trauma rooted in colonial legacies, about the main character's battles with polio and her experience of being sent a long way from home to hospital in Sydney where she is surrounded by white people. When she finally meets her parents again to journey back home, they are strangers to her. She writes, 'For a long time I lived in two worlds, one white, one black, and never really fitting into either.'[7]

Jayapraga Reddy, a South African writer, born in Durban, writes her own experiences of disability and disabled characters. In her short story 'A Gift for Rajendra,' a young man who uses a wheelchair 'refuses to go out to crowded places and … won't go to barber shops.'[8] I interviewed Jaya in 1994 and corresponded with her after that. She spoke of declining muscle function including the discomfort associated with eating and why she refused to go to parties where a meal would be served. She says, 'I can't enjoy it … people … feel I'm so rude … because they're eating with gusto. I'm just nibbling ….'[9] Her writing intersects with experiences of race, gender, and class and often reflects upon the trauma and struggles of people living under the Apartheid system, building community, strong, supportive women and South African 'Indian' identity characterized by different origins, languages, and religious beliefs.

As disabled writers, most of us are also aware of and choose not to use disablist language, shallow and pejorative impairment metaphors, and impairment as a tool

---

[4] Johnson (2005).

[5] Samatar (2013).

[6] Ibid.

[7] Kennedy (2008).

[8] Reddy (1981).

[9] Gaele Sobott interview with Jayapraga Reddy 11 August 1994 at her home in Durban.

to create villains or neurodivergent-coded characters as comic relief. This means we replace pervasive and damaging pejorative disability metaphors with 'innovative', politically accountable uses of metaphor that make people think more deeply and alternatively. This also means better writing. But I believe there is more to utilizing our impairment as a resource and disrupting disablist narratives than being aware of negative metaphors and/or consciously writing the material experience of disability. Disabled Australian writer, Honey Brown notes,

> When we create, we're tapping into our most private self, we're making our own rules and revealing our uniqueness. My first completed manuscript reminded me of who I was. There I was, on the page in front of me—not spelt out in memoir fashion, but in the subtext, in the descriptions, within character reactions, in the ideas fuelling the story. Each manuscript revealed a little more of me.[10]

Our embodied experiences of the world as disabled writers may also reflect in the way we organize sounds and silences, symbols and spaces, rhyme, assonance, metre, and alliteration. The pace, narrative structure, imagery, and rhythm of the text; even the grammar and spelling. I am suggesting that disabled writers may both consciously and/or without realizing it, bring concrete or imprecise traces of our bodies and cognition to our style of writing, to the logic and aesthetic of writing. In this way, our writing has the potential to disrupt current literary expectations.

Bessie Head, the South African/Botswana writer, is an example of a disabled writer writing their embodied experiences in a way that may be said to create a disability aesthetic. She is one of a few African writers and I believe, the first to write convincingly of the complexity and intensity of madness, and the intersection of madness with varied facets of racism and patriarchy. Bessie Head's mother was a white woman who after falling pregnant to a black man in Apartheid South Africa was committed to the Fort Napier psychiatric Hospital in Pietermaritzburg, Natal, where she gave birth to her daughter, Bessie. Presumed white as a baby, Bessie was initially fostered out to a white family who returned her because she did not appear white. She was then reclassified as 'mixed race' and given to the Heathcotes, a poor 'coloured' family. As a child, she believed these people were her biological family. When her foster father died, she was sent to an Anglican missionary orphanage in Durban to attend high school. It was at this school that the principal told her of the real circumstances of her birth. Bessie's upbringing was fraught with insecurity and cruelty. She experienced extreme prejudice and hardship as a young adult. She eventually fled to Botswana where she lived for 15 years as a political refugee until she was granted citizenship in 1979. Her book, *A Question of Power*, is an experimental, introspective novel written on two levels; one is 'an everyday level'[11] that involves a communal garden and the people who work with the main character, Elizabeth on that garden, the second level is what Bessie Head describes as 'a journey inwards to the soul.'[12] It offers a narrative structure which is not a rational account of madness but a hectic and sometimes illogical, paranoid, and delusional conversation; a struggle

---

[10] Brown (2014).

[11] Head and Vigne (1991).

[12] Ibid.

between Elizabeth and voices of the people who exist in her hallucinations. Dan, Sello of the brown suit, Sello the monk and Medusa fight ferociously with Elizabeth about power, evil and the nature of God, sexuality and guilt.

Bessie Head describes the book as 'totally autobiographical.'[13] She says the material for the book largely came from the 'tremendous disturbance' she 'began to experience from 1968 until late 1970.'[14] Her writing is both a raw testimony to madness and a literary work that, as Elizabeth says in the beginning of the book, proposes an argument where 'the barriers of the normal, conventional, and sane [are] all broken down, like a swimmer taking a rough journey on wild seas.'[15] The reader cannot be passive if they are to gain an understanding of this narrative, they must engage with discontinuity and uncertainty.

Speaking at the 2019 Queensland Poetry Festival, poet Andy Jackson said he believes that disabled poets may often bring embodied experiences of brokenness, difference, and deformity to the form of poetry. In free verse poetry, 'strange and unusual shapes are important, fractured speech is important ... even the idea that a poem is supposedly potentially defined by line breaks is significant'[16] to the disabled aesthetic. Denise Leto, a core participant in the Feminism, Embodiment, Disability, Poetry, Performance project (FEDPP) in the US writes:

> As a poet with a neurological voice/body 'disorder' my utterances are sometimes perceptually indistinct units of sound-artifice, breaking. Pieces of a word revise as they are being spoken (fluent and dysfluent communication). The chasm between the given voice and the constructed voice is a field of query: polyvocality, syntactic fracture, chance constraint, and a recommunion with self and other. On the page, the poetic line becomes a sensory encounter with orality.[17]

Amber DiPietra is also a core member of the project. She is a San Francisco-based Latina disabled poet who also blogs for Kelsey Street Productions, a press with a focus on feminist poetics. She writes about her poetic labour intertwined with her particular embodiment as a physically and visually impaired woman:

> This is my blog, full of errata and gaps. Typos should read as the blips and darts and granularity you get when listening to records. My eyes operate on phonograph time. Copy editing only scratches the surface and causes lines that grid an already tenuous visual field to wobble and converge more often.[18]

When Bessie Head wrote *Question of Power*, she knew she was taking a commercial risk, and that it was not going to be easy to get the book published. In letters to Randolph Vigne, she describes the work as 'a huge hotch potch like a Van

---

[13] MacKenzie and Clayton (1989).

[14] Ibid.

[15] Head (1974).

[16] Andy Jackson speaking at the 2019 Queensland Poetry Festival on Verity La Poetry Podcast Episode 14, Disrupting the (Dis)Ableist Narrative, October 2, 2019, https://verityla.com/2019/10/02/verity-la-poetrypodcast-episode-14-disrupting-the-disableist-narrative/.

[17] Denise Leto, unpublished fellowship statement, Movement, Somatics and Writing symposium, University of Michigan, 2011 as quoted by Kuppers (2011).

[18] DiPietra (2011a).

Gogh painting' and 'a sprawling run across the universe' (Head and Vigne, 168) with a subject matter that 'makes people react very emotionally' (165). Gillian Stead Eilersen summarizes various agents' and publishers' damning responses to *Question of Power* when it was still in draft manuscript form: it was "too dense and intractable", it "did not get across" to readers, was "a draft of a novel, not a completed one", and the language was a form of "prose poetry" bordering "on the meaningless" (Eilersen 1995: 150). There is risk involved when we allow our impairment, the way we move through the world, and the way the world receives us to bubble up into our writing. In many cases, such acts of embodied writing; disruptive, vulnerable, imperfect are silenced by the gatekeepers of literary worth, teachers, editors, publishers, and critics. Instead of treating learning-disabled texts as dialectal expressions of language, many editors either straight out reject the work or impose dominant editorial and discursive paradigms in such a way that they destroy the integrity of the work. We do not always need to enforce standard grammar and spelling when non-standard word choices are important to communicating experiences and emotions or affording rhythms.

In his poem, 'Dear Hearing World', Jamaican-British poet, Raymond Antrobus writes:

> … your judgment made my syllables disappear, your magic master trick hearing world—drowning out the quiet, bursting all speech bubbles in my graphic childhood, you are glad to benefit from audio supremacy, I tried, hearing people, I tried to love you, but you laughed at my deaf grammar, I used commas not full stops because everything I said kept running away, I mulled over long paragraphs because I didn't know what a "natural break" sounded like, you erased what could have always been poetry (strike that out). You erased what could have always been poetry.[19]

Skotaville Press was originally going to publish Jayapraga Reddy's autobiography, *The Unbending Reed* but it remains unpublished to this day. Sam Naidu in her chapter, 'Negotiating Home and Homeland through Women's Life-Writing' in *Diaspora Poetics and Homing in South Asian Women's Writing* writes that Jayapraga's 'memoir … concentrates almost exclusively on her disability … and her struggle to become a writer as a black woman in Apartheid South Africa', and that 'the language of Reddy's life-writing is colourless, almost lifeless at times, resembling reportage rather than creative writing.'[20] I have not yet read the manuscript, so it is difficult for me to comment, but I have read an excerpt from The Unbending Reed, published in 1994 in *Like a House on Fire: Contemporary Women's Writing, Art and Photography from South Africa.* I find it an emotive read about the death of Jayapraga's brother, Kesa, at four and half years of age, from breathing and lung complications related to the muscle-wasting condition Jaya and her brothers inherited. The coffin was brought into the front room. Mourners are gathering around, wailing. The narrator is a child. She realizes the finality of death based on the actions of the family cat, Prill. 'He put his front paws on the coffin and peered in. The mourners were sufficiently roused

[19] Antrobus (2016).

[20] Naidu (2018).

out of themselves to stop weeping and watched as he turned and walked out the way he came in.

We never saw him again.'[21]

I strongly believe that our writing as disabled people is important to imagining other ways of being human that disrupt and transcend current limitations. I hope our writing will encourage more committed, deep, and radical reading of our texts and cultural studies approaches that analyse our varied disabled aesthetics and embodiments. This will in turn feed back into our writing and reading, and the writing and reading of others, and into changing who makes and creates the evaluative criteria that determine what literature is and in turn what those criteria are.

Disabled writers do face many barriers. Sometimes, the struggle is simply to be 'heard', especially when disabled people experience intersecting oppressions and discrimination. Sometimes, it is finding the support we need to write and this too may vary in different socio-economic, political, and historical contexts. In her essay, '*From* My Notebook Has a Rigid Spine or How to Operate the Body in Writing', Amber DiPietra describes some of the difficulty she faces. Apart from the event being up a steep flight of stairs, 'the approaching date of the talk coincided with the realization that I needed to find ways to spend less time at the computer doing my writing because this work exacerbates my chronic pain and physical limitations.' Her solution lies within the form she chooses for her writing, a '... porous, a membrane.'[22] 'A text that sucks the reader through its many holes and vaporous areas while offering also a sampling of real tissues, body-systems that another body can assimilate.'[23] It is a text that 'exists as notes ... an artificial joint that has not been installed in a human body.'[24]

In my writing practice, I seek out and nurture collaboration with others for various reasons, including the need for support in helping me around barriers and discrimination. Where possible, I also provide collaborative support and solidarity when called upon. I have learnt to identify my access requirements and I try my best to organize ways to meet these requirements. I join with disabled and non-disabled activists in fighting to build the vision of a better world where the shared human project ensures people with impairment can effectively live full lives in this world and future worlds. And yes, not very often but sometimes, I can hear her breathing. As part of this struggle, I ask that while we, disabled writers are learning to craft, crafting and recrafting our material, that we also look to developing methods that utilize our impairment as a resource, that we build the know-how and confidence to write from our embodied experiences. Nalo Hopkins writes,

> I struggle with every day: the mental diligence and stamina needed to sit in front of the computer, open the file, start writing and to keep doing so, word after word, until I've created the next story. A combination of learning disability and chronic health issues make that the hardest thing for me. And if I can't write, I'm not a writer. I know that's eminently

[21] Reddy (1994).

[22] DiPietra (2011b).

[23] Ibid., p. 273.

[24] Ibid., p. 274.

> survivable, but still, I can scarcely bear to contemplate it. So I'm constantly coming up with new strategies for getting to the mental place where writing is so joyous and playful that I almost can't help putting the words down.[25]

I wish this for disabled writers that we constantly come up with new strategies for getting to the mental place where writing is so joyous and playful that we cannot help but to write.

References

Antrobus, R. (2016, August). Dear hearing people. *Deaf Poets Society*, Issue 1. https://www.deafpoetssociety.com/raymond-antrobus

Brown, H. (2014, September 2). Focus on Australian women writers with disability: Guest post by Honey Brown. *Australian Women Writers Challenge.*

DiPietra, A. (2011a). Falling in real time. http://adipietra.blogspot.com

DiPietra, A. (2011b). From my notebook has a rigid spine or how to operate the body in writing. In J. Bartlett, S. Black, & M. Northern (Eds.), *Beauty is a verb: The new poetry of disability* (p. 272). Cinco Puntos Press.

Eilersen, G.S. (1995). Bessie head thunder behind her ears

Findlay, C. (2019). *Say hello* (p. 210). Harper Collins.

Head, B. (1974). *A question of power* (p. 15). Heinemann International.

Head, B., & Vigne, R. (Eds.). (1991). *A gesture of belonging: Letters from Bessie Head, 1965–1979* (p. 165). SA Writers.

Hopkinson, N. (2015, August 21). I'll take my chances with the 21st century. *The Globe and Mail* 'Books', updated May 15, 2018. https://www.theglobeandmail.com/arts/books-and-media/nalo-hopkinson-ill-takemy-chances-with-the-21st-century/article26048188/

Johnson, H. M. (2005). *Too late to die young: Nearly true tales from life* (p. 4). Picador.

Kennedy, G. (2008). *Me, antman & fleabag* (p. 97). University of Queensland Press.

Kuppers, P. (2011). Poetry-ing: Feminist disability aesthetics and poetry communities. *English Language Notes, 49*(2), 78.

MacKenzie, C., & Clayton, C. (Eds.). (1989). *Between the lines: Interviews with Bessie Head, Sheila Roberts, Ellen Kuzwayo, Miriam Tlali* (p. 24). NELM.

Naidu, S. (2018). Negotiating home and homeland through women's life-writing. In S. D. Bhat (Ed.), *Diaspora poetics and homing in South Asian women's writing: Beyond Trishanku.* Lexington Books.

Reddy, J. (1981). A gift for Rajendra. *Staffrider, 4*(3), 40.

Reddy, J. (1994). The unbending reed. In COSAW Women's Collective (Ed.), *Like a house on fire* (p. 76). Congress of South African Women Writers.

Samatar, S. (2013, February 25). "Write your heart out": An interview with Nalo Hopkinson. *Strange Horizons.*

Tink, A. (2019, May 27). A history of reading: Alan Marshall and Helen Keller. *Sydney Review of Books.*

[25] Hopkinson (2015).

Chapter 2
Pilot Research Study: Utilizing the EMDR Integrative Group Treatment Protocol Online to Help Parents with the Stresses of Having a Special Needs Child

Dana Elken Terrell and Cecily Resnick

Abstract Eye movement desensitization and reprocessing (EMDR) therapy using the integrative EMDR group treatment protocol was adapted for provision of treatment online during the COVID pandemic. Six parents of special needs children were given assessments before treatment, immediately after and one-month post-treatment. This is an exploratory pilot research study that used quasi-experimental and qualitative designs, with pre-assessments and multiple post-measures and by qualitative data taken after each session of the two-part treatment plan. The results of the pilot study show decreases in anxiety, depression, parenting stresses, and distress about the child's disability. EMDR seems an effective treatment for the stress experienced by parents of special needs children. Considering the importance of the role these parents play, further and more rigorous research with randomized control studies and large samples is recommended

Keywords EMDR · Integrative EMDR group therapy · Online group therapy · Parents of special needs children · Trauma of parents with special needs children

---

D. E. Terrell (✉)
San Diego, CA, USA
e-mail: danaterrell.lcsw@gmail.com

C. Resnick
Encinitas, CA, USA
e-mail: drresnick@cecilyresnick.com

R. Uniyal and F. Rizvi (eds.), *Understanding Disability*,
https://doi.org/10.1007/978-981-99-4925-0_2

Overview Special Needs Children: Research of PTSD and Treatment

Special needs children include children with three categories of disability: intellectual/developmental, emotional, or medical needs. In the current cultural context in industrial countries, children with special needs receive a fair amount of attention from family, school, community, and research.

Fortunately, in the past decade, there are studies in America and Europe exploring the question of whether persons with intellectual or verbal disability have trauma or PTSD (Kildahl et al., 2019; Wigham et al., 2011). Some studies have demonstrated that in fact, special needs children experience more trauma than their typical counterparts (Brenner et al., 2018; Mandell et al., 2005; Sullivan & Knutson, 2000).

Studies have explored whether special needs children respond positively to trauma treatment (Mevissen et al., 2011). Some focused specifically on EMDR treatment of children with developmental disabilities (Adler-Tapia, 2011; Ford & Adler-Tapia, 2010; Mevissen, 2011) or on the use of trauma-focused cognitive behavioural therapy (TF-CBT) (Holstead & Dalton, 2013), and another employed an integrative approach using EMDR, CBT, and other modalities (Scharloo & Coppens, 2010). One study focused on children with medical trauma (Lempertz, 2014). Additionally, there is a study of adults with developmental disabilities receiving EMDR treatment (Giamp, 2004).

Parents of Special Needs Children

Status of Support

Across the world, how much attention, understanding, and healing do the *parents* of special needs children receive? They are often given practical help to cope with their added responsibilities and stresses. However, parents may be disappointed in the quality of service offered by professionals: "Parents are often dismayed at having to be such strong self-advocates to professionals who serve them and their special needs child. Rather than experiencing a helpful, concerned and cooperative relationship, parents sometimes experience the parent-professional relationship as conflictual and adversarial" (Petr & Barney, 1993, 250). Sloper (1999) found that the most effective service models for parents are guided by full involvement of both parents and professionals. The literature indicates that in addition to special needs children being stigmatized and discriminated against, the parents report their own experiences of stigma-related discrimination, generally from professionals or strangers (McHatton & Correa, 2005). All of these concerns were chosen as topics to address with EMDR by many of the parent participants in the present study.

Once awareness of a problem surfaces, perhaps inspired by the disability and human rights movement, we hope for improvement for parents as well as children. Many programmes for helping these parents have focused on practical matters, such as financial assistance, navigating complicated systems to access help for their children, potential respite services, improving special education opportunities designed for the children's needs. But how often has there been the opportunity to address the diagnosis of a disability as a highly stressful event, in and of itself? Though it has likely been addressed by individual counsellors with their clients, it has not been reported in the literature.

Most parents of children with special needs devote such an extraordinary amount of time tending to the needs of their children that they often have little time for their own needs. With all their potential feelings of shock, grief, denial, guilt, anger, embarrassment, depression, overwhelm, or fear for the future, it may be very difficult for parents to share these vulnerable, distressing feelings. For these parents, receiving the awareness of their child's diagnosis was stressful, and for some, potentially traumatic.

Since we have begun to appreciate the greater need for emotional healing of special need children, can we also recognize that their parents experience more stress and trauma than the general population? They also need effective methods of healing and recovery.

In San Diego, California, USA, when parents received news of this opportunity to receive EMDR therapy as research subjects, several reported that it took time to realize the opportunity was not for their children but instead for themselves. Three parents reported the realization brought them to tears.

EMDR

Eye movement desensitization and reprocessing (EMDR) has been shown to decrease the distress of traumatic or stressful memories. It was developed and researched by Shapiro (1989) and has since been reported in over 400 research studies, including over 40 randomized control studies (EMDR Foundation).

There is no current research on EMDR for parents of special needs children. As Barol and Seubert (2010) reported, until as recently as 2010, it was considered that children with a dual diagnosis of intellectual and developmental disabilities (IDD) with a mental health diagnosis and consequent challenging behaviours would not be appropriate to treat with psychotherapy. However, their study of six clients showed that their young patients could benefit from EMDR focused on the trauma they had experienced, and it could help them to overcome their challenging behaviours.

One of the present authors was asked by the owner of a private special education school in Lucknow, India, to provide group EMDR therapy in March 2020 to parents of special needs children. After two sessions in one day focusing on stressful experiences related to their children, these parents responded positively. Thus, it was decided to study the effects of a more thorough treatment plan.

No studies of potential PTSD in parents of special needs children could be found.

Current Study: The Purposes of This Study

The purposes of the present study are threefold: *first*, to determine what psychological effects a child's disability may have on their parents. They will be assessed for scores reflecting depression, anxiety, stress level, PTSD, and distress level about their child's diagnosis.

Second, this study attempts to determine the value of a comprehensive group EMDR treatment programme (in an online format for safety during the COVID-19 pandemic) focusing on the EMDR 3-pronged protocol. This divides treatment into three foci for treatment on two days: Part 1 clears the distress of three past events related to their child to include the first experience that is still disturbing, the worst experience, and the most recent experience; Part 2 addresses two current triggers for distress and concludes with addressing a future concern for their child and strengthening a future template for handling stress.

Third, no research has been published to date on using EMDR therapy in an online format. Research in this area is greatly needed at a time when for many, online formats are the safest way to offer therapy. Potentially, online group treatment may also offer a more affordable way for more to receive healing opportunities.

Qualitative assessment was done after Part 1 on the first day (via an emailed handout to return afterwards) and after Part 2 on the second day was completed, while the group was still together online. This immediate feedback guides future efforts to serve this population. Additional qualitative feedback was part of every stage of follow-up.

The same set of assessments will be given at one-week post Part 1, one month after Part 2, and 12 months after completion of the two-part group EMDR experience.

Method

This is an exploratory pilot research study that used quasi-experimental and qualitative designs, with pre-assessments and multiple postmeasures and by qualitative data taken after each session of the two-part treatment plan.

Each participant experienced 6 h of EMDR therapy and an approximate total of 30 min of preparation time and closure time before and after each half-day session.

Participants

Participants in this study were recruited by three ways: making the study public by posting notices, seeking potential parents known by local special education teachers (serving special needs students), and inviting therapists to inform their contacts of the opportunity. Of the six participant parents of special needs children, four were therapists.

Each of the participants consented to participate in the study, complete the pre- and postevaluations (postevaluations were taken at 1-week and 1-month follow-up and will be taken again at 12-month follow-up). Preliminary findings will be reported in the present paper after 1-month follow-up.

Assessment Tools

In the pretreatment assessment, a history questionnaire was used to prescreen individuals to make sure that they would be candidates for an online group treatment.

1. History survey.
2. Burns Depression Checklist (Burns, 1995).
3. Burns Anxiety Inventory (Burns, 1995).
4. PCL-C found at PTSD.VA.gov.
5. Differentiation of Self Inventory, This test was developed and researched by Skowron and Friedlander (1998) and Skowron et al. (2009). It may show an indication of improvement in relationship functioning.
6. Parent Experience Scale. This scale is adapted from Burden Assessment Scale with permission from Reinhard (1994) and Duchovic et al. (2009) measures factors associated with parental distress.
7. A Qualitative Survey asking what was most helpful and what was most challenging about this group therapy? What was most surprising about the EMDR experience?

In post-assessment, all items but the first were offered again.

EMDR Treatment Provision

EMDR consists of an eight-phase protocol. Phase 1 is the *history* stage. A prescreening questionnaire (Terrell, 2020) was used to screen for any parents who needed more individualized screening to make sure they were good candidates at this time for the EMDR treatment. Two questions concerned any negative experience in a group setting or with a therapist in the past. There was no research subject who had one of these issues or other significant red flags, such as dissociation, (Bernstein and Putnam, 1986) that would either require more individual attention before the group experience, or could rule out a group EMDR experience altogether.

Phase 2 is *preparation*. This consisted of educating about the EMDR process, and teaching two self-help techniques including Container Exercise ("imagine a container big enough and strong enough to hold all the distress you need a break from now and place your distress in the container and shut it securely"), and the

4 Elements Exercise (Shapiro, 2014) which includes a grounding technique, deep breathing, swallowing saliva to exit the "fight or flight" state and shift to "rest and digest" and an imagery technique to recall a positive memory; and the Butterfly Hug (BH), a method of self-administered bilateral stimulation (Jarero & Artigas, 2012).

Phase 3 is *assessment* of the visual, auditory/cognitive (negative belief), emotional, and physical aspects of the memory. Phase 4 accomplishes *desensitization* of a memory through gentle bilateral stimulation through the sense nerves related to sight, sound, or touch. Stimulation may include repetitive eye movements or sounds or taps (as in the Butterfly Hug technique) delivered bilaterally to the two sides of the body. Once the distress of the memory reaches 0 or what is accepted as ecological at this time, Phase 5, *installation*, begins. The preferred positive belief chosen during Phase 3 is now strong and can be held in the mind with the initial negative image. This is paired with bilateral stimulation to strengthen the stability of the positive belief.

Phase 6 is the *body scan*. While holding the original memory image in mind, and concentrating on the positive cognition, the client is directed to scan the body from head to toe. This step was omitted from the Group protocol, because it was not always the case that each individual reached a distress level of 0 in the time allowed for group processing.

Phase 7, *closure*, concludes the session in a way that assures that members are feeling comfortable and stable. This is done by asking each one to share what they gained from the experience and what was challenging for them. Then as a group, the container exercise is used to imaginatively "put away" any remaining distress.

Phase 8, *reassessment*, is usually a check to determine whether the result held at the time of a follow-up session. That step was not feasible, and instead, the closure activity was used to learn if a participant remained distressed at the close of the session and may have needed individual attention.

The EMDR integrative group treatment protocol was developed by Artigas and reported by Jarero and Artigas (2012) and Jarero et al. (2015). It has been beneficially applied with children who survived natural or man-made disasters and for adult female cancer patients. It utilizes art therapy as well as the Butterfly Hug (BH) as a self-administered form of bilateral stimulation. This procedure allowed a group to receive EMDR therapy from one practitioner for the first time. Participants can maintain a high degree of privacy through the drawing format. Participants think of the worst image associated with their distressing memory and draw it with simple stick figures and then do bilateral stimulation using BH. They then draw another drawing reflecting how they feel now and use the BH. This process is repeated a total of four times, allowing distress to decrease. Participants are instructed to share in group a general idea of what they are working on, without the details. The goal is to concentrate completely on calming and neutralizing their own memories, and prevent secondary traumatization, or acquiring distressing new memories shared by other group participants.

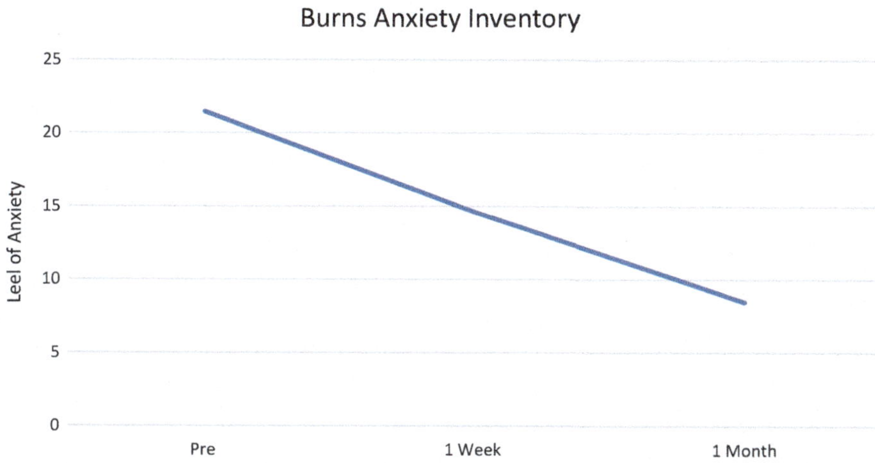

Fig. 2.1 Average Burns Anxiety Inventory score decreased from a moderate level of 21.5 at pretest to 7.8 at one-month post-test, which is considered a borderline anxiety level

Results

Note: All scores represent averages of all participants' scores. The subjects were under the cutoff for a PTSD diagnosis, except for one individual who initially qualified for PTSD with a score of 59. There was no consistent change in Differentiation of Self Inventory scores. Some people showed gains, while some showed decreases. The parents had a lot of stress. Figures 2.1, 2.2, 2.3, 2.4, and 2.5 show improvements on a number of variables.

Discussion

This was a pilot study with a quasi-experimental design. To truly validate it, it would need a randomized control study with a much larger sample size to validate the efficacy of this intensive group treatment experience for the population of parents of special needs children.

The *first* purpose for this study was to determine what psychological effects a child's disability may have on their parents. Parents were assessed for initial scores reflecting depression, anxiety, stress level, emotional response to their child's diagnosis, and PTSD. The parents had anxiety, depression, and stress not qualifying for PTSD. Four had high levels of distress about their child's disability diagnosis.

The *second* purpose was to see the effect of the treatment on the initial distress. The anxiety measures decreased. Interestingly, their depression first increased at 1-week post and then decreased from original levels by one-month post. It is not possible to determine the exact reason for this, because the 1-week qualitative data

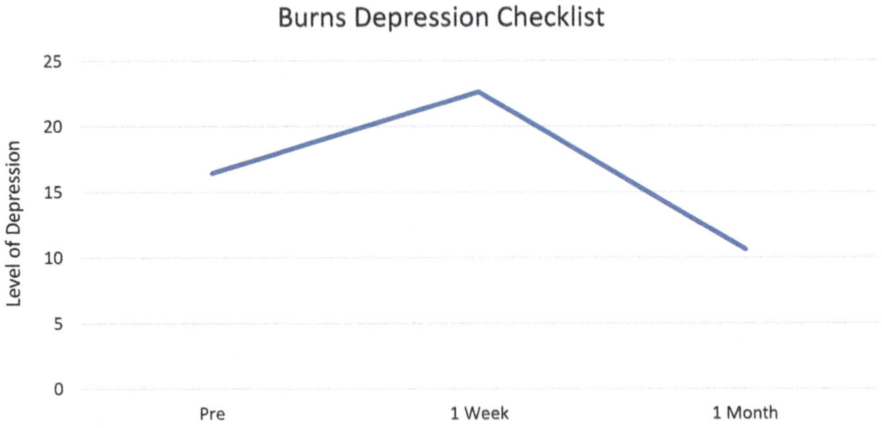

Fig. 2.2 Average Burns Depression Checklist at pretest was 16.5. At one week, the average scores increased to 23.6. By one-month post-test, the average score dropped to 10.8. An initial average of mild depression increased to a moderate average depression score of 21.5 at one-week post and then dropped to a normal but unhappy average score of 7.8 at one-month post-test

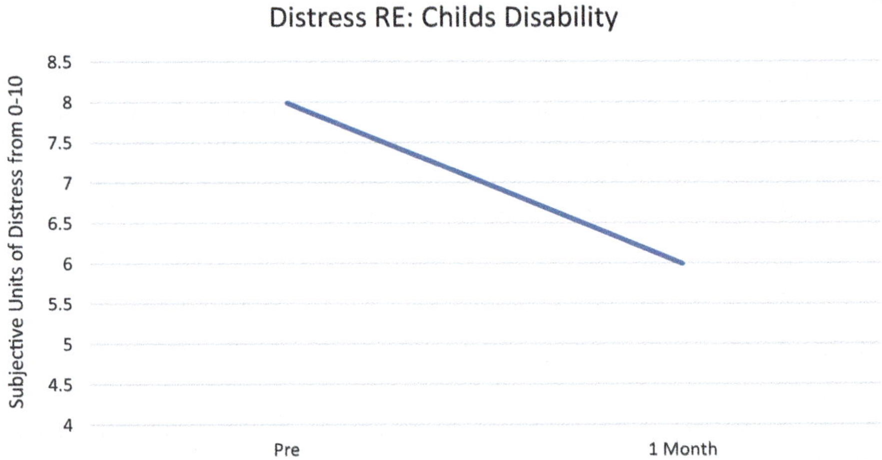

Fig. 2.3 SUDS measure of distress regarding the child's disability decreased from an average of 8 to an average of 6 (potential scores range from 0 to 10). Data from one subject, as an outlier, were omitted from this chart. That subject's initial score of 1 increased to 5

were not submitted by four of six parents. That information could have clarified if the depression scores were due to the intervention. In their qualitative responses by 1 month, parents listed many confounding variables having to do with COVID-19 stresses, such as children returning to school or to online learning while parents still worked from home, less support from family and workers due to COVID restrictions, etc. It is not clear why this affected depression scores but not anxiety scores.

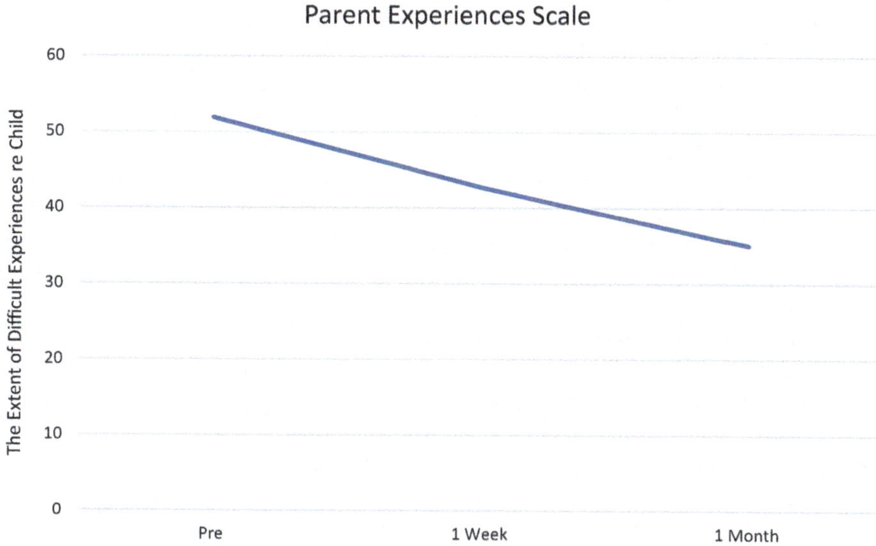

Fig. 2.4 Average score for the extent of difficulty with child-related experiences decreased from an average of 52.0, decreasing to 44.6 after one week, and decreasing further to 35.0 after one month

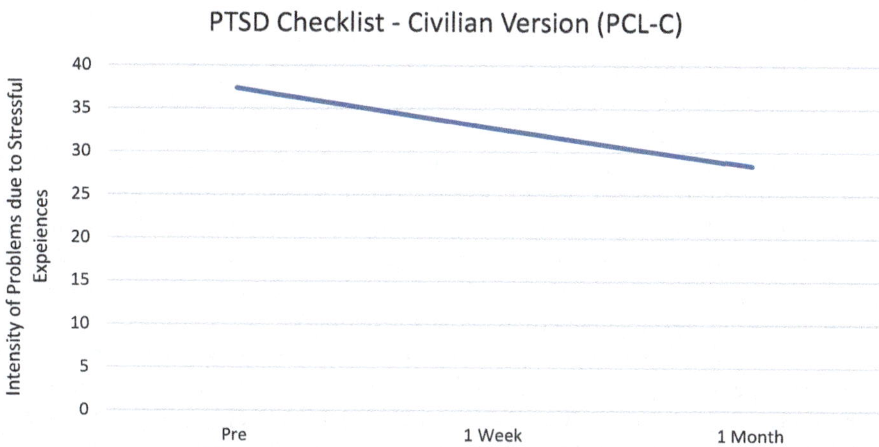

Fig. 2.5 Intensity of difficulties as measured by PCL-C decreased from an initial average of 37 to 28 by one-month postintervention. 44–50 indicates probably post-traumatic stress. Thus, these parents did not have PTSD, on average, and after intervention their scores dropped. As mentioned above, one parent did qualify for PTSD at the pretest with a score of 59, which reduced to 43 at one-month post-test

All parents expressed difficulty facing their feelings about their child's disability diagnosis. In one case, the parent believed initially that her distress level was low and was surprised to discover strong feelings during the EMDR treatment. For that parent, the distress began at a 1 and increased to a 5. She commented that she had been good at ignoring the distress. A second parent began at a 5 and increased to a 6. The other four parents started out with higher distress levels as measured at pretest, between 8 and 10. One month later, their scores ranged from 5 to 7.

The Parent Experience Scale scores indicate that the parents were stressed to begin with. Their stress score average began at 52.0, decreased to 44.6 after one week and to 35.0 after one month.

The beneficial improvements in levels of anxiety, depression, parent experiences scale, and distress regarding their child's diagnosis indicate that a comprehensive integrative EMDR group treatment plan focusing on the EMDR 3-pronged protocol had a positive value for parents of special needs children.

The *third* purpose was to report the results of offering the EMDR integrative group treatment protocol in an online format with six participants. The parents reported that they were surprised that online EMDR could work. Comments included,

- "I was surprised at how effective [EMDR online] was to reduce my bottled-up stress."
- "I was nervous about strangers, but our special link made it comfortable to meet virtually." "I forgot we were online and felt connected to others."

The 3-h format for parents of young children was hard on everyone. It was hard for the children and their co-parent to manage the children for three hours. Parents were unanimous in preferring a two-hour format offered on three days.

For several parents, the pandemic meant that children were in the home while they were trying to process trauma. Parents feared a child suddenly entering their space (which did happen) causing a loss of confidentiality and distraction from their purpose in the group treatment. In future, therefore, participants should be advised to coordinate with other caregivers so that they have no parenting responsibilities or interruptions during an online group therapy experience.

In a more rigorous study with a large number of subjects, would results be improved by guiding parents to protect their privacy and confidentiality by choosing a more private location for the online therapy? Alternatively, could they arrange for their children to be cared for in another location? Also, could the reassessment phase be strengthened? Participants could be informed in advance and at the end of the day's session that if they have distress remaining after the closure steps, that individual follow-up can be scheduled as needed.

When parents were asked their opinion about what percentage of parents of special needs children would benefit from a similar opportunity for group EMDR therapy, five parents reported 90–100% needed it. One parent, who had the most difficulty with interruptions by family, reported that 60% of parents need it. Either way, training more EMDR therapists to meet this need could make a significant difference in the reducing stress indicators of parents living with these varied ongoing challenges concerning their special needs child.

Limitations and Questions for Further Study

1. There was variety of factors and activities occurring in participant homes at this time during COVID-19, including fear of COVID, financial stresses, parents working at home, children studying at home; providing many confounding variables beyond the children's disability. Thus, it is very important to do an experimental study with randomized assignment and control group with larger numbers of subjects.
2. Given that systems' theory indicates that helping one part of a system can help the entire system, this small pilot study gives hope that the rest of the nuclear family may benefit from a calming process. For that to be ascertained, the family as a whole, including the special needs child, would need to be studied before and after the intervention with a parent.
3. Since parents of special needs children have higher rates of anxiety and depression, and greater stresses than the general population, would it help to offer EMDR *early* in the child's life? Would it be helpful to offer it not only to parents, but even interested members of the extended family using the EMDR integrative Group protocol (which allows for privacy) while they are processing distressing events concerning the child's diagnosis? Would this leave parents and family calmed earlier on in the child's life and better able to face together the challenges with which the child will live?

Conclusion

The results of the pilot study show decreases in anxiety, depression, parenting stresses, and distress about the child's disability. EMDR seems an effective treatment for the stress experienced by parents of special needs children. Considering the importance of the role they play, further and more rigorous research with randomized control studies and large samples is recommended.

References

Adler-Tapia, R. (2011). Improving lives: PTSD and the use of EMDR in psychotherapy for people with intellectual and developmental disabilities. Presentation at the *16th EMDR International Association Conference*, Orange County, CA.

Barol, B. I., & Seubert, A. (2010). Stepping stones: EMDR treatment of individuals with intellectual and developmental disabilities and challenging behavior. *Journal of EMDR Research and Practice, 4*(4), 156–169. https://doi.org/10.1891/1933-3196.4.4.156

Bernstein, E. M., & Putnam, F. W. (1986). Development, reliability, and validity of a dissociation scale. *Journal of Nervous and Mental Disease, 174*(12), 727–735.

Brenner, J., Pan, Z., Mazefsky, C., Smith, K. A., Gabriels, R., Siegel, M., & Autism and Developmental Disorders Inpatient Research Collaborative (ADDIRC). (2018). Behavioral symptoms of reported abuse in children and adolescents with autism spectrum disorder in inpatient settings. *Journal of Autism and Developmental Disorders, 48*(11), 3727–3735. https://doi.org/10.1007/s10803-017-3183-4

Burns, D. D. (1995). *Therapists toolkit: State-of-the-art assessment and treatment tools for the mental health professional*. Author.

Duchovic, C., Gerkensmeyer, J. E., & Wu, J. (2009). Factors associated with parental distress. *Journal of Child and Adolescent Psychiatric Nursing, 22*(1), 40–48. https://doi.org/10.1111/j.1744-6171.2008.00168.x

Ford, G., & Adler-Tapia, R. (2010). Improving lives: Diagnosis of PTSD and EMDR treatment for people with I/DD. Plenary presented at the *Annual NASDDDS (National Association of State Directors of Developmental Disabilities Services) Conference*, Arlington, Virginia.

Giamp, J. S. (2004). *Honoring their voice: Eye movement desensitization and reprocessing through the eyes of inmates with developmental disabilities* [Dissertation]. Walden University.

Holstead, J., & Dalton, J. (2013). Utilization of trauma-focused cognitive behavioral therapy (TF-CBT) for children with cognitive disabilities. *Journal of Public Child Welfare, 7*(5), 536–548. https://doi.org/10.1080/15548732.2013.843495

Jarero, I., & Artigas, L. (2012). The EMDR integrative group treatment protocol: EMDR group treatment for early intervention following critical incidents. *Revue Europenne De Psychologie Applique/European Review of Applied Psychology, 62*(4), 219–222. https://doi.org/10.1016/j.erap.2012.04.004

Jarero, I., Artigas, L., Uribe, S., Garcia, L. E., Cavazos, M. A., & Givaudan, M. (2015). Pilot research study on the provision of the EMDR integrative group treatment protocol with female cancer patients. *Revista Iberoamericana de Psycotraumatologia y Dissociacion, 6*(3), 1–16. https://doi.org/10.1891/1933-3196.9.2.98

Kildahl, A. N., Bakken, T. L., Iversen, T. E., & Helverschou, S. B. (2019). Identification of post-traumatic stress disorder in individuals with autism spectrum disorder and intellectual disability: A systematic review. *Journal of Mental Health Research in Intellectual Disabilities, 12*(1–2), 1–25. https://doi.org/10.1080/19315864.2019.1595233

Lempertz, D. (2014). EMDR in the treatment of medically traumatized children. In *EMDR Clinical Practice Symposium* (M. Luber, Chair) Symposium presented at the *15th EMDR Europe Association Conference*, Edinburgh, Scotland.

Mandell, D. S., Walrath, C. M., Manteuffel, B., Sgro, G., & Pinto-Martin, J. A. (2005). The prevalence and correlates of abuse among children with autism served in comprehensive community-based mental health settings. *Child Abuse and Neglect, 29*, 1359–1372. https://doi.org/10.1016/j.chiabu.2005.06.006

McHatton, P. A., & Correa, V. (2005). Stigma and discrimination: Perspectives from Mexican and Puerto Rican mothers of children with special needs. *Topics in Early Childhood Special Education, 25*(3), 131–142. https://doi.org/10.1177/02711214050250030101

Mevissen, L. (2011, June). Treatment of people with developmental disabilities. How far can we go? Presentation at the *12th EMDR Europe Association Conference*, Vienna, Austria.

Mevissen, L., Lievegoed, R., Seubert, A., & De Jongh, A. (2011). Do persons with intellectual disability and limited verbal capacities respond to trauma treatment? *Journal of Intellectual and Developmental Disability, 36*(4), 278–283.

Petr, C. G., & Barney, D. D. (1993). Reasonable efforts for children with disabilities: The parents' perspective. *Social Work, 38*(3), 247–254. https://doi.org/10.1093/sw/38.3.247

Reinhard, S. C., Gubman, G. D., Horwitz, A. V., & Minsky, S. (1994). Burden assessment scale for families of the seriously mentally ill. *Evaluation and Program Planning, 17*(3), 260–269. Adapted from Burden Assessment Scale and used with permission from Susan C. Reinhard and Catherine Duchovic.

Scharloo, A., & Coppens, L. (2010). Trauma treatment after sexual abuse for people with developmental disabilities. Presentation at the *2nd Bi-Annual International European Society for Trauma and Dissociation Conference*, Belfast, Northern Ireland.

Shapiro, F. (1989). Efficacy of the eye movement desensitization procedure in the treatment of traumatic memories. *Journal of Traumatic Stress, 2*(2), 199–223. https://doi.org/10.1002/jts.2490020207

Shapiro, E. (2014). Four elements exercise for stress management. In M. Luber (Ed.), *Implementing EMDR early mental health interventions for man-made and natural disasters: Models, scripted protocols, and summary sheets* (pp. 133–142). Springer Publishing Co.

Skowron, E. A., & Friedlander, M. L. (1998). The differentiation of self inventory: Development and initial validation. *Journal of Counseling Psychology, 45*, 235–246. https://doi.org/10.1037/0022-0167.45.3.235

Skowron, E. A., Stanley, K. L., & Shapiro, M. D. (2009). A longitudinal perspective on differentiation of self, interpersonal and psychological well-being in young adulthood. *Contemporary Family Therapy, 31*, 3–18. https://doi.org/10.1007/s10591-008-9075-1

Sloper, P. (1999). Models of service support for parents of disabled children. What do we know? What do we need to know? *Child: Care, Health and Development, 25*(2), 85–99.

Sullivan, P. M., & Knutson, J. F. (2000). Maltreatment and disabilities: A population-base epidemiological study. *Child Abuse & Neglect, 24*(10), 1257–1273. https://doi.org/10.1016/S0145-2134(00)00190-3

Terrell, D. E. (2020). History of adult adverse experiences for parents of special needs children.

Wigham, S., Hatton, C., & Taylor, J. L. (2011). The effects of traumatizing life experiences on people with intellectual disabilities: A systematic review. *Journal of Mental Health Research in Intellectual Disabilities, 4*(1), 19–39. https://doi.org/10.1080/19315864.2010.534576

Chapter 3
Social Role Valorization Theory in India: An Idea with Consequences

Elizabeth Neuville, Percy Cardozo, Mitu De, and Raymond Lemay

Abstract Simply put, the goal of Social Role Valorization is to make the *good things of life* available to devalued and marginalized people (Caruso and Osburn in J Policy Pract Intellect Disabil Res 8:191–196, 2011). Such good things include a home, relationships, a decent reputation, belonging, a robust self-image, opportunities, and a comfortable lifestyle, and these are near universal in terms of their values across peoples and across cultures. SRV first recognizes and gives a detailed accounting of the impact of systematic devaluation on the lives of certain societal groups.

Keywords Inclusion · Inclusive practice · Social role valorization · Social incusion · Integration · Normaization de-institutionalization · Individualization · Social role theory · Social roles · Social devaluation

What Is Social Role Valorization?

Simply put, the goal of Social Role Valorization is to make the *good things of life* available to devalued and marginalized people (Caruso & Osburn, 2011). Such good things include a home, relationships, a decent reputation, belonging, a robust self-image, opportunities, and a comfortable lifestyle, and these are near universal in terms of their values across peoples and across cultures. SRV first recognizes and gives a

E. Neuville (✉)
Keystone Human Services International, Delhi, India
e-mail: Eneuville@khs.org

P. Cardozo
Sangath, Socorro, Goa, India
e-mail: percy.cardozo@sangath.in

M. De
Gurudas College, Kolkata, West Bengal, India
e-mail: mitu.botany@gurudas.education

R. Lemay
International Social Role Valorization Association, Ottawa, ON, Canada
e-mail: raylemay@rogers.com

R. Uniyal and F. Rizvi (eds.), *Understanding Disability*,
https://doi.org/10.1007/978-981-99-4925-0_3

detailed accounting of the impact of systematic devaluation on the lives of certain societal groups. These wounds of devaluation, as they are called so descriptively in SRV theory, are inflicted in highly predicable ways on individuals and groups and are very resistant to change because they are often inflicted without conscious intent to harm (Osburn, 2006). The consequences of social devaluation include the experience of profound rejection, congregation and segregation, symbolic stigmatization, de-individualization, time- and life-wasting, and role-casting into such devastating negative roles such as object of pity, menace, garbage, eternal child, and burden of charity. The infliction of these wounds sets up entire classes of people, as well as individual persons, to experience very poor treatment at the hands of society (Wolfensberger, 2013).

Social Role Valorization postulates that such wounds can be most effectively addressed using principles that "work" for typical members of society. If one studies typical society, it becomes apparent that the good things of life tend to come to people who have highly valued roles, and these, in fact, serve as a gateway for such good life experiences. In other words, valued social roles serve as a potent vehicle for many good life outcomes (Wolfensberger, 2013). This relatively simple precept forms the background for a multitude of implications about how, if one wants certain people to have the good things of life, certain things may be done which make that more likely, and certain other things will make that less likely. All of SRV is based on such "if this … then that" propositions, offering extensive guidance to practitioners, service workers, activists, and people with disability and their families (Wolfensberger, 1995).

Social Role Valorization describes how people come to be at the bottom of the social ladder and what really works in people's lives to lift them out of this social devaluation (Neuville, 2019). The central strategy is to help people who are entrenched in deeply harmful social roles—such as burden, eternal child, menace, sick, "better off dead", human service client, and object of ridicule to name a few—instead be assisted to move towards valued roles, like citizen, taxpayer, neighbour, big brother, student, employee, homeowner, amateur artist, and club member. These valued roles carry great weight for all people, as they are the means through which all people gain access to important elements of life such as acceptance, belonging, a good reputation, a strong self-image, opportunities, and a full, rich life (Osburn, 2006). Services which support and assist people with disabilities to have valued social roles as a focus point seem to be the ones which provide the greatest well-being to the people they serve.

Unfortunately, many programmes intended to make life better for people with disabilities tend to focus on providing activities and keeping people busy, rather than working towards positively valued roles for each person, individually, and providing activities directly related to the development of valued roles. SRV offers a fundamentally different understanding about how to guide people towards good lives. Competency development is one way to build towards valued roles—for example, assisting someone to be in the role of an amateur artist involves learning at least some of the skills needed to create art, but also involves helping someone to have the image of the role—by having the equipment, the materials, the right clothing, and be in the physical places that artists spend time. In addition, one would help a person be with the typical people in society that artists tend to spend time with.

Much more remains to be said about valued roles, their benefits, and how to support people with disability to grow into them successfully, but a deeper study of SRV can be pursued elsewhere. SRV has been referred to as an "elegant theory" (Flynn & Lemay, 1999), meaning that it is a simple concept from which many programmatic lessons can be drawn. An organization does not use SRV as a checklist or standard set of practices—but if used as a base, it seems that whatever methods are used can be used better, more fully, and with more positive benefit and less unintentional harm if designed and carried out on a strong foundation of SRV (Caruso & Osburn, 2011).

Inclusive education will likely more truly inclusive and successful with an understanding of the power of imitation and modelling and role circularities offered by SRV theory. All things being equal, helping people who have been rejected and isolated actually gain life-giving relationships is more likely if SRV theory is put to use. Creating community-based services that are integrative rather than segregating can be aided using SRV. It is helpful in addressing issues of service design, as well, and may result in programmes that successfully meet the most pressing needs of people and that are effective at helping people enter into valued roles successfully. SRV study and use appear to help professionals, families, and advocates, and everyday citizens see more keenly the wounding experiences that disabled people must contend with, identify more closely with such people, and work more fruitfully towards better futures.

Historical Roots and Impact of SRV

The ideas that developed and coalesced to become Social Role Valorization theory emerged in the 1950s–1960s at a time of widespread disenchantment with congregate care settings for children and adults with intellectual impairments. Residential institutions in North America and Western Europe were essentially custodial, of poor quality, even dehumanizing (Wolfensberger, 1969), and not a few were the subject of negative exposés in the popular press (Blatt & Kaplan, 1974). In his history of the principle of normalization, Wolfensberger (1999) recounts that though many were in agreement that the institution had to go, it was not at all clear what it should be replaced with. There was no available organizing idea to direct the establishment of a new approach to serving people with disabilities.

However, there were, here and there, attempts at change and innovation. Wolfensberger (1934–2011), while on a postdoctoral research fellowship in the early 1960s, visited cutting-edge services in Germany, Switzerland, Belgium, and parts of the UK and wrote up what he found (1964a, 1964b, 1965). With the participation of many families of people with intellectual disabilities, Wolfensberger was also a leader in designing and setting up a new community service system in the state of Nebraska in the USA (Schalock, 2002), where many new service modalities were imported from Europe or were original in design.

In 1969, Kugel and Wolfensberger (1969) were asked to bring together a group of leaders in the field of disability to describe residential alternatives for people with cognitive impairments. "Changing Patterns in Residential Services" to which contributed a number of the leading lights of the era included Nirje's (1969) first systematic description of what he was first to call the "normalization principle" and defined it as "making available to the mentally retarded patterns and conditions of everyday life which are as close as possible to the norms and patterns of the mainstream of society." The book and Nirje's chapter ended up becoming quite influential. More detailed histories of normalization are available (Lemay, 1995; Nirje, 1999; Wolfensberger, 1999).

Wolfensberger further elaborated the principle of normalization to apply to all groups of people at risk of marginalization (Wolfensberger, 1970). His 1972 book on "The principle of Normalization for Human Services" was a best seller; however, the term "normalization" generated some controversy and many misconceptions (Wolfensberger, 1980). Also, Wolfensberger's definition of it had evolved considerably with the "social role" concept becoming a key element (Wolfensberger & Tullman, 1982). In 1983, he suggested that the principle should be called something else and proposed the expression "Social Role Valorization" (SRV) as the name of a theory that reached beyond normalization. In line with his goal of defining it as a social science theory, he evacuated much of the ideological content. SRV thus became a descriptive theory that elucidated how social roles were the mechanism through which devaluation or valorization was transacted and later (Wolfensberger et al., 1996) that would emphasize how valued social roles opened up access to objective well-being or "the good things of life."

From the very beginning, normalization and then SRV have been very influential (Flynn & Lemay, 1999), particularly in the English-Speaking World (Canada, the USA, the UK, Ireland, Australia and New Zealand). Twenty years after its publication, the "The Principle of Normalization in Normalization" (Heller et al., 1991) was judged to be the most influential text on intellectual disabilities of the past 50 years. The 1983 article unveiling Social Role Valorization (Wolfensberger, 1983) was judged the 17th most important work over the same period of time (Heller et al., 1991).

The community-based service agency structure first developed in Nebraska has been widely replicated (Schalock, 2002). In 1994, the United Nation's hosted a conference in Reykjavik, Iceland, titled "Beyond Normalization: Towards a Society for All" (Lemay, 1994a) to unveil the new "Standard Rules for the Equalization of Opportunities for Persons with Disabilities" that owed much to the seminal contributions of normalization and SRV (Lemay, 1994b).

Over the past 40 years, many thousands of people around the world have attended multiday workshops that explain SRV theory. Many human service "best practices" find their origin in SRV such as support for individualization and autonomy and rights that are now commonplace (Caruso & Osburn, 2011). SRV's teaching on the issues of imagery and particularly language has gained widespread adherence. Inclusion/integration is broadly acknowledged as a primary goal of intervention, once again with SRV leading the way conceptually and through practice innovations

(Flynn & Aubry, 1999). Intervenors who engage in these best practices do not always acknowledge and possibly do not even know their provenance, but they are nonetheless products of SRV. However, SRV is best practised comprehensively; otherwise, applying a single best practice might end up being incoherent if the general thrust of intervention is counterproductive.

Though SRV and its concepts are well known in the Anglosphere, there are current Social Role Valorization initiatives ongoing in France, the Netherlands, Ireland, Republic of Moldova, and also to a limited degree in Japan and South Korea. Billimoria (1993) described the possible application of normalization in India, but normalization and SRV were first written and taught about in India by Dr. Akhilesh Kumar and various colleagues (Kumar et al., 2015) and with Dr. Thomas Thressiakutty (Kumar & Thressiakutty, 2012, 2020) and also an article by Saha (2017). In the scheme of things, Social Role Valorization is still a relatively new idea that continues to generate insight and innovation for those who sample its rich structure of concepts and practices.

Establishing the Foundation: SRV Teaching Across India

Apart from a few UK-educated scholars and practitioners exposed to the theory, SRV was not taught or used in any sort of a systematic way in India until about 2016. A few papers were written, including one highlighting a small-scale use of PASSING (Kumar et al., 2015), but it is clear that the full foundation for SRV understanding and use was not in place. In 2015, several influential partners, The National Trust, Rural India Supportive Trust, and The Hans Foundation collaborated with Keystone Institute India to support the inaugural introductory workshop in India, with highly experienced SRV international experts leading and providing the main aspects of the theory over 30 classroom hours in Delhi. In attendance were some of the most influential persons representing advocates and activists, parent leaders, and professionals, hailing from 13 states across India. The level of government and private sector support for this workshop was exceptional, especially considering that it was a leap of faith to believe that the ideas would be embraced, given that the faculty were from out of country (USA, Australia, and Republic of Moldova). In fact, the workshop was well received and resulted many of those course graduates sponsoring a host of brief, one-day workshops across the country over the next 18 months. Course graduates were also mentored to serve as faculty and resource persons at these smaller workshops.

This first wave of SRV teaching followed the preparation of in-country faculty for intensive courses, as well as thoughtful recruitment for all courses. Most of the initial course graduates nominated their own proteges and promising colleagues to attend the second intensive course offered in 2018. As well, across India, those teaching brief courses consistently kept a list of "bright spots" attendees showing both interest and promise as future SRV leaders. All these promising people were invited to apply to the courses offered in 2018 and again in 2019. The same sort of measured and intentional follow-up was taken after each, and each workshop cohort showed more and more excitement and intention to use SRV in the lives of their sons and daughters and the people they serve in their organizations. A high proportion of family members gave great strength to each of the cohorts. As has been the case in other countries, there were very few people with lived experience of developmental and other disabilities participating at each intensive workshop event.

A Platform for SRV Leaders

It should be said here that the formation of strong and experienced SRV educators is a committed process by those who mentor new trainers as well as those who aspire to be SRV trainers. Teaching even very brief workshops on SRV requires a much deeper knowledge of the theory and its use. It also requires much more than a theoretical grasp of the concepts and how they relate to each other. Those who teach SRV credibly must have significant experience with people with disability and their families and have experience assisting such persons to move into valued roles. Trainer formation in is a lengthy and intentional process (SRV Development, Training & Safeguarding Council, 2005), a far cry from the typical "train the trainer" events.

Some of the indicators of creating successful trainer formation process in India is that 100% of the faculty in the 2016 intensive workshop were from outside India, with admittedly little experience in-country. By the second course, named SRV 2.0 and offered in 2017, 40% of the lead trainers were Indian, and by the SRV 3.0 course offered in 2019, fully 60% of the leadership was Indian. Each course produced significant numbers of highly motivated persons hungry for more opportunities to put the ideas to work. In 2020, the All-India SRV Leadership Network was founded with over 100 members, with a mandate to offer a platform for the development of SRV course graduates.

At the time of this writing, there continues a small but active vanguard of people across India who are engaged in a mentoring process to conduct both brief and more extended high-quality workshops covering SRV basics. These courses are designed to give a conceptual overview of the consequences of devaluation along with the utility of valued social roles in moving people with disability towards access to the good things of life—belonging, acceptance, relationships, a positive reputation, true home, personal growth, and opportunity. As well, the workshops have been conducted in both Hindi and English and gave participants practical ideas and examples of implementation in the Indian context. These workshops have been helpful in exposing over 6000 people from nearly all Indian states to SRV in the first five years and have created fertile ground for recruiting standout participants for further engagement with the ideas as potential trainers or implementors. A number of these referenced emerging leaders have taken advanced training in the USA, and these potential senior trainers in India form the core of SRV teaching in India. In addition to developing capable and experienced SRV trainers within the country, another working group is focusing on aspects of writing and research, to generate a foundational Indian body of writing on SRV. A third thrust of activity is geared towards gaining experience in conducting SRV-based programme evaluation and assessment. These two activities, alongside the development of SRV trainers, will be essential in fleshing out the understanding of SRV across India as well as the actual implementation of Social Role Valorization.

SRV in Practice

SRV principles can be applied in the life of an individual person with a disability, a family, a programme or organization, or an entire society (Osburn, 2006), which gives it great relevance to any change efforts intended to benefit people with disabilities. In fact, SRV is not a method, but it is a foundational idea set which often means that methods rooted in it will be more successful and more likely to result in good outcomes in the lives of marginalized and oppressed people. As mentioned, inclusive education seems to be more successful when an understanding of Social Role Valorization informs it, as does person-centred planning, individual educational planning, vocational and livelihood ventures, and certainly residential services (Caruso & Osburn, 2011). Across India to date, SRV has taken strongest root within numerous organizations and among thought leaders in the field of developmental disability, but especially in programmes supporting people with autism. As implementation moves forward, experimental changes in programme practices towards both image enhancement as well as competency enhancement have been adopted across many services. Some of these changes are being captured in online resources and prepared for publication (Keystone Institute India, 2020).

SRV relies on modelling the design of supports and services to what typical valued people have, do, or want, making the ideas quite sensitive to culture. Efforts to assist people with disabilities to be in the normative pathways help with integrative efforts and access to valued roles. For example, children go to school, have standards and classes, and get together with their classmates after school. Most adults work, and if they do not, occupy their days by contributing in other ways to the society. Implementation efforts across India have focused on helping people with disability engage in typical activities, with typical people, in typical ways, in typical places, and in recognizable social roles (Lemay, 2006). The following case studies are intended to help illustrate the ways that SRV has been applied within organizations and within individual lives.

Case Studies

The case studies were undertaken with two organizations and one individual with a view of uncovering the implementation experiences of SRV in India. The founding members of these organizations and a guardian of the individual were interviewed.

The intent of the interviews was to understand the participants' motivations for the change, their experiences as they embarked on the journey, and the impact of SRV on their organizations. The interviews revealed that although the organizations have not been able to implement all principles/elements of SRV, they have made an excellent start. Data also showed that SRV had not only affected the organizations positively but has also influenced the personal lives of individual people to a large extent. As a start, the organizations and individuals have used SRV theory as a lens to evaluate their services delivery and interactions with people.

Fictional names have been used in place of the people and the organizations.

Case Study 1—Rani Y, the Founder Director and CEO of Pumpkin Patch Design Studio

Rani describes herself as a 21-year-old woman who loves dogs, horses, computers, travelling, and cycling. She adds that people not turning up on time upsets her the most and that she does not like her routine being shuffled. She says her family, friends, and her teacher have been her greatest supports. "Keep trying and learning" is the message she wants to convey to young people like her.

Rani, whose strengths are visualization and designing, was diagnosed with autism at a very young age. Her mum, Ritu, reminisces that her first session on SRV was an eye-opener and a life-changing experience. It subsequently led to a deeper engagement with the SRV leaders in India to plan a PATH (O'Brien et al., 2010) session for Rani. PATH is a creative, inclusive planning process that helps envision a future of valued roles and a plan to work towards that future. Ritu believes that elements from SRV have helped her clarify her expectations, focus on her daughter as an individual in her own right, and accept and respect her views. She liked the central focus that PATH accorded to Rani; for the first time, it gave her the control of her life and the freedom to plan it the way she envisioned. This empowering experience changed her life forever; it helped her discover her goal, built her self-confidence, and enhanced her social networks. Engagement with SRV networks has helped Rani carve a valued role for herself—that of an entrepreneur and an employer. It has allowed her to find a place for herself in society, gain respect from the community, and live an enriched life.

For Rani and the team who supports her, intentionally using highly valued imagery and helping her to gain the competencies to take the lead authentically at Pumpkin Patch has been an equal effort contributing to role success.

Case Study 2—The Axis Foundation (AF), New Delhi

The AF is a not-for-profit organization established more than a decade ago catering to the needs of children and adults with autism and developmental disabilities. Their vision is to transform communities to value every individual with developmental challenges and support them to lead a fulfilling life. To achieve this, they operate an early intervention centre, a special school, a vocational training centre for young adults, and they extend mentoring and training supports for families and advocate about disability issues.

AF is one of the earliest organizations in India to have embraced and adopted the teachings of the SRV theory. Its founder was introduced to the SRV network in India through one of AF's partner organizations. Her initial brief encounter with SRV attracted her to the concept and its relevance to the organization. She immediately got the board members, senior staff, and families involved in SRV training and requested a collaborative evaluation to discern pathways to move forward.

The first shuffle was the set-up of the classrooms to diminish the wounding and the stigmatization that resulted from "branding" the classes according to functional levels of students. They based the new structure on age levels, which matches the norms applied in the general education schools. Also, they embarked on a journey of "unlearning" the segregating terminologies and methods by pairing up with a neighbourhood school. In this way, they studied the schedule, the curriculum, the physical appearance inside and out, and the typical language used and matched it as best they could within AF. They created a separation between the school portion of the service and the vocational portion, so that there was normative separation between school and work, as well as young adult and child. The school aims for complete inclusion, but there are practical challenges that they have to deal with. Over the long haul, they can envision shifting to a more inclusive model but in the meantime have shifted towards integrated, community-based learning activities, maximizing experiential learning and increasing the potency of learning.

With a new understanding of the power of employment roles, specifically the role of employee, in-house vocational skills training was shifted towards authentic supported jobs in the community. The leadership of this organization is optimistic about the futures for the people served at AF as they move, more and more, towards using a framework of SRV in promoting valued roles. One important component is gaining the widespread support of the entire school community—board members, staff, families, and young people who access their services.

Case Study 3—The ABC Society, Kolkata

ABCS is a non-government organization working towards education, empowerment, and entrepreneurship development for young people with disabilities. They are striving to enable young people with disabilities to gain control over their lives and establish financial independence. ABCS envisions a place where young people with disabilities will be celebrated as valuable contributing members of the community.

The organization holds a strong belief that financial independence is the key to improve the status of young people with disabilities. When young people earn their own "bread and butter" through valued work, they enjoy a valued status in society, which will naturally allow them to enjoy some good things in life. Through a social enterprise model, ABCS reaches out to other organizations to provide support for skill-building, setting up business enterprises and mentorship. They have worked alongside a number of young people with disabilities to launch real careers. They plan and carry out image enhancement strategies in the form of community sensitization activities. In this way, they work to shape positive perceptions to enhance the status of young people with disabilities. When the organization was transitioning itself to function through an SRV-based approach, the biggest barrier was battling the negative attitudes that people hold towards persons with disabilities. ABCS has worked on both sides of the SRV equation. They use direct and explicit strategies to help people move into valued roles such as shareholder, colleague, tax payer, employee, entrepreneur, and trendsetter and also work to put good things into the minds of the typical citizens of Kolkata about people with disability and their contributions. SRV has inspired their model of inclusive social entrepreneurship, which focuses on capabilities and strengths, rather than deficits.

Future Directions

India is a nation whose roots are steeped in diverse cultural soils. As a nation, Indians have associated a negative value to many marginalized groups, viz. religious minorities, widows, poor people, individuals belonging to low castes, tribal or ethnic minorities, disabled people, refugees, migrant labourers, people with different sexual orientation, etc. An important consequence of this is that people operate within their cultural context but are often unaware of it (Stangor et al., 1996). Our close environment and culture influences prejudice because members of a culture hold sets of beliefs in common, including beliefs about behaviours, values, attitudes, and opinions. Michael Kendrick mentions in one of his paper "throughout history, one of the great commonalities in the human condition has been our propensity to devalue one another" (Kendrick, 1994).

The introductory course on "The Principles of Social Role Valorization (SRV)" created a powerful paradigm shift in consciousness of most of the SRV graduates in India. The course was an eye-opener, as it revealed how mainstream society devalues groups of people in India and how parents had preconceived notions about disability. It was particularly painful for many parents to realize how they had devalued their children or the people they served earlier, thinking it was good for them.

The SRV introductory courses and the several follow-up workshops across India gave the participants the courage to question their own beliefs about disability. SRV offered a lens through which they could view their role in society. SRV taught the course graduates to question themselves. This term "wounding" triggered a trail of reflective thinking among many of the anguished participants. They wondered who and how they had "wounded" unconsciously.

Participants were introduced to the power of "valued social roles" and how important they were so that the individual "experienced the good things in life". Image enhancement and competency enhancement were discussed as the primary means of getting people into valued social roles (Thomas, 1999; Wolfensberger, 2013).

Across India and some parts of Bangladesh, individuals set about implementing the principles of SRV. The case studies are examples.

An important consequence of the SRV training in India was helping parents of individuals with disability to have a vision for their children. Of course, the obstacles that came in the way were identified and paths were envisaged either around it, or over it or through it. PASSING (Wolfensberger & Thomas, 2007) is an evaluation tool that helps take a disciplined look at the rights and wrongs of human services through the lens of SRV. SRV theory and the PASSING evaluation instrument together provide a very useful theoretical framework and operational methodology for the analysis of the quality of human services. Mainstream and higher education and teacher training education are some of the areas where SRV, if introduced, may create a stronger foundation for inclusive strategies.

Conclusion

United Nations (UN) Secretary-General António Guterres said "When we secure the rights of persons with disabilities, we move our world closer to upholding the core values and principles of the United Nations Charter". Inclusion exists where people are enabled to take part in the activities and roles that are part of mainstream society such as having a job (Wistow & Schneider, 2003).

The future is yet to be shaped, and we all have the power of influencing it. How we perceive ourselves and others will have implications where we are heading as a society in the future. We humans share basic wants and needs that are the hallmark of humanity. It is the collective mindset of a nation which determines the future. An understanding of Social Role Valorization (SRV) can lead to an inclusive mindset which could improve the lives of people who are devalued by society.

References

Billimoria, R. B. (1993). *Principle and practice of normalization: Experiences from Sweden and application to India*. Uppsala University.

Blatt, B., & Kaplan, F. (1974). *Christmas in purgatory: A photographic essay on mental retardation*. Human Policy Press.

Caruso, G., & Osburn, J. (2011). The origins of "best practices" in the principle of normalization and social role valorization. *Journal of Policy and Practices in Intellectual Disability Research, 8*(3), 191–196.

Flynn, R. J., & Aubry, T. (1999). Integration of persons with developmental or psychiatric disabilities. In R. J. Flynn & R. A. Lemay (Eds.), *A quarter-century of normalization and social role valorization: Evolution & impact* (pp. 271–304). University of Ottawa Press.

Flynn, R. J., & Lemay, R. A. (1999). Normalization and social role valorization at a quarter-century: Evolution, impact, and renewal. In *A quarter-century of normalization and social role valorization: Evolution and impact* (pp. 3–16).

Heller, H. W., Spooner, F., Enright, B. E., Haney, K., & Schilit, J. (1991). Classic articles: A reflection into the field of mental retardation. *Education and Training in Mental Retardation, 26*, 202–206.

Kendrick, M. (1994). Some reasons why social role valorization is important. *SRV/VRS: The International Social Role Valorization Journal/La Revue Internationale de la Valorisation des Roles Sociaux, 1*(1), 14–18.

Keystone Institute India. Jhalak: Portraits of SRV and person-centred practices. https://www.jhalak.org. Accessed November 24, 2020.

Kugel, R., & Wolfensberger, W. (Eds.). (1969). *Changing patterns in residential services for the mentally retarded*. President's Committee on Mental Retardation.

Kumar, A., Singh, R. R., & Thressiakutty, A. T. (2015). Quality of special education services in India: A PASSING analysis. *European Academic Research, III*(7), 7331–7347.

Kumar, A., & Thressiakutty, A. T. (2012). Social role valorization (SRV): A strong voice of disability. *Scholarly Research Journal for Interdisciplinary Studies, I*(II), 284–292.

Kumar, A., & Thressiakutty, A. T. (2020). Impressions of principle of normalization on special education services in India. *Scholarly Research Journal for Humanity Science & English Language, 8*(37).

Lemay, R. (1994a). A Reykjavik Journal. *SRV/VRS: The International Social Role Valorization Journal/La Revue Internationale de la Valorisation des Rôles Sociaux, 1*(2), 42–44.

Lemay, R. (1994b). A review of the "standard rules on the equalization of opportunities for persons with disabilities". United Nations Department for Policy Coordination and Sustainable Development. *SRV/VRS: The International Social Role Valorization Journal/La Revue Internationale de la Valorisation des Rôles Sociaux, 1*(2), 47–51.

Lemay, R. (1995). Normalization and social role valorization. In A. E. Dell Orto & R. P. Marinelli (Eds.), *Encyclopedia of disability and rehabilitation* (pp. 515–521). Simon & Schuster, Macmillan.

Lemay, R. (2006). Social role valorization insights into the social integration conundrum. *Mental Retardation, 44*(1), 1–12.

Neuville, E. (2019). Pathways to the mainstream: The promise of social role valorization. In S. Dutta & M. De (Eds.), *Understanding autism* (pp. 32–46). The Asiatic Society.

Nirje, B. (1969). The normalization principle and its human management implications. In R. Kugel & W. Wolfensberger (Eds.), *Changing patterns in residential services for the mentally retarded* (pp. 179–195). President's Committee on Mental Retardation.

Nirje, B. (1999). How I came to formulate the normalization principle. In R. J. Flynn & R. A. Lemay (Eds.), *A quarter-century of normalization and social role valorization: Evolution & impact* (pp. 17–50). University of Ottawa Press.

O'Brien, J., Pearpoint, J., & Kahn, L. (2010). The PATH and MAPS handbook. In *Person-Centered Ways.*

Osburn, J. (2006). An overview of social role valorization theory. *The SRV Journal, 1*(1), 4–13.

Saha, S. (2017). Difficulties and exploitation in inclusive schooling: In-field reflections in mental disorder/disability inclusion in India. *Journal of Psychosocial Research, 12*(2).

Schalock, R. L. (2002). Out of the darkness and into the light: Nebraska's experience with mental retardation. *AAMR.*

SRV Development, Training & Safeguarding Council. (2005). *A brief overview of the North American SRV Council's trainer formation model.*

Stangor, C., Jonas, K., Stroebe, W., & HEWSTONE, M. (1996). Influence of student exchange on national stereotypes, attitudes and perceived group variability. *European Journal of Social Psychology, 26*(4), 663–675.

Thomas, S. (1999). Historical background and evolution of normalization-related and social role valorization-related training. In R. J. Flynn & R. A. Lemay (Eds.), *A quarter-century of normalization and social role valorization: Evolution and impact* (pp. 353–374). University of Ottawa Press.

Wistow, R., & Schneider, J. (2003). Users' views on supported employment and social inclusion: A qualitative study of 30 people in work1. *British Journal of Learning Disabilities, 31*(4), 166–173.

Wolfensberger, W. (1964a). Some observations on European programs for the mentally retarded. *Mental Retardation, 2*(5), 280–285.
Wolfensberger, W. (1964b). Teaching and training of the retarded in European countries. *Mental Retardation, 2*(6), 331–337.
Wolfensberger, W. (1965). General observations on European programs. *Mental Retardation, 3*(1).
Wolfensberger, W. (1969). The origin and nature of our institutional models. In R. Kugel & W. Wolfensberger (Eds.), *Changing patterns in residential services for the mentally retarded* (pp. 59–171). President's Committee on Mental Retardation.
Wolfensberger, W. (1970). The principle of normalization and its implications to psychiatric services. *American Journal of Psychiatry, 127*, 291–297.
Wolfensberger, W. (1980). The definition of normalization: Update, problems, disagreements and misunderstandings. In R. J. Flynn & K. E. Nitsch (Eds.), *Normalization, social integration, and community services*. Baltimore.
Wolfensberger, W. (1983). Social role valorization: A proposed new term for the principle of normalization. *Mental Retardation, 21*(6), 234–239.
Wolfensberger, W. (1995). An "if this, then that" formulation of decisions related to social role valorization as a better way of interpreting it to people. *Mental Retardation, 33*(3).
Wolfensberger, W. (1999). A contribution to the history of normalization, with primary emphasis on the establishment of normalization in North America between 1967–1975. In R. J. Flynn & R. Lemay (Eds.), *A quarter-century of normalization and social role valorization: Evolution and impact* (pp. 51–116). University of Ottawa Press.
Wolfensberger, W. (2013). *A brief introduction to social role valorization: A high-order concept for addressing the plight of societally devalued people, and for structuring human services* (4th ed.). Valor Press.
Wolfensberger, W., & Thomas, S. (2007). *PASSING: A tool for analyzing service quality according to social role valorization criteria. Ratings manual* (3rd rev. ed.). Syracuse University Training Institute for Human Service Planning, Leadership & Change Agentry.
Wolfensberger, W., Thomas, S., & Caruso, G. (1996). Some of the universal "good things of life" which the implementation of social role valorization can be expected to make more accessible to devalued people. *SRV/VRS: The International Social Role Valorization Journal/La Revue Internationale de la Valorisation des Rôles Sociaux, 2*(2), 12–14.
Wolfensberger, W., & Tullman, S. (1982). A brief outline of the principle of normalization. *Rehabilitation Psychology, 27*(3), 131–145.

Chapter 4
Hold Your Breath: Promoting Health for Individuals with Intellectual Disabilities

Naval Chandra Pant

Abstract Understanding the value of the breathing exercises as taught in the ancient yoga practices which help the learners with special needs in various areas of skill development is need of the hour. At PYSSUM (Paramahansa Yogananda Society for Special Unfolding and Moulding), we practise these yoga practices for the individuals with intellectual disabilities to enhance concentration and improve behaviour patterns for the individuals with intellectual disabilities.

Keywords Asana · Bharstrika · Double breathing · Hath Yoga · Pagal Bachchon Ka School · Prana · Religious practices

Introduction

Understanding the value of the breathing exercises as taught in the ancient yoga practices which help the learners with special needs in various areas of skill development is need of the hour. At PYSSUM (Paramahansa Yogananda Society for Special Unfolding and Moulding), we practise these yoga practices for the individuals with intellectual disabilities to enhance concentration and improve behaviour patterns for the individuals with intellectual disabilities.

These are very interesting times when people are making an effort to involve religious practices in educational systems and breaking the shackles of the superstitions imposed thereby. Since ancient times, the social systems, which also included the education, were guided by the spiritual giants of those time. For many centuries, the spiritual practices were replaced by outer traditional rituals without helping the society in their true evolvement. With progress in science and technology, the new generations are questioning the relevance of religious practices that become the integral part of the life of parents of special needs individuals. This paper "*Hold your Breath*" values the religious sentiments of the all parents and institutions but urges

N. C. Pant (✉)
PYSSUM, Lucknow, India
e-mail: navalpant@pyssum.org

R. Uniyal and F. Rizvi (eds.), *Understanding Disability*,
https://doi.org/10.1007/978-981-99-4925-0_4

them to make a sincere effort to analyse the scientific basis of these traditions and rituals. As we know special breathing exercises are part of all religions, PYSSUM has been attempting to help children with intellectual disability with yogic system of breathing exercises and achieved great results. We wish that every institution can implement scientific methods of breathing exercises founded on spiritual principles/philosophies, as it will create a positive and creative environment for not only the children with special needs but also the mainstream learners.

Understanding the Phrase "Hold Your Breath"

Generally, the phrase, "Hold your Breath", would be considered part of a literary expression. I have actually lived this phrase and seen miracles happening with this. So, when do we "hold our breath"? Dictionary meaning (www.collinsdictionary.com/dictionary/english/hold-your-breath) of the phrase is "To wait in an anxious or excited way to see what happens next". Here "wait", "anxious", and "excited" are the prominent words to describe the phrase. Let us try to understand each of these words individually to make sense of the phrase.

"*Wait*" means a position or a state of expectancy (www.merriam-webster.com/dictionary/excited). It appears to be a stationary position of mind, which may or may not be visible, but in a state of expectancy, one is usually restless. When one waits for someone to say, arrive, or some situation to unfold, the mind visualizes multiple outcomes. In other words, the longer the wait, the more the *restlessness.*

"Anxious" if we look at the meaning, again reflects *experiencing worry, unease, or nervousness*, the state of mind. The words *experiencing worry, unease, or nervousness* individually or collectively would naturally cause *restlessness* in a person.

"*Excited*" (www.oxfordlearnersdictionaries.com/definition/english/anxious; www.psychologytoday.com/us/conditions/intellectual-disability-intellectual-developmental-disorder)—an excited person is the one who is in a state of enthusiasm or display of excessive energy. Such a person is always ready to work, which, without being judgmental, may be a positive quality but may cause uneasiness or nervousness in their environment. Enthusiasm may be productive, but the excitement if not accompanied by the right attitude may cause *restlessness.* The focal point of discussion, at the moment, is not to argue or justify the enthusiasm; rather, to look at the state of mind of an excited person. Let us take it positively as enthusiasm generally causes positive outcomes. So, what happens, if someone with a lot of enthusiasm does not get the expected outcomes? Consequently, most of us become worried, depressed, or even lose hope. One with lost hope may not be expected to be calm. Lack of calmness in any situation would be called *restlessness.*

So, the definition of words in the phrase, "*Hold your breath*", does not display a state of comfort. What happens if one holds one's breath for ten seconds? I actually tried this. Nothing much happens, but if one goes beyond twenty seconds, one starts feeling discomfort and beyond twenty-five seconds, one would start feeling the sense of choking. Why something like "breath" if put on hold for more than twenty-five seconds starts causing the loss of life. Let us try to understand this using a bit of common sense.

Breath and Disability

When we say *hold your breath*, are we actually holding the breath? To go a step beyond, let us try to understand what actually is the breath? Breathing is the activity, in fact, the most important activity of sustaining our life. It is the process of taking oxygen into our lungs and bringing carbon dioxide out of our body. This is what the science of the body says. So, if something like breath signifies a process that sustains life, then how could *holding our breath* be exciting. Instead, it is a process of choking our life and consequently throwing away the life from the body. However, it is quite interesting that literature goes beyond the imagination of truth revealed by physical science. It is not easy to understand its nuances, but I got the answer from the sources that could be called 'literature with a difference'. But before we go to the source, let us dive a little deeper into the breath through my own experience.

I actively began working in the area of intellectual disability when I decided to start a voluntary organization PYSSUM for people with special needs. It was not an "intellect-based activity" for me as I was not a trained professional in the area of intellectual disability. In fact, when I started recognizing the disability, I simply thought it to be 'Mental Retardation'. Gradually it began to be addressed as Intellectual Disability or Learning Disability and even a Cause for Special Needs. However, in day-to-day life most of the people I come across do not much know or care about the difference. Even after working for so many years in this field many people sometimes refer us as a "*Pagal Bachchon ka School*" (School for Mad Children) or a centre for people with "Mental Diseases". I have also come across medical doctors who lack knowledge or exposure about intellectually challenged individuals. Generally, it is a disabled person or a parent or sibling or close associate of these persons who understand the true nature of the intellectual disability.

Let us now review as to why intellectual disability happens. As per the understanding of the medical sciences in today's world, it is considered either due to some genetic disorder in the family or due to brain trauma which happens during the birth of a baby. By brain trauma, it usually means loss of oxygen supply to brain due to many causes which happens at the time of birth. And this leads to mental disability.

Breath: Possibilities of Reducing the Impact

Let us look at the possibility of easing the struggle of an individual with intellectual disabilities through the basis of the problem and looking at possibilities of opening up an area that has not been discussed in a scientific mode.

The success of the entire process of childbirth begins with the crying of the newborn. Medically speaking, the beginning of the crying is the beginning of the first inhalation of the child. This is the first breath of a new life. If there was accident prior to the first inhalation, the impact is enormous.

Besides medical science, most religious scriptures talk of this first breath. However, we may keep the explanations given in religious scriptures out of the scientific paradigm, but let us be open to scientific discussions in the background of references given in the scriptures.

Not many might have understood the new thought process, initiated by Paramahansa Yogananda on 6 October 1920, the day he gave his maiden talk in Boston, USA. The talk was titled as '*The Science of Religion*', a title good enough to shake the traditionalists of the USA (Yogananda 1946). One could easily wonder if there is any science in religion in the early twentieth century, close to the First World War, when science was thriving in the defence sector besides many other areas. America could still be considered the last place for people to talk about religion, but it was the land of opportunities, although Swami Vivekananda had already aroused interest among many Americans towards Indian philosophy and culture.

Though India was considered downtrodden, it was on its way to break the shackles of slavery under British Raj. Gandhi's philosophy of non-violence had started attracting people's attention the world over. In those times of political turbulence in all parts of the world, Paramahansa Yogananda started talking about the scientific principles prevalent in the religions and their universality (Yogananda 1946). It initially sounded unbelievable, but people in America found it worth trying. Since his first talk till he breathed last in March 1952, Paramahansa Yogananda talked about the Scientific Techniques of God Realization and his literature continues to spread far and wide to this day. It may sound completely conflicting, but the scientific discoveries have started talking about the possibilities of science behind religion. The most interesting part of his techniques even for a complete novice about religious practices begins with "breath".

The discussion on breath-based techniques is beyond the scope of this article; however, we can always look at the context of his repeated mention of the breath. I would particularly refer to his book *Autobiography of a Yogi* that has made its place in the first hundred spiritual classics in the twentieth century. The first mention of the breath comes, when he talks about his encounter as a child with Bhaduri Mahasaya, a yoga expert in Kolkata. Bhaduri Mahasaya displayed one of the pranayama techniques, namely *Bharstrika* before two young lads, Yogananda being one of them.

The credit for making the *Bharstrika* and other breathing exercises a household name in India and abroad goes to Swami Ramdev. Through his Hath Yoga Asana discourses in the last two decades, he connected the Yoga Asanas with the physical well-being and health care of an ordinary person. Somehow, he misses out on the essential reason of getting the benefits of his breathing exercises best known to him. Yogananda highlighted the hidden reason behind any breath-based yoga practice, which if not captured carefully, one might miss out on an important indicator about the role the breath plays in physical well-being.

> Method of controlling life force (Prana) through regulation of breath, The Bhastrika ("Bellow") Pranayama makes the mind steady. (Yogananda 1946)

Interestingly, Paramahansa Yogananda talked about the role of breath even in animals when he introduced the system of scientific techniques. Revealing his experience of cosmic consciousness, he indicates the connection between the breath and the mind.

> The breath and the restless mind, I saw, are like storms that lash the ocean of light into waves of material forms – earth, sky, human beings, animals, birds, trees. (Yogananda 1946)

These two references suggest that breath should not be taken as a simple physical process to sustain life from the conventional medical point of view. We can find many such instances where Paramahansa Yogananda talked about the impact of our breathing patterns on our thought process. Its deeper connections with life need to be studied and considered for a serious and conscious implementation in our day-to-day life.

> Fixity of attention depends on slow breathing; quick or uneven breaths are an inevitable accompaniment of harmful emotion states: fear, lust, anger. (Yogananda 1946)

While many exponents of Hatha Yoga have shown many advantages with the regular though superficial practices of breathing techniques like *Bhastrika*, but in my opinion, these techniques could be helpful in bringing better mental and physical health in people at large. If our children and all learners are given training in the areas of breath regulations, it will not only improve their concentration but also mental health.

Breath: A Foundation of Healthy Body and Healthy Mind

So, it could be a matter of research to find out the root of the phrase "Hold your breath" what it actually means and not as it is perceived. Holding the breath has some deeper meaning. The intellectual disability may not be an area of active interest for the teaching community, but as such the education system always aimed to train students to have a healthy body and healthy mind. Healthy body may not be much of an issue as games and gyms are generally on the priority list of the parents and students, but developing a healthy mind is gradually becoming a serious challenge.

Mind is a faculty that has been given to human beings with unlimited freedom to choose. Human race has come a long way from the limited resources to vast exposure and unlimited choices. In the last three decades, there has been an explosion of information with technological advancements, but communities have not thought much of the impact of these advancements on the thinking process. The communities in their social or education policies have not cared much to develop a system that would naturally move towards developing a healthy mind.

Mind does not have a physical existence, but it reflects its presence through the physical tools. As suggested by Bhaduri Mahasaya and Paramahansa Yogananda, one of the physical tools is breath, which has a direct visible impact on the mind provided the method is learnt as a yoga science. Through various research backed evidence, the efficacy of yoga has now surpassed the traditional notion of being merely a religious practice. Today its popularity has increased tremendously, and therefore, 'World Yoga Day' is celebrated on 21 June every year all over the world. People are learning Yoga Asanas without their inherent affiliation of faith and are benefitted. However, yoga science is a system that has a methodology which must be learnt under the guidance of an expert. Swami Ramdev has taught the exercises inherent in Hatha Yoga as a science, and likewise, PYSSUM has been using the science of breath as mentioned in the teachings of Paramahansa Yogananda to see the possibilities of improvement in children and adults with intellectual disabilities.

BREATH: A Practical and Scientific Application

PYSSUM has been working for individuals with intellectual disabilities. Even when the name "intellectual disability" was not much in use although it had a direct connection with the mind. Intellectual abilities are measured with IQ tools. Many names have been given to the abilities that reflect the human personality. Any missing ability of human personality from our day-to-day activities may be termed as a disability. This disability may be physical or intellectual depending upon the cause.

Most of the time, a physically challenged individual may be intellectually sound and may find her or his way to lead an almost normal life in mainstream society. There may be issues pertaining to the emotional expressions due to psychological impact; however, it is easier to deal with these issues by giving emotion-oriented support to the physically challenged individual. In the case of intellectually challenged individuals, the life of the individual and the people around her/him may become extremely vulnerable. The intellectual impairment has its impact on not only at an intellectual level but also psychological, emotional, social, and physical levels requiring mostly individual and group support.

In the First Hand Report (FHR) submitted by parents of intellectually challenged persons, in their understanding, intellectual impairment is due to the damage in the brain caused by the lack of breath. As it is, we have been hearing so much of the breath in general. Therefore, a system was developed at PYSSUM to introduce the use of breath as a lifeline along with the other tools recommended in the special education books. The tool was "to regulate the breath" in order to enhance the intellectual capacity of challenged individuals (Yogananda 1990).

Starting a process of "Regulating the Breath" in those who have a learning disability was not an easy process. To teach them to get into the process required the tools taught in the books of special education. However, the simplest methodology which could be called Parrot Learning or copying what is observed was used. This is one of the most common techniques used in the learning of vocal or instrumental music or any performing arts. Initially, one learns what one observes or hears. One can recall, how a child learns to smile or to use the words of its mother tongue growing through infancy (Yogananda 1990). Children challenged or not learn through familiarity with their surroundings.

In India, we still have a system of morning assembly at schools and prayers are a part of this assembly. In the Western countries, this practice of assembly is not there except in faith schools. The interest of students in morning assembly is limited to those, standing on the dais either to sing the prayers or read the latest news or those who are to receive some accolades for their achievements.

However, this is not an issue in case of the children with special needs as for them everything is a joyous activity until or unless the activity causes some discomfort. It has been observed that even the most severely disabled children were able to sit without causing any serious disturbance. So, an environment of breathing exercises was created in the form of a prayer service around these children without judging the extent of their intellectual disability. Everybody, the head, the leader, the special educators, and the class teachers would sit for the prayer session during morning assembly.

It takes time to get adjusted with the new system. Even the staff members are not used to sitting in prayers for a dedicated time. Everybody has to work hard to create an environment that motivates children as well as adults to follow the instructions. It took around six to eight months to completely accept this system. The first impact that became visible in the children was the sense of calmness. We noticed that, however difficult a child may be in its challenged situation, she or he would look forward to joining this morning session. This was observed even in the children and adults who joined the school even at later months or years. The environment of calmness touches everyone.

The second impact which was observed was in individual behaviour and personality. In most of the cases, the behaviour develops and changes as a response to the challenges come across by an individual throughout lifetime. It was noted that the individual child's and adult's behaviour was becoming less challenging for the educators. Encouraged by these results, the functionaries of PYSSUM introduced special breathing exercises of a particular nature and got more profound positive results.

Initially, the reference for comparison was the behaviour and personality at the joining time and at the end of three to six months. Once the children and adults were fully settled into their routine at school, the reference of comparison became the behaviour at the school and behaviour at home. It was overwhelmingly noticed that the child was performing much better at school than at home. This can also be argued that the change could also be because the parents are not professionally trained to handle a challenged child in comparison with the structured system at school. However, the outcomes were the same even in case of the parents who are educated or trained to handle the child by the rules of special education. Even in the case of the families, where the home environment provided a routine system of prayers, the behaviour outcomes were not as good as seen after this new system was introduced in school.

If we focus only on the behaviour of these children and adults in terms of silence, it showed amazing results. Let us look at the patterns of behaviour displayed during the prayer session. At PYSSUM, the entire prayer session of 30 min duration consists of five slots of activities: **Prayer, Chanting, Breathing Exercises, Period of Silence, and Scientific Healing Technique**. Let us try to study each one of these activities individually.

Prayer—An Activity for a Positive Impact

Prayer is where something is spoken, mostly in Hindi, occasionally in English. The word pray is first found in Middle English, meaning to "ask earnestly" (Richert). Whatever may be our understanding of prayer, the dictionary meanings explicitly say that prayer is the use of words to ask for something depending upon where the prayer is being presented. Generally, the social understanding of any community with some religious or spiritual affiliation would be to believe that prayer always has a positive impact on an individual or a group. Here the context is kept limited to the impact of the words in the routine on the individuals with intellectual disabilities.

So, for an individual with intellectual disability, a prayer is a group of words, which she or he is uttering because everyone else is doing so. The word may or may not be really meaningful to the individuals in the group depending upon their previous acquaintance with the word or the system of the prayer. More so in case of the individuals with special needs, who are generally not equipped or expected to understand the meaning or the context of the prayer.

However, the ardent follower of an individual spiritual or religious system may have some convictions about the vibratory power carried by a prayer which may not require the literary understanding of the meaning of the prayer words. For a spiritual or religious aspirant, the feeling or the devotional aspect may be more convincing if they follow a system of faith. In the present context, even though the uttering of words in prayer an individual with special needs may not understand its literal meaning, it is understood that purely the scientific use of a technique can have a positive impact on an individual or a group with special needs.

Chanting—The Joy That Brings a Positive Change

Group chanting is generally a joyous musical activity. It has been observed that individuals with intellectual disability enjoy the activity. Their participation may not be well co-ordinated due to their lack of understanding of the rhythm or the words, but it is observed that gradually over a period of time an individual and even the group touches the peak when everybody is one with the lead singer. The well-co-ordinated peek appears effortlessly without any external discipline and may vary from time to time.

If we try to peep into the process of chanting, it can be divided into many segments. A simple chanting has Meaningful Words uttered at regular intervals, the rhythm and the control over the utterances of the words. On repeated practice, chanting brings amazing coordination. The coordination brings a joyous feeling and great sense of participation. But there is another hidden aspect of the well-co-ordinated chanting. Let us try to study it from the principles of music. The best practice focuses on the best possible control over the rhythm, both in case of vocal or instrumental music. Since here the focus is on the chanting by individuals with intellectual disability, we shall be discussing the process of vocal music.

Any vocalist would vouch for the impact of achieving control over the rhythm which means the rhythmic control over the breathing patterns of the vocalists. In fact, most of the music trainees are asked to coordinate their breathing while practising their lessons. It is applicable both at highly classical pieces of training, as well as at the basic level. Many a time, the trainers are seen asking the music students to focus on their breathing. The expert vocal classical singers, Indian or Western, display their expertise by displaying their control over breath in their best compositions.

Here while chanting in a group, the rhythm importantly regulates the breath of the special needs individuals. Chanting in a group allows them to capture the rhythm and thereby regulate their breath. Better regulated is the breath, calmer would be the mind of an individual, whether challenged or not. This is true of any group in any setting. The most popular party songs seem to have some kind of joyous impact on groups and individuals. But if we observe the singing in a religious setting, the singing with the choir in a church, Kirtans in temples and Qawwalis by Sufis, they have a deeper impact in the form of joyous calmness.

However, if we take this to another level, the spiritual chants go much deeper and display the impact to the level to bring healing in the individuals. That is why, in all cultures, there were norms and traditions to take the sick people to spiritually charged places. The group or individual chanting as in Buddha Monasteries, sound of bells in Churches or Temples, or any other place of spiritual importance has an impacting environment. It has definitely been observed in case of challenged individuals.

Breathing Exercises—A Process with an Impact on the Mind

Breath, as mentioned earlier, is not just a process of inhalation of oxygen and exhalation of carbon dioxide but has a connection with the inner realms of human existence, a science that is gradually being discovered by the world. Paramahansa Yogananda with his own experience talks of the deeper relationship between the breath and the mind.

> The breath and the restless mind, I saw, are like storms that lash the ocean of light into waves of material forms – earth, sky, human beings, animals, birds, trees. (Yogananda 1990)

The relationship between the breath and the mind is also revealed in many verses by the seers from the times of Bhakti movement, namely Kabir, Tulsidas, Nanak Dev, and many. Kabir talks about "God as the breath inside the breath", whereas Ramana Maharishi calls, "the breath being a mind restraint".

At PYSSUM, the very basic technique of this science of breathing is being applied, and it can work well with anyone who has the interest and intent to draw benefit out of the Science of Yoga, which gradually becomes the Science of Religion.

PYSSUM as a part of its prayer session encourages its teachers as well as students with special needs to practise the special breathing, what Paramahansa Yogananda called **Double Breathing**. It is simple and very effective as it increases the oxygen intake and expelling of carbon dioxide from the body and calms the mind. The children and adults with special needs like anyone, generally, do not understand the process in one go; however, they copy it very well by observation. It has been observed that this brings a calming impact on their excessive physical movements.

The Double Breathing—The Foundation of Mental Health

Normally, the natural breathing is inhalation and exhalation. This process varies from person to person due to the lung capacity of the individual and the physical activity performed. However, in double breathing, as introduced by Paramahansa Yogananda there are two parts "double inhalation" and "double exhalation". Double inhalation is the conscious inhaling of air through the nose—in two steps, short inhalation and then long inhalation. Short inhalation takes in the short amount of oxygen instantly followed by long inhalation. In the normal inhalation in the usual breathing process, one does not fill the lungs to the fullest capacity, but with double inhalation, the blood gets much more oxygen than the normal casual inhalation.

The second part of the double breathing is "double exhalation". In the natural process of exhalation, we exhale through the nose, but in the double breathing the carbon dioxide is exhaled through the mouth, again first in short exhalation followed by long exhalation. In double inhalation, one breathes in excess oxygen; likewise, in double exhalation, one throws out excess carbon dioxide consequently helping the heart to purify the blood with less effort.

The Impact of Double Breathing

Double inhalation and double exhalation if practised with regularity help the body gain increased stamina of lungs and reducing the stress on the heart. This is the physical part of the process. There is also extremely important subtle mental reflection of this simple exercise, which normally takes place without our knowledge and that is its calming impact on the mind. Emphasizing on the deeper connection of the breath and mind, Paramahansa Yogananda assures calming of the mind and consequently its positive psychological impacts on all individuals.

PYSSUM gets a good number of children and adults with special needs in various categories, namely mental retardation, autism, Down syndrome, and multiple disabilities, technically divided into educable and trainable groups. It has also been educating children without any intellectual disability but socially and economically challenged from slum dwelling. Socially challenged children come with the severe social issues like child abuse, overexposure to the adult environment, parental infighting and separation, drugs and alcoholism, and so on. On the other hand, intellectually challenged children come with their intellectual challenges along with ignorant parents, non-accepting, and over expecting parents. The only common ground for them where both groups could meet each other without any judgement was the yoga platform. Paramahansa Yogananda philosophy offers the fundamental arena of integration through yoga for all.

As observed by the special educators and functionaries, the mixing of the two broader groups could have been extremely difficult, but for these specialized breathing techniques and the spiritually charged environmental support, children, as well as adults, respond positively.

The second part of this double breathing practice is emptying the lungs by exhaling the air completely with the double exhalation. Once the lungs are emptied, one should "Hold the lungs in the emptied position as long as one can do comfortably" in other words "**Hold the breath**", gradually allow the breath to come in and go out naturally without controlling it, and just watch the breath going in and coming out without any control over it and keep watching it.

This simple practice of double breathing and watching the breath not only brings calmness but also invisibly develops the will power. One could really ask, what is the connection between the breathing exercise and the will power. Ask any fitness culturist or artist, what happens if the practice of the exercises is forced upon a willing student. The same thing happens even with the challenged individual and not only the challenged individuals but with anyone, if motivated to practise these breathing exercises with a precise discipline, would develop the same calmness and will power. A calm and willing individual can do much more than the one with a restless mind.

In this entire process, the breathing exercise plays an extremely important role in moving on to the next part of the whole session, that is, **Watching the Breath** an exercise that may sound little confusing to the one who has not practised it earlier.

Watching the Breath—A Science, Not a Belief

Generally, the question asked is, how one can watch the breath. To make it simpler for our children, we also say, try to **feel the breath**. Most of the time, it is not possible to explain to the individuals with intellectual disabilities, how one can **watch or feel the breath**. Another phrase that is used to convey the message is "**Be Silent**" which they hear quite often even beyond the school environment. However, they generally go silent and practising intense double breathing, withdrawal from the double breathing is the process of watching or feeling the breath that helps them become silent. Even if the entire group goes silent for 10 s, it is a great success, as this silence period helps them for the whole day.

Scientific Observations

The children or adults with autism, Down syndrome, or attention deficit hyperactivity disorder have been observed entering the PYSSUM campus, troubling the parents or helpers but becoming quiet once they reach the assembly hall. The assembly has at PYSSUM is not very big. It can only accommodate about 40 people comfortably. Generally, 10–15 children and adults come late to school every day due to the vehicle issues or morning temperaments of the children and then, the entire group has to sit in a compact sitting arrangement in assembly hall. We must take into consideration that touch and smell sensitivity is normally felt by coming in close proximity to anyone. However, this troublesome behaviour becomes more aggravated when they come back after either a weekend or a long break. The troublesome behaviour is a generalized term here and does not mean violent behaviour. It would generally mean not sitting at one place, making a sound, looking at each other, looking at a visitor, which are very general traits we see in children. However, after the long breaks, this becomes the worst if the parents switch over their environment with no familiarity or extend the weekends or some disturbing activity at home during those days.

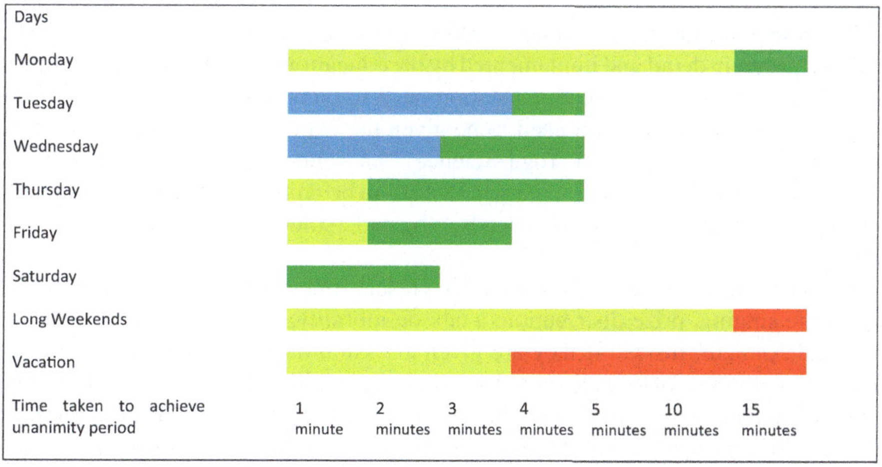

We studied the pattern of behavioural disturbance of all students during the various days of the week at the school. If we place red as very high disturbance, yellow colour as high degree disturbance blue is a mild disturbance, and green as minimum disturbance during the prayer session and chart them in the graph.

As the week advances from Monday to Saturday, the calmness in all the children and adults enhanced to a significant level. We found that after weekends, generally the disturbance is maximum and the minimum disturbance level reaches only after sitting the prayer session for 10 min which covers the breathing and chanting session.

The role of the proper breathing exercises and the calming of the mind needs to be studied further in detail and implemented by the educational institutions. The learners and students of the mainstream education need to come out of the clutches of the present era's distractions and need to be given the exposure of the higher sciences inherent in India's legacy of Yoga Science. Our school goers and the university students have tremendous potential which need to be tapped by using these methods given in our spiritual culture. This needs to be understood as a science not simply as a belief.

Schools' morning assembly sessions in present times have just become activities with little singing, prize distribution, a talk on morality, news reading, and then the National Anthem. Instead if they are given a session of proper breathing exercises with a few minutes of silence on a daily basis, it would help them better. It will be of great advantage to instruct them in calming breathing exercises. This would help not only an average student but also the backbenchers and slow learners who are generally ignored due to their poor intellectual performance.

The morality taught to the students has to be practised on the foundation of a calm mind. The restless minds causing unprovoked disturbances in society on a day-to-day basis can be handled if the students in schools and colleges are introduced to the science of "**hold your breath**" using the simple exercises exemplified by their teachers and mentors. It is high time that they withdraw the attention from the celebrities who do not display any discipline in their personal life and look for the higher values of life from their cultural heritage. To begin with, practising proper breathing, from any system as **the training in the breathing**, does not need to go against any faith, any religion or any system. It, in fact, connects one with the inner system of life. That is why it helps the individuals, particularly younger individuals with intellectual disabilities better as they are more connected with their inner system. So, just try it once, **hold your breath!!**

Declaration The pictures used in the article are from the PYSSUM Activity Centres. PYSSUM has the written undertaking from the stakeholders to use the pictures of the beneficiaries for the purpose of awareness activities in all modes and research articles.

References

Psychology Today. *Intellectual disability (intellectual developmental disorder)*. Sussex Publishers; www.collinsdictionary.com/dictionary/english/hold-your-breath

Richert, S. P. What is prayer, and what does it mean to pray? *Learn Religions*. www.thoughtco.com/what-is-prayer-542573

www.merriam-webster.com/dictionary/excited

www.oxfordlearnersdictionaries.com/definition/english/anxious; www.psychologytoday.com/us/conditions/intellectual-disability-intellectual-developmental-disorder

Yogananda, P. (1946). *Autobiography of a yogi*. Self-Realization Fellowship.

Yogananda, P. (1990). *Science of religion*. Self-Realization Fellowship.

Part II
Disability in Literature, Film and Theatre

Chapter 5
The Mad Mother in the 1BHK—Hallowing and Harrowing Positions in Jerry Pinto's *Em and the Big Hoom*

Ega Peter

"Mad is an everyday, ordinary word" (Pinto 207).

The medical sciences have done a huge disservice to the understanding of disability. By locating disability in the individual, "the medical perspective views disability as pathology (a physical, sensory, or cognitive failing that tragically 'handicaps' those 'afflicted')" (Goodley 6). In fact, one of the earliest attempts of disability studies was to distinguish between disability and impairment. The Disabled Peoples' International, a cross disability NGO, in its constitution maintains that "impairment is the functional limitation within the individual caused by physical, mental or sensory impairment", while "disability is the loss or limitation of opportunities to take part in the normal life of the community on an equal level with others due to physical or social barriers" (Goodley 8). Language, or the lack of it has done immense damage to comprehending disability. That there is a dire need for respectful vocabulary (as well as the omission of derogatory ones) has found consensus among those involved in the discourses on disability—for language often marks, stigmatizes, and stereotypes. This very complication is alluded to by Jerry Pinto's young narrator halfway through the novel:

> It [Madness] fits into songs. As the old Hindi film song had it, *M-A-D mane paagal*. It can become a phrase, "Maddaw-what?" which began life as "Are you mad or what?" It can be everything you choose it to be: a mad whirl, a mad idea, a mad March day, a mad heiress, a mad mad mad mad world, a mad passion, a mad hatter, a mad dog … (Pinto 207)

E. Peter (✉)
Vimala College (Autonomous), Thrissur, India
e-mail: 571peter@gmail.com

St. Mary's College, Thrissur, India

R. Uniyal and F. Rizvi (eds.), *Understanding Disability*,
https://doi.org/10.1007/978-981-99-4925-0_5

The everyday-ness and ordinariness of the word 'mad' are precisely what is problematic for disability studies.[1] The enumeration here delineates the variegated shades of madness. Thrown around casually with no thoughts of the repercussions, madness becomes a trope to evoke everything except what it really encompasses—a serious health condition that demands medical aid.

"I only knew that something was wrong with all of us and that it had something to do with my mother and her nerves" (Pinto 9).

Even as the young narrator lists out his ideas of madness, the one that is most familiar to him remains absent—that of having a 'mad' mother. There is an improbable ring when 'mad' and 'mother' are uttered together, like an unpoetic oxymoron; two contrary words violently put together, for Indian culture doesn't permit the existence of a 'mad mother'. Hailed as the epitome of sacrifice and grace, the Indian mother simply cannot be imagined to have a debilitating mental condition. But it needs to be pointed out that it is not permissible for women in general to have a mental disorder, with their condition often being reduced to labels of 'mood swings', 'emotional outbursts', and 'female hysteria'. Alice Hall asserts that feminists have frequently attacked the pathologization of what is generally called 'female conditions' such as premenstrual tension and postnatal depression (41).

Em and The Big Hoom follows a nonlinear narrative style—an instance of form imitating content. Narrated from the point of view of Em's adolescent son, the novel straddles the boundary between fiction and memoir.[2] Taken back and forth in time as and where Em's (Imelda Mendes) conversations with her children take the readers, the novel is interspersed with anecdotes, letters, and diary entries describing the Big Hoom's (Augustine Mendes) twelve yearlong courtship of Em. The narrative style serves two purposes—firstly, it allows the reader a peak into Em's perception of time, how for her time doesn't seem to pass linearly, but flits back and forth. Cathy Caruth expounds this experience of time in her book as:

> … the wound of the mind—the breach in the mind's experience of time, self, and the world—is not, like the wound of the body … but rather an event that … is experienced too soon, too unexpectedly, to be fully-known and is therefore not available to consciousness until it imposes itself again, repeatedly, in the nightmares and repetitive actions of the survivor. (3–4)

And secondly, the inclusion of anecdotes, letters, and diary entries to progress the story offers a glimpse of the many facets of her identity—of a loyal friend, a faithful lover, and a firebrand of a young woman. PhebeAnn Wolframe claims that "mad people undermine the fixing of madness as identity, instead carefully negotiating their identifications and affiliations, and consciously blurring boundaries" (44). Pinto

[1] "Despite the overlaps between Mad Studies and Disability Studies, the two disciplines are an uneasy fit in some ways. A deep rift between the approaches exists because many psychiatric survivors do not identify as being disabled, and likewise, many disabled people do not identify as psychiatric survivors" (Brewer 15).

[2] In an interview with Penguin Random House, Pinto claims: "… it was supposed to cure me, this novel. It was supposed to help me deal with what I had just learned was called a skewed family".

takes utmost care to develop the character of Em—she is flamboyantly intelligent, who uses her disability to make statements that her 'normal' self wouldn't have been allowed to make. A couple of lines uttered by Em over the span of a few pages offer a peak into her wisdom and helplessness. She says: "Sometimes I would see myself as a book with bad binding. You know, like one more reader, one more face-down on the bed and I was going to spill everything, lose control" (95); followed by, "I didn't go to bookshops to buy. That's a little bourgeois. I went because they were civilized places … It was lovely. Like standing in the middle of civilization" (101). Read together, these lines have immense consequences—that Em dislikes social interactions cannot be more evident. The general population tends to be exhausting and emotionally draining towards people with disabilities. Furthermore, she compares herself to a book, the repository of society's knowledge, as if to say that the leaps and bounds human civilization has made have done little to alleviate the stigma surrounding mental disabilities.

"One day I told him about the boys of the neighbourhood, about their mocking" (Pinto 73).

Lerita Coleman Brown develops the description of stigma to suggest that "all human differences are potentially stigmatizable … stigma also indicates that those possessing power, the dominant group, can determine which human differences are desired and undesired" (148). Stigmatization then, it has to be understood, creates a social hierarchy where the 'normal' bodymind[3] takes a superior position at the cost of the disabled body/neuroatypicals.[4] A lot of stigma is attached to being 'mad' or having members in the family diagnosed with mental illness; it can be distressing for everyone involved. Especially for the people themselves who are suffering from it, since it is, more often than not, an invisible suffering. As for the rest of the members of the family, especially the children of the one afflicted, there is an impending sense of inevitably succumbing to mental conditions. This fear of biological determinism[5] pervades the narrator's thoughts throughout the novel.

Em is a perpetual victim of this discrimination where insulting taunts are hurled at her owing to her condition; she is also confined to the claustrophobic 1BHK—a metaphorical indication of how limited the space that she is allowed to inhabit is. Le Corbusier once wrote: "Taking possession of space is the first gesture of living things … a fundamental manifestation of equilibrium and duration. The occupation of space is the first proof of existence". Seen in the light of this statements and

[3] Margaret Price uses the term "*bodymind* to emphasize that although "body" and "mind" usually occupy separate conceptual and linguistic territories, they are deeply intertwined. This theory is drawn in part from Babette Rothschild's *The Body Remembers*" (Davis 306).

[4] According to Margaret Price, *Neuroatypical* was primarily used to indicate people diagnosed with the Autism Spectrum Disorder, but has later been used to include persons with bipolar disorder and traumatic brain injuries (Davis, 303).

[5] Jerry Pinto, in an interview with *India Ink* says: "I remember reading somewhere that neologism, creating new words, is a sign of schizophrenia, and I thought, oh, man, there I go, this is it" (Bearak).

assuming that existence is proportional to spatiality, it can only be imagined how less of a being Em ends up being within the confines of the private recesses of her home, forbidden to occupy public spaces. A study undertaken by Meekosha could explain Em's confinement: "… disabled women are more likely to be poor than disabled men … are more likely to experience public space as threatening; are more likely to live in the parental home and experience sexual abuse" (Goodley 35).

Another important aspect that the novel touches upon is society's apathy towards those suffering from BD. Mental health, despite being a very important subject, is often neglected. Em often makes insightful jibes at the vacillating nature of the society: "You can cry in public as long as you do not sob. Tears are transparent … Sobs intrude. They push their way into people's consciousness. They feel duty-bound to ask what has happened" (Pinto 213). 'Duty bound' not 'worried' or 'concerned'. Nothing captivates human mind like tragedy—to be a spectator and taking in things from afar, to be silently thankful that it was 'them' and not 'us' and to silently move on. This is what society does best—"In this city, every deserted street corner conceals a crowd. It appears in a minute when something disrupts the way in which the world is supposed to work. It can disappear almost as instantaneously" (Pinto 162).

Em's story about the Big Hoom's pet name 'Limb of Satan' is deeply insightful on how institutions like religion play a dominant role in pushing people at risk over the edge. With its strict moral codes and rigid laws, religion has played an influential part in the upbringing of Em. With hints of hyperreligiosity[6] in her personality and ironically adept in Freud's theory of Psychoanalysis, a young Em could never negotiate between faith and desire. Replying to her son's questions about the Big Hoom's pet name, she says: "Because he was always tempting me to sin … it's always a sin according to the Wholly Roaming Cat Licks … I think you're only supposed to do it if you want babies" (Pinto 3).

Em then goes on to talk about how she managed to terminate her pregnancies twenty-six times, since abortion was a sin according to her religion: "I'd just climb down five stairs and jump six … six steps and land with a thump, six times, to shake those little mites from their moorings" (Pinto 4). This horrifying incident repeated twenty-six times is undoubtedly traumatic. Em also tells her children about her friend Gertie who had eaten "three platefuls of papaya" and drank "three gins as if they were tonic" to "bake the poor things out of there" (Pinto 4). This goes on to suggest the kind of pressure religion exerted in her youth and the lack of a supportive family that ought to have understood her dilemma. She lends the support she lacked from her mother to her daughter: "Anyway, only doctors do it. So when you're knocked up, you'll get a proper doctor to fiddle with your middle, you hear? No back-street abortions for you" (Pinto 4).

Em further narrates how the church had opposed the use of painkillers in the maternity ward. She says, barely hiding her rage against religion as an institution:

[6] Clinically known as Geschwind Syndrome, hyperreligiosity is characterized by intense religious feelings that hinder normal, everyday functioning.

"It had to do with Adam and Eve and their apple … birth was supposed to be painful and we were suffering in expiation of Eve's sin. Adam got away, of course. Men do" (Pinto 169). If women have it hard, mothers have it harder and disabled mothers hardest of them all.

"… the doctor showed me how to carry her, to feed her, and I thought, "I should know this stuff, shouldn't I? I mean all those dolls. They were about learning the rope, no?"" (Pinto 53).

Religion wasn't the only institution that was asserting enormous pressure on her—it was also the perception and ideals of motherhood shaped by the society. According to S. B. Mintz "motherhood, marriage and home-making are heteronormative roles that, when enacted by disabled women with others, may actually be seen as taking on a subversive quality" (Goodley 162).

This uncontrollable pressure to fit the mould and the realization of being unable to had a deep impact on Em. Numerous studies have been undertaken to elucidate the gendered function of toys in young children—that active ones like cars and balls for boys and passive ones like dolls and kitchen sets for girls have deep cultural impact is textbook knowledge. Shashi Deshpande had succinctly put it into words when she wrote the essay 'Learning to Be a Mother'—that motherhood is not an acquired skill, but a learnt one. It is then no wonder that women when conditioned from such a young age to nurture the next generation go through immense despair at not being able to carry out these functions properly. The point is, such wrongful notions can be highly distressing to mothers, especially disabled mothers.

There are numerous instances in the novel where Em vehemently talks about motherhood and society's idealization of mothers. In one of her conversations with her children, Em declares she would have preferred to stay child-free:

> Oh God, no. I saw what children do. They turn a good respectable woman into a mudd-dha. I didn't want to be a mudd-dha. I didn't want to be turned inside out. I didn't want to have my world shifted so that I was no longer the centre of it. (Pinto 133)

The shockwaves these few lines send down the readers' spines are enough to indicate how the Indian culture has failed its women. Women are judged and labelled once they become mothers—the measure of goodness most often depends on the amount of unrealistic expectations the mother seems to meet. According to Goodley, "the 'good' mother is where our pleasures are gratified, our nurture met, our psychoemotional needs addressed. The 'bad' mother is the barrier to these pleasures and is quickly associated with feelings of pain, frustration and anger" (96). It's not hard to pinpoint why Em would have been labelled a 'bad' mother.

"Home was where others had to gather grace. Home was what I wanted to flee" (Pinto 147).

Em and The Big Hoom does not celebrate mothers or motherhood, simply because there is no version of an all sacrificing, all forgiving mother of divine virtues present in the novel. The narrator sums it up: "It wasn't. Not in my world … The Big Hoom was my rock and my refuge. He knew what to do, how to handle stuff … I tried imagining my life without him and immediately grew cold with fear …" (Pinto 80).

For the narrator and his sister, home is a hollow word. For them, it does not evoke a sense of security or warmth. Home was filled with fear of living with a bipolar mother, as the narrator describes here:

> Home was a blood-stained bathroom which, when it was scraped down for repainting, revealed an old suicide note, scrawled in pencil. Home was uncertainty: who would open the door? Em in a panic of sorrow? Em in a rage against some unnamed enemies? Em in a laughing fit with a beedi fuming in her hands? (Pinto 148)

The impact of disabilities on family relationships is extensive. Sufficient long-term disease management depends on good family relationships, but often family members do not know how to emotionally support each other. Partners of the disabled person suffer tremendously and often face crisis in their marital life. Difficulties are also faced due to the changing role of the family member in the disabled person's life, where the family member or partner often ends up being the primary care-giver—a role that is traditionally attributed to women. This is precisely what Anita Ghai reflects upon: "Yet another strand of this cultural construction conceives of disability as eternal childhood, where survival is contingent upon constant care and protection" (51).

"Mad people don't want sex" (Pinto 5).

Em's rejection of her sexuality could be in tandem with what McRuer and Wilkerson claim as the 'routine infantilization of disabled people and their construction as helpless and asexual, or conversely as possessing uncontrollable sexuality'. Em does not have the luxury to lose herself in personal urges because she already has a lot on her mind. But she is thoroughly aware of what marital life entails. Em is so utterly concerned about sex that she ends up writing a letter to the Big Hoom prior to their marriage talking about her terror of physical intimacy. Even after marriage, she plays out her insecurities by asking him to have an extra marital affair since she herself could not satisfy him. Although the Big Hoom laughs it off, the hurt from such statements cannot be overlooked. Her disinterest could also stem from problems of self-esteem. Her low self-esteem can be thought of as a consequence of what Harlan Hahn calls "asexual objectification"[7] (Thomson 25)—when disabled people are perceived to be devoid of any sexuality.

The medication also strips them of their personality. Em, quite fond of reading, had to give it up because she could no longer concentrate. Neither do the people with BD have privacy. In the novel, the narrator makes a comment that those who suffer from mental conditions and those who suffer from the mental conditions of someone they know get accustomed to invasions of their privacy. Privacy cannot exist because the private recesses of their minds, their deepest, darkest most intimate thoughts are to be spelled out to be put under scrutiny. Nothing is exempt—sexual history, childhood, adolescence, it is all out on the table for the prying eyes of medical professionals.

---

[7] Ghai states "This kind of reasoning is echoed in North Indian Punjabi culture, where, although girls are allowed to interact with their male cousins, they are not allowed to sleep in the same room. Disabled girls, on the other hand, are under no such prohibitions" (55).

"What can mental health mean in a nation that wants an injection to put it back on its feet the next morning?" (Pinto 65).

Invasions of privacy are just one part of the problem in a nation looking for a one-pill solution to its disability issues. Mental health awareness and health care, or maybe the dearth of it, are remarked upon in *Em and The Big Hoom* countless times. In a poignant scene in the novel, the narrator talks about how his sister tried to make sense of their mother's episodic lapses into mania by charting her changing moods against the phases of the moon. Beliefs as such where natural phenomena are thought of as the causality or the cure for certain disorders are common in many cultures.[8] There is also a serious gap in administering the right type of treatment to people with BD. The narrator says:

> But it seemed as if all psychiatric medicine was aimed only at the symptoms. Mute the paranoia. Calm the rage. Raise the endorphins. Underneath, the mysteries continued, unchanged. Underneath, somewhere in the chemistry of her brain, there was something that could not be reached. (Pinto 113)

According to Ghai, the legislation for disabilities too has a very gendered approach—not many addressing the problems of disabled women. Rukmini Sen argues that "although women got included in the Bills, there was not a feminist perspective yet to disability legislation" (70) and disabled women lived "everyday reality of a 'culture of fear' … in trepidation and vulnerability" (71). This approach reflects the general attitude towards disabled women in India. This lack of visibility is suggested to in *Em and The Big Hoom*:

> It occurred to me that the mad in India are not the mentally ill, they are simply mad. They have no other identity. Here, everyone was mad. They had lost their hair so that the institution could keep them free of lice. They had lost their clothes because their families had abandoned them, and they had lost their lives because they had lost their families. They were now free in a bizarre sort of way. (Pinto 196)

"My buaji says god listens to the prayers of mentals because they are touched by his hand" (Pinto 66).

Sensitivity is not the strongest suit of the society. During one of her visits to the hospital after a failed suicide attempt, a young man asks Em to pray for him so that he may clear his interview. Em finds this amusing because it is in stark contrast to what her religion had taught her. People had always discredited her, a point the narrator makes when he passionately asserts how he tried to believe her in everything she said because everyone else found her incredulous. There is also a prevailing notion regarding them that people with BD have superhuman abilities, not one that needs to be marvelled upon, but instead one that evokes a sense of terror. Em sums it up: "Mad people are telepathic, clairvoyant and everything that should frighten you" (Pinto 102). This is the dual experience of disability in India—deification or

---

[8] During the solar eclipse of December, 2019, several families in Kalburgi, Karnataka, followed the superstitious belief of burying their mentally and physically disabled children neck-deep in sand hoping to cure them of their illness (Chowrasia).

discrimination. Ghai writes about the intertwining of disability with religion within the Indian cultural context:

> … disability implies a "lack" or "flaw" leading to a significantly diminished capability; images of the disabled also are associated with deceit, mischief, and devilry. Disabled people sometimes are depicted as suffering the wrath of God, and being punished for misdeeds that either they or their families have committed-a kind of penance or retribution for past misdeeds. (51)

Numerous studies have been undertaken to examine how persons with disability can lead a fulfilling life by being accommodated and accepted within the family and society by creating opportunities for them to function as per their capacities. As Shubhangi Vaidya writes, "interdependence, relatedness and affiliation are valued above individual abilities" (101). Interdependence, relatedness, and affiliation are what makes us all human, indeed.

Bibliography

Bearak, M. (2014, January 21). A conversation with: Author Jerry Pinto. *India Ink*. https://archive.nytimes.com/india.blogs.nytimes.com/2014/01/21/a-conversation-with-author-jerry-pinto/

Brewer, E. (2018). Coming out mad, coming out disabled. In E. J. Donaldson (Ed.), *Literatures of madness: Disability studies and mental health* (pp. 11–30). Palgrave Macmillan.

Campbell, F. K. (2009). *Contours of ableism: The production of disability and abledness*. Palgrave Macmillan.

Caruth, C. (1996). *Unclaimed experience: Trauma, narrative, history*. The John Hopkins University Press.

Chowrasia, S. (2019, December 31). Karnataka's 'buried' kids: Faith eclipses anti-superstition law. *The Quint*. www.thequint.com/news/india/anti-superstition-law-fail-disabled-childrenburied-kalaburagi-karnataka

Coleman Brown, L. (2013). Stigma: An enigma demystified. In L. J. Davis (Ed.), *The disability studies reader* (pp. 147–160). Routledge.

Ghai, A. (2002). Disabled women: An excluded agenda of Indian feminism. *Hypatia, 17*(3), 49–66.

Goodley, D. (2011). *Disability studies—An interdisciplinary introduction*. Sage.

Hall, A. (2016). *Literature and madness*. Routledge.

Linton, S. (1998). *Claiming disability: Knowledge and identity*. New York University Press.

McRuer and Wilkerson. (2003). An overview of queer and critical disability studies.

Penguin Random House. (2020, September 20). *Em and the Big Hoom reader's guide*. www.penguinrandomhouse.com/books/314819/em-and-the-big-hoomby-%20jerrypinto/9780143124764/readers-guide/

Pinto, J. (2012). *Em and the Big Hoom*. Aleph Book Company.

Price, M. (2013). Defining mental disability. In L. J. Davis (Ed.), *The disability studies reader* (pp. 298–307). Routledge.

Sen, R. (2016). Right to care, home and family: Ethics of responsibility towards persons with disability. In *Interrogating disability in India: Theory and practice*. Springer.

Thomas, C. (2007). *Sociologies of disability and illness—Contested ideas in disability studies and medical sociology*. Palgrave Macmillan.
Thomson, G. R. (1997). *Extraordinary bodies: Figuring physical disability in American culture and literature*. Columbia University Press.
Wolframe, P. (2018). Going barefoot: Mad affiliation, identity politics, and eros. In E. J. Donaldson (Ed.), *Literatures of madness: Disability studies and mental health* (pp. 31–49). Palgrave Macmillan.

Chapter 6
(No) Shared Towers: Performing the Bipolar in *Em and the Big Hoom*

Richa Joshi Pandey

Abstract The current paper discusses the novel *Em and the Big Hoom* with a view to unmask the weight borne by an assemblage of authoritative figures. Read through the lens of the cultural critic Raymond Williams, such figures, widely, pervasively and in an immersive manner, typify rules about the dramatization of individual consciousness, that necessitate response in the form of performance as coping mechanisms. The novel traces Em's staging of her personal and her professional roles; the stage, meanwhile, is occupied only by actors who belong to its own discursive integrity. In fact, characters, once part of the plot, are pushed into waiting in the wings. It is their presence that not only delineates the contours of the stage, but also raises questions about the issue of spectators and spectatorship. Such an enquiry into bipolar illness gestures towards the psychic blindness of the spectators, who are, in fact, either actively or tacitly, responsible for a particular (re)presentation of bipolar illness. This opens up questions about the manufacturing of exploitative structures that pathologize individuals and also about what, if at all, are we, as the dramatis personae of this medicalizing script, willing to offer as reparations.

Keywords Bipolar illness · Stage · Performance · Spectators · Language · Dramatization of consciousness

> Somehow it seems to fill my head with ideas. Only I don't know exactly what it is. (Carroll 12)

> A diagnosis helps cure. But it also pigeonholes the patient. She's manic depressive. He's schizophrenic. Into your box. (Pinto 212)

The current paper discusses the story of Em's life, with a view to unmask the weight borne by an assemblage of authoritative figures that widely, pervasively and in an immersive manner, typify rules about the "dramatization of consciousness" (Williams 15) and that necessitate response in the form of performance as coping mechanisms. The novel throws a spotlight on Imelda Mendes, whose life-world becomes her

---

R. J. Pandey (✉)
Department of English, School of Languages, Doon University, Dehradun, India
e-mail: richa.j.pandey@doonuniversity.ac.in

R. Uniyal and F. Rizvi (eds.), *Understanding Disability*,
https://doi.org/10.1007/978-981-99-4925-0_6

stage, within which, she feels subjected to an assemblage of authoritative stage directions regarding her professional and domestic roles as daughter/mother/wife. These assumptive directions standardize physical/mental ability in visual terms that signify her social behaviour. The current paper discusses how such assumptions underlying cultural ableism are particularly counterproductive to individuals with altered psychic states, as in the case of bipolar illness, by acting as potential 'triggers'. Alternatively, these assumptions also tend to pathologize individuals through language by homogenizing, trivializing, and stereotyping mental illnesses as 'madness'.

The novel, *Em and the Big Hoom* is a story about the narrator's mother called Em. Em's journey through manic-depressive disorder/bipolar illness, an extremely debilitating mental condition, is one that also severely limits and complicates the lives of her family members. The novel charts the life of Imelda Mendes (fondly called Em) and her courageous battle with her mental condition, her family's undaunting belief in her own strength and their fears and insecurities around their individual predicaments, as she constantly battles her severest vulnerabilities and inner demons. Notably, the narrative particularly draws attention to the ambivalences and insecurities in the lives of those who love Em, her children Susan and her son, the narrator as well as Em's husband and the children's father, called Augustine Mendes (fondly called Big Hoom).

The novel is a deeply personal narrative by the narrator, who tries to understand and thus share his mother's pain. He tries to come to terms with the deep and enduring scars that her inevitable and lonely battle with the disease have rendered. He soon realizes that he must always remain outside her locked-in mental state, which is like the dark tower where "You're a (mere) tourist; she's a resident" (Pinto 75) and that it was possible "only to make contact by mistake" (73). Though the family doggedly manages to save Em from death after her repeated attempts at suicide, her death by a heart attack, is something that they have been completely unprepared for. Em's life and mental state are typified by the Mendes's home, a one bedroom hall-kitchen in Mahim, Bombay, a city exemplified by its severely constrained urban spaces. Her story, narrativized through her conversations with her children as well as her scraps of writing in the form of letters/scribbled notes, is one of innate courage and immense grit in the face of her own illness and the presence of an assemblage of pervasive authority structures. These structures together constitute the dominant medico-sociocultural discourse that typifies how we come to perceive our own world and its various fellow actors, through a gaze that legitimates its own medicalization.

An article by Anderson et al. in the British Medical Journal summarizes the following salient features of bipolar disorder:

- Bipolar disorder is characterized by recurrent episodes of elevated mood and depression, together with changes in activity levels.

- Elevated mood is severe and sustained (mania) in bipolar I disorder and less severe (hypomania) in bipolar II disorder. Disinhibited and violent behaviour in mania may be the cause of harm to others.
- Depression is usually more common and longer lasting than elevated mood, and—together with interepisode milder symptoms—contributes most to overall morbidity.
- Other psychiatric disorders, such as anxiety disorder and alcohol and drug misuse, are common.
- Risk of death from suicide and from natural causes, most often cardiovascular disease, is increased.
- Treatment is with drugs and supplemental psychotherapies; for both acute episodes and maintenance, treatment is guided by whether mania or depression predominates (27). The diagnosis of bipolar illness is based on "the presence or history of hypomania or mania" (28). The treatment is challenging for various reasons and co-morbid psychiatric conditions are common. The diagnosis has a variable course and is often delayed due to a symptom overlap with related symptoms; for example, psychotic symptoms may be mistaken for schizophrenia, or unrelated (irritability may appear as a manic state) mental illness(es). Deliberate self-harm is also relatively common. Importantly, patients cycling between mania, hypomania, and depression are especially difficult to treat (27–29).

Life and Theatre: The World Is a Messy Stage

Life and theatre have, for the longest time, been hierarchically and porously interrelated. From the point of view of Indian poetics, for example, drama brings about an identification with the focus of the dramatic situation, to the effect that the audience realize through the experience of such an identification, the need for pursuance of the highest human goals (Pandey 4). Moreover, it is not theatre alone, that prompts us to re-imagine and renegotiate life in terms of the external situations that necessitate and elicit response. Life, as it is lived in non-homogenous, nonlinear, freely flowing time, prompts and focalizes a re-imagining of the story of life, as it is lived in its theatrical moments. Life-in-art and art-in-life are the paradoxically interrelated aspects of our lived existence.

The contemporary cultural critic Raymond Williams uses the term "dramatization of (our) consciousness" (15). Lizzie Eldridge (80) explains that William's use of the term is rooted in 'typification' (a term used by Lukacs) in referring to the way we perceive our own world, peopled by our fellow actors and conscious of our own behaviour in typical terms vis-a-vis generalized categories. These categories have been formed through a range of experiences, that are, in turn depicted through a range of media. The existence of such a hegemonic process has serious implications for the nature and possibility of dissent.

Performance is a powerful political tool to engage with and explore the world's stage. Drama, per se, is scripted by impersonal, timeless, and invisible forces of power and authority. The call to perform various roles is spontaneous and authoritative, and it assumes pliant actors, who do not question or 'mess up' the script. There is a deep-rooted sense of entitlement assumed by an increasingly powerful authoritarian assemblage which consists of hegemonic processes that arise from a conglomerate of religion, family, personal history, ethnicity, physical/mental ability, and gender. The performativity evinced by this conglomerate involves pervasive acculturation processes that act by and through the creation and internalization of normative subjects. While the call to perform gets louder, the performance itself is ironically elided over as the natural way(s) of being; the stage loses its contours and its special status as performance ground(s) where human agency and subjecthood may be (re)enacted and dissent may be put to test. Moreover, how an individual (re)enacts and improvises on gender-based roles often tends to mask the individual's embeddedness in other structures, for example, in those that define physical/mental ability or those that define the consciousness of class and ethnicity for individuals, who as the novel suggests, "work in the ABC professions … Ayahs. Butlers. Cooks … who have to work ten times as hard because they see us (migrant Goan Roman Catholics) as boys in the band" (Pinto 94).

Madness and Culture: Who's Stage Is It Anyway?

There is a profound gap between the norm and the constru(i)cted sense of the routine on the one hand and what constitutes our sense of pathology on the other. While entitlement and privilege accrue to the norm/normal/routine which justifies itself in discursive terms, pathology is derived from the norm in terms of the extent of deviation from the latter, in this case, knowledge about the illness and its treatment. Interestingly, ethnopsychological approaches reveal that mental illnesses are culturally specific, with culture determines how we shape, conceive, name, and treat mental illnesses (Pewzner-Apeloig, n. pag.).

Thus, each culture creates a milieu of potential pressures/triggers for the individual psyche which determine the roles taken up by her/him. The novel traces Em's own staging of her personal and her professional roles. Growing up, Imelda is split between the deep desire of what she really wants to do and what she is co-opted into doing. Hailing from a displaced, immigrant family, her maiden life is preoccupied with her effort at enacting the role of a dutiful daughter, who must abide by the rules of her religion, class and family, in particular, and her culture, at large. Her professional life too, is beset by anxiety over her capacity to sufficiently stage the act of being accepted, first as a teacher and later as a stenographer. Interestingly, the tenacity and creativity inherent in the drama of everyday life are (re)modelled and (re)channelled through the hegemonic potential of icons and their iconography. Every culture goes on to venerate, idolize, and bar-specific forms of reading against the grain. This sets the tone for their inherent creativity. Cultures also tend to consolidate various kinds of psychic slavery that typically perceive and create legally and biopolitically produced normative subjects. These subjects are produced within the confluence of medical and social discourses through the exertion of disciplinary biopower on the individual body as well as, at a different level, on the species body.[1]

Cultures assume a kind of blindness to their own deploying of censorship, biases, and validation to the contours of what inheres as normalcy. Cultural icons become the pegs/pivots around which physical/mental normalcy constructs, challenges, and restores itself. These icons signify a paradox in that they define the limits of a culture and hence restore appropriateness and legitimacy to certain aspects of culture that can/must be followed, desired, emulated, and preserved; yet their desirability ensues from their radical strangeness, queerness, and maverick-ness that (re)defines art and the artist. Both the art and the artist then become available for pluralized displays/debates and can be staged for and through the simultaneous resistance and perpetuation of a widely acknowledged ethic of public morality, that is culturally underpinned.

While icons and iconography conditionally determine what should be behaviourally, emotionally and/or physically desired/pursued vis-a-vis what should not be pursued/desired, their ready availability elides over the invisibility of their action. For instance, a culture of heroes and hero-worship is produced, sustained, narrativized, challenged, and bolstered within and through structures of the theatrical real. These figures legitimize and pervade culturally specific ideas of body image, physical/mental states, and abilities as well as sexual disgust and repression. Thus, Em's world is neatly divided around strict sexual dos and don'ts that emanate from the centres of religion, family, and popular culture and thus become identity markers that validate her moral status.

As long as the maverick remains on stage, entertaining the audience with the comic irony of the world without actually polluting the neat goings on of a constru(i)cted moral code derived through hierarchies based around the intersectional frame of sex, gender, class, religion, age, species and mental/physical abilities, he/she is tolerated, fetishized even. As discussed by Emily Martin in her work *Bipolar Expeditions: Mania and Depression in American Culture*, notably, the manic-depressive is often stereotyped in popular culture as the garrulous, hypersexualized artist, whose psychic excess rewards him/her with their gift of creativity. Their legitimacy is premised on their presence in art and not in life. Their creativity operates as a kind of wish fulfilment for those who are entertained by their spectacle, for the manic depressive or the schizophrenic is pathognomonically liberated from the regime of normalcy and traditional/received wisdom.

Sharon Packer reveals that mental illnesses, at large, become the avenue/template/conduit for otherwise dangerous or harmful behaviour but acknowledged as cultural/creative liberty in popular culture; that popular culture fetishizes an individual with mental illness as an enfant terrible, for example like the homme/femme fatale. Our cultures parasitically draw on their creativity without acknowledging their debt, reparations owed, and the manufacturing of exploitative structures that pathologize them. Studies reveal that only mild cases of hypomania may spur "imaginative, especially artistic creativity" (Greenfeld 226) and that the "delusion of grandeur" that it produces is ultimately "unproductive" (227), "deceptive" (226), and "destructive" (226). For Emily Martin, "manic depression is actually a malady of social conformity" (200). The literary fetishization of bipolar illness tends to become a roundabout apologia for this parasitic creative debt. The psychic excess that undergirds their creativity is premised on a psychic slavery enforced by the spectators/consumers in terms of the *enterslavement* (entertainment + slavement) that individuals with such an illness provide. This opens a nasty Pandora's box about bipolar illness, which bears not only suffering, pain, loneliness, stigma, and alienation on the part of those who are diagnosed with the illness (along with their loved ones) but also remorselessness, violence, and blindness on part of the pathologizing public.

Em's social performance is conditioned by the "panache of Anna Magnani" (21) or "the chin of that lovely girl in *Anarkali* … the poise of Merle Oberon … (or) Angela Brazil" (Pinto 12022). Her appearance is conditioned in terms of strict body discipline that demands limbs to be waxed (123), beheld according to a certain body image and body schema, accompanied with the appropriateness of dress which could be either "like the other Roman Catholic and Anglo-Indian girls of Byculla or … the Coelho sisters in their khadi sarees and Kolhapuri chappals" (24).

She starts off as "a fey frightened creature … a frigging woodland nymph" (131). She sees herself as a hybridized entity—a prop in the drama scripted by her mother—that explores its/her agency as vibrant matter as she is "trying my (her) best to be the immovable object (furniture being re-arranged) against which the irresistible force (Mae, Em's mother) must expend itself" (106). She battles her own nervousness (as performer) in confronting schoolchildren (as the director), whose power is vested in their ability to "anneal into a single organism: the class" as they "let slip the dogs of war" (29) and thus spontaneously invert the code underlying actor-director. The demand on her to stage her performance as a math teacher is immense and deeply personal, for she hates Mathematics and loves English and History. Soon, she must combat her inhibitions and fears around being sexually objectified and infantalized vis-a-vis "All those cartoons about 'Come in and take some dictation'" (24). At work, people like Brigette, a scheming, conning, vamp-like figure of tyranny from popular culture, who "thought (thinks) only she had the right to wear lipstick" (37), evinces a challenge that she must win, in order to keep her own role intact. When addressed "Hello. Buttercup" (18) by a prospective, partner, she must respond favourably. She must marry/court within the terms set by her lower-middle class, Goan, Roman Catholic family.

Moreover, she must configure her own sexuality in terms of either maiden chastity and/or sexual surrender to her husband.

Em writes prodigiously in the form of letters, notes, and scribbles. Her first-hand writings reflect her preoccupation with the roles that she has been called upon to play at various stages in her life. In one of her letters, for example, she writes like a playwright, giving stage directions while in the middle of her own monologue, in response to another actor from amongst her script's various dramatis personae. Writing/speaking to her future husband, she takes a sly textual dig by addressing him as Angel Ears:

Dear Angel Ears,

I know we have agreed to pledge our troth and etc. …

(She takes a long steadying draught of tasteless tea. Just so you should know how difficult this is to write.)

I do not think I am much interested in the business of copulation … (154).

Stylistically, the parenthetical stage directions given by Imelda, the director, to Imelda, the character, produce a deliberate distancing effect so as to foreground the acute and unrelieved stress at her self-awareness of the present. This indicates her ongoing discomfiture around sexual initiation after marriage. It also exposes the gap, while superimposing[2] the difference between an asexual discipline, that is encouraged for the female sex just before the couple 'pledges their troth' and complete sexual surrender towards legitimizing heterosexual reproductive autonomy, soon after. Here, the gaping threat inherent in the clash of competing/reversed but co-terminous moralities is unaccounted for. Surely, the gap cannot be part of the solution. However, it prompts a differential reading practice, one that offers an orientation towards the psychically 'triggering' potential of this anomalous gap and the ambiguous demands of cultural discipline.

In Em's case, there is also the experiential gap between the norm and pathology, which is further widened by her 'slow consciousness' of the latter and is typified by the norm's public entitlement. Tracing the genealogy of her condition, Em recounts, "At first it was only a drip, a black drip, and I felt it as sadness … There was no drain. There isn't one even now … It's like oil. Like molasses, slow at first. Then one morning I woke up and it was flowing free and fast. I thought I would drown in it. I thought it would drown little you, and Susan" (12). Em's experience of her illness is intense and protracted, even when she expects the action to build up and finish fast. In this theatrical framing of everyday life, a suicidal occasion presents itself as dramatic irony, which operates as the gap between promise and performance. Speaking of the same occasion, Em recounts getting dressed, going out on the road and jumping in front of a bus, thinking "it would be a final thing, quick like a bang. Only, it wasn't … The bus stopped and the conductor had to take me to a hospital in a taxi. He sat in the front, lotus pose." The driver, buddha-like, sits in a 'Lotus pose' and has "had to take me (her) in a taxi" (13). Primarily a demotic response, this appears, at best a legally sanctioned public/moral etiquette. Em's confusion about the experience of her illness owes itself to the huge psychic cost borne by the dramatic irony of the situation itself. This is intensified by the contrary entitlement evinced in an apparent clarity that the world and its actors have about what should or should not be said/done. From a Foucauldian perspective, subjects are produced within discourse, and, as in Em's case, it is the dominant medico-sociocultural discourse that "constrains and enables" (Barad 819) the validation of certain statements and acts vis-a-vis others, which, in turn, become habitual and perpetuate their own entitlement.

It is only recently that the attempt to suicide has been decriminalized in case of patients diagnosed with certain mental illnesses. At the time that this novel was written, the law did not have such a caveat. In Em's case, the diagnosis and treatment of her condition have been difficult. This is partly because of the very nature of the disease and its insidious and intense manifestations, and partly due to external triggers that complicate treatment. These triggers, like the demands made by the various societal roles she must internalize, in order to befittingly perform for an invisible, disciplining[3] audience, are further intensified by the discounting of Em's own effort. Eventually, the stages of Em's performance are mapped on to the stages of her illness. For Em, unable to find a drain or an outlet, suicide is a performative coping mechanism. "My blood was flowing across the floor of the taxi. There was no drain there either … In the taxi. With the world outside clear … Oh, not the world. It was inside my head" (Pinto 13). She has had no internal drainage mechanism; neither has the floor of the taxi, as public infrastructure, offered her one. Clarity is not to be had, not in the world, neither inside her head. She must, moreover, deal with the semantic consciousness of 'drains' and 'clarity'—textual traces that are only available to her in negative terms. The physical and emotional demands on motherhood, too, are left unacknowledged, except ironically in the understated terms of "tolerance and generosity and deep Mother Courageousness" (77). Em has had to transition from wanting to be a "nun … none" (133) into marriage, orchestrated by her mother and aunt as a guarantee of stability and respectability. But the psychic demands of such invisible coercion have cost her dearly. Her choice to pray to 'Our Lady' rather than 'surrender' to an all-demanding male Jesus is telling: "I can't take too much more male will in my life. No thy-will-be-done for me. I surrender nothing. I surrender nothing. I'll take my chances with a woman's kindness" (193). Religion and kinship systems hegemonically configure motherhood as a self-elevating, self-sacrificing act and children as God's gift, meant to be unequivocally and universally desired. To trace the affective and emotional cost borne by motherhood is to deviate from the sacred norm of motherhood and thus risk "being practised upon" through a cultist directorial ingenuity by those who "quote" from the book of "history" (132). She feels the pressure of the performance in the most intimate corners of her home. On being accosted by her husband about spending the emergency bank fund, her sense of guilt and shame present as a spontaneous reaction from within the fault lines of her fragile identity. Prima donna-like, from the movies that tend to readily dispense with secondary female roles, she uses stock phrases to evince her reaction: "… Stay the Course … Face up to the Consequences. Then maybe I should put a gun in my mouth and shoot myself before I am blackballed at the club" (174).

In Em's words: "Oh God, no. I saw what children do. They turn a good respectable woman into a mud-dh-dha. I didn't want to be turned inside out. I didn't want to have my world shifted so that I was no longer the centre of it" (133). The word mud-dh-dha, inflected with "rage and contempt" (51), bears the threatening and grotesque stamp of a buddha-like figure, who is universally venerated for his sacred code of religious and philosophical elevation. Buddha, the God, is self-referential and draws his followers to the centre of peace. In its play on the lexical similarity with the word bud-dha, Em disrupts its supposed clarity and elevation and implodes into an engagement with motherhood in hitherto unexpected ways. While in a casual conversation about being a "*mud-dh-dha*" with her family, she suddenly breaks into a chant, "Mother most horrible, mother most terrible, mother standing at the door, mouth full of dribble" (51) that she remembers from her childhood games. Her context and timing of the speech act involving the 'mother' in her chant and her use of the '*mud-dh-dha*' concomitantly, have the perlocutionary effect of referring to childhood and motherhood as tainted ideals in the first place and bear the illocutionary force of visibilizing this taint upon the consciousness of her own children, who, as is wont, frame her more as a mother, and one who is in fact "messed up", rather than as an individual, whose agency and choice are constantly up against an intimate and unassailable ante. The conversation progresses towards an infant-devouring mother-temptress figure from Greek mythology. She puts up the question to her children, "Do you think I'm that kind of mother? The kind who'd devour her children?" (51). Notably, if her son recognizes that she is playing out her insecurities because "this was allowed by her 'condition'. She could say what 'normal' women could not" (55), such a dialogue is a promising step towards the (re)claiming and (re)defining of madness in the area of language and identity politics.

For the narrator, his mother is the bricoleur, who can't get work done, whereas his father engineers their home and their place in the world. "My mother: incapable. My father: capable. My mother's mind belonged to the humanities. My father was the engineer" (90). His father has been bred on a steady reading of the Reader's Digest (91), a popular magazine that set the standard to which Em could never belong, for she (and by extension, her family) is "all messed up" (28). Her stories are eclectic and her conversations are like "wandering in a town you had never seen before … You had to keep finding your way back to the main street in order to get anywhere" (26). During these occasions, it is possible even to "frolic with her through van Goghian fields of free association" (103). She is creative and entertaining, casually discussing the religious code of sexuality as "a sin according to the Wholly Roaming Cat Licks" (3), where she is referring to the Holy Roman Catholics. As long as she envisages a fantasy world through her unique ways of inverting the norm while keeping the referential structure intact, she could be let off as a stereotype. But Em is more than a stereotype. By laughing at her own stereotype, she thereby inverts it and exercises agency. "Mad people are telepathic, clairvoyant and everything that should frighten you. Be afraid of me" (102). Here, Em's brand of the messianic madness stereotype, may be considered an inversive and socially enabling interventionist practice, as it draws attention to the way religion and popular culture together create the conditions of possibility for a pervasive s(t)ilt of the norm. Until now, Em is not culpable of the charge of discursive obsolescence. She is still a human actor. However, the onus is on her to be the sine qua non of human behaviour and language. The invisible cost of her use of language is not borne by her spectators, but by Em, alone.

Thus, while her manic state "as a rough, rude, roistering woman" (58) is "often ugly" (58), her depressive state, like a "wild animal with flecks of foam at its mouth" (59) is worrisome and she is called "the disgusting bitch" (135) by her son, who is later jolted by how his mother "assessed the flood of information that was her world for new threats to all of us …" (199). The narrator recounts an incident at the Staywell Clinic, where his sister and he admit Em, because they can't face the "terror and embarrassment" of her manic episode without their father, who is out on a work visit. On discharge, Em appears like a lifeless mechanical doll, a plastered puppet and not a live actor, devoid of any semblance of agency or choice: "Em sat like any of a million perfectly correct Roman Catholic women, her knees pressed together, her elbows off the table her head inclining courteously to the person speaking. She was a caricature of herself' (205). She had been administered electroconvulsive therapy (ECT).

Much research has shown ECT to be a controversial, but often useful treatment method for mental illnesses. For example, Dukart et al. show differential, highly specific, spatially distributed effects of ECT on regional brain structure in two separate populations of patients with unipolar or bipolar disorder, who are shown to respond differentially to ECT. According to Blease, in cases of particularly severe forms of depression, when all other treatment options have failed, the use of electroconvulsive therapy (ECT) is a recommended treatment option for patients; despite this, uncertainties over the mechanism of action of ECT and the risk of serious side effects prompt insight into aspects of informed consent in an attempt to value patient autonomy. On an optimistic note, in India, the Mental Healthcare Act, 2017 is supposed to have changed the fundamental approach on mental health issues including a patient-centric health care, instead of a criminal-centric one (Mishra and Galhotra, n. pag.). This act not only decriminalizes the attempt to suicide by a mentally ill person, it also prohibits the use of electroconvulsive therapy, referred to as shock therapy, without the use of muscle relaxants and anaesthesia on a patient suffering from mental illness.[4]

Notably, Em's shadowy appearance after treatment is a moment of rupture that will continue to haunt her children. For example, the narrator remembers his mother's ECT episode years later during his training at the Thane Mental Hospital, when he actually sees the larger implications of 'how' ECT is, in fact, administered to patients. Here, he witnesses how they are treated like shadow-like stick figures devoid of identity, except that "they are simply mad" and "free, in a bizarre sort of way" (Pinto 196); free, perhaps from being approached for consent regarding their own treatment.

Language and Mental Illness: No Escape from the Madd(en)ing Crowd

Language is an important tool in brokering the cultural constructedness of mental illness. The terms 'madness' and 'mad' connote the colloquial and pre-emptive use of language and may range from denigrating someone and comically abusing them, to accusing them of 'not fitting in enough'. Aarguably, often enough an attempt is made to realign normative categories, while assuming language to be an innocuous, alternative device, that can label, medicalize, and stigmatize with impunity.

Trans-coding madness with a disruption of the norm is representative of a kind of 'soft threat' posed by culture to madness and vice versa. Clearly, there are hidden tensions, anxieties, and fears underlying garbled words as "vedi" (82), which a colloquial Marathi term for a mad woman and "maddaw what" or usages in popular culture like "*M-A-D, mad mane pagal*" (207), a song from Indian Cinema, specifically in their easy and slippery usage. 'Vedi' is reflective of an exclusionary practice that normalizes discriminatory behaviour such as psychic blindness towards the un-coercible 'other'. Such terms mask a culture's discomfiture around altered/heightened psychic states and have profound and lasting effects on those being labelled.

On the other hand, Em's creativity underlying her use of language, is a smoke-screen for the tremendous repression she has experienced—a measure of her own spillage/slippage. Madness here a reductive majoritarian term. For Em, madness means the blurring of outer and inner demons.

External situations, like the threat from "Black Pants" (158), are magnified in her pre-existing hall of repressive/repressed psychic mirrors. Agency and choice are potent coping mechanisms or improvisations on her difficult roles, that enable her to come to terms with her own 'madness'. She must exert herself tremendously to "let this one (word/action) out of its cage and that should make the other cage stronger" (100).

Em is an eloquent "survivor" (202). She re-(in)scribes an existing sociocultural script in reverse, by deploying non-sequiturs. When she says, "Put me in a home", home for Em, is an aporia, signifying tension. Home signifies (be)longingness; it signifies an emplacement within the world's plot. It is a place that everyone is assumed/feels entitled to have, a place that signifies the start and end of life, and a place that justifies life. But home is also a potential pathological ground, like for Em, for identity construction. Ironically, it is the building up and sustenance of her 'home' that has taken its toll on Em. However, her plea for a home is not answered/answerable unless "you wanted to take your chances with mental hospitals and ECT" (202). Thus, while she exercises her agency in articulating a language that can bring itself to a crisis of representation, the world and its linguistic range—both semantically and ethically—fail to offer Em a relatable register or a metaphorical/literal home. Like their family's submerged piano and her own objectified status as furniture, she is a metaphor for what can be discarded. Given her existing intrinsic psychic pressures to perform, what consequences would this feeling of being on the brink of getting discarded have on her? Is it not likely to trigger a feeling of persecution, a feeling of homelessness within the contours of home?

Em is never proffered the stage. In her own story, she is waiting in the wings to be part of the main script. However, whether her role will get cultural validation or no—whether Godot will ever come or no—is uncertain. Given the complexity and challenges in the diagnosis and treatment of mental illnesses, Em's story enjoins a powerful message/moral: Advocacy in the form of societies and support groups is only a partial step towards the recognition of our responsibilities (along with their individual rights) towards individuals with specific psychic states, as these groups presuppose homogeneous categories, medically labelled as diagnoses, that are scientifically studied in terms of statistical data.

Read through the lens of life as a 'dramatization of consciousness', the stage unravels actors who belong to the discursive integrity of the stage. However, characters, once part of the plot, are often pushed into waiting in the wings. It is their presence that not only delineates the contours of the stage, but also raises questions about the issue of spectators and spectatorship. Such an enquiry into bipolar illness gestures towards the psychic blindness of the spectators. It also opens up questions about the manufacturing of exploitative structures that pathologize individuals and also about what, if at all, are we willing to offer as reparations. The solutions are never final, nor complete. They are evolving, situational, activist, culturally specific, and based on praxis. However, an approach sensitized to the psychic costs incurred due to normative categories that operate as invisible power/authoritative structures, warns against the risks which stem from new ways of keeping the violence intact. Without critically addressing and visibilizing these dominant power structures. Such a reading of Em's illness becomes a call for advocacy towards the restructuring of spaces that concern life-as-theatre. It is imperative that the emotional and psychic burden of social roles is not discounted through the invisibilizing process of normalization and homogenization. While (re)brokering mental illness, the role of pathology and its intensive range of afflictions in the lives of individuals and their families cannot be dismissed; for they must endure and combat both the disease and its social implications, that are as different as individual coping mechanisms are. Evidently, we need to progressively, transactionally, and affirmatively make a self-conscious attempt at reflection, mediation, and the restructuring of these dramatic spaces and (re)orient ourselves to the psychically 'triggering' potential of an irreconcilable and ambiguous cultural discipline. This involves a shift from a culture of apathology (apathy + pathology) that tends to compartmentalize mental illness and pathologize people in culturally specific ways, towards a culture of empathology (empathy + pathology), that focusses on the interconnectedness between testimonies of suffering and strength, experienced within and through culture, explicitly highlighting its salient/silent pressures. Instead of normal/pathological as "initial and originary subjectivities" (Bhabha 1), based on reductive binarisms, we need to critically visibilize the huge psychic effort required in performing normatively configured social roles, re-examine the creativity underlying performances as coping mechanisms, recognize the brave effort/agency involved in producing psychosocial bridges, formulate, foster, and endorse a language of empathy and testimony as well as re-orient viewing behaviour to include and tolerate with empathy, the 'slow consciousness' that mental illness entails.

Conclusion

In creative terms, the writing of stories such as *Em and the Big Hoom* is important to initiate a new culture of empathology. Imelda Mendes's story is predominated by the *karuna rasa*. Pinto dedicates his novel to his mother. He writes in his epigraph to the novel "… my mother said, 'Baba? Oh he's trying to write.' Still trying, Meem" (Pinto, n. pag.). As indicated in the epigraph, the rest of the novel, too is written in the form of Em's personal testimonial interwoven with his own. Though, the current paper focuses largely on Em's journey through bipolar illness, a broader work may profit much from exploring her entire family's journey with Em's illness. This paper, brings to light, Pinto's empathetic approach in narrating his mother's story though the fictional character Em. Thus, Pinto explores and comes to terms with his own "ambivalences" and "fears" (Pinto 23) in (re)negotiating those of his mother's and her increasingly self-conscious and brave responses to her pressures, shame, alienation, and loss. The success of such writing inheres in Pinto's style that exudes pride, frankness, vitality, and empathy without any embarrassment or reserve. Beyond advocacy, this kind of literature crucially creates an expansive milieu and a terrain for recognizing and (re)asserting alternative response strategies to cultural pressures that may potentially trigger unprecedented or unexpected psychic states.

Notes

1. In *The History of Sexuality: An Introduction*, Foucault writes of biopower: this power over life evolved in two basic forms; these two forms were not antithetical; however, they constituted rather two poles of development linked together by a whole intermediary cluster of relations. One of these poles—the first to be formed, it seems—centred on the body as a machine: its disciplining, the optimization of its capabilities, the extortion of its forces, the parallel increase of its usefulness and its docility, its integration into systems of efficient and economic controls, all this was ensured by the procedures of power that characterized the disciplines: an anatomo-politics of the human body. The second, formed somewhat later, focused on the species body, the body imbued with the mechanics of life and serving as the basis of the biological processes: propagation, births and mortality, the level of health, life expectancy and longevity, with all the conditions that can cause these to vary. Their supervision was effected through an entire series of interventions and regulatory controls: a bio-politics of the population (139).
2. Foucault discusses Nietzsche's idea of goodness in terms of a special space that involves a superimposition of the dominant and the suppressed: the concept of goodness is not specifically the energy of the strong or the reaction of the weak, but precisely this scene where they are displayed superimposed face to face. It is nothing but the space that divides them, the void through which they exchange their threatening gestures and speeches (Foucault, "Nietzsche, Genealogy, History" 150).
3. "The perpetual penalty that traverses all points and supervises every instant in the disciplinary institutions compares, differentiates, hierarchizes, homogenizes, excludes. In short, it normalizes" (*DP*, Foucault 182–183).
4. The Mental Healthcare Act, 2017 under the column of prohibited procedures, writes: 95. (1) Notwithstanding anything contained in this act, the following treatments shall not be performed on any person with mental illness—(a) electroconvulsive therapy without the use of muscle relaxants and anaesthesia; (b) electroconvulsive therapy for minors; (c) sterilization of men or women, when such sterilization is intended as a treatment for mental illness; (d) chained in any manner or form whatsoever (39).

Bibliography

Anderson, I. M., Haddad, P. M., & Scott, J. (2013). Bipolar disorder. *BMJ: British Medical Journal, 346*(7889), 27–32. www.jstor.org/stable/23493486. Accessed August 23, 2020.

Angermeyer, M. C., & Dietrich, S. (2006). Public beliefs about and attitudes towards people with mental illness: A review of population studies. *Acta Psychiatrica Scandinavica, 113*(3), 163–179.

Barad, K. (2003). Posthumanist performativity: Toward an understanding of how matter comes to matter. *Signs, 28*(3), 801–831. https://doi.org/10.1086/345321. Accessed August 26, 2020.

Bhabha, H. K. (1993). *Location of culture*. Routledge.

Blease, C. R. (2013). Electroconvulsive therapy, the placebo effect and informed consent. *Journal of Medical Ethics, 39*(3), 166–170. www.jstor.org/stable/43282689. Accessed August 23, 2020.

Carroll, L., & Tenniel, J. (n.d.). *Alice's adventures in wonderland: And through the looking-glass*. Three Sirens Press.

Dukart, J., Regen, F., Kherif, F., Colla, M., Bajbouj, M., Heuser, I., Frackowiak, R. S., & Draganski, B. (2014). Electroconvulsive therapy-induced brain plasticity determines therapeutic outcome in mood disorders. *Proceedings of the National Academy of Sciences of the United States of America, 111*(3), 1156–1161. www.jstor.org/stable/23770444. Accessed August 23, 2020.

Eldridge, L. (1997). Drama in a dramaturgical society. In J. Wallace, R. Jones, & S. Nield (Eds.), *Raymond Williams now: Knowledge, limits, and the future*. St. Martin's Press.

Foucault, M. (1977). *Language, counter-memory, practice: Selected essays and interviews*. Cornell University Press.

Foucault, M. (1978). *The history of sexuality: An introduction*. Vintage Books.

Foucault, M., & Sheridan, A. (1975). *Discipline and punish: The birth of prison*. Penguin.

Greenfeld, L. (2013). Madness muddled: Manic-depressive illness. In *Mind, modernity, madness* (pp. 211–308). Harvard University Press. www.jstor.org/stable/j.ctt2jbvq5.8. Accessed August 25, 2020.

Martin, E. (2007). Revaluing mania. In E. Martin (Ed.), *Bipolar expeditions: Mania and depression in American culture* (pp. 197–233). Princeton University Press. www.jstor.org/stable/j.ctt7sxt0.14. Accessed August 25, 2020.

Mishra, A., & Galhotra, A. (2018). Mental Healthcare Act 2017: Need to wait and watch. *International Journal of Applied & Basic Medical Research, 8*(2), 67–70. https://doi.org/10.4103/ijabmr.IJABMR_328_17

Packer, S. (2017). *Mental illness in popular culture*. Praeger.

Pandey, K. C. (1959). *Comparative aesthetics*. Chowkhamba Sanskrit Series Office.

Pewzner-Apeloig, É. (2005). Psychologie universelle, psychologie plurielle: La psychologie est-elle une production culturelle? *Annales Médico-psychologiques, revue psychiatrique, 163*(2). Elsevier Masson.

Pinto, J. (2012). *Em and the Big Hoom*. Aleph.

The Mental HealthCare Act. (2017). Available from: https://www.indiacode.nic.in/bitstream/123456789/2249/1/A2017-10.pdf. Accessed August 15, 2020.

Williams, R. (1975). *Drama in a dramatised society: An inaugural lecture*. Cambridge University Press.

Chapter 7
Disability, Sexuality, and Postcoloniality in Bengali Fiction

Arunabha Bose

Abstract Manik Bandyopadhyay's *Pragoitihishik* (1937) gives recognition and value to disabled sexuality which Bengali fiction has either been disinclined to acknowledge or has mis-recognized as absent/non-existing. Bandyopadhyay offers a positive representation of disabled sexuality which had either been represented through medical discourse as pathologized or cultural discourse as asexual/non-sexual. A cultural co-relation between disability and femininity is borne out by Bandyopadhyay's narrative; in fact, he uses the concept-metaphor of pregnancy to signal the maimed protagonist, Bhikhu's "rebirth" as a feminized self. Bandyopadhyay deflates the biological absolutism of categories such as whole/defective to show how disability is a cultural production ideologically reorganized around narratives of Normativization/Masculinization. Denied a socially sanctioned expression, the libidinal economy of differentially embodied and morphologically defective bodies is repressed as primeval, barbaric, and unstable id which violently resurges through a hypermasculine reassertion of bodily aggression through murder at the end of the story. Mahasweta Devi's *Shishu* (1979), a parodic fantasy-horror story, withholds the climactic transformation of deformed and morphologically stunted adivasis through "magic" since in reality there is no miraculating agency that can transform the aboriginal (premodern, disabled, non-subject) into the citizenry (modern, abled-bodied, constitutional subject).

Keywords Disability · Pathologized · Corporeal · Feminized · Embodied

Introduction

The disabled body in the fiction of Manik Bandyopadhyay and Mahasweta Devi, by virtue of its "defects" or inadequacy is an aberrant distortion and deviation from the norm of the stable and normative body. It reduplicates and reproduces the primary

A. Bose (✉)
Vivekananda College, University of Delhi, New Delhi, India
e-mail: arunabhabose@vivekanand.du.ac.in

R. Uniyal and F. Rizvi (eds.), *Understanding Disability*,
https://doi.org/10.1007/978-981-99-4925-0_7

"lack" or castration in the psychosymbolic regime that Lacan speaks of in the socio-economic regime. Using Julia Kristeva's idea in *Powers of Horror: An Essay on Abjection* (1982), one can designate the disabled body as *Abjected*, since by virtue of its deformity and distortion; it unsettles the ego boundaries of the stable and definitionally male body (2–3). Shildrick and Price (1999) using Foucault show that power circulates through the disciplinary procedures by which bodies are rendered manageable or useful under forces of capitalism thus producing a "Social Body" (433). Similarly, Tom Shakespeare disputes the fixity and absoluteness of binary categories such as disabled/able-bodied and pathological/normal since disciplinary regimes through practices of manipulation and repression first produce "normal" bodies which they claim to govern (16). Disabled bodies tend to occupy an ambivalent place in the discourse of public surveillance and monitoring; sexuality of disabled people remains in the grip of sociologically induced mythification. Responses to the sexuality of disabled people in modern Bengali literature range from denial, disacknowledgement, and silencing to morbid scopophilia, medical curiosity, invidiousness, and repugnance. Disabled bodies are pathologized/medicalized and often divorced from the erotic and pleasurable body. This chapter attempts to explore the multiple registers of differential impairment and limitation—physiological, sexual, and ethnic—in order to examine the co-relation between disability and emasculation on one hand and disability and citizenship on the other in two Bengali short stories.

Disability and Embodiment

Dominant hegemonic narratives of disability derecognize, silence, and disavow the problematic aspect of sexuality of disabled people; Manik Bandyopadhyay's *Pragoitihishik* (*Primeval* 1937) gives utterance to this culturally repressed and forbidden aspect. Disability breeds alienation and self-estrangement from the body; Bandyopadhyay's story reverses this culturally resonant archetype as the (disabled) body is retrieved back as a functional corporeal materiality for sexual fulfilment. "Pragoitihishik" or "Primeval" suggests barbarism and cultural primitivism; disabled bodies in Pre-Partition rural Bengal remained sedentary and alienated from mobilizing forces of colonial and capitalist modernity and thus being differentially embodied metonymically stage a primeval and premodern tribal ethnicity. To be primeval is to be excluded from operations of civil society, similarly differentially embodied people are outside of organized structures of labour production and thus marginal. Denied a socially sanctioned expression, the libidinal economy of differentially embodied and morphologically defective bodies is repressed as primeval, barbaric, and unstable id which violently resurges through a hypermasculine reassertion of bodily aggression through murder at the end of Bandyopadhyay's story. In the Deleuzean schema, the social technological machine and the collective semiotic machine (regime of signs) are both structurally built upon the substrate which is the anthropomorphic level constituted by the body which is non-formed, non-organized, non-stratified, and in essence deterritorialized (Holland 22). One can use this Deleuzean model to suggest that the disabled body is the substrate or *content* which is *expressed* as emasculated/feminized when inserted in the semiotic system by the collective semiotic machine, which in this case is the circulation of dominant morphological archetypes in the cultural imaginary.

Pragoitihishik looks at the social production of disability in premodern, colonial societies as a discourse and empirical category. The unobtrusive presence of the three disabled beggars, Bhikhu, Panchi, and Bashir in the muddy lanes and alleys of rural Bengal, serves to confirm, sustain, and generate the deterministic and culturally sanctioned hegemonic distinctions between clean, uncontaminated physiologically functional bodies and unclean, contaminated, pathologized, and dysfunctional/non-functional bodies. In fact, their respective pathological deformities expedite and sustain their abjection from the regulative regime and normative socio-economic discourses of rural society. Bhikhu because of his shrivelled and dysfunctional right limb and Bashir because of his amputated leg are located outside the modes of labour production; similarly Panchi because of the festering sore having disabled the normal physiological "performance" of her legs is outside the biological mode of sexual reproduction. Thus, the three main protagonists of Bandyopadhyay's story through their corporeal dysfunctionality personify what I would like to call *Embodied Difference*; they are differentially embodied phantasms who only exist to confirm the logocentricity of the normative body.

Bandyopadhyay's narrative shows the social production of disability as an epistemological and ethico-political category since Bhikhu, Panchi, and Bashir both embody and are embedded in a power differential. In the cartographies of premodern and provincial power relations, their visual deformity confirms historically invariable structures. The three disabled beggars internalize rather than resist a dominant representational discourse that (medically/taxonomically) classifies their bodies as deviant, transgressive, and pathologically abnormal. The disabled subject interestingly is arrested in time (genealogical aspect) and space (geopolitical dimension) because he/she is no longer structured by other regulative material variables such as caste (Bhikhu is a social untouchable, Bagdi), gender (Panchi is the gendered subaltern), and religion (Bashir is a religious minority) but by the superseding variable of disability. Thus, Bandyopadhyay shows the materialist mappings of embedded and embodied subject positions since the rural colonial state invents new modes of legitimation and power to replace/displace outmoded structural categories such as ethnicity, caste, and gender in order to justify the exclusion of deviant bodies. There is effected a social reconfiguration of what Foucault calls a Disciplinary *dispositife* or *Disciplinary Regime* which recalibrates variables, institutional operations, and material practices of identity formation and through a transmutation of value accords disability an over-determined position in constitutive relations of exclusionary power (Hekman 213). Because of their location within a visual and scopic economy, disabled bodies are inordinately more contaminated, unclean, and monstrous than bodies inscribed with invisible determinants such as caste, religion, or ethnicity. Rather than defining himself as a low caste Bagdi or a robber, Bhikhu reconstitutes and reconfigures his marginal and minority-centric identity through the new discourse of disability. Disability unseats older forms of discrimination and prejudice such as caste or criminality and becomes an over-determined, reorganizing social category that enlists the backing of formal legal exclusions and disqualifications from social workforce and organized capitalist political economy.

Disability and Emasculation

Bhikhu's former identity, that of being a murderer, rapist, and robber, is predicated on the Universalized Masculine code of violent and aggressive assertionism. Interestingly, even after his physical disability and enfeeblement, he refuses to disassemble the universality of the phallocentric model of hyper-masculinity in order to see alternative modes of identity reconstitution. His "distorted" physiognomy and morphological deviance does not alert him to power dissymmetries and the unnaturalness of culturally produced bodies as stable/normative/functional and vulnerable/non-normative/dysfunctional. Disability renders Bhikhu almost a socio-economic mutant, a vulnerable and docile subject, but even this dislocation from his earlier dominant subject position does not make him probe and question the materiality of differentially valued enfleshed and embodied selves. His bodily dislocation from masculine wholeness, inhabiting a vulnerable state of disintegrated/fragmented masculinity, only makes him hunger for an aggressive recuperation of lost masculinity, thus uncritically reproducing the same disciplinary power structures which penalize him.

Shakespeare et al. in *Sexual Politics of Disability: Untold Stories* (1996) alert us to the engendering of the disability narrative since masculinity in the phallocentric cultural imaginary is associated with wholeness, able-bodied activism, independence, penetration, strength, and invulnerability (16–17), whereas female bodies, by virtue of being genitally deformed or castrated, are culturally inscribed with vulnerability, passivity, sexual reception, weakness, and dependency. Moreover the female body because of its mutable nature as it undergoes change during menstruation, pregnancy, and lactation, is uncontainable, indeterminate, and unstable. Unlike the male body, the female body has porous and shifting ego boundaries and its secretions such as blood and milk constantly threaten to erode the boundaries of the contained body. Similarly just as the female body during pregnancy or menstruation requires medical care, protection and constant surveillance and not to mention are removed from the (male) public sphere and gaze; the disabled body too is subjected to constant medical surveillance. Like the pregnant body, the disabled body is vulnerable and dependent, incapable of unsupervised existence and not a facilitator but a hindrance to free movement in space and realization of goals. Using Iris Marion Young's phenomenological theorization of the female body, one can state that the male/healthy body is *transcendent*, while the female/disabled body is *immanent* (Marion Young 48–49). This cultural co-relation between *disability* and *femininity* is borne out by Bandyopadhyay's narrative. In fact, Bandyopadhyay uses the concept-metaphor of pregnancy to signal Bhikhu's "rebirth" as a feminized self. Like a pregnant woman, Bhikhu is hidden in the womblike darkness of the forest in Chitalpur surrounded by sinjuri trees, thus removed from social community and productive labour. Like a woman undergoing labour pain, Bhikhu's body is subjected to immense pain, "his wound suppurated the next day" and his functional right arm "swelled to the size of the drum, he could not move it at all" (226). His broken and leaking body ejecting exudations mimics the pregnant/lactating body; moreover his immobility and complete dependency on his friend, Pehlad for survival dispossesses his "masculine" body of activism, agency and sociability. Bhikhu's loss of bodily autonomy, material independence, and embodied corporeal subjectivity (like the fetishized female body being subjected to patriarchal surveillance is objectified) is depicted by Bandyopadhyay as re-enacting a cultural ritual of becoming feminized, devitalized, and dependent. In the cultural semantics of phallocentric signifying regime, the disabled body is inscribed with signs of stigmatization, abnormality, and deformity; Bandyopadhyay deflates the biological absolutism of categories such as whole/defective to show how disability is a cultural production ideologically reorganized around narratives of normativization/masculinization.

Bhikhu's inability to overpower Pehlad's wife sexually and his eventual physical castigation at the hands of Pehlad and his brother-in-law, Bharat whom Bhikhu could have once pummelled to ground in a mortal combat symbolically enacts his castration; Bhikhu, the lascivious and habitual molester, is rendered impotent. His stigmatized existence as a disabled person repulses Bhikhu not because it dislocates him from modes of labour production but because it dematerializes, dissolves, and disallows his masculinity. "He was filled with regret as he felt his right arm in the darkness. Despite all his *physical prowess* amidst so much human weakness and cowardice, the lack of a mere arm made him as good as dead" (229–230). His inability to sexually tame the Bagdi woman emasculates him in a rural society where material relations of power are determined by corporeal materiality of an unfragmented body. Bhiku is *defamiliarized* from his sexual/normal bodily self; he is dislocated from his former subject position as vengeful, rapacious, and aggressive. His body which was till now an instrument of sadistic overpowering gets transplanted from a libidinal economy of phallic excess and plenitude to a "feminized/disabled" bodily economy of lack. One of the ways of reading Bandyopadhyay's title is to see the primitivism and barbarism in Bhikhu's ritual embeddedness in a hypermasculine, tribal discourse where masculinity is a cultural derivative of bodily aggression and disabled/enfeebled bodies are deemed feminine. "He who once used to take such delight in killing people was now reduced to seeking solace in impotent jeers. Physically strong as ever, he had forever lost he means of using his strength" (229). The teleology of Bhikhu's narrative with his murdering of the Muslim beggar, Bashir and successful sexual conquest of Panchi can be read as a re-suming and re-establishing of his former familiarity with the male body, thus accomplishing a successful de-feminization and consequent normativization of the body.

Disability and Violence

However, *Pragoitihishik* makes an interesting departure from the regulative practices of the dominant cultural imaginary. Men suffering from disability try to disguise/hide their disabled/feminized bodies and simulate the morphology of normative masculinity by using prosthetics, thus hoping to metonymically erase their disability (although something only possible with physical impairment and not mental disability). But Bhikhu stages and "performs" his disability; by carefully choreographing his disabled appearance, "his head with its unkempt hair, the dirty, brown, torn rag around his waist, the emaciated arm dangling like a length of rope" he publically *displays* his crippled body (227). Thus, there is a double movement in the narrative; on the one hand, there is a theatrically managed exhibition of abnormality and on the other hand, a desire to contain that abnormality and normalize it to simulate masculine able-bodiedness and rather over-emphasize one's community/conformity with "whole" and non-castrated men. This can be explained in two ways; Bhikhu's physiological abnormality allows him to live in the plain sight of police, grants him a certain social invisibility (even at the cost of being subjected to a more hostile and repelling gaze which fetishizes him as pathologically ill-formed) and legal immunity. It serves as a stealth mode granting the runaway convict a new identity which he endlessly rehearses in a public exhibition of disabled vulnerability and its moral by-product, innocence. "He begged himself a torn coat which he wore even in the warmest weather to hide the scar on his shoulder, but tore off its right sleeve, as it won't do to keep the right arm covered: it was after all the greatest asset of his trade" (227). This, performative gesture serves as a *gestalt*, simulating Bhikhu's self-negotiation with the altered corporeal equivalence between *self* and *soma*. Bhikhu seeks to conceal the scar from the spear wound on his shoulder sustained during his flight from Baikuntha Saha's house after the armed robbery as it is a humiliating reminder of failed enactment of virility and bravado, significantly this wounding is also the inaugurating moment of the maiming and mutilation of Bhikhu's whole masculinity and bodily aggression. It shows him embracing the entrenched cultural script of masculine invulnerability. However, after the mutilation, Bhikhu learns to artfully display his "feminized/disabled" body thereby reinscribing the mutilated body within the newfound discourse of dependency, physical inadequacy, vulnerability, and scopic fetishism to invite attention. It becomes an economically necessary but ambivalent display of disadvantaged and differential identity which culturally relies on reduplicating negative, resentful, and disavowed images of the body.

In a comic scene, Bhikhu's masculinity on confronting Panchi's effrontery is mortified and he makes a gift of phallic banana to her after she insensitively rejects his overture. Being disposed of an unfragmented bodily self and mimicking a structurally splintered position culturally associated with femininity, Bhikhu's "giving" of the phallic fruit can be read as an overcompensation for sexual inadequacy since phallocentric representations of femininity designate it as inadequate/deformed which shows Bhikhu's uncritical acceptance of and imprisonment within a psychic framework of oppositional thinking modelled on able-bodied/masculine and disabled/feminine dialectic.

The most obvious sign of performative recuperation of his lost masculinity is his proposal to "provide for" Panchi, thus reconciling disability with masculine independence and subsuming Panchi within the disability discourse of dependency, passivity, and incompetence. He tries to seduce her by insisting, "I shall feed and clothe you, keep you in comfort. You can put up your feet and do nothing at all" (230). Bhiku's courtship of Panchi with the climactic triumph over the sexual rival, Bashir both culturally and metonymically re-inscribes him within the masculine ritual of contestation; the unleashing of his savagery when he punctures Bashir's skull with his spear serves as a rite of passage accomplishing the recuperation and re-institution of masculinity in a blood orgy before Panchi's eyes. Bhikhu had always made a psychic connection between the sadistic torture of unprotected women made to watch in horror the sight of blood squirting out from the lynched bodies of their fathers/husbands/sons and a hypermasculine reassertion of sexual identity/sovereignty. "What could be more exciting than to watch in flickering torchlight the indescribable horror of a woman's face as she saw her husband in ropes, being mercilessly beaten in her presence?" (229)

Disability, Sexuality, and Subjectivity

Disabled bodies tend to occupy an ambivalent place in the discourse of public surveillance and monitoring; sexuality of disabled people remains in the grip of sociologically induced mythification. By virtue of being defective, the disabled boy is dissociated from all established traffic with the orgasmic body which by nature denotes libidinal excess, plenitude, and what Lacan in *Écrits* (1999) calls *jouissance* (208). Disabled people having an active sexual life are seen to threaten and destabilize regulatory practices of heteronormativity, so power regimes seek to medically classify, sanitize, and contain disabled sexuality. Any form of sexual pleasure which transgresses the sanctioned parameters of normative coupling, which is not genital or generative is seen as unnatural since mutilated or ill-formed bodily organs cannot function as erogenous zones. Foucault in *History of Sexuality* (1990) talks about disciplinary and regulatory regimes which *produce* the "docile body"; sexuality and eroticism threaten normative stability, so the biopolitical regime tries to contain bodies and their pleasures and materiality. So, non-normative or anomalous sexualities pose an added threat to *governmentality*. Margrit Shildrick sees disabled people as *sexual outsiders* since by virtue of their *Embodied Difference* they cannot fulfil normative expectations and hence must be deficient in fulfilling "prescribed" sexual practices or sexual normativities (64–65). There is a culturally prescriptive and pragmatic materialization of the disabled body as struggling to function as an instrument of survival (*Use Value*) and thus robbed of erotic function which is a *Surplus Value*. Bandyopadhyay's story is of particular interest as it rematerializes the *de-Sexed* disabled body as *Sexed*. Bhikhu feels most acutely the hungers of the flesh, " Despite all his daring courage and physical prowess amidst human weakness and cowardice, the lack of a mere arm made him as good as dead. But even that was bearable. Regret and self-pity helped it subside. But loneliness was unbearable" (229–230); Bandyopadhyay gives recognition and value to disabled sexuality which Indian fiction has either been disinclined to acknowledge or has mis-recognized as absent/non-existing.

Bandyopadhyay offers a positive representation of disabled sexuality which had either been represented through medical discourse as pathologized or cultural discourse as asexual/non-sexual. Bhikhu's impairment does not lead to a repression or disavowal of libidinal drives; the disabled body which is emptied of sexual signification is re-invested with sexuality and enfleshed corporeality, "He increasingly wearied of his unfestive, *womanless* life" (228). Bhiku's deformed and "devitalized" body thus embodies approved, natural, and heteronormative sexual desire or what Merleau-Ponty calls *corporeal subjectivity* (Grosz 308). The *Lived Body* in space is thus a psychosomatic unity which is both meaning producing and meaning making in its relation to the world even if the relation has altered. Pre-evident cultural assumptions tend to create a rift between the physiological needs/limits of the disabled body and its sexual needs/limits; both these ontological and biological anchoring points are seen as mutually independent. But ironically, Bhikhu's narrative shows them to be mutually co-dependent, thus giving rise to a single undifferentiated body. Since Bhikhu's body is visually "distorted", it is assumed that he cannot participate in normative sexual practices and sex (most probably non-consensual) with an able-bodied woman would transgress ethical and biological norms. Bhikhu starts hanging around women's bathing places pretending to beg; his status as physically enfeebled and thus emasculated makes him less of an active phallic threat to women thus permitting him the voyeuristic pleasure of fetishizing naked female bodies. But this sexual encounter remains distant, scopophilic and ultimately thwarted by social constraints and regulating procedures enforcing "normalization". Bhikhu may have successfully avoided custodial surveillance, but he is now subjected to a different and more intrusive control. The disciplinary gaze of society subjects Bhikhu's body to active surveillance; by extension forestalling his sexual encounter with able bodies on cultural, ethical, and now legal grounds since traditional understanding of a sexual encounter between a functional and an anomalous body has to be forced, non-consensual, and thus unlawful. In fact, the criminal body subjected to penal servitude can be reformed and rehabilitated, but the disabled body cannot be reclaimed or re-installed within normative social discourses. His sexual desire for able-bodied women strains and challenges the permissible limits of natural, institutionally regulated, and reproductive heteronormative practice. Thwarted in his attempt, he tries to coerce Panchi into erasing "visual" signs of her bodily anomaly and acquiring a corporeal wholeness by the intervention of medically reconstitutive practices; "Put medicine on and cure it (sore) quickly" (230); being shrivelled and dismembered, the male body seeks compensatory completion by/through the penetration of the docile, receptive, unresisting but whole female body.

Disability and Ethnicity

Mahasweta Devi's *Shishu* (*Little Ones*), first appearing in *Nairitey Megh* (*Clouds in the South-western Sky*, 1979) stages a complex interplay between political/physical abnormality, literal/metaphorical marginalization, aboriginality/abnormality, normative evolution/pathological devolution, and production/appropriation of disability. In an infernal and accursed mining town called Lohri, located on the outskirts of Ranchi, Sarguja, and Palamau; newly appointed government officers tasked with distribution of relief material to the draught hit tribes are terrorized by unearthly nightly apparitions. These "apparitions" who plague the nightmarish hallucinations of the government officers turn out to be a tribe of iron workers, the *Agariyas* who resisted the mining lobby in an armed uprising thus inviting governmental retribution in the form of genocidal violence. Sheltered in the dense forests without food, these forgotten adivasis (as distinct from the *bharatvasis*) have devolved into primitive (*adi*) and primeval (*adim*) spectres indistinguishable from stunted infants or "shishus". In *Shishu*, the disabled, infantalized, and emaciated aboriginals can only rub their grizzly genitals and "cackle in ghoulish and vengeful glees" (Devi 20); there can be no communication between these stunted (emasculated) men and able-bodied Indian men since the adivasis have not yet "emerged" into the non-genital *metaphorics* of linguistic reality. Language according to Judith Butler is the constitutive and regulatory force that causally configures sex/gender (pre-ontological reality of substance) and social "self" (the cultural metaphysics of substance) (Butler 68). There is no "outside", "before", or "beyond" the postcolonial signifier, and since the stunted aboriginals are outside of this signifier, they cannot be represented through dominant linguistic regimes and postcolonial cultural practices. The aboriginals as victims of decolonized development are expelled from the postcolony and regress into becoming atrophied and emasculated aberrations.

Can the difference between the citizen and the native, subject and the subject-in making be understood through the framework of *Embodied Difference*? Can indigenized subjectivity be represented as differential, disadvantaged, and female? Can the figure of the disabled indigene be read as an invention of the dominant culture? Disability is thus not only associated with physiological, psychological, and sociological models of self-hood but also with ethnographic narratives which reduce the native to the status of an inappropriate and invalid entity lacking a stable and representable self-hood. Thus, differential subjectivity as a by-product of cultural identity is not determined entirely by the mechanism of biological classification but also by ethnographic taxonomy and its internal colonization as well. Disability becomes a metaphor for the political abnormalization of adivasis. Hence, what Mahasweta Devi invents is a grotesque parody of the beloved genre of Bengali ghost story popularized by Rajshekhar Basu (Parashuram) and Shirshendu Mukhopadhyay in works such as *Bhushandir Mathe* (1924) and *Monojder Adbhut Bari* (2004). *Shishu* brings the folk carnival logic to the *bhadralok* (urban literate upper-middle class genteel elite) genre of the *bhautik galpa* (horror story). This carnivalesque story of blood red earth, fire eating demons, bodily transformations, and regressed nocturnal spectres brings forth the hitherto defamiliarized/alienated realm of postcolonial reality within respectable official-ideological discourse through the use of sanskritized and officialized Bangla. The carnivalesque "cackle" of the disabled *adivasis*, their morphological aberrations, and blasphemic genital playfulness turns the aesthetic-ideological logic of the *bhadralok bhautik galpa* (bourgeoise Gothic) inside out. The postcolonial "spell" of capitalist modernity backfires turning adivasi men into infants. There is not only a profanization/parodization of transcendental divinity by eulogization of demons, but a celebration of the disfigured, de-aestheticized, and defamiliarized human form which inverts the modern Indian man's physiological normality. According to Irigaray in *Speculum of the Other Woman*, "All Western discourse presents a certain isomorphism with the Masculine sex; the privilege of unity, form of self, of the specularisable, of erection" (63–64). The deformed/disabled tribal bodies incorporate the distorted and demonic to caricaturize the institutional narrative of development; and in doing so, the tale *historicizes* a phenomenon mistakenly recognized as *supernatural*, "the undernourished body and laughable height of the ordinary Indian male appear a heinous crime of *civilisation*" (21). Against the "natural bodily growth" of the metropolitan Indian citizen; the *adivasi's* "laughable height" stages a distinctively ideological revolt.

Corporeal and Spectral Bodies

In *Shishu*, the tribal male bodies are precisely denied specularization/visualization; dominant fictional discourse does not produce the male tribal body as phallic, this presocial and prelinguistic body lacks morphological *becoming* in form. Postcolonial signifying practices are suited for an isomorphism between bourgeois male sexualities and language and thus the "naturalized" or anatomical tribal body which is not a sociolinguistic construction cannot in effect have meaning for the bourgeois relief worker, "Men hold their penises, women their breasts. Their penises rub against him, reminders that they are men, adult, Indian males" (19–20).

The ghoulish heroes of *Shishu* refuse to re-integrate themselves with the postcolonial nation's modernizing apparatus. The realm of marvellous and implausible is actually *not* the tribal fantasy tale with its anthropomorphic prehistoric reptiles and mythological apparitions but the "fairy tale" of promised decolonized development. As the enchantment of the neocapitalist fable wears off, it reveals remnants of a foregone world and the forgotten keepers of that civilization now reduced to myths, devoid of their humanity. For Mahasweta Devi, the postcolonial nation and its epistemological frames of neo-colonialism appropriate the structuring apparatus of fairy tale to perpetrate a mythical fable of national modernity; this *postcolonial fairy tale* estranges the citizen-reader from tribal reality. In Mahasweta's hands, the tribal "horror story" counteracts the mythological "fable" of capitalist modernity and thus becomes an epistemic performance which contests the dated chronologizing machinery of history and serves as postcolonial history's ethnological corrective and not surrogate.

Mahasweta's parodic postcolonial fantasy constitutes a counter-discourse to the "fairy tale" of decolonized development. The government relief worker in *Shishu* brings the broadest possible range of anthropological and epistemological modes of comprehension to understand this "regression", the dwindling of adult Indian males into infants, only to confront the vanishing point of postcolonial reason. In *Shishu*, Mahasweta invokes the Netherworld Tribal God, Jwalamukhi and shows a complex social-ecological-physiological relationship between the diseased ecosystem of Lohri and its shrivelled humanity. The Aagariyas are descendants of the demon (*asur*) clan–Lohasur (patron demon of iron), Koilasur (patron demon of coal), and Aagaiyasur (patron demon of fire). Aagariyas ate flames, dug deep into the bowels of the earth to mine iron from the netherworld and the Aagariya King Logundih only allowed the Lohri tribe to forge iron implements. King Logundih's wife gave birth to a son, Jwalamukhi (He of flaming mouth) who fought a legendary battle with the Hindu deity, Sun. The Aagariya youth consider, Jwalamukhi their hero since it is because of him that the venerable Hindu God cannot mate with his wife, Chandrika except on a full moon night (4–5). The historical reality of the iron workers of Lohri can only be understood from the standpoint of the folkloric parable about Jwalamukhi's battle with the Hindu deity, Sun. In a grotesque parody of the marvellous fable, Mahasweta shows a pathologized ecosystem ruined by governmental apathy and mining lobby as well as the physiological abnormalities plaguing its stunted and disfigured tribal population. The Aagariyas of Kubha who attacked mining contractors and governmental lobbyists in collusion with Naxalite insurgents ran away and merged with the forest thus becoming ghostly apparitions haunting the imagination of government relief workers. The re-emergence of the old Aagariyas as shrivelled, stunted, and impotent "shishus" shows a terrifying return of the repressed as a regressive spectre. The devolution of grown Aagariya men and women into infertile, dwarfish ghouls metonymically stages the modern aboriginal's relapse into infantilism as if to mock the evolutionary teleology of technocratic and ecocidal progress. The Aagariyas attempt to unsettle *capitalist technocracies* by evolving *ecological democracies* in which the subject merges with the habitat, thus demolishing what Marx called alienation and almost inventing a unique version of ecological Marxism in which social relations are contingent upon ecological affinities. The unrepresented disabled bodies of aboriginal insurgents in this fable are not transformed in the end through a magical spell.

Disability and Postcolonial Difference

The folklore about Jwalamukhi constitutes the genealogical *intertext* transposed from Aagariya oral narrative to Mahasweta's historical-realist text. Unlike a typical realist fiction, Mahasweta's text is a mixed collocation of differing signifying systems; there is a redistribution of sign systems be it folkloric, hagiographic, epic, mythological, anthropological, or journalistic without privileging one over the other. Now, the folklore about Aagariyas inheriting their hereditary caste trade from demon clans of Lohasur, Aagaiyasur, and Koilasur is just one version of genealogical origin, and hence, I would like to call it *intertext a.* According to another version, they are the descendants of King Logundih and his twelve brothers who were married to one woman in a tribal mimicry/mockery of the Kshatriya Pandavas, this can be called *intertext b.* And according to another, King Logundih's wife was sheltered by a Gond (tribal), smarting from the Sun God's flame, she gave birth to Jwalamukhi who fought against Sun bringing curse upon the land since "all wealth earned from iron by the Aagariyas will turn to ash" thus explaining their hereditary poverty, this serves as *intertext c.* Now, unlike a singular and complete subaltern history, this originary narrative is plural and varied. No single version is preconstitutive of origins but all are collectively poly-constitutive; Mahasweta's text adheres to this genealogical polyvalence rather than prioritize one source over another. Julia Kristeva in *Revolution in Poetic Language* (1984) believes that "transposition is the signifying processes' ability to pass from one sign-system to another, to exchange and permutate them" (60); Mahasweta's polysemic fiction by exploding the unitary origin tale into intra-genealogical fable allows the folkloric semiotic to displace rather than disavow the historical realist. By rehabilitating fable, folklore, and myth within the generative grammar of the communicative realist text, it becomes a *metalinguistic text.*

In Mahasweta's parodic fantasy/horror story, climactic transformation is deliberately withheld since in reality there is no miraculating agency that can transform the aboriginal (pre-modern, disabled, non-subject) into citizenry (modern, abled-bodied, constitutional subject). The dysmorphic masculine aberrations in *Shishu* hold out their scaly genitals for the modern Indian citizen to touch at the end of the story; the phallic lack and the symbolic castration of the aboriginal male show his inability to reconcile morphological and sexual difference (penis and phallus) as well as the biological Father and symbolic Law Giver. The aboriginal man has not emerged into the symbolic register as he has failed to merge the penis with the cultural metaphor, the phallus. The incomplete disavowal and displacement of sexual/symbolic lack shows that he is much closer to what Kristeva calls the "semiotic" (maternal imaginary) or the presymbolic *metonymic* as opposed to the postcolonial *metaphoric.* The intergenerational folktale of Jwalamukhi and his descendants shows an alternative mode of subaltern representation in which unaffiliated/unrepresented bodies of *khadanmajdoors* are embedded in non-agrarian systems of economic transformation, thus displaying a unique bodily materiality of subaltern history. Perhaps this is a *Neo-Deleuzean Desiring-Production* in which aboriginal subjectivity is rooted in geographical materialism. Epistemological modes of capitalism see historical subjectivity of the bourgeois as dematerialized abstraction, but in *Shishu,* we see the barrenness of ferrous-rich soil imitating the impotence of its populace.

References

Bandyopadhyay, M. (2010). Primeval. In K. Bardhan (Ed.), *The Oxford India anthology of Bengali literature: Volume 1* (D. Chattopadhyay, Trans., pp. 232–239). Oxford University Press.
Butler, J. (1993). *Bodies that matter: On the discursive limits of "sex"*. Routledge.
Devi, M. (2009). *Bitter soil* (I. Chanda, Trans.). Seagull Books.
Grosz, E. (1994). *Volatile bodies: Towards a corporeal feminism*. Indiana University Press.
Hekman, S. J. (Ed.). (1996). *Feminist interpretations of Michel Foucault*. The Pennsylvania State University Press.
Holland, E. W. (2013). *Deleuze and Guattari's: A thousand plateaus*. Bloomsbury.
Irigaray, L. (1987). *Speculum of the other woman*. Cornell University Press.
Kristeva, J. (1982). *Powers of horror: An essay on abjection*. Columbia University Press.
Kristeva, J. (1984). *Revolution in poetic language*. Columbia University Press.
Lacan, J. (1999). *Écrits* (B. Fink, H. Fink, & R. Grigg, Trans.). W.W. Norton and Company.
Shakespeare, T. (2006). *Disability rights and wrongs*. Routledge.
Shakespeare, T., Gillespie-Sells, K., & Davis, D. (1996). *The sexual politics of disability: Untold stories*. Cassell.
Shildrick, M. (2002). *Embodying the monster: Encounters with the vulnerable self*. Sage.
Shildrick, M. (2009). *Dangerous discourses of disability, subjectivity and sexuality*. Palgrave Macmillan.
Shildrick, M., & Price, J. (Eds.). (1999). *Feminist theory and the body*. Routledge.
Young, I. M. (2005). *On female body experience: "Throwing like a girl" and other essays*. Oxford University Press.

Chapter 8
Stigmatizing the Other: Treatment of Disability in Franz Kafka's "The Metamorphosis"

Jaya Upadhyay

Abstract This paper takes into account symbolic interactionist approach to understand the constructedness of difference and stigma in Franz Kafka's "The Metamorphosis". It looks at the story as a representation of behaviours and responses of individuals towards the other (non-normative body) and the dilemmas and anxieties of this non-normative body in managing and maintaining its sense of self around the other (normative body). It also looks at how interactions between the two lead to the fortification of the categories of normal and the not normal (deviant). The paper draws from the ideas of Erving Goffman to facilitate an understanding of micro-level interactions between individuals and from poststructuralist ideas to understand embodiment and subjectivity. It also emphasizes on a mixed approach including both social interactionism and poststructuralism to understanding disability and disabled identity.

Keywords Stigma · Symbolic interactionism · Embodiment · Subjecthood · Disability

Introduction

The words stigmatizing and other in the title of the paper bear a connection with regard to the construction of a disabled subject. *Other* is not a materially existing category but one that comes to pass in the process of *othering*. The othering process takes place within social interactions when one confronts a category of persons which disrupts the usual expectations of *socio-cultural normalcy*. This category is then otherized, devalued and discriminated against, i.e. stigmatized. The issue of stigmatization is significant in relation to disability, since the concept of *disability* and *disabled identity* is to a great extent an effect of stigmatization. Theorists working in the field of disability have dealt with the issue of what constitutes as *disabled*, and

J. Upadhyay (✉)
Department of Humanities and Liberal Arts, DIT University, Dehradun, Uttarakhand, India
e-mail: mailjayaupadhyay@gmail.com

R. Uniyal and F. Rizvi (eds.), *Understanding Disability*,
https://doi.org/10.1007/978-981-99-4925-0_8

most of them think of disability as something that is produced when a body is judged through the socio-cultural lens of physical/mental well-being or completeness and is found lacking in one or more respects. The above view is informed largely by poststructuralist ideas of construction of identities through an opposition, for e.g. the binaries of male and female or normal and deviant, etc. These views have greatly benefitted researches in the field of critical disability studies.

In the present paper, I have employed the notions of identity as realized within symbolic social interactions, pioneered and applied to the field of disability studies by the sociologist Erving Goffman. I have studied the plight of the character, Gregor Samsa in Franz Kafka's novella, "The Metamorphosis," as representing the plight of a disabled person and the state in which such a person finds himself in anticipation of others' reaction towards his condition. I have analyzed his family members' and his boss's responses to his condition drawing from Goffman's views on stigma and disability. Goffman's ideas are particularly useful in informing our understanding of production and maintenance of categories of disability or deviance through ritualized patterns of behaviours within micro-level social interactions. His views on symbolic interactions as laid down in his work, *Stigma: Notes on the Management of Spoiled Identity,* are important for the field of disability studies to perceive the various ways in which the abled and disabled manage themselves around each other to ease off social interactions, how the *so called disabled* engage in various strategies to cope up with the dilemma they find themselves in around the *so called abled*. I also bring in the ideas of Margrit Shildrik and Janet Price, Susan Wendell, Lerita. M Coleman, and others, whose work on disability is informed by poststructuralist approaches to selfhood. A poststructuralist view to disability is especially important to understand the constructedness of all forms of embodiments including disablement and also make sense of the processes through which the non-normative body types are viewed as different and deviant.

This analysis tries to make sense of disability through the lens of symbolic interactionism and poststructuralist readings on embodiment. This paper makes a case for including both approaches to the study of disability and impairment. Both these approaches provide a well-rounded understanding of how bodily identities are perceived as disabled or abled through a socio-cultural discourse on them, and how these perceived norms are actualized within micro-social encounters between individuals. This mixed approach will be able to minimize the limitations of both approaches in making sense of disability; it will then be based on as Fountain and McLaughlin (2013) mention in their work, "materiality of bodies and in the stories that give meaning to those bodies." (135). The connection between both points of view is that individuals never enter social situations or encounters without cultural narratives about their identities; they are never blank slates when they participate in social interactions. The socio-cultural imagery embedded in people's psyche determines how they act as bodies. The dynamics of interactions, as well as the socio-cultural grounding that individuals possess, are what give birth to disabled and abled identities; these micro-level interactions further secure the cultural social imagery through ritualization. Fountain and McLaughlin (2013) emphasize the importance of a mixed approach when they argue how categories of disability are secured and become socially significant by what actual bodies "do" and interpretations made of them within social interactions. Franz Kafka's story can be interpreted in numerous ways owing to the surrealist stance it takes. The central character, Gregor Samsa's metamorphosis into a "gigantic insect" on getting up one fine morning, pushes the narrative in various existentialist directions of analysis; at the same time, this transformation and the accompanying incapacity that he is shown to suffer make "The Metamorphosis" a perfect metaphor for disability.

The Discredited and the Discreditable Subject

The story begins with Gregor witnessing his transformed body, struggling to keep it stable and in control of its movements. His initial reaction to his condition is "What has happened to me?" Kafka (2011) As he tries to get out of the bed to start on his train journey to his office, he finds it difficult to get the lower part of his body out, and when he tries recklessly, he collides against it. He then tries to get the upper part of his body to the edge of the bed first, but scared of hitting his head in the process, stops and decides against trying to get out of the bed on his own. Gregor's struggles can be equated with the struggles of people who acquire disability at a later stage in their lives. Not only is the actual physical incapacity that they undergo a challenge for them, but so is accepting their disabled identity and learning newer coping up mechanisms and managements of self. Erving Goffman (1963) talks about the socialization process that individuals go through when coming to understand the dynamics of their conditions and acquiring a conception of their self. According to him, the people acquiring a disability later in their lives have the greatest difficulty in adjusting to their situation and are more prone to disapproving themselves. Part of their problem stems from the fact of their being fully aware of the categories of normal and stigmatized. They have as a point of reference the socially normative life that they had led in the past and their changed situation which they know fully well is discredited in the society. "The painfulness, then, of sudden stigmatization can come not from the individual's confusion about his identity, but from his knowing too well what he has become" (133). In his work, Goffman mentions the experience of someone who gets polio later in life and experiences dissociation from their condition or an inability to come to terms with their newer self. "I was like everyone else—normal, quarrelsome, gay, full of plans, and all of a sudden something happened! Something happened and I became a stranger. I was a greater stranger to myself than anyone. Even my dreams did not know me" (35). It is similar to abandoning a previous life, a break from the meanings of their self that is imposed on them.

Consequently, Gregor's refusal to come out of the room after his transformation despite several entreaties from his family members also mirrors a newly disabled person's apprehensions about the reaction of people to his condition. One of the first coping mechanisms of such an individual under the given conditions are limiting social encounters or avoiding company of others. It should also be stated here that Gregor's condition signifies that of a "discredited" (Goffman, 1963, p. 4) person, an individual whose difference is apparent directly, similar to a visually impaired or a physically challenged person who walks on crutches. Goffman mentions instance of one such Mrs Dover in his work, *Stigma: Notes on the Management of Spoiled Identity,* who avoided leaving her house after the amputation of the distal half of her nose. He mentions how Mrs. Dover, who was previously independent, friendly, and outgoing, confined herself to the four walls following her disfigurement. "The first two or three years she seldom left her daughter's home, preferring to remain in her room or to sit in the backyard, "I was heartsick," she said, "the door had been shut on my life" (qtd. in Goffman12). However, the discredited individual must be distinguished from the "discreditable" (4) individual, whose difference is not immediately apparent, such as a person using a colostomy bag or suffering from chronic fatigue syndrome. According to Goffman, discreditable individuals try to manage the information regarding their difference through trying to pass as a non-deviant; the discredited might try to do so through cowering in social situations or completely avoiding them.

Disability: A Performance of Discourse

From a poststructuralist point of view, an individual produces his identity as a disabled subject through adhering to the societal norms of health and illness. Society expects and respects a body that is capable enough to perform mobility without external help or is capable of performing simple daily chores independently. Independence of bodily functions defines wholeness of a body, anything less signifies incompleteness, brokenness. An individual with impairment first tries to define himself through the norms of normativity where he finds himself lacking, and his act of avoiding social intercourse or trying to pass as a normative body is then prompted by the same definition. Margrit Shildrik and Janet Price (2013) discuss the idea of a disabled identity from Michel Foucault's perspectives in their work, "Breaking the Boundaries of the Broken Body." Their work surrounds the analysis of the ways in which discourse on health and ability creates disabled subjects out of individuals. They are concerned particularly with medical/governmental demands made to individuals with impairments for providing details on the nature and the degree of their impairment. The process of constant reporting and addressing the details of their issues is what according to Shildrik and Price creates and maintains their identity as a disabled person. "The subject herself effects a normalising judgment on her own modes of being by submitting to what Foucault calls a power that 'produces domains of objects and rituals of truth' (1977: 194) Moreover, she acts not as a pre-existent bounded being, but constructs her very selfhood in the process of normalization" (Shildrik and Price, 2013, p. 436). Thus, Identities are negotiated, produced and maintained between people through difference.

Deconstructionist and poststructuralist contention is with the defining of identities in absolute terms. When it comes to disability studies, these approaches are concerned with deconstructing the absolutes of ability and disability. The narratives and discourse that circulates within the society are what gives these absolutes meaning. The actual production of disability then comes through the performance of it on the basis of societal narratives within micro-level social interactions. Be it Gregor Samsa or Mrs. Dover, both are socialized in a way that their actual behaviour within social interactions is motivated by a discourse on disability. Their avoidance or cowering produces and maintains their identities as disabled subjects.

Stigma: Actual Social Identity Versus Virtual Social Identity

Gregor finally decides to open the door of his room and reveal himself to the chief clerk who had come to enquire about his absence from the office. When he exposes himself in the presence of the clerk, he receives a reaction that is summarized as, "[...] he heard the chief clerk utter a loud "Oh!"—it sounded like a gust of wind—and now he could see the man, standing as he was nearest to the door, clapping one hand before his open mouth and slowly backing away as if driven by some invisible steady pressure" (Kafka 81) in the story. His mother is dumbfounded clasping her hands while his father "knotted his fist with a fierce expression on his face as if he meant to knock Gregor back into his room, then looked uncertainly round the living room, covered his eyes with his hands and wept till his great chest heaved" (81).

The above reactions to Gregor's situation can be analyzed to understand stigmatization of individuals with impairment within social interactions. Goffman's works majorly deal with a discussion of how humans perform within social interactions. According to him, we all work on the basis of some ritualized behaviours which are established within the dynamics of social interactions itself. There are frames and patterns of behaviour which guide daily human encounters, and these patterns are accepted and maintained to make participation within social settings natural and convenient. For better or for worse human beings don't enter social settings as clean slates but with certain narratives and preconceived ideas regarding people and things. Daily discourse is governed by cultural and social narratives, and social interactions partly reflect the narratives that people have in mind and those they tell themselves when they are in specific settings.

In case of any discrepancy in what we witness in individuals and the anticipation we have in mind regarding them, we tend to discredit them. "He is thus reduced in our minds from a whole and usual person to a tainted, discounted one" (Goffman 3). In short, the individual is stigmatized or otherized. The aggressive reactions that Gregor gets from those that witness his transformation can be equated to reactions against any individual who possesses an attribute that is different and less desirable in the category that he constitutes. While explaining "stigma", Erving Goffman mentions that it arises when a discrepancy is found to exist between a person's "actual social identity" (3) and "virtual social identity" (3). The former is the attribute the individual actually possesses and the latter is the anticipated attribute that he is assumed to possess. "Such an attribute is a stigma, especially when its discrediting effect is very extensive; sometimes it is also called a failing, a shortcoming, a handicap. It constitutes a special discrepancy between virtual and actual social identity" (3).

Stigma and the Dilemma of Difference

As we move further through the story of Gregor's metamorphosis, we find that after initial overt rejections and displays of disregards, he is confined to his room within the house. It happens when his father takes up a newspaper in his hand and shoos him away towards his room locking the door behind him. "[…] Pitilessly Gregor's father drove him back, hissing and crying "Shoo!" like a savage" (Kafka 86). Later Gregor's sister started bringing his food to his room which she used to push ahead by opening the door of his room slightly, and Gregor used to remain confined to the room, contemplating, listening to his family's conversations from behind the door. There were momentary encounters between him and his sister, especially, at the times of the day when she came to pick up the empty utensils and to open the windows of the room. But never did he move out of the room after his metamorphosis. Staying away from public life Gregor became isolated and alone. Before his transformation, he had a routine, and he had a job and the satisfaction of looking after his family, but all that came to an end once he became impaired. He wasn't allowed to move out of the house, not even out of his room.

Gregor's confinement within the four walls of his room came as a result of his family's dilemma about his situation. The way his father got disappointed over the fact that the chief clerk felt disgusted at the sight of him explained his locking up of Gregor. His father wanted to avoid social questions regarding his son's situation; he was ashamed of Gregor's situation and found no other way to manage it than to limit Gregor's public view. One way of explaining Gregor's family's segregation of him and also the violent reactions at the sight of him could be the fear resulting from what disability means symbolically for humans. On a philosophical level, we can say that witnessing disability results in a fear of losing control of one's body or even death. For a person (the so-called abled/normal) witnessing, a disability can evoke the fear of losing his own ability, freedom, independence, strength and vitality, traits that are supremely priced in our society. Coleman and Lerita (2006) mention in their study, "The unpredictability of stigma is similar to the unpredictability of death. […] note that the development of a stigmatized condition in a loved one or in oneself represents a major breach of trust—a destruction of the belief that life is predictable" (149). They call it "dilemma of difference" (149). Stigmatization of the disabled person through isolation and confinement are ways in which people around him deal with their own fears. "Many stigmas, in particular childhood cancer, remove the usual disguises of mortality. Such stigmas can act as a symbolic reminder of everyone's inevitable death" (149).

Stigma and the Unstable Body

Coleman and Lerita make an interesting point in their study when they say that stigmatization of disabled individuals also results from awareness of stigma as being unstable in nature. Stigma is something which is defined on the basis of societal norms regarding deviancy or abnormality. The unpredictability of stigma then comes from the unpredictability of societal norms, from the fact that they can change, and at some point, even the traits regarded normal can become stigmatized. They mention that stigmatization is the denial of this truth. "To deny this truth by attempting to isolate stigmatized people or escape from stigma is a manifestation of the underlying fear" (149). Gregor's interactions with his sister could be read in the light of the preceding statement regarding the fear of instability of stigma. Gregor's sister Grete while being concerned about his condition on the one hand is also repulsive of the sight of him. Every time she came to his room, and she tried to leave as soon as possible without getting a glimpse of Gregor by all means. Once or twice Grete catches a glimpse of him momentarily and leaves banging the door shut in such a rage that Gregor realizes the repulsion she might have felt at the sight of him. As a result, Gregor made sure that every time he heard the key in the door turn, he would hide himself so as to spare Grete the horror of looking at him "[...] yet when she caught sight of him under the sofa [...]she was so startled that without being able to help it she slammed the door shut again. But as if regretting her behaviour she opened the door again immediately and came in on tiptoe, as if she were visiting an invalid or even a stranger." (Kafka 90).

Grete's despising the sight of Gregor also hints to a point that Wendell (n.d.) in her work "Disability as Difference" makes. She says that the process of othering involves making the individual present before us into an object, someone we would avoid identifying with, he/she would represent symbolically our fears and uncertainties, "When we make people 'other', we group them together as objects of our experience instead of regarding them as subjects of experience with whom we might identify, and we see them primarily as symbolic of something else—usually, but not always, something we reject and fear and project onto them" (60). Wendell mentions that disability and incurable illnesses have many symbolic meanings for people who are non-disabled. For them, disability and illnesses would signify among other things a "failure to control the body". It also brings to surface an awareness of body's uncertainty, an awareness that the body can refuse to being tamed. Wendell alludes from Susan Griffins writing "The Way of All Ideology", an instance of how fear and dilemma are projected onto people around us. Susan Griffins describes an incident where she felt hatred and disgust towards an older lady who looked pale and sick. She says that witnessing her in a restaurant made her hunger subside and she felt nauseous instead. She comments further that through that, "I had projected on her, my own fear of death, of the possibility that my body might fail me, instead of giving me hunger, give me nausea?" (61).

Exclusionary Cultural Paradigm and Isolation of the Stigmatized

As a result of his isolation, Gregor becomes dull and depressed. "Often he just lay there the long nights through without sleeping at all, scrabbling for hours on the leather" (Kafka 97). His sister kept coming to his room for arranging the furniture or for putting his food, but never was he allowed to go about the house on his own. In fact, his sister expected him to not come directly in her sight every time she came to his room. Gregor's guilt was also accentuated by the fact that he was the sole bread earner of the family and every mention of the family's weak finances made him feel helpless. Kafka mentions, "[...] At first whenever the need for earning money was mentioned Gregor let go his hold on the door and threw himself down on the cool leather sofa besides it, he felt so hot with shame and grief" (97).

Susan Wendell discusses the cultural paradigm of non-disability that creates and maintains the otherness and stigmatization of the disabled. She mentions that the culture of otherness excludes the representation of experiences of the disabled within its narratives and that keeps the stigmatization of the disabled intact. The disabled population is not assimilated within the mainstream culture which keeps the non-disabled from knowing their struggles and experiences, and as a result, they remain being the other to one another symbolically. She mentions, "This is a self-perpetuating social system, since the exclusion of people with disabilities from many aspects of life in a society prevents the non-disabled to know them, and also prevents people with disabilities to make their own mark on culture, both of which contribute to the remaining the symbolic 'other' to the non-disabled people." (Wendell 64).

The anxiety of the disabled regarding their reception within social situations is to a great extent a result of the fact of their awareness of the cultural paradigm which isolates and otherizes them. This awareness may also lead the disabled individual to self-isolate and avoid participation in society and culture, again perpetuating this otherness. This anxiety a stigmatised person experiences when participating in circumstances where non-stigmatized people are present is explained by Erving Goffman in his work, Stigma: Notes on the Management of Spoiled Identity as, "The fear that others can disrespect a person because of something he shows means that he is always insecure in his contact with other people; and this insecurity arises, not from mysterious and somewhat disguised sources, as a great deal of our anxiety does, but from something he knows he can't fix" (13). Wendell also mentions that a part of the anxiety of the disabled in participation within social interactions comes from the fact that they are always at a higher risk of undergoing physical, verbal, and even sexual abuse at the hands of many. "[...] For people whose disabilities are readily apparent, every appearance in public world means risking insult, ridicule and embarrassment, but also physical assault" (64–65). She refers to an incident reported by a woman, Diane DeVries who was born with short arms, no hands, and no legs that she had a kid come to her once while she was in a park and tell her, "[...] 'aw, you ain't got no arms, you ain't got no legs, and now you're not gonna have no head.

He held me right there, by the neck, and had a little knife" (65). Even Gregor had to undergo similar abuse at the hands of his family, especially his sister.

When Gregor decides to come out of his room in the presence of the lodgers that his family had kept in order to meet the family's finances, his father's and sister's reactions were of anger and hate. His sister decided that it was time they had to get rid of Gregor when the lodgers were stunned and appalled at the sight of him. Subsequently there were many things she said in her rage that hurt Gregor immensely. One way in which we can explain his sister's rage is through Goffman's idea of "courtesy stigma". Goffman mentions in his work that many a times a disabled person's associates might feel that even they are at the receiving end of the stigma by virtue of being his close associate or kin. Grete's anger pelts up after the lodgers complain to them and refuse to pay them for their lodging. She and her family were being called out by people just because they were associated to Gregor and Grete couldn't deal with it. It is then when she loses all her sympathy and concern for her brother, "We must try to get rid of it," his sister now said explicitly to her father, "[…] it will be the death of both of you, I can see that coming. When one has to work as hard as we do, all of us, one can't stand this continual torment at home on top of it. At least I can't stand it any longer" (Kafka 124).

His sister uses the word 'it' in place of 'him' to address his brother which also points to the fact of how totally she had dehumanized Gregor owing to his condition. She further callously discredits Gregor when she mentions to her father, "[…] you must just try to get rid of the idea that this is Gregor. The fact that we've believed it for so long is the root of all our trouble. But how can it be Gregor? If this were Gregor, he would have realized long ago that human beings can't live with such a creature, and he'd have gone away on his own accord" (125). Grete categorizes Gregor as a "creature" sharply contrasting him to "human beings" which is suggestive of the stigma attached to him as a result of his condition. She in fact overtly expresses her desire for him to willingly leave the house in consideration of the compromised situation of the family. Kafka doesn't mention the cause of Gregor's demise in the story later when he is found lying pale and unconscious on the floor of his room, but we can think of suicide as one possible reason for it, especially since he was dejected over the fact that his family and especially his sister didn't want him any longer in their lives.

Abled and Disabled (Perspectives) Not Types

Erving Goffman's study of disability from the point of social interactions is especially significant to understand that identities because they are negotiated within interactions aren't stable. One point of his enquiry is that both disabled and abled people's identities can be reversed within social situations. What he means to say is precisely this, that there are times in life where an abled person may act as vulnerable and disabled and at times a disabled may act as abled. According to him, disabled and abled are roles or performances that individuals give within social interaction owing to their unconscious adherence to socio-cultural norms, "The normal and the stigmatized are not persons but rather perspectives. They are generated in social situations during mixed contacts by virtue of the unrealized norms that are likely to play upon the encounter" (137–38). In other words, these are not fixed categories but rather "perspectives."

Within Kafka's story also an abled individual who was the income earner of his home, who had a socially significant life, becomes stigmatized and isolated due to his sudden metamorphosis (disability). In fact, his family members also were disabled in a way before his condition. His father who was out of job for five years had grown fat and sluggish. His mother who had asthma kept lying on the sofa near a window and his sister, "[…] was still a child of seventeen and whose life hitherto had been so pleasant, consisting as it did in dressing herself nicely, sleeping long, helping in the housekeeping, going out to a few modest entertainments and above all playing the violin?" (96–97) His family members become abled as a result of his condition, the father started working, the mother started sewing, and the sister started taking French and music classes.

Gregor's family members breathe a sigh of relief after his demise as they are unburdened of the role of being his caretakers. They decide to take a small journey through the city as a gesture of celebration, all three of them got into a tram which was "filled with warm sunshine" (Kafka 132). They were finally free of the presence of a *body with defect* and as a result free of the psychological discomfort it caused them. They could finally get rid of the "Courtesy stigma" that ensured to them for being the close associates of Gregor. The three of them looked forward to the possibilities of their future and the things they could do with their newly achieved freedom; they would as the father said, "let bygones be bygones" (Kafka) and embark on a life devoid of the discomfort of adjusting and managing themselves around a *body with difference.*

Towards the end of the story Gregor's father and mother are described noticing Grete's physical features and concluding that she had grown up to be a beautiful lady. The words Kafka uses to describe Grete's body are the standard cultural terms used to identify a healthy, abled (normal) body. "[…] she had bloomed into a pretty girl with a good figure" (132). Grete's body can be seen as a contrast to the deformed, disabled (abnormal) body of Gregor, and her metamorphosis into a pretty girl with a good figure as a contrast to Gregor's metamorphosis into a gigantic insect in the beginning of the story. While Gregor's metamorphosis made him stigmatized and isolated, Grete's transition according to the parents opened her prospects of finding a nice husband. She is also described standing steady on her feet and stretching her body in the lines that follow, these acts could be read as acts characterizing a body as abled and independent within socio-cultural contexts, Gregor's body on the other hand which could not be turned or straightened without his bumping himself into one thing or another was a cultural specimen of a disabled body. The concluding lines of the story state, "And it was like a confirmation of their new dreams and excellent intentions that at the end of their journey their daughter sprang to her feet first and stretched her young body" (132).

Conclusion

Franz Kafka's novella makes a compelling read and a potent document for understanding disability and the socio-cultural dynamics of it. It is especially significant for making sense of how identities are negotiated between individuals interactionally. This article makes a case for approaching disability from a mixed perspective (sociological and philosophical) which would help in developing more inclusive action plans to educate individuals on causes related to disability. Educating individuals on the line of this model shall also help them understand disability and ability not as fixed but unstable categories that are affected by several parameters ranging from societal narratives, institutional and other discourses on bodily identities. Bringing in social interactionism within its ambit will benefit in understanding how identities are generated within micro-interactions through individual performances and also how these interactional spaces can become areas where counter narratives of bodily identities can be created and sustained. Fountain and McLaughlin mention, "This take on symbolic interactionism thus 'emphasizes human beings as active and creative agents [and] a human world that both shapes the doings of people and is fashioned by the doings of people " (qtd. in Fountain & McLaughlin, 2013, p. 146). These "micro dynamics of enhancement" will deny power to dominant stories that portray people as disabled and in turn help produce counter narratives that would give free space to those that would like to have themselves expressed more freely as bodies that "cannot do certain things, but which can do so many others" (146).

The conclusion can include some concluding remarks on your reading of the story.

References

Coleman, V., & Lerita, M. (2006). Stigma: An enigma demystified. In L. J. Davis (Eds.), *The disability studies reader* (pp. 141–152). Routledge. https://uniteyouthdublin.files.wordpress.com/2015/01/lennard_davis_the_disability_studies_reader_secbookzz-org.pdf

Fountain, E. C., & McLaughlin, J. (2013). The interactions of disability and impairment: Stories of different embodiment. *Social Theory and Health, 11*(2), 133–150.

Goffman, E. (1963). *Stigma: Notes on the management of spoiled identity*. Simon & Schuster

Kafka, F. (2011). The metamorphosis. In *Selected short stories Franz Kafka* (W. Muir, E. Muir, Trans.) (pp. 67–132). Srishti publishers &distributors

Shildrik, M., & Price, J. (2013) Breaking the boundaries of the broken body. In *Sites.middlebury* (pp. 432–444). http://sites.middlebury.edu/soan191/files/2013/08/ShildrickBrokenBody.pdf

Wendell, S. (n.d.). *Disability as difference* (pp. 57–84). http://www.dsfnetwork.org/assets/Uploads/DisabilitySunday/31206.-Wendell-Disability-as-Difference.pdf

Chapter 9
Notions of Normalcy and Changing Definitions: Defeating Stereotypes and Creating Acceptance of Disability

Akshata Jaiprakash

Abstract This research paper attempts to examine notions of normalcy in a diverse set of texts such as 21st Chromosomes and Other Narratives (2017), a few children's literary texts such as Clumsy (2016), Why are You Afraid to Hold my Hand? (2005), Abba's Day (2016), Wings to Fly (2015), I Didn't Understand (2018), and Machher Jhol (2018), in which 'disability' on the one hand is labelled, judged, criticised, and on the other, embraced and normalised. The paper examines concepts such as 'acceptance', 'labelling', and stereotypes connected to a person with disability by the society and its consequences in the Indian context. India being a country of multiple cultures and vast differences, several stereotypes are attached to the concept of disability. Apart from the aspects of disability, people with disability also tend to combat gender concerns. Societal perspectives on the disabled are extensively studied through these texts.

Keywords Disability · Acceptence · Equity · Normalcy · Labelling · Embracing the difference

Introduction

Disability studies in the Indian context are an important arena of study. Studies state that India has a population of about 2.68 crores who are differently abled (as per the 2011 census). Despite constituting such a large number, people with disability live tough lives because their disability is often projected as 'inability' and their 'ability' are questioned. Disability in the Indian context is as significant an issue as race, caste, or gender. However, disability cannot stand alone in seclusion without recognizing its relation to various aspects such as gender, sexuality, religion, caste, class, or race. Society's idea of people with disability is clouded with misconceptions and

A. Jaiprakash (✉)
Department of English Studies and Research Centre, Kuvempu University, Shankarghatta, Karnataka, India
e-mail: akshataj@gmail.com

R. Uniyal and F. Rizvi (eds.), *Understanding Disability*,
https://doi.org/10.1007/978-981-99-4925-0_9

stereotypes which further lead to sympathy, discrimination, and isolation of people with disability from the rest of the society.

This research paper attempts to study notions of normalcy and changing definitions of disability in a diverse set of texts, such as *21st Chromosomes and Other Narratives* (2017), a few children's literary texts such as *Clumsy* (2016), *Why are You Afraid to Hold my Hand?* (2005), *Abba's Day* (2016), *Wings to Fly* (2015), *I Didn't Understand* (2018), and *Machher Jhol* (2018) where 'disability' is labelled, judged, and criticized on one hand and on the other, embraced, and normalized.

Objectives

This research paper presents a transitional change in the characters depicting persons with disability. It is an attempt to throw light on the following objectives:

- To represent the notions of 'acceptance' of a person with disability by parents, family members, the society, and their consequences.
- To portray varied perceptions of the society on persons with disability.
- To identify the stereotypes associated with disability.
- To focus on the 'ability' of the person, rather than disability.
- To illustrate layman's act of labelling persons with disability.
- To bring awareness and burst myths about disability.
- To examine aspects of gender in the world of disability.

People with disability encounter several challenges, especially, in a society with vast cultural differences and numerous religious practices. The first and foremost is 'acceptance'. Studies state that family plays a major role in bringing a positive attitude towards disability. *The Child with a Disability: Parental Acceptance, Management and Coping. 2007*. There are instances where parents have failed to accept the child with disability or accept the disability of the child, which results in not addressing the issue or providing timely intervention. There are instances of the parent abandoning the child only because the child is born with a disability. Acceptance of the child along with his/her disability is crucial—when the child is accepted and not the disability, due to the societal image and misconceptions, the child is not given interventions and therapies at the right time. Acceptance of people with disability by the parents, family members, and the society helps them in having a better morale. For instance, in *Wings to Fly* (2015),

> When Malathi was about a year old, she had high fever and lost the strength in her legs. For two years, her parents took her to doctors in Bengaluru, where they lived. Finally, they took her to Chennai for treatment. (Rajendran 7)

Acceptance by the people the child lives with is a vital aspect for the child. At the same time, it is a traumatic situation for a mother to 'accept' the disability of the child. Every parent has dreams and aspirations associated with their child right from the stage of conception. When reality strikes, it becomes difficult for parents to understand and accept the child with disability. For instance, in "Mandara—You can do it!" from *21st Chromosome and Other Narratives* (2017)

> Though the doctor was careful in her choice of words, an instant damage to Vasanthi's psyche had occurred. She was still a very young mother who was at the early post-natal stage. The words of the doctor seemed very harsh, her body was weak and couldn't withstand the trauma. She showed erratic behaviour, started laughing and sobbing, blurting words out of context…to take care of Vasanthi. (Jaiprakash 38)

Another example of an extreme condition, as presented in "Transcending the Tsunami" from *21st Chromosome and Other Narratives* (2017) Dear Durai Paul.

My dreams have always been different from what I could get from living with you. I have somehow managed to suffer with you all these years. I have given birth to your insane, crippled children, that has shattered my hope of happiness…. Don't ever try to search for me and spoil my future (Jaiprakash 163).

Every parent has their pattern of acceptance of disability in their child. When the parents accept the child with the disability, the problem can be addressed at the earliest with the right medical intervention and therapies. Consequently, the outcome can be positive. For instance, in "21st Chromosome" from *21st Chromosome and Other Narratives* (2017), she knew that the doctor had deliberately used sweet-coated words to reveal the bitter truth.

> She realised that her son, a scientist's son, a musician's son, could never lead the life of a normal person…. She wiped her cheeks and beamed a broad smile at her son. (Jaiprakash 78,79)

Acceptance from the society is imperative to live a contented social life. In India, stereotypes about disability co-exist with religious superstitions and believes. While the society acts as a carrier of different perceptions of stereotypes, persons with disability tend to feel isolated and inferior. For instance, as Dhir expresses in *Why are you Afraid to Hold my Hand?* (2005).

> People say all sorts of things.
>
> I limp, I lisp, all this and more.
>
> Sometimes I feel so sad and sore.
>
> Folks make fun, it's nothing new.
>
> If you were me, what would you do? (Dhir 1)

Research states that the notions of normalcy are notions constructed by the ableist society, rather than concepts that existed naturally (*Valle, Connor 22*). Notions of normalcy have been examined in the selected primary texts to understand the complexities for the disabled that exist in the Indian society. While India is a country of multiple cultures and vast differences, there are several stereotypes attached to the concept of disability, such as—disability as a curse for the sin of the past birth, disability as a contagious disease, sympathy, and discrimination, considering a person with disability as subhuman (*Cooper 31*).

For children, to be part of the peer group matters a lot. Bullying, teasing, and ragging frail ones in the group is an appalling but common sight to see in schools. For children with disabilities, when put in an exclusive setup, they tend to be the victims of such unruly behaviour. Many a times, because of their disability, they would not be able to express or bring the incident to the notice of an adult, which might have a traumatic consequence. In *I Didn't Understand* (2018), Srinivasan depicts the little girl expressing her plight,

> Suddenly, I fell down. I don't know why. I heard someone laughing. It was Shwetha from my class. Her foot was sticking out from her desk, and she was laughing. Some of the other kids were laughing too. I did not understand why. (Srinivasan 7)

Acceptance from the peers makes a lot of difference to the child with disability. In Sheila Dhir's *Why are You Afraid to Hold My Hand (1999),* exquisitely pictures the boy with disability trying to assert his position to the world that looks at him with a pitiful eye.

> She drools all the time.
>
> Yes, I have a problem.
>
> No, it won't go away.
>
> Take me for who I am,
>
> Just a child who wants to play. (Dhir 2)

The societal perspectives of the disabled will be broadly studied through these texts. For instance, in Champa Jaiprakash's "Mandara—You can do it!" from *21st Chromosome and Other Narratives* (2017), Mandara's grandmother utters words that hurt and haunt Vasanthi, when she comes to know that the child is born with disabilities.

> Seethamma commented, "She made such a big fuss to bring out this dumb child" … Alamelamma was no better. While carrying the child she said, "Why were you born at all? Was it only to rob all the happiness of my daughter?" (Jaiprakash 39)

Literature contributes a great deal in moulding and constructing notions in the society. Classics in literature do carry such responsibilities (*Margolis and Shapiro* 5). One such instance, where the person with disability is sympathized and discriminated, is in *Why are you Afraid to Hold my Hand?* (2005)

> So Sad.
>
> Please don't cry or feel bad. I'm doing fine, so why be sad?
>
> Here, let ME do it for you.
>
> Don't smother me. Give me space to live my life at my own pace. (Dhir 3, 4)

Every person, undeniably, has one ability or the other. In a common man, the ability is revealed spontaneously, but when it comes to a person with disability, the ability must be identified, brought out, nurtured, and nourished in order to be expressed and be visible to the outside world. The society plays a significant role in bringing out the 'ability' of a person with disability. For instance, in "Beyond Autism" from *21st Chromosome and Other Narratives* (2017),

> Pandu's teacher had observed that he used to be preoccupied with tapping the desk in rhythmic beats. She suggested that he needed tabla classes…. Pandu could construct his own musical instrument, something that resembled Shivamani's instrument. The way Pandu brought out music from that junky instrument was amazing! (Jaiprakash 121,122)

There are also instances where people with disability are self-motivated and have proved themselves capable of displaying their abilities. In Richa Jha's *Machher Jhol (Fish Curry)* (2018), we can see how Gopu, the visually impaired child, takes up a challenging task of travelling alone to his grandmother's house in a tram and brings fish curry for his ailing father.

> "Who will believe you can't see, Gopu?" said Baba. "How did you do it alone?" "I had you with me Baba; you have shown me everything, Baba" said Gopu…
>
> "Unbelievable!", said Baba. He was already sounding better. (Jha 32, 34)

Yet another instance from Sowmya Rajendran's *Wings to Fly (2015)* depicts an extra ordinary strength, will power, and self-motivation in Malathi, who wins over extreme circumstances and loves the encouragement that she receives. "Malathi found that she liked doing this. She liked to exercise, she liked to play. She liked the medals, too, that she began to win (Rajendran 34)."

The society contributes significantly in facilitating persons with disability. Though there are psychological studies that state that there are several advantages of labelling, *(Rix 28)* the act of 'labelling' persons with disability may also break their self-esteem. To illustrate this, an instance from Mini Shrinivasan's *I Didn't Understand* (2018)

> Most of the children in my school are not mentally challenged. But there are three children in wheelchairs. They cannot walk. And two children are blind. That means they cannot see anything. We six are called Children with Special needs. Our school has a special room for us. We also have a special teacher; we go to our special room every day for one hour. (Shrinivasan 4)

There are several phrases that are used to label persons with disability that focus on their disability rather than their ability. These labelling phrases are mostly culturally imbibed. Legends, folk tales, mythological stories have depicted disability in a negative light, not just in the Indian context but also worldwide. *(Graham 8)* Labelling leads to a drop in the self-esteem level of children and adults. For instance, in Manjari Chakravarti's *Clumsy* (2016), the drop in self-esteem in the little girl, who's been labelled by people around her, from her parents to her teachers to her friends, is evident.

> "Clumsy!" her mother said, when she found a puddle of milk on the table.
>
> "Slowcoach," grumbled her father as she fumbled with her shoes.
>
> "Careless," moaned grandfather, as she knocked down his walking stick…. These words scared away all other words. (Chakravarti 1–9)

An instance from Champa Jaiprakash's "Write Fast, Famida" from *21st Chromosome and Other Narrative* (2017)

> When she was asked to read in the class, in order to test her reading skills, she wished she was not present there at all…. The teacher would shout at her, "Famida, can't you read these simple lines? Come on read fast." The pressure would mount. Famida would feel that she was entrapped by her enemies with no way out to escape. (Jaiprakash 48)

Another instance from Sheila Dhir's Why are you Afraid to Hold my Hands? (2005) shows how the society's outlook makes people with disability feel uncomfortable.

> "You look so...so different!
>
> I'm a person. I feel shy. From staring eyes, I want to hide." (Dhir 7)

Many assumptions and myths about disability that exist in the society can be dispelled by bringing awareness to the people. These assumptions and myths have been a part of the society from time immemorial through mythological stories and oral traditions. As Dr. Somdev Banik rightly suggests in his article 'Representation of Disabled Characters in Literature' (2016), in *International Journal of English Language, Literature and Translation Studies*:

> The great Indian epics Ramayana and Mahabharata have given us two such prototypes, immortalised though, through their Machiavellianism, namely DasiManthara and Shakuni. …Disabled characters in classics are often not portrayed as real—life people, rather as literary devices to suggest their potential for mischief and evil doing. They are one-dimensional and type-characters, not realised fully. (Banik 12)

These myths and assumptions exist as a cultural entity among people. Creating awareness about disability facilitates in changing the stereotypical mindset of the society. Disability is often thought to be an ailment which could be cured by medication. Parents of children with disability expect their child to turn out to be 'normal' children. The parameter of their comparison lies in what picture the society has constructed for them, which comes from the lack of acceptance of the child for what he/she is and the lack of awareness about disability. For instance, in 'Beyond Autism' from *21st Chromosome and Other Narratives* (2017),

> Saroja asked Sarala, why he behaved like a mad fellow, and would he be alright? …. "Madam, I beg for your help, please do something and make him alright." She was in tears again. (Jaiprakash 110)
>
> "Saroja asked with utmost sincerity, "If I do that, and send him to school regularly will he be alright? Will his madness go away? Will he become like other children?"" (Jaiprakash 114)

The right kind of awareness can bring transformation not only in the parents or caregivers, but also in the society. This facilitates the person with disability to lead a respectful and productive life. For instance, in "21st Chromosome" from 21st Chromosome and Other Narratives (2017):

> Dr. Mohandas explained the features of the down's child. "All of you can observe Sanjay's eyes. They are slant. See, there is a line of fold near the eyes… If you regularly consult her, your child will improve a lot." (Jaiprakash 76)

Apart from the social injustices and discriminations, people with disability also battle issues like gender bias, caste differences, religious, and even racial discriminations. Encountering fears of societal taboos and pressures has an impact on the mental state of the already stressed individual. Studies state that the global literacy rate is three per cent for all adults with disabilities and one per cent for women with disabilities. However, persons with disabilities encounter barriers to employment, and studies show that men with disabilities have been found to be almost twice as likely to be employed as women with disabilities. *(Arthur 31-33)*

For instance, from Sowmya Rajendran's *Wings to Fly (2015)*, barriers of gender, disability are encountered, but optimistically.

> Around this time, Malathi went to Ahmedabad for a sports meet. She entered her name for a track event. Then she found there was a problem. No other woman had given in name. "But I want to participate!" Malathi said. (Rajendran 18)

Over the years, how the society views disability has significantly altered. Today, people have access to a wide range of information, which acts as a path to create awareness among the masses. The media industry—advertisements, cinema, print, audio, and visual media, have facilitated in bringing about this change, however minor the change might be. From being a taboo, or a curse, to holding open discussions about disability, is a positive step towards building an inclusive society for persons with disability.

For instance, in "21st Chromosome", from *21st Chromosome and Other Narratives* (2017).

Srihari was restless. He wanted to go home and sit in front of his computer to know more about his son through the internet. As soon as he reached the house, he went straight to Sangeetha's room… …He said, "Sangeetha, it is a big challenge for both of us. We will dare it boldly. Never think it is a curse. Both of us will do our best for his progress. I will be with you always. Don't lose courage." (Jaiprakash 79,80)

Literature also has a significant share of contribution in not just creating awareness, but also in defeating stereotypes and bursting myths about disability. From legends and mythological narratives that considered disability as a curse for the sins committed in the previous birth, to stories and narratives that are filled with success stories and achievements of persons with disabilities, the transition is phenomenal. However, the journey of this transformation was filled with struggles, embarrassments, humiliations, and hardships. NGOs, social and human rights activists, special educators, parents of children with special needs have put in tremendous efforts after several dark phases, to see the day's light.

For instance, in Champa Jaiprakash's "Write Fast Famida", from *21st Chromosome and Other Narratives* (2017),

> She began, "Respected Sr. Stella, dear parents, I am happy to see you all assembled here… …Your child's education, which is the responsibility of the school, depends on the child's intelligence, learning abilities, memory, comprehension, attention span, emotionality, and mental health. How much a child can learn, retain, remember and express it when needed is an important concern of the school and the parents." (Jaiprakash 140)

Introducing the concept of disability in children's literature to children and young adults gives a fresh perspective to children about disability. This would also help the child to understand and build an inclusive world for persons with disability.

For instance in *Machher Jhol: Fish Curry* (2018), the little boy's disability is not labelled right through the narration, except for a few subtle hints that state that he cannot see.

> Stop one, Stop two and three. Gopu got off at fourth…
>
> …Only three turns and 1849 steps before he handed Baba his favourite food.
>
> Baba would be so happy! (Jha 25)

Similarly, in Sunaina Ali's *Abba's Day* (2016), there is no mention of disability of the little girl, unless one observes keenly on the illustrations. The little girl Aaisha narrates the events that take place at her house on a particular Sunday. The book triumphs in breaking the stereotypes of gender roles in a house.

Abba and I make masala chai for Ammi. It's Ammi's holiday too!... When we come back, Abba takes charge of the kitchen. (Ali 6-8)

At another instance from *Wings to Fly* (2015), where the narrator describes Malathi in a wheelchair, the tone is void of sympathy or sadness and it is merely a description.

> She wants to catch one as it falls…
>
> For that, she will have to run out. But how can Malathi do that?
>
> She is in a wheelchair. (Rajendran 3,4)

Disability in children's literature is a necessity for children and young adults to be aware of the individual differences that prevail in the society. Children need insights into the various attributes of the society so that people of differences are not isolated from the rest. ('We need children to see disability as part of the norm—not as a weird phenomenon').

According to Children's Literature Review, Encyclopaedia,

> The presentation of disabilities in children's literature, while historically infrequent, has nonetheless offered a breadth of insight into as well as perpetuated stereotypes for an otherwise underrepresented minority group. Often by necessity, studies of how individuals with special needs are represented in children's literature link a disparate variety of handicaps together in their examinations of the issue, regularly classifying mental, physical, cognitive, and emotional impairments together under a broad definition of the term "disability." (12)

Preconceived notions that the society has constructed about disability can be rejected only when the right awareness and the real problems of the disabled are brought to the forefront. Children's literature is a great medium where the 'citizens of tomorrow' can be moulded with appropriate knowledge and not stereotypes or labels that the society has created.

> Several themes emerged from a discourse analysis of the transcriptions, including defining disabilities, questioning and critiquing notions of normalcy; idealizing disabilities; identifying with characters; developing an advocacy stance; and using imagination to open up

> perspectives towards people in the real world. Through exploring characters in books, children not only learned about various disabilities, but they came to understand characters with disabilities as full and complex beings, similar in many ways to themselves. (Adomat 3)

Children's literature can act as a bridge that enables children in not just understanding and empathizing the differences prevalent in the society but also learn to appreciate the similarities that they share. When children learn to celebrate the similarities and embrace the differences, the world turns into a better place to live in.

Conclusion

'Disability' is a social construct. Every person on the planet has certain abilities and disabilities. The society has constructed a set of prescribed standards for people who are a part of it. With these norms in mind, the society also brands people for their abilities and disabilities. A person's ability needs not be defined by the norms set by the society. Parallel to gender norms and stereotypes that a society predominantly constructs and practices, stereotypes about ability and disability are also stipulated. This construct does more harm to the people concerned in breaking their morale and making their lives difficult, than helping them cope or supporting them in their work.

However, the disparity between the number of people with disability and the number of people working for the betterment of the disabled is vast. Very few people opt to work in this field because it is not a well-paid job, especially in India. Rehabilitation of the disabled requires professional help. Professionals who are trained here fly away to different countries for better prospects, therefore discriminating the disability field, by and large.

Even in literature, the disabled are side lined and discriminated. The real problems of the disabled are hardly represented. The need of the hour is not just stories of persons with disability, but a broader outlook on the kind of lives they lead, their parents' struggles, and measures taken by the society to take them along in all walks of life. As Dr. P Hanumanth Rao rightly put, "There is a thin line between 'ability' and 'disability'". (citation)

Bibliography

Adomat, D. S. (2014). Exploring issues of disability in children's literature discussions. *Disability Studies Quarterly, 34*(3), 3865.

Ali, S. (2017). *Abba's day*. Katha.

Banik, S. (2016). Representation of disabled characters in literature. *International Journal of English Language, Literature and Translation Studies, 3*(2), 198–202.

Bolt, D. (2007). Literary disability studies: the long awaited response. In: *Presented at the inaugural conference of the cultural disability studies research network*. Liverpool John Moores University. www.disability-studies.leeds.ac.uk/wpcontent/uploads/sites/40/library/bolt-Long-Awaited-Response.pdf

BookTrust. (2017). *We need children to see disability as part of the norm: Not a weird phenomenon.* BookTrust. www.booktrust.org.uk/news-and-features/features/2017/december/we-needchildren-to-see-disability-as-part-of-the-norm-not-a-weird-phenomenon/
Chakravarti, M. (2016). *Clumsy*. Tulika Publishers.
Cooper, H. (2019). The oppressive power of normalcy in the lives of disabled children: Deploying history to denaturalize the notion of the 'normal child'". In: T. Curran, K. Runswick-Cole (Eds.), *Disabled children's childhood studies*. Palgrave Macmillan.
Dhir, S. (2005). *Why are you afraid to hold my hand?* Tulika Publishers.
Encyclopedia.com (2020). *Children's literature review*. Encyclopedia.com. Retrieved from August 28, 2020, from www.encyclopedia.com/children/academic-andeducational-journals/disabilities-childrens-literature
Graham, H. R. (2019). Disabled gods: A critical disability studies analysis of ancient Greek Myths. In: *Undergraduate research symposium*.
Helander, E. (1998). Prejudice and dignity: An introduction to community based rehabilitation (2nd edn.). New York UNDP. http://hrw.org/women/disabled.html
Jaiprakash, C. (2017). *21st Chromosomes and other narratives*. ChinthanaPusthaka.
Jaiprakash, A. (2019). Notions of normalcy: Breaking stereotypes and generating acceptance of disability. In: *Deglobalizing disability: Texts and contexts*. University of Lucknow.
Jha, M. (2016). The damaging depiction of disability in Indian mythology. In: *HuffPost India*. HuffPost India. Retrieved from November 3, 2016, from www.huffingtonpost.in/martand-jha/the-damagingdepiction-of-disability-in-indian-mythology_a_21591083/
Jha, R. (2018). *Machher Jhol: Fish curry*. Pickle Yolk Books.
Kandel, I., & Merrick, J. (2007). The child with a disability: Parental acceptance, management and coping. *The Scientific World Journal, 7*, 1799–1809. https://doi.org/10.1100/tsw.2007.265
Kurtts, S. A., & Gavigan, K. W. (2017). Understanding (dis)abilities through children's literature. *Education Libraries, 31*(3), 23.
Margolis, H., & Shapiro, A. (1987). Countering negative images of disability in classical literature. *The English Journal, 76*(3), 18–22.
Munyi, C. (2012). Past and present perceptions towards disability: A historical perspective. *Disability Studies Quarterly, 32*(2), 3197.
O'Reilly, A. (2003). The right to decent work of persons with disabilities. In: *Skills working paper No. 14* (pp. 31–33). International Labour Organization.
Rajendran, S. (2006). *Wings to fly*. Tulika Publishers.
Rix, J. (2006). Does it matter what we call them? Labelling people on the basis of notions of intellect, Ethical Space. *The International Journal of Communication Ethics, 3*(4), 2228.
Shrinivasan, M. (2018). *I didn't understand*. Tulika Publishers.
SigurjonsdoTtir, H. B. (2015). Cultural representation of disability in children's literature. *Childhood and Disability in the Nordic Countries*. https://doi.org/10.1057/9781137032645.0016
Traustadóttir, R. (2006). Disability and gender: Introduction to the special issue. *Scandinavian Journal of Disability Research, 8*(2–3), 81–84. https://doi.org/10.1080/15017410600831341
Valle, J., & David, C. (2019). Examining beliefs and expanding notions of normalcy: A disability studies approach to inclusive practices. *Rethinking Disability*. https://doi.org/10.4324/9781315111209-3
Wilson, J., & Lewiecki-Wilson, C. (Eds.). (2001). *Embodied rhetorics: Disability in language and culture*. Southern Illinois University Press.
Yorke, S. (2015). Disability, normalcy, and the failures of the nation: A reading of selected fiction by Salman Rushdie, Rohinton Mistry, Indra Sinha, and Firdaus Kanga. *ORA*.

Chapter 10
Normalizing Disability: Discourses of the Decolonized Body

Dipanwita Mondal

Abstract Disability Studies is a recent development that seeks to extricate the idea of 'disability' or 'impairment' from the existing cultural myths, ideologies and stigmas that heavily influence socio-cultural interaction, policies and movement. I, therefore attempt to reconsider the idea of 'ability' or 'normalcy' within the socio-cultural construct through a Bengali short story by Rabindranath Tagore named titled Subha where I have tried to explore the different ways of representation of the disabled character. My paper therefore, attempts to reconsider the idea of 'disability' which according to me, metaphorically functions at two levels here-firstly, there is the clinical or physical 'disability' suffered by the poor girl Subha being deaf and mute, and secondly, the 'disability' of the apparently 'normal' world which is 'blind' enough to not look deeper into reason and also 'insensitive' enough to feel or understand the inner workings of a dumb girl's mind.

Keywords Disability · Ability · Power · Politics · Normal

Critical disability theory, more than a specified area or branch of study, is a certain methodology which focuses more on 'how' than 'what' to study in the field of disability studies. According to the methodology, the theory involves scrutinizing not physical or mental impairments but the social norms that define particular attributes as impairments, as well as the social conditions that concentrate stigmatized attributes in particular populations.[1]

The concept of power and its inevitable presence and importance in a society is irrefutable. We all belong to a constructed societal structure where exists a certain set of accepted norms which we are designated as 'normal'. This concept of 'normal' has different interpretations. The overall idea of norm, unlike that of ideal, implies that

[1] Schalk (2017).

D. Mondal (✉)
Department of Comparative Indian Language and Literature, University of Calcutta, Kolkata, West Bengal, India
e-mail: dmcill@caluniv.ac.in

R. Uniyal and F. Rizvi (eds.), *Understanding Disability*,
https://doi.org/10.1007/978-981-99-4925-0_10

the majority of the population must or should comply and somehow be part of that constructed norm. Therefore, the idea of normalization refers to a socially certified standard through which ideas and actions are tagged as 'normal' or 'acceptable' or 'natural' and thus become 'usual' in mainstream life. This twenty-first century once again redefined the idea of normalcy in the COVID-19 era where humans are struck by the most disastrous pandemic devouring lives. In this era, humans have yet again known the concept of normalcy in a different way where they are bound to wear masks and gloves and sanitize themselves every now and then. This avatar of humans wearing masks has globally been referred to as the 'new normal' because that is what is expected from humans to do at that particular point of time; they are not being treated with surprise or curiosity because it has been 'normalized' by the human society for their own safety, health, and hygiene. So, we see that the idea of normalcy is very relative and it is nothing but a social construct which transforms with time. It is something which is designed by the society, for the society itself mostly prioritizing its own convenience and benefit. The issue of social stigma regarding disability, too, is linked with this politics of social construction which quite evidently goes in favour of the ones who are socially certified abled section of the mass and unfortunately goes against the victims who are not as 'able' as far as the social certificate of fitness is concerned. In this connection, I would focus on the issue of disability—be it physical or mental of humans, which is a matter of great concern in our society.

Disability as a social edifice results in the stereotyped perceptions of qualities inherent in people with disabilities. The disability concept often directs a society to create and enforce its standards, which invariably are accomplished by imposing vindictive qualities onto disabled people. The disabled bodies, therefore deprived of their own voices and power, may easily be considered as 'marginal' or 'subaltern' in the mainstream 'able' societal structure. The emerging field of disability studies therefore rejects the notion of disability as 'otherness', endorsing rather a scale of abilities and limitations. The disabled, as conventionally understood, manifest differences, but they are in no way radically 'other'. It is different, not the other, it is quite articulable like anything else if articulated in the right way. Metaphors of disabilities thus function as dual mechanisms of subjugation: they create disability as aberrant, and they prevent people with disabilities from voicing their rights. Therefore, disability metaphor becomes a political threat, for every metaphor administers norms of able-bodiedness. And these norms are false in their essence as disability studies contend for ability and disability as merely relative positions on a spectrum. Disability scholar Link systematically explains the semantic connotation of—the normal and traces it back to the eighteenth century and attempts to describe the evolution and modes of dissemination of the idea of—'the normal'. He however concludes that the normal is not an isolated idea, but an extensive and complex discursive field. In everyday conversations—the normal manifests in the form of stereotypes, truisms, idioms, and laymen's terms.[2] What needs to be done before trying to understand the disabled body is to turn to its invisible, apparently neutral, and usual 'other'. As

[2] Link (2004).

disability studies scholar Lennard Davis puts it, the core of the problem is not the person with disabilities; the problem is the way that normalcy is constructed to create the problem of the disabled person.[3]

All of us are born into a condition of vulnerability and dependence; all of us rely throughout our lives on technological interventions to amplify physical abilities and compensate for physical limitations; all of us experience illnesses; and most of us grow old and face increasing losses of physical and mental power. Ability, then, is both relative and temporary. It is in no way an invariable norm. It is disability, rather, the use of prostheses, that is universal, and without the narrative prosthesis provided by cultural constructions of disability, the ideology of —ability cannot function. We are a part of a world which is constituted of a set of norms. There is a particular framework, a structure which is regarded as 'normal'. This concept of 'normal' has different interpretations. The overall idea of norm, unlike that of ideal, implies that the majority of the population must or should somehow be part of the norm. Therefore, normalization refers to a socially certified standard through which ideas and actions are tagged as 'normal' and become 'usual' or 'natural' in everyday life. The concept of normalization is detailed by Michel Foucault in his *Discipline and Punish*, where he used the term associated with the construction of an idealized norm of conduct and then rewarding or punishing individuals for conforming to or deviating from this idealized standard. While interrogating into the realms of normalcy, one may ponder upon the fact that the idea of norm must have existed earlier as the idea of *mimesis*[4] suggests that the real world is a representation of the ideal world which also echoes the basic idea of translation. The real world has a tendency to conform to the ideal world, that is, to satisfy the conditions of being normal. Therefore, it is clear that it is a general affinity to be normal and to comply with the accepted standard and it is not desired to be anything other than that. The benchmark of pre-assumed normalcy is accepted widely and anything other than this constructed normalcy is somehow unacceptable.

Regarding the politics of construction of the 'body', scholar Siebers states, I am claiming that the body has its own forces and that we need to recognize them if we are to get a less one-sided picture of how bodies and their representations affect each other for good and for bad. The body is, first and foremost, a biological agent teeming with vital and chaotic forces. It is not an inert matter subject to easy manipulation by social representation. The body is alive, which means that it is as capable of influencing and transforming social languages as they are capable of influencing and transforming it.[5]

It may be assumed that idea of norm must have existed earlier as evident from the concept of 'mimesis' where Plato suggests that the real world is a representation of the ideal world. The real world has a tendency to conform to the ideal world, that is, to satisfy the prerequisites of being normal. Therefore, it is clear that it is a general affinity to be normal and to comply with the accepted standard and it is not desired

---

[3] Davis (2006).

[4] Plato Republic (2013).

[5] Siebers (2006).

to be anything other than that. The benchmark of pre-assumed normalcy is accepted widely and anything other than this constructed normalcy is somehow unacceptable.

The basic principle of Disability Studies and that of feminism seems to be similar on the grounds of marginalization, as Garland-Thomas points out,—Disability—like gender—is a concept that pervades all aspects culture: its structuring institutions, social identities, cultural practices, political positions, historical communities, and the shared human experience of embodiment.[6]

Surprisingly in the Indian context, the philosophy of Karma is also irrelevantly associated with the perception of disability. Karma, an inseparable part of Indian religious faith, is regarded as the accumulation of our past actions which control or influence our present and future. It is very much related to the Western philosophy of Destiny or Fate. Within the Indian cultural space, Karma is often associated with other things as well. For instance, the idea of disability or physical and mental deformity is believed to be the consequences of Karma. That is, disability or physical and mental deformity is like the punishment that Karma heaps upon, i.e. penalty for the misdeeds of the previous life. People with disabilities are often viewed as inferior and therefore shunned. They are even pitied and considered to be supported by charity and sympathy which calls for a power play between the abled and the disabled.

Criticism based on disability calls for the literary analysis of the literary incompetence to associate reversely to a culture's socio-political realities. In this regard, Moody comments, "Such an approach has to draw on literature from the broader humanities and disability studies. It is concerned with the role, appearance, discursive treatment and resonant meaning of the characters in the narrative; and their dealings with, or the absence of, representations of a disabling environment; and power relations between able-bodied and disabled interests."[7]

Literature and narratives in general are traditionally considered a base of the whole idea of construction of the normal and the disabled body. Jürgen Link identifies literature as a platform for cultural practice, seems to be above all, functional for subjectivation—that is, the production and reproduction of subjectivities.[8]

After a close study of the classical and modern works of literature and film, Mitchell and Snyder have observed that the theme or idea of disability has been a common narrative motif. As they comment, "Disability provides a common formula for differentiating a character's uniqueness through the identifying features of physical and behavioural quirks or idiosyncrasies."[9]

In my paper, I attempt to deal with this issue of disability as portrayed in a literary character. Certain literary characters have always been considered as quite influential and relatable to our real lives, characters which are strong, full of positive vibes, and also characters which are negative and repulsive. But then, there are also characters which might not be very popular or desirable, but they tend to signify or symbolize certain real-life characters who are also very much present around

---

[6] Garland-Thomson (2002).

[7] Moody (1997).

[8] Link (2013).

[9] Mitchell and Snyder (2001).

us but not paid enough attention or it might be said who are deliberately pushed aside by the mainstream society thinking them to be incapable of qualifying for a normal respectable life. People with disabilities may be regarded as such people who are somewhat disregarded and treated as the 'other' by the conventional normal society. I take up such a disabled character for discussion in this regard from one of Rabindranath Tagore's short stories named *Subha.*

Subha is a story of a mute and deaf girl whose two elder sisters having married off her parents are eager to get her married too at their earliest possibility, but her 'disability' becomes a matter of hindrance in doing so. While Subha lacks speech, her large expressive eyes do the talking which unfortunately is understood by none. While her mother considers her 'disability' to be her own imperfection and despises her, her father seems to be somewhat considerate towards her initially. But as the preconceived notions of a regressive society go—there is probably no other burden more painful for parents than having a 'disabled' unmarried daughter at home. While being a woman in this patriarchal society involves enough reason for neglect or domination, the fact that the woman is disabled or physically not fit becomes an even more curse for her. So Subha is married off soon and even sooner she is detected to be 'defective' at her in-laws' house and her husband brings in an 'able' second wife. Subha's parents wash their hands off the responsibilities of their 'disabled' daughter having married off and she is destined to live a life where happiness is the most uncommon word.

Subha's life therefore chronicles the life of an unfortunate mute girl whose inability to speak is regarded as an unpardonable crime. Even her parents are ashamed of her and consider her to be a burden which should be gotten rid of at the earliest possibility. Her mother considers Subha's inability to speak to be a grave deficiency of her own having been transmitted to her daughter. Though her father seems to love her dearly despite her physical inefficiency, he cannot restrain himself from thinking that he needs to get her married off soon as that is the only suitable and safe future plan, he can make for her.

Subha possesses a pair of large black eyes which seem to compensate for the lack of communication she can make through her speech. In a world where her own parents mistreat her, she finds solace in her communication with nature, with the domestic cows in her backyard, and expresses her inner thoughts and fears and happiness through the language of silence. She often sits at the riverside by her home and gets mesmerized by the charm and beauty of nature and the ever-flowing water of the river. It seems as if the ripples of the river-water console her reminding her that she is not unwanted in this world and perhaps provides the inspiration to continue with her otherwise mundane life. Her mute but unique communication with nature has made her feel that nature understands her, appreciates her, consoles her, and protects her even more than her parents do. This very sense of secure shelter and safety that nature provides her is one of the factors that keep her going. She is accustomed to the impertinent treatment she often faces due to her lack of speech and has somehow convinced herself to bear it for the rest of her life. When her parents want to get her married like their two other prospective daughters, they realize that they can find no one who would agree to marry a dumb girl like her. So, they decide to take her away from their village home to Calcutta where they can somehow manage to get her married off to a wealthy prosperous groom and thus feel free from the social allegations of keeping an unmarried girl at home for long. When the groom came to examine the decked up would-be bride, quite naturally, he could not make out that she was dumb because an ideal bride was not supposed to or it may be said, not allowed to speak. Therefore, Subha's speechlessness in a way worked in her favour as she could prove herself to be eligible for the groom's approval. This exactly was what Subha's parents wanted, i.e. suppress the truth about Subha's dumbness and get her married in any way possible.

After the marriage rituals were over, Subha's parents returned to their village home being happy and content to have their burden shed off their shoulders forever. On the other side, within a week or so it was discovered by Subha's in-laws that she could not speak and started treating her in a manner even worse than that of her own parents. Her husband marries again in no time and this time seems to be more careful in selecting his bride through thorough scrutiny of the girl's physical functions. Thus, Subha's life was doomed into eternal sorrow and darkness having failed to communicate her inner thoughts. Her large black expressive eyes attempted to communicate everything, but the world of abled-bodied persons who claimed to have all the senses right could not understand Subha's inner feelings, her pain, her story. It is not like she is unable to express her intentions, it is only that there was no one who she could try to make understand.

In fact, the concept of 'disability', according to me, metaphorically functions at two levels here—firstly, there is the clinical or physical 'disability' suffered by the poor girl Subha, and secondly, the 'disability' of the apparently 'normal' world which Subha interacts with. It is because that world is full of insensitive people who are dumber than she is, because they fail to utter a word of relief to her, they are blind because they cannot look at her with the same esteem, they treat any other 'normal' person with, they are even deaf because they do not have the ears to listen to her inner voices and aspirations, and they can even be called senseless because they cannot feel the pain and humiliation she is bound to go through. They belong to a class of people who are regarded as normal by societal norms and thus exert their power over people like Subha. A person who cannot speak can very much feel and perceive things this simple fact seems to be a distant reality to the people around her. Her physical disability heightens her misery in the sense that she is unable to express her inner intentions and feelings verbally. She is completely nurtured and guided by her instincts and creates her own world where things function differently. She creates a domain of her own where she is free to move.

Subha's physical activities may be restricted due to her physical or clinical disability, but her active mind along with its imagination balances that deficiency. Being dumb, she observes, perceives, and feels the beauty of the world through her vision and senses. Her intentions are never properly understood and she is used to it. In a society, where being a girl proves to be a tale of utter misery, being 'disabled' added to that, is the worst curse possible and that is why she is doubly dominated here—first for her disability and second for her gender. Just as the concept of ability and disability is relative in the world, her ability and disability too are manipulated according to the needs of the selfish people around her. She is inaudible to the normal world just like the supersonic sound which is beyond our sense perception. Just like our inability to hear or perceive the supersonic sound does not dismiss the existence of it, likewise, our incapacity to hear Sudha's cry or perceive Subha's world does not disqualify or dismisses it. It is only, therefore, remains a matter of relativity.

To come back to the question of power, it may be said that it is omnipresent. According to Michel Foucault, power is everywhere—inherent and embodied in discourse, knowledge, and regimes of truth, and it comes from everywhere. The idea of power is thus something which produces knowledge and reality and even produces domains of objects and also rituals of truth. It creates an authority to bring about societal changes on a larger scale and also governs the behaviour of individuals be it positive or negative. And this sense of power also defines 'normalcy' in a society. There is a subtle political power play in the way things are being defined and tagged. The issue of disability also gets defined as something which is way distant and different from what is being tagged as normal and acceptable. Here, power generates knowledge which is again relative and may vary from different perspectives. Knowledge produced by power therefore is not absolute or universal but varies and differs both in terms of time and space. When power and knowledge are connected, the obvious notion that comes out of it is that knowledge is power, whereas it is not completely true. It hints at a point how power manipulates the definition of knowledge; how certain knowledge system is preferred or imposed over the other. Similarly, it has been imposed on society that certain types of behaviour or action or physical requirements are considered acceptable in the mainstream society and certain are not. And that is where the discrimination starts, that is where marginalization starts. Likewise, disabled bodies are abandoned or ignored or considered incapable of performing normal action.

It is therefore a story about how this 'able' world mistranslates and misinterprets her. The story also chronicles how her aspirations and imaginative consciousness are thwarted by the apparently 'sane' world of people. While the whole idea of the study of the subaltern or marginality revolves round the basic idea of looking for an alternative source for verbalization of the otherwise oppressed voices, the disabled bodies also require a more articulate, coherent, and pronounced channelization of their accumulated fears, insecurities, and inferiority complexes. And it may be possible through a collective and corrective measure taken by each one of us who represent 'society', by treating them with respect, care, humility and more importantly as 'one of us'.

References

Berger, J. R. (2013). *Introducing disability studies*. Lynne Rienner Publishers, Inc.

Davis, L. (2006). Constructing normalcy: The bell curve, the novel, and the invention of the disabled body in the nineteenth century. In L. Davis (Eds.), *The disability studies reader* (2nd ed.). Routledge.

Davis, L. J. (2013). *The disability studies reader*. Routledge.
Foucault, M. (1995). *Discipline and punish: The birth of prison*. Vintage Books.
Garland-Thomson, R. (2002). Integrating disability, transforming feminist theory. *NWSA Journal, 14*(3), 1–32.
Goodley, D. (2010). *Disability studies: An interdisciplinary introduction*. Sage Publications.
Link, J. (2013). Crisis between 'Denormalization' and the 'New Normal': Reflections on the theory of normalism today. In: M. Uecker, et al. (Eds.), *Norms, normality and normalization: Papers from the postgraduate summer school in German studies*. Nottingham.
Link, J. (2004). From the, power of the norm to, flexible normalism: Considerations after foucault (Trans. M. M. Hall). *Cultural Critique, 57*, 14–32.
Linton, S. (1998). *Claiming disability: Knowledge and identity*. NYU Press.
Mitchell, D., & Snyder, S. (2000). *Narrative prosthesis: Disability and the dependencies of discourse*. U of Michigan P.
Mitchell, D. T., & Snyder, S. L. (2001). *Narrative prosthesis*. University of Michigan Press.
Moody, N. (1997). Untapped potential. The representation of disability/special ability in the cyberpunk workforce. *Convergence, 3*(3), 90–105.
Plato Republic. (2013). *India*. Maple Press.
Schalk, S. (2017). Critical disability studies as methodology. *Lateral, 6*(1), 13.
Siebers, T. (2006). Disability in theory. From social constructionism to the new realism of the body. In: L. J. Davis (Eds.), *The disability studies reader* (2nd ed.). Routledge.
Tagore, R. (1939). *Subha galpaguchha*. Visvabharati.

Chapter 11
Disabled Identities and the Linguistic World: Exploring Dysfunctionalities in Leela Gour Broome's *Flute in the Forest*

Saumya Srivastava

Abstract Corporeal inefficiency prevents disabled individuals from actively participating in societal development. The social injustice and incarceration that the disabled face in our society are completely unjustified. Disability studies' theorists aim at deconstructing the myths associated with disability. Disability studies confer a central position on the disabled while allocating a peripheral position to the non-disabled. According to Jacques Lacan, it is the language that constructs our conscious and unconscious minds. The whole question of identity formation is based on language. The aim of this paper is to deconstruct the conventional meaning of disability and to develop and redefine the concept of 'disability'. Leela Gour Broome attempts to liberate disabled women through the portrayal of a female character as the protagonist in her novel with a significant disability. She redefines the social construction of femininity and disability, deconstructs gender roles and roles imposed on people with disabilities, and probes hard into the consciousness of the disabled female. By highlighting the issues related to female disability, Leela Gour Broome attempts to challenge the standardized and absolute thinking of normal people. This research is an interdisciplinary study that focuses on the social, political, and cultural interpretation of disability. This work presents an investigation of the human mind.

Keywords Disability · Phallogocentrism · Normalcy · Dhvani · Identity

Aristotle, a famous Greek philosopher, equates disabled men with women. He considers women disabled. This problematizes the identity of disabled individuals within the domains of the society, where one section enjoys a higher status, while other is pushed towards the margins. Female bodies are considered deviant. Historically femininity is compared usually with disability and mental infirmities like hysteria, agoraphobia and anorexia are accepted as popular feminine traits. It is

S. Srivastava (✉)
University of Lucknow, Lucknow, Uttar Pradesh, India
e-mail: saumya.sri16@gmail.com

R. Uniyal and F. Rizvi (eds.), *Understanding Disability*,
https://doi.org/10.1007/978-981-99-4925-0_11

also observed by people in general that females usually possess diminished intellectual potential. Women are appreciated for their bodies by the masses. Bodily form becomes important for women, and any deviance from the normal structure of corporeal form can prompt gaze. The aspect of beauty of a woman increases the value and cultural capital of a woman in the society as women are appreciated more for their bodies than minds.

Leela Gour Broome has tried to position her disabled protagonist within the domains of the linguistic world. Various cultural forces deny positioning of disabled women within the category of women. Therefore, their identification as women remains a blurred category.

In the story *Flute in the Forest*, Atiya's experience of the outside world is depicted. Leela Gour Broome's *Flute in the Forest* is an account of a thirteen-year-old girl named Atiya. Due to her disability, she is not liked by the students of her class. They used to treat her differently. Therefore, she remains isolated from the world. She is not fond of school and friendship is out of question for her. She used to spend most of her time in the forest. School is a monotonous place for her and she is unable to establish a bond with her classmates. They used to consider Atiya dimwitted and nincompoop. Atiya suffers discrimination because of her disability. "Limping along on her strong foot, the other being a little shorter, she used her wooden walking stick to balance herself" (Broome 2).

Metaphors which usually surround the distinct category of disability are isolation, desolation, alienation, marginalization, social ostracization, distantiation, deprivation, etc.

Disability studies are a critical inquiry and it presents an investigation of human mind, behaviour, and cultural perceptions. Cultural perceptions are fabricated by the social narratives. The position of disabled individuals is usually perceived as diminished and far away from the position acquired by the normals. Atiya, who is contracted with polio, is identified as deviant. Doctors tried their best to heal her but all in vain. Her parents find it difficult to bear this pain. Sarojini, Atiya's mother, wanted Atiya to fulfil her dream of becoming a famous dancer, though the dream now seems unrealistic and impossible. This does not mean that she is devoid of other career prospects.

Disability studies' theorists aim at subverting the prevalent notions by questioning and unravelling the fixed concrete notions. We define categories and people around us based on our experiences. Hence, we do not define the world, instead we define the world view. Perfect corporeal form is the utopian concept for disability studies' theorists. They believe in relative existences where cultural influences play a huge role in defining the capacities of the individuals.

As the narrative progresses, we see Atiya's mother being appalled and equally disturbed by Atiya's infirmity. Atiya's mother could not bear this pain of having a disabled child. She leaves her husband Mr. Ram Deva Sardare and her little daughter behind and moves ahead in life with a desire to fulfil her dream of becoming a famous dancer. There is a constant desire in each individual to become better each day which is reflected through the portrayal of the character, Sarojini.

Ram Deva Sardare is a Forest Officer, who used to reside near a forest. Being deserted by his wife, he becomes a little disillusioned, though content with the fact that he has his daughter to look forward to.

Atiya is not a beautiful girl, but she has a beautiful mind. She has an inclination towards studies. Her interest in studies develops further during the course of her journey in life. Her hand would go first, if a question asked by her teacher in class is related to science and geography. She is amicable and friendly. Atiya longs to have a friend. She did not have any friends. Her situation is saddening and disheartening. She has been deserted by her mother and the society in which she is living does not want her to be a part of any social group. "How she craved for a friend- just one friend. But other than Thampu, the 11-year-old son of their Kurumba driver and that drivelling, snotty-nosed Suriamma, whose parents owned the only milking cow in the entire village, there really wasn't anyone at all" (Broome 10).

In the ancient times, women were not allowed to read or write. The structural laws were narrated and written by men. The reason behind it was 'language' or 'education,' which empowers a person. Learning language means acquiring identity. One can be identified only when one acquires the power to speak. The lack of education has relegated women to the secondary position. Women are considered as the 'other.' The cultural predominance of the patriarchy has led to the marginalization of women.

Social inequalities, labelization, and increasing polarization of the categories of normal and non-normal has troubled the situation for varied existences.

Forest is a symbol of solace and tranquillity in the narrative. Atiya finds immense satisfaction amidst trees. Rustling sound of the leaves and wind elevates her spirit. Sound of animals like—chirping of birds, barking of dogs, etc., is all like music to her. Atiya's father has prohibited music in the house because music reminds him of his wife, Saroj. Atiya, being a young girl, could find solace only amidst nature. Therefore, she started spending more time amidst the woods.

The second chapter of the novel presents an investigation of the idiosyncratic behaviour of Atiya's father. His anxieties and dilemmas are talked about and explored in detail. Something seems to bother him all the time. This is none other than Atiya and her age which is in constant flux, and as the years are passing by, she seems to resemble more and more like her mother.

Atiya in the story is shown as a perfect human being with little imperfections. She is treated by the author as a normal figure with extraordinary abilities. These extraordinary abilities should be the focus of attention for the members of the society, but many a time we witness that her disability takes the centre position and she is treated as a subhuman. "The term normate usefully designates the social figure through which people can represent themselves as definitive human beings" (Thomson 8).

The marginalized position of the disabled person is explicitly visible in the narrative. It seems like disabled identities possess no happiness to share with other people as they are doomed to live their life in isolation. At one instance, Atiya urges her father to give her permission to visit aunt Deepti in Bangalore. This again throws light on the fact that disabled people are usually controlled and directed by people. They do not have rights to choose for themselves.

When Atiya finally reaches Bangalore, Dips sits with Atiya and prepares a list. On the list, she mentions a visit to Dr Gyan first. She wants to inquire about a new set of callipers for Atiya's legs. She further mentions that this will not take much time, and after this, we can go to '*mela*' and have a blast. "For a fleeting moment Atiya wondered how they planned to have a blast with her leg in braces and going thack-thack, clonk-clonk on the ground as she tried to get walking with the new ones fitted on" (Broome 37).

Disability is considered to be a state where there is no hope. Metaphors like joy, happiness, merriment, etc. can never be associated with disabled existences. Therefore, the perception of people largely defines the concept of disability rather than the disability itself. This category is largely a fabricated concept.

Further in the narrative, we witness Atiya's passion for studying geography. Her new teacher Mrs. Naina Pillai seems to be supportive in her academic journey. She is the first person to have identified Atiya's potential. She offered to help her in her studies whenever she is in need. Mrs. Pillai's son Gopal is Atiya's batchmate and is interested in Botany. Since Atiya and Gopal share common interests, therefore, they seem to share a unique bond. Their fondness for each other is depicted in the story. Being isolated from the world for a long period, Atiya finally has a friend and a companion in the real world. "It meant that Gopal would be more often in their home and she would have a friend... finally" (Broome 49). Atiya and Gopal plan to explore the forest on their own on the weekend. Their adventurous expedition helps them to come closer. Atiya again confesses the fact that "It felt good to have a friend at last" (Broome 56). It is sad to notice that people refrain from being friends with disabled people. This ignorance of the normal people towards the non-normals inflicts soft violence on the people with significant disabilities and it further relegates them to a diminished status.

Disability studies' theorists attempt to unveil the dominant ideologies and cultural paradigms which govern the social system and create heterogeneous politicized identities.

Atiya's passion to learn flute is actually a serious effort which she undertakes and tries to learn with all her might. She is a quick learner. Her curiosity helps her to learn things quickly and easily. She later becomes fascinated with the old-aged man who plays flute in the forest. Despite being polio-stricken, Atiya is a girl, full of endless mental and physical capacities. She never gives up on anything. She is adamant to learn flute. She also wants to treat Ogre's illness and the infirmity of the rogue elephant of the forest, Rangappa. She never considers herself shackled to her illness. She always tries to find out ways to become better everyday. She looks forward to new things to explore each day. Her intellect knows no boundaries.

"Little did they know it, but he too had suddenly realized how much this girl and the flute lessons had done for him, both mentally and physically! Even though his muscles and his legs became weaker and weaker, his self-awareness had grown even stronger. He seemed to have earned his self-respect again" (Broome 147).

This is the magic of Atiya's disposition. She helps in curing Ogre's illness. She also brings about a great change in the temperament of Ogre. He becomes more calm and patient in the latter part of the narrative.

Leela Gour Broome claims for the authority to speak about women's desires and ambitions which consequently marks a new phase in the empowerment of womanhood. The voice of Broome's protagonist is so profound that it can be heard by the masses. She stands against the exploitation of women and helps in raising the consciousness of the society. Leela Gour Broome in her works tries to liberate disabled women from their degraded status by putting them into the centre and by establishing a feminine narrative. She attempts to form a new cultural poetics so that women acquire their new found place in literature and history. Leela Gour Broome challenges the gendered assumptions and questions the conventional roles played out by women within the domestic realm.

Broome highlights a characteristic specific to Atiya, that is, her calm attitude. She maintains her composure all the time throughout the narrative. She used to tolerate Ogre's ill-temper. Her drive to learn music is so huge that she used to tolerate harsh comments and ill treatment given to her by Ogre. We usually witness that people with significant disabilities develop an aversion towards the normals, but here, we can notice that Atiya's company acts as a therapy to all. We witness major transformation happening in the disposition of Ogre and Rangappa. Atiya's nature proved to be therapeutic. Ogre's comment is a proof of Atiya's endless potential to metamorphosize people into better human beings. Ogre at an instance in the narrative says, "'We'll see you next week, my child!' he said with the first gentle farewell wave he had allowed himself to give anyone for a very long time, 'And from now on please call me Ogre Uncle!'" (Broome 137). Her everyday adventure in the forest and her struggle to cover a significant distance with the help of callipers in order to learn flute are commendable.

Atiya has so much to give to the world. Her position in the society is not confined within the domains of her disability rather she has much more to explore and learn. Her intrinsic motivation and desire to acquire knowledge are immense. She is self-reliant and self-sufficient. She is not dependent on others. Therefore, her journey and struggle have that warmth and excitement which can never be found in commoners. Her character has a special charisma.

Mr. Ogre's meaningless life has found a reason to live. This reason is none other than Atiya. She has taken a prominent place in Ogre's heart. "He knew she had the makings of a great musician and the clarity of thought of a true researcher" (Broome 147).

A disabled girl, deserted by her own mother, eventually carves her future. Her constant instinct of learning paves her way to become an achiever in her life. Mrs. Pillai is humane and considerate. She used to encourage Atiya to perform better in class. She never discriminates people on the basis of their physical appearance. She is fond of Atiya's inner beauty, but lately she has been noticing that Atiya is becoming physically attractive as she is advancing in age. There is a glow on her face which is starkly visible. For Mrs. Pillai, Atiya's identity is not confined within the realms of her disability rather her immense potential is what makes her special.

Disability studies' theorists question the power struggle which exists between the powerful and the powerless. Language is heavily influenced by the socio-political and cultural narratives. It is inherently ideologically and politically motivated. Powerful voices their opinions, desires, and longings, whereas powerless is usually devoid of attention as they do not have language of their own. Therefore, it is the language which gives shape to the identities.

French psychoanalyst Jacques Lacan considers women outside the "Symbolic" system. Symbolic system refers to the entire domain of culture which controls human consciousness. It stands for the world of predefined rules where gender differences, language, and social roles come into play. These predefined rules have been falsely accepted as truth.

Lacan believes that a woman's identity is defined by masculine tradition of thought. Lacanian philosophy has excluded women from the "Symbolic" order. According to Lacan, the patriarchal order is synonymous to the symbolic order. Symbolic order is preoccupied with phallus and the language that is structured around the symbolic phallus. Therefore, 'language' and the whole 'Symbolic' order which stands for culture is preoccupied with masculinity.

We can witness the same argument coming from a distinguished disability theorist, James Berger. He professes that "The dys-/disarticulate is the figure at the boundary of the social-symbolic order, or who is imagined to be there, and at that liminal place, there is no adequate terminology" (Berger 2).

Broome also throws light on the importance of music according to the Indian tradition of thought. In the narrative, Mr. Sardare exhibits strong aversion towards music. On one hand, we see that music is the only thing at home which is prohibited by Atiya's father. On the other hand, Atiya's fondness for music of the flute which she hears in the forest grows day by day. That music allures her to such an extent that she eventually started craving for learning an instrument, though aware of the fact that music can never enter her house. Atiya finally finds uncle Ogre who used to play the flute in the forest. She requested uncle Ogre to give her lessons on the art of playing flute. From here, her secret journey of learning flute has started. Her passion towards learning this art form is so intense that she started imitating Ogre's way of answering via playing the tune.

Indian philosophical and cultural texts talk volumes about the importance of music, sound, and dhvani. At one instance in the narrative, Atiya sees an ill-tempered Rangappa from a distance. In order to calm Rangappa, she immediately starts playing her flute. Her melodious tune soothes and calms down the rogue elephant who eventually retires to the forest after a while. At another instance, we also witness that Atiya plays a tune and Ogre plays another tune in answer to the tune played by Atiya. Hence, it is obvious that a tune, sound, and dhvani have a language of its own. This language is liable to multiple interpretations.

While referring to the significance of sound and its impact and meaning, the first text of Indian tradition of thought, which comes to our mind, is *Natyashastra*. *Natyashastra* is a seminal text of Indian dramaturgy. Dhvani theory is one of the important poetic theories of ancient India. "...the locus of dhvani was determined by the concept of meaning" (Barlingay 78). Anandavardhana is the main propounder of this theory, but at the same time, a major contribution has been made by yet another classical theorist, Abhinava Gupta. Dhvani theory focuses on the semantic part of the words. The verbal structures and the potency of word structures are given the central position. In a work of art words, meanings, emotions, and suggestions all play a major role in conveying the appropriate emotions. "Dhvani theory is a theory of meaning…" (Barlingay 79). A word has two contexts, i.e. semantic and emotive. Meanings can be of two types, literal and suggestive. Literal meaning is the exact meaning of the word, but suggestive meaning is the hidden meaning. The tune played by Atiya suggests a hidden meaning which is grasped by uncle Ogre. Therefore, Mr. Ogre plays a tune in answer to the tune played by Atiya. Dhvani theory has wider applications. It is not limited to the domains of words, rather it can be applied on any kind of sound or music.

Meaning also can never be separated from the sound of the word. They are interdependent terms and help in building the suggestiveness of a word. There are myriad music and different musics have distinctly different impacts on people. We can see the therapeutic impact of music on a rogue animal like Rangappa. Music changes its character and inherent nature. Rangappa becomes docile after listening to the tunes played by uncle Ogre and Atiya. We can witness that Rangappa no longer remains a fierce and terrifying rogue animal. "'Rangappa has changed, in a strange way.' Papa was telling her, a little perplexed. 'He doesn't seem half as fierce as before, which is most unusual. The rangers do not see him with a herd, so he is still on his own, but he doesn't enter the surrounding farms and sugar cane fields any more...'" (Broome 172).

Further in the narrative, we can see an emotional bond developing between uncle Ogre and Atiya. For uncle Ogre, Atiya and flute have become a constant source of motivation.

We can witness a strange kind of telepathy at an instance in the narrative between Atiya and Rangappa. Atiya possesses a special ability to understand non-verbal cues of animals and Rangappa has a sixth sense to understand the consequence of the situation beforehand. Therefore, Rangappa in the latter part of the story comes to Atiya's house to convey the serious condition of uncle Ogre. Mr. Sardare is awestruck after witnessing this strange conversation which happens before his eyes between Atiya and Rangappa.

We have often witnessed that mass consciousness is usually preoccupied with the lack or corporeal disfiguration rather than with the abilities or potential of the deviant existences. Deviance is stigmatized within the cultural system. Serious efforts are made by the disability studies' theorists to deconstruct these hegemonic ideas.

Indian cultural narratives are usually preoccupied with music and rhythm. The therapeutic effects of music are beautifully laid down by Leela Gour Broome in her account.

Atiya's music has the capability of casting a spell on her father and everyone else present at the tenth-day death ceremony of uncle Ogre. To this, even Mishora proclaimed that this is the most precious and beautiful tribute to her father. Music has the capability of bringing a transformation in people's disposition and we can witness this transformation in the disposition of Mr. Sardare, when instead of being angry he praises his daughter for the talent which she has inculcated recently.

Leela Gour Broome through the feminine discourse of Mishora and Atiya seems to establish a female identity free from male assumptions. It appears as if by establishing a feminine narrative, Broome is putting 'women' and their desires at the centre, thus challenging the notion that centre belongs to patriarchy and normals. By dealing with disabled women's thought processes, oppressions, and victimizations, Leela Gour Broome seems to deconstruct the idea of phallogocentrism.

> The modern world is composed of thousands of cultures, each with its own ways of thinking about other people, nature, family and community, social phenomena, and so on. Culture is sustained through customs, rituals, mythology, signs and symbols, and institutions such as religion and the mass media. Each of these informs the beliefs and attitudes that contribute to disability oppression. These attitudes are almost universally pejorative. They hold that people with disabilities are pitiful and that disability itself is abnormal. This is one of the social norms used to separate people with disabilities through classification systems that encompass education, housing, transportation, health care, and family life (Charlton 219).

Uncle Ogre knew that Atiya was polio-stricken, but he was also aware of her immense potential. He knew that Atiya will return to the forest to carry out his research on the life and music of Kurumbas. He seemed to be certain of this fact and knew her interest in Anthropology, before she could think for herself. Here, we can see that there are many strong and supportive figures associated with the life of Atiya. All of them knew her capacities and were aware of her willingness to achieve great heights. Mishora, uncle Ogre, Mr. Sardare, and Mrs. Pillai, all of them have seen a beautiful dream and a successful career for Atiya. Throughout the narrative, her potential has been emphasized. Hence, despite taking a disabled character as the protagonist of her story, Leela Gour Broome centralizes the abilities of the disabled person.

The constant concentration on men and masculinities leads to the marginalization of women. Leela Gour Broome by bringing out the feminine discourse of women into the public domain compels the readers to look at the feminine perspective. She also wants the readers to accept the protagonist of her novel in the disfigured shape or in the shape given by the author. The condition of disabled women is saddening and dehumanizing in India. Broome's work raises many questions like—how a disabled woman is silenced behind the veil; how she is unheard by the majority; and how she remains unidentified? The binary system relegates disabled people to the secondary position and the cultural and social construct pushes women to the margins. Leela Gour Broome in her work projects an authentic account of disabled woman's emotional and psychological experience under patriarchal authority and the authority of the normals.

By the end of the narrative, we can see that Atiya plays a tune on the flute for the Kurumba children. "Mishora and the children listened as Atiya began to play. As the notes washed over all of them, the children fell silent. First she played a quiet melody to calm them, leading them into a tranquil, contemplative mood. The notes became stronger and louder as she increased her tempo and then, with swift, lightning and yet light and easy touch she skimmed over the flute, blowing and breathing skilfully as she played. The children sat glued to their seats. They loved it! She charmed them completely" (Broome 191).

The narrative has an optimistic ending. Atiya is supposed to come back in order to complete the research work initiated by uncle Ogre. The potential of the non-normal people is usually undermined by the normals. Atiya is depicted to have a bright future with much more to give to the world. Her contribution towards the growth of the society is going to be a significant one.

"Disability studies, in contrast, focuses on the external variables: the social, political, and intellectual contingencies that shape meaning and behavior." (Linton 6) There were numerous socio-cultural variables which were responsible for giving a perfect shape to the demeanour of Atiya.

A distinguished French feminist, Helene Cixous believes that writing about women; their desires; needs; longings; etc. can help in developing a new feminine consciousness. This feminine consciousness will help in subverting the phallocentric symbols embedded in the narratives.

Disability studies' theorists stand against social inequality and attempts to bring about the reformation in the society at large. Their main motive is to expose and resurface the unsettling and disquieting issues of the society. They rebel against the powerful structure of culture which leads to the oppression and marginalization of many people.

> Thus, there is an inherent hierarchy in the very understanding of disability which is reflected in the categories that are used to define the character of the disabled versus the able-bodied. For instance, able/disabled, civilized/savage, rich/poor, rational/emotional, mind/body, normal/abnormal are the polar/binary opposites. In every set, one pair is the privileged. One is seen as 'having', while the other is seen as 'lacking'. Understanding disability is thus loaded with such binary oppositions of inclusions and exclusions the dominant ideologies in Indian culture have continued to operate paradoxically in characterizing the binaries that define social realities (Ghai 81).

Leela Gour Broome believes that literature can bring about social awakening and cultural transformation in the society. She believes that those customs should not be followed which inhibit the growth of the society. Raising awareness and transforming consciousness were integral to her writings. Her work confronts and smashes the codes followed by normals. Leela Gour Broome intends to profess that even the upper class women are oppressed by the social norms defined by normal people. Broome deeply penetrates into the consciousness of disabled females and boldly speaks about the repression faced by the women with significant disabilities. She attempts to bring periphery to the centre, by breaking the silence of the oppressed. Leela Gour Broome asserts that women with disabilities are subjected to subjugation in all the public spheres as normal people carry a privileged position in the public domain. "Social constructionism and performativity seemed to offer the way out of the problem caused by the worm of essentialism, but it also created severe problems in shaping notions of identity" (Davis 233).

Leela Gour Broome's latent subversion against hegemonic force of normalcy is clearly exhibited in her work. Abled people take the 'center' position and disabled are always pushed to the margins. The aim of this paper is to unveil these hidden issues and to reconstruct new identities of people with significant disabilities. She asserts the desires, needs, and longings of the disabled women which are generally repressed by the hegemonic forces of patriarchy and normalcy. The truth defined by normal people facilitates the articulation of desires of normals while completely neglecting the desires of the non-normals. The socio-cultural narrative underrepresents women with disabilities. Most of the ancient scriptures and mythological texts are predominantly written by able-bodied people who belong to the linguistic world. The mythical structures created by able people are prejudiced against disabled. Leela Gour Broome vehemently attacks social injustice and strictly opposes the gender roles imposed on women with disability.

Bibliography

Berger, R. J. (2013). *Introducing disability studies*. Lynne Reinner Publishers.

Broome, L. G. (2010). *Flute in the forest*. Penguin.

Charlton, J. I. (2000). *Nothing about us without us: Disability, empowerment and oppression*. University of California Press.

Ghai, A. (2015). *Rethinking disability in India*. Taylor & Francis Group.

Linton, S. (2006). Reassigning meaning. In L. Davis (Ed.), *Disability studies reader* (pp. 161–172). Routledge.

Davis, L. (Ed.). (2006). *The disability studies reader*. Routledge.

Thomson, R. G. (1997). *Extraordinary bodies: Figuring physical disability in American culture and literature*. Columbia University Press.

Chapter 12
From Narrative Prosthesis to Disability Counternarrative: Reading Cognitive Difference in Aparna Sen's *15 Park Avenue*

Meenakshi Pawha

Abstract Norms control our world, and we are conditioned to conform to society's notions of normality. What does not fit into the quintessential discourse of our lives is mediated. It is only natural that the disabled body becomes deviant in societies that have imposed these ideas. This places disabled people in an ambiguous connection to the cultures and narratives they inhabit. This sense of being in a 'special condition' makes them a prominent literary subject, a 'stock element of characterisation', and an 'opportunistic metaphorical device'. David Mitchell and Sharon Snyder call this continual discursive dependency on disability, narrative prosthesis. Focusing on physical disability and evaluating against able-bodied norms, writers, filmmakers, and artists have excluded many persons and groups with cognitive disabilities. Cinema and other visual cultures can play a pivotal role in challenging these exclusions. In reading Aparna Sen's *15 Park Avenue*, the present paper endeavours to offer a more humane model for the embodiment of cognitively different people. It attempts to explore and initiate a re-imagination of literary and cultural history.

Keywords Disability · Narrative · Prosthesis · Cognitive difference · Cinema

Introduction

Cinema is perceived to be a powerful and effective medium that mirrors the realities of society. Despite getting mired between the real and the imaginary lives, it is an effective medium for entertaining people, instructing them, and helping to change their attitudes and behaviours. Due to the international reach of the Hindi film industry, it has been potent in transforming people's perspectives and deconstructing socio-cultural presumptions. This paper situates and examines the portrayal of disability

M. Pawha (✉)
Independent Scholar, Whispering Palms, 9-B, Tilak Marg, Lucknow, Uttar Pradesh 226001, India
e-mail: meenakshipawha@gmail.com

R. Uniyal and F. Rizvi (eds.), *Understanding Disability*,
https://doi.org/10.1007/978-981-99-4925-0_12

and the influence of Indian popular cinema on the country's disability movement. It uses specific films as examples and explores the representation of disability from the 2000s to contemporary times. In addition to analyzing the impact of these films on the disability movement in the country, it traces its preoccupation with the physical. This paper also explores how cinema in recent years has played a pivotal role in challenging the exclusion of portrayal of cognitively different people. In reading Aparna Sen's *15 Park Avenue,* the paper endeavours to make a plea for a more humane model for the embodiment of cognitively different people that inhabit our society. It attempts to explore and initiate a re-imagination of literary and cultural history.

The definition of disability has, in specific contexts, been expanding in the twenty-first century. Critical disability theorists have frequently suggested that disability sparks imagination and narration. For example, Michael Bérubé states that: disability "demands a story" (570). This "demand for explanatory narrative" works on an elementary level in everyday life: people with disabilities are often expected to describe and even explain their bodies and histories in ways that those perceived as normal are not: "the scar, the limp, the missing limb, or the obvious prosthesis—calls for a story" (Couser 457). This demand for the story also inspires literary narratives about disability. For Lennard Davis, narrative reconfigures the relationship between disability and time: "When one speaks of disability…[it] immediately becomes part of a chronotope…." (3–4).

The first step in understanding the social dynamics around/in disability is to concede that interdependence is the law of human societies. Apart from food, clothing, and medical treatment, we are all reliant on others for support networks and social opportunities. The difficulty is that individuals with disabilities have historically had to contend with an able-bodied majority whose institutions, attitudes, and ideas characterize disability as a problem. This ingrained perspective has numerous implications, including marginalization, neglect, medicalization, and direct violence against the disabled. It is further compounded by social stigma, especially against the mentally disabled and ill.

Stigma is a term that refers to the practice of stigmatizing specific individuals as being inferior and different. It is a badge of shame, insignificance conferred on the stigmatized. As a result, avoidance and even exclusion from society occur. It can be considered as a type of social surveillance or exclusion of minorities from specific competitive areas, serving as an intangible form of control over groups of people with mental illnesses, which Goffman defined as an "attribute that is deeply discrediting." (3). A combination of cognitive, emotional, and social factors results in the individual losing social status. Social status, in this sense, refers to an individual's position in society, as well as his or her reputation and influence.

Stigma is commonly recognized as a substantial impediment to recovery and inclusion for people who struggle with mental health issues. Furthermore, mental disease stigma is intimately linked to discrimination towards those with mental illnesses, including perceptions of danger, incompetence, and irresponsibility. Aware of this scenario, the World Health Organization (WHO) issued a statement in 2001 that summarized the most widely held assumptions about mental illness and demystified them with scientific facts, as detailed below:

"Mental disorders are not imaginary; they are real diseases that result in suffering and impairment of function. It is not true that persons who are mentally ill or have suffered brain injury are helpless. As with all mental illnesses, they can be treated and mental health restored. Suffering can be relieved, symptoms managed, and many patients totally recover. Mental illness has nothing to do with the nature of an individual, as it is always the outcome of biological, psychological, and social variables. Additionally, the link between genetics, lifestyle, and environment and illness is as well-established as the link between physical illness and genetics. Mental disease care requires not just the patients' concerted efforts, but also expert aid. Treatments are available, but nearly two-thirds of people with a known mental disorder never seek help from a health professional. Stigma, discrimination and neglect prevent care and treatment from reaching people with mental disorders, says the World Health Organization. Where there is neglect, there is little or no understanding. Where there is no understanding, there is neglect." (WHO).

The WHO emphasized the necessity of avoiding moralizing and putting patients and their families on the defensive. Individuals with mental health challenges should not be treated only in hospitals and asylums, as they have the same right to special care and proximity as other individuals. They should be handled individually in their homes, clinics, and mental institutions. Rehabilitation may occur in cooperative housing developments, job training programmes, or support groups. Only 20% of patients are permanently unable to work.

Myths are stigmatizing signs. One of the most pervasive myths about the mentally ill is that they are a threat and dangerous to others in society. The WHO attempted to demystify it by emphasizing that the vast majority of people with mental illness do not constitute a threat to others. When a mentally ill person becomes dangerous, it is frequently for the same reasons that other people do, most notably drugs and alcohol abuse. The likelihood that an ill person will be hazardous increases if the individual exhibited violent behaviour before the illness, suffers from delusions and hallucinations, has untreated psychosis, and abuses alcohol and drugs. Numerous studies have established this. These risk factors are moderate and comparable to those identified in groups without mental health problems, such as those with a poor education level, adolescents, those socially ostracized owing to their gender, and those with a history of aggressive behaviour (Corrigan, 2005). Additionally, this risk factor is significantly diminished because violent behaviour among the mentally ill is linked with a discrete set of psychotic symptoms that a professional may clearly identify. Mentally ill people are twice as likely to be victims of violence as other social groups (Chappel et al., 2004).

As Feminist/Disability Studies' philosopher Licia Carlson summarizes in her 2010 book *The Faces of Intellectual Disability: Philosophical Reflections:*

Historically, impairment has been defined medically—as a characteristic of the individual that deviates from what might be called normal species functioning. As various disability theorists have noted, this model is accountable for many beliefs and practices around disability and the disabled. The view that disability is objectively abnormal and thus undesirable generates a related set of assumptions known as the 'personal tragedy model': that disability is objectively bad and thus something to be pitied, a personal tragedy for both the individual and her family, and something to be avoided and, if possible, cured. This belief that disability is a stain on the otherwise optimistic medical research and society's well-being justifies a slew of connected policies, ranging from involuntary sterilization, institutionalization, and forced rehabilitation to social marginalization, euthanasia, and 'mercy killing.' (*Faces* 5, also see Kittay and Carlson).

Similarly, Harlan Lane, an academic, uses the mask of kindness as a metaphor for what the medical paradigm of disability has habitually accomplished—institutionalized oppression of persons with disabilities under the pretext of just reaching out to those indigent. Thus, the inclination for a 'social model' elevates the concept of 'disability' as a relational term (Carlson, *Faces* 5). That is, disability is not an objectively existing distinction but one manufactured within a particular cultural context and must be managed socially. By and large, Disability Studies' scholars deploy the social model to expose how it has been formed in the common imagination as opposed to equally constructed (and socially negotiated) concepts such as 'normalcy'.

Mitchell and Snyder make this argument in their book *Narrative Prosthesis: Disability and the Dependencies of Discourse.* It develops a narrative theory of disability's extensive use as a contrivance of characterization in literature and films. It contends that while other excluded groups have faced cultural isolation as a result of a scarcity of pictures reflecting their reality, disabled people have faced marginalization as a result of the continuous circulation of images of disability in print and visual media. Mitchell and Snyder adduced that narrative functions as a type of prosthetic response to the structure of disability that it initiates—the notion that it proceeds on the basis of something in need of repair, some flaw in the natural order, frequently embodied by a disabled character—are cogent, astonishingly radical, engaging, and provocative.

It is appropriate to discuss the etymology of the term "prosthesis". It originated in ancient Greece and was introduced into the English language in the sixteenth century through linguistics. Its root "pros" means "adding, advancing, progressing, providing greater power" and so stresses the prosthetic as an "additional power source" rather than an extension of an already existing term (Funk 3). Because the prosthetic provides strength for what is lacking, it is feasible that the literal definition lends itself to a variety of metaphorical expressions that have little or no basis in an amputee's everyday prosthesis experience. Indeed, the term suggests that losing an arm or a leg is debilitating and traumatic; hence, the prosthesis is viewed as a "saviour" equipped with a special aptitude to fill in a void or a loss. Similar to the term handicap, the dominant culture may prefer to define prosthetics and their ostensibly ugly connotations to anyone with physical disabilities. Despite this fact, it is difficult to ascribe a "prosthesis" to any individual with mental "disabilities". Finally, prosthetics' status, value, relevance, and metaphors ultimately depend on ingrained cultural assumptions that must be brought to a standstill (Cachia, 252).

When we look at mainstream cinema in India, social observers and media experts have long lamented the lack of authentic representation of disability in it. With few exceptions, Indian filmmakers have lacked the tenacity to face the complexities of disabled people's lives and address them. Disabled people have historically been marginalized, whether as Oscar-nominated Kachara (trash) in *Lagaan* (2001) or Langra Tygai in *Omkara* (2006). *Koi Mil Gaya* (2003) narrates the story of a developmentally challenged protagonist, Rohit, but it is a science-fiction musical in its treatment! In Salman Khan and Kareena Kapoor's in *Kyon Ki*? (2005), Salman Khan's (Anand) illness bears no resemblance to any realistic mental illness documented in the history of psychiatry. In our films, we rarely see Hollywood's splash of realism as in films like *One Flew Over the Cuckoo's Nest* (1975), *A Beautiful Mind* (2001), *Rain Man* (1988), *My Left Foot* (1989), *Born on the Fourth of July* (1989), *and Scent of a Woman* (1992). Occasionally, in the past, in popular Indian cinema, a perceptive director such as Gulzar provokes us with a sensitive film such as *Koshish* (1972) or Sai Paranjpe crafts an intense film such as *Sparsh* (1984). To varying degrees of success, these two films truly represented the lives of people with disabilities. They sought an apolitical equilibrium in resolving the complexes lurking in the psyches of the disabled and the able-bodied individuals.

Recently, there has been a cornucopia of mainstream Indian films that deal with mental illness in some form. Perhaps, the most well-known of these is *Black* (2005), which is about a girl, Michelle (Rani Mukerjee), who suffers from visual and hearing impairment, but her tutor, Debraj (Amitabh Bachchan), helps her to realize her dormant potential as she confronts the challenge of graduating from college; *Iqbal* (2005) deals with a young boy Shreyas Talpade) who is hearing-impaired and aphasic, but is good at playing cricket and his perseverance stands him in good stead. The depiction of Indraneel Thakur (Ajay Devgn) in *Main Aisa Hi Hoon* (2005) offers a rather precise representation of autism; and *Anjali* (1990) recounts the story of a young girl with an intellectual disability and how her family and the larger community transform as time passes by. Apart from a few exceptions mentioned above, the majority of films in India use mental illness to create pathos, making a concentrated effort to elicit pity from the audience. Moreover, nearly all of them end up being insignificant since they are bound by a set of rules for dealing with mental illness that is entirely predictable and safe. For example, the Indian Stammering Association submitted a petition in protest of the film *Golmaal 3*s portrayal of a character with a speech impediment, noting that while the industry has improved, a character with a speech debility was derided in the film. This is congruent with Harnett's (21) argument that films commonly "employ characters not for their complexity as individuals, but for their easily identifiable impairment, which scriptwriters exploit for dramatic effect, emotional appeal, or overt symbolism."

Aparna Sen, one of the most innovative filmmakers in contemporary Indian cinema, belies this statement. *15 Park Avenue* (2005) is a poignant film about a young woman named Mithi, who has schizophrenia. It is an outstanding film, sandwiched between Aparna Sen's finest films, *Mr and Mrs Iyer* (2002) and *The Japanese Wife* (2010), and alludes to one of her central themes: reality perception. It has a terrific cast, each of whom excels in their various roles. The film is predominantly in English, with brief ventures into Hindi and Bangla to establish the plot and characters, verisimilitude in locations where one may reasonably expect to see them (in situations when characters speak to strangers on the streets of Calcutta). Sen has returned to her serious art-house roots following *Mr and Mrs Iyer*, in which she was dabbling with a more commercial aesthetic. *15 Park Avenue* is filled with educated, cosmopolitan characters, heated dialogues, and detailed descriptions of schizophrenia, its symptoms, and treatment options, all of which appear to be extremely current and medically infallible.

In *15 Park Avenue*, Mithi (Konkona Sen Sharma), the chief protagonist of the story, becomes increasingly entangled in her illusions to the point where she eventually vanishes from our and the other character's perception of reality. The story's tracks do not provide answers; instead, as the film unfolds, they inspire an increasing number of questions. Anu (Shabana Azmi), Mithi's elder sister, is a physics professor who is deeply immersed in quantum theories, which profoundly alter our perception of physical reality. She posits innumerable questions to the doctor (Dhrittiman Chatterjee) who is treating her sister. Using a little vase from a neighbouring table, he depicts how subjective reality perception may be, in a critical discussion with Anu. Mithi, who continues to live in delusory worlds with her ex-fiancé and five children, once asks Anu what she would think if Mithi was to admit that her profession as a physicist is purely fictitious.

Aparna Sen's film opens with the most distressing montages. At first glance, one of the most intriguing scenes appears to be a standard parallel montage, implying the simultaneity of Anu lecturing on quantum physics and Mithi being treated at home by a shaman. However, the soundtracks for Anu's lecture and Mithi's treatment begin to overlap, and the rhythmic exchanges between Mithi and Anu have nothing to do with a parallel montage; instead, this moment appears to be two moments occurring concurrently but wedged together, a montage that does not lead to some order, but is on the verge of chaos at this moment. For the time being, there is a reasonable grasp of this, at least in terms of our human perception of the dreadful chaos of invisible matter processes.

Aparna Sen's films have never shown an unstable universe like *15 Park Avenue*. The montage of the film now begins to shift between locations. Mithi's family travels to Bhutan, and we find ourselves without much preparation, a seemingly incredibly dreamlike logic. In another scene, Joydeep, Mithi's former fiancee, is also in Bhutan with his wife and children. To his amazement, he discovers Mithi, follows her to her bungalow, and speaks with her elder sister. But he notices that Mithi is oblivious to his presence.

Despite its meticulous filming, one of the most horrific scenes is Mithi's gang rape sequence. In *Yugant* (1995), one can recollect a scene of mental warfare between Anjan Dutt and Rupa Ganguly. The scene depicted in *15 Park Avenue* is one of physical aggressions. There is little evidence that has to be shown. We are aware of Mithi's fate. However, the scene in which one of the rapists destroys her tape recorder and smashes her camera against the wall is as terrible and unbearable as Hitchcock's renowned *Psycho*'s (1960) death scenes. We need not observe how they rip her garments asunder, as the camera is damaged against the wall. The camera is a metaphor for the invisible image-making equipment used to generate cinema. As a woman ultimately creates this film, this moment is one of the most intimidating in Aparna Sen's oeuvre.

The most striking narrative pieces concerning the protagonist come from secondary sources: Anu's report to the doctor about Mithi's story and Joydeep's memories and subsequent account to his wife. Each account of Mithi is interpreted differently by each individual based on their ideas of reality, akin to Akira Kurusawa's *Rashoman* (1950). Her final departure from what we refer to as a "normal sense of reality" occurs towards the film's finale. She vanishes between realms, leaving no trace.

Sen's *15 Park Avenue* is about the human condition following a medical disaster. A fundamental theme of the film is the nature of reality, both for the sick girl and for others around her. Who is to determine which is the most genuine? *15 Park Avenue* is a monument to subjectivity—an ode to the inescapable duality that pervades all existences. The narrative of the film begins *in medias res*—in the middle of nowhere. Sen briefly darkens the screen to amplify the film's emotional resonance; in a manner reminiscent of Satyajit Ray, the darkness surrounding Mithi's environment is instantly communicated to the audience.

According to her doctor and others, she has schizophrenia. She believes her address which is *15 Park Avenue*, where she will be reunited with her husband and five children. She makes a brave attempt to locate the house (and is eventually successful. We are aware of it due to our observations. Her family members, on the other hand, are ignorant). Occasionally, her family and friends attempt to assist her in locating the residence. They periodically attempt to talk her out of it. Mithi's search continues—at times blatantly, at times, discreetly.

Moreover, as she explores, we learn more about her magical mind's complicated structure. The effortless and subtle delivery of her views is a very poignant moment in the film. Mithi's most emotional scenes involve her conveying her convictions about her husband, her children, her job at *The Illustrated Weekly*, her bank account, and her home at *15 Park Avenue*. She does not expect her five children to be looked after by others. She is self-assured in her capacity to raise children on her own. Mithi is seen in a terrifying night scenario expressing her love, often reprimanding, comforting, and guaranteeing her children's safety. This indicates her libertarian disposition. She is always optimistic and convinced that she would eventually find a home on Park Avenue. Her intrinsic self-assurance drives us to wrestle with oneself in the dreary darkness of the auditorium. Why do the so-called normal people lack Mithi's innate serene confidence? Why can we not love our husbands and children with the same intensity as she does? Her opinions are rarely fully heard because she always speaks in a calm, reasoned tone—hardly ever in the style of a vehement outcry. Frequently, she is effective in this endeavour. This is a tremendous accomplishment for anyone, particularly for someone as marginalized as Mithi. She voices her opposition only once, and it is similarly philosophical in tone—"Who are you… you look like my parents… who are you?" (Mithi inquires when employees from the mental hospital arrive to take her away). The question is philosophical, as is the one we all wish to ask so many individuals regularly throughout our lives.

Mithi screams as an unidentified group of men carries her off. She is wholly appalled as this was happening not outside the precincts of her home but inside it. At that moment, she screams, 'This is my Home!' Moreover, for the "last time" in her life, she considers her mother's house her own. After witnessing her parents' conscious hesitation to protect her from strangers' unpleasant touches, she permanently relocates. The "new address" is *15 Park Avenue.*

The narrative of the film lucidly unfolds how intelligent she is. It is palpable when she pays a visit to the Presidency College with a plan for her elder sister, Didi. Mithi seeks Didi's company on her journey to a little town near Dhanbad. She is now working on a report on post election violence. Mithi does not attempt to persuade. 'My job is in jeopardy,' she admits respectfully. 'They would believe that I lack the necessary fortitude… Jojo will be outraged…'. Mithi's politeness is frequently interpreted as a manifestation of her general insecurity. On the contrary, her inner confidence enables her to be pleasant.

Mithi gradually gains an appreciation for life and living as the film proceeds. She is going through an inward shift about which her family is unaware. Only observers are afforded the rare opportunity to watch a person's most intimate transformations. This is, without a doubt, a defining trait of a great film. She is not particularly forceful at first, which is demonstrated in the opening image when she searches for her "Home"as she, views it, via Didi's automobile's windscreen. Mithi's voice is confusing—reserved and vaguely suspicious—given her newfound fear of Didi. Didi, on the whole, is intolerant of her. 'You instruct me… this is your house, not mine', says Anu in anguish. She cries, 'Mithi,I am sick of you'. Ironically, Mithi is the most debilitated character in the film, as she is always seeking to convince her family of her new reality—her new address. She is the only one who is unable to raise her voice to Didi's level. Mithi yawns, exhausted and withdrawn, and reclines in the car next to Anu. Nevertheless, she begs Anu for another five minutes, claiming, 'My children want to see the new baby as well,' and 'Let us pick them up.' She has an intuitive feeling that she has arrived near *15 Park Avenue.* All she requires are a few extra minutes and the final scene embodies her sentiment.

Mithi's optimism grows even stronger in the second section—the days and nights spent in Bhutan—despite her agonizing spasms. She regains her composure. Even the mere presence of Joydeep Roy (Rahul Bose) cannot account for anything. In Bhutan, he is solely known as Mr Roy.

Only a brilliant poet can imbue a character with such a shift so spontaneously. Aparna Sen is a renowned poet of cinema. *15 Park Avenue* is brimming with these poetic illuminations, which depict Mithi's thoughts, conscience, and sense of commitment to her husband and five children. Is she rediscovering herself in Bhutan due to Mr Roy's sudden appearance in her life? Is she reacquainted with love? Is it possible that Mithi's incomprehensible memory recognizes Jojo's face in some strange way that she nor we are aware of?

The audience is indicated the answers to the questions in the closing scene. In the last scene, Mithi turns away from Mr Roy, bidding a "nomoshkaar" (in contrast to Mrs Iyer, who returns her gaze to her 'Mr. Iyer'). This reveals that Mr Roy is merely a conduit for her in everyday reality. Her gesture—embodied in the slight bend of her neck—epitomizes humility as she bids the ultimate "nomoshkaar." A quiet sadness is associated with departure, mirrored in the bronze-coloured shadow on her left cheek. Additionally, there is the prospect of locating house number 15. When these three seemingly incongruous feelings—humility, optimism, and grief—coalesce, Mithi's gesture serves as a final farewell to Mr Roy and the prosaic world. She immediately detects the white walls that follow the "nomoshkaar" and recognizes house number 17! Mr Roy and the others accompany her, and the white walls and homes nos. 17, 16, and 15 vanish. Mithi reappears in full frontal close-up, laughing and repeating "Nayantara," her daughter's name. She now assumes the role of a young mother, delighted, stooped, and shy at the long-awaited reunion, dressed in her outmoded, unironed salwar-kameez with untidy greyish hair. She is seen stooping and smiling in front of the camera—a cinematic depiction of her confronting her world for the first time—the actual world.

Despite her schizophrenia, Mithi possesses an instinctive sense of when to respond to her inner calls. She puts the inner voices pleading with her to accompany her children in rescuing her injured spouse ahead of anything else. Mithi, on the other hand, becomes even more determined—and confident of her convictions—upon her return to Calcutta. Throughout her first hunt, she was pessimistic. However, she smiles and even exits the van during the final search to converse with unknown individuals. Mithi found it difficult, as she lacks the support of society. Dr Verma (Dhrittiman), Mr Roy, a "new" acquaintance, and her Didi accompany her on her final exploration.

However, they are either sympathetic or merely uninterested. Scientific curiosity as delineated by the doctor and familial sympathy as expressed by Anu are incompatible with the warmth and confidence Mithi currently seeks from her ones. At times, curiosity paired with sympathy can be detrimental. Nonetheless, this is the compensation she now receives, even under ideal circumstances. Her war becomes incredibly lonely at this point; yet, one of the advantages of loneliness is the inherent seclusion. Finally, Mithi discovers the location of house number 15. Following that, Park/Palm Avenue and the boomerang-shaped road—alternatively, the cul-de-sac—remain deserted. Contrarily, she argues that the route is neither blind nor boomerang-shaped and is accessible. Moreover, she is acquainted with it which is evident by her unbolting the wrought iron gate. She is the only person authorized to enter the cul-de-sac.

Mithi's fight is intense. On the one hand, she attempts to conceal her inner compulsions (by failing to warn Didi in Bhutan that her children are in danger and have phoned their mother), while on the other hand, she is adamant about the existence of *15 Park Avenue*. She is confident that her family and friends will not interfere with her efforts to locate house no. 15. These two motives appear to be mutually exclusive. Nevertheless, she is able to successfully navigate the conflict due to her compassion and inner confidence.

She is conscientious about her tasks which is evident throughout the two phases of her life—prior to joining the 'Mental Home' and following her return—she maintains a maximum level of commitment to her tasks. As a result, some may assume Mithi is an entirely different person after returning from the 'Mental Home.' This, however, is a wholly incorrect assumption. She maintains the same level of commitment as ever for the following reasons:

She possesses the courage to address political reality in her political journalism. However, she is not engaged in political journalism purely to establish her worth in Jojo's eyes. That is a secondary motivation; the primary motivation is to contribute substantially to society through her journalistic writings.

After being released from the 'Mental Home,' her primary emphasis shifts to her five children. Each of her five children is anxious for their Mamma. Her treatment of the small children is without a trace of insincerity. She is now a proud mommy. What is notable is the joy provided by a strong sense of commitment that connects these two seemingly unlike persons. Mithi is the film's most unified figure. Each of her decisions is sensible. Others in the film, as in life, veer in and out of character at various periods. The night is unforgettable because Mithi assures her children that she will come to them—undetected by Didi or Charu, the maid. She is steadfast in her commitment to return to them and remain with them until the bitter end.

Another very gripping scene is one of Professor Anjali Mathur's classes. She quotes Erwin Schrödinger[1], who once attempted to define life: 'An organism possesses an extraordinary capacity for concentrating a "stream of order" on itself and avoiding collapse into atomic chaos—for "drinking orderliness" from a suitable environment. Mithi is more alive than the other characters in the film by this definition; no other character is as committed to her/his cause. Furthermore, she can ensure a constant flow of order by never breaking her obligations. Mithi, as a result, defies Entropy. However, after we locate Anjali on the phone—'The signals are faltering… I cannot hear you…'—a sign of imminent collapse, an echo of Entropy. Professor Anjali Mathur's classes in the film extensively use references to thermodynamics and quantum physics.

According to quantum physics, a sub-nuclear particle can exist in two states: wave and particle. As with 'day' and 'night', 'trough' and 'crest', the 'wave' and 'particle', existences of sub-nuclear matter are both true at the same time. Is 'Mind' a manifestation of 'Life' on the outside? If this is true, then 'Mind' must have originated from 'Matter.' Due to the fact that the activities of subatomic particles fall under the purview of quantum physics, even the most subtle 'Mind,' activities can be logically understood in terms of this duality concept.

Mr Roy embodies the particle aspect of 'existence,' whereas Jojo embodies the wave aspect of the same existence. Mr Roy, the particle, is palpable to everyone who comes into contact with him. Jojo, the wave, exists entirely for the benefit of one individual—Mithi. The irony is that although they are two representations of the same existence, they cannot sense or feel one another—just as day and night cannot co-exist on the same face of a solar planet. Only the observer, specifically Mithi, can see both of them in a brief period—but not concurrently. As a result, the observer is unaware that the two manifestations are identical twins of the same entity.

[1] An organism possesses an extraordinary capacity for concentrating a "stream of order" on itself and avoiding collapse into atomic chaos- for "drinking orderliness" from a suitable environment.

The concept of truth is highly subjective. Mr Roy—this is how the people in society address him. To Lakshmi, his wife, he is Joy and Joydeep. He is Jojo to Mithi—and only to her. Sen's film is genuinely stimulating because—while Mr Roy ultimately leads Mithi to her Jojo—the particle illustrates the path to the wave. Thus, she is liberated from the ordinary world of particles, dust, and ashes. The hypothesis also applies to her final glimpse of *15 Park Avenue.* The wave functions are interpreted as expressing the likelihood of detecting a particle at a given point in space. Thus, if one is looking for a particle (in this case, Jojo), one may come across one. Therefore, every decision she makes is rational.

15 Park Avenue delves into more than one deranged character; it contends with the entire family and friends. It is not just about Mithi, who lives with her imaginary husband and children in a fictitious address, but also about her helpless mother (Waheeda Rehman), who, out of sheer desperation, resorts to any means necessary to treat her, even exorcist; it is about Anu, who has put her life on hold to care for Mithi, and Jojo, her ex-boyfriend, who abandons her after realizing he does not have the strength to deal with her misery. Additionally, it is about the webs of relationships that bind them and how each is renegotiated.

Conclusion

In conclusion, films, like literature, do not exist in a void. They mirror the realities of the humankind around them. *15 Park Avenue* depicts the different perceptions of realities as interpreted by the director. Sen portrays Mithi who has schizophrenia, as a person having cognitive difference rather than someone inflicted with a cognitive disability. The narrative in the film is not used as a 'prosthesis', rather the story is told in a manner that Mithi's centrality is not lost at any point of time. Sen states, "*15 Park Avenue* is my most honest film. It is born completely out of the first-hand experience. I have lived through the trauma of dealing with mental illness in the family. I love dealing with the question of who and what is normal". These are concrete reasons to believe that, barring few filmmakers, prior to Aparna Sen, were capable of expressing this philosophical reality—both scientific and human—through a theme involving embodied persons in a tangible society in contemporary times. The findings of this study indicate that in the portrayal of Mithi's cognitive difference, Sen has been successful in desisting the prevalent social, economic, and religious climate of India ever since independence which has influenced and continues to influence how mental illness is portrayed in Indian popular cinema. Sen uses the cognitive difference in perceptions of reality as a predominant trope in the narrative rather than perceiving it as a disability. She redefines the notions of normalcy, and her film is about ferreting a reality with reference to the challenging phenomenon known as schizophrenia: it is exceedingly tough and perplexing to comprehend, but that does not imply we should not attempt. Everyone's mental health is precarious. It benefits us to participate in the discourse.

Appendix 1: Notes

1. Erwin Schrodinger (1887–1961). Austrian theoretical physicist who made significant contributions to the wave theory of Matter and other fundamentals of quantum mechanics. He was an incredibly talented individual. After completing his studies and chemistry, he spent several years studying Italian painting. He and the British physicist P.A.M. Dirac shared the 1933 Nobel Prize in Physics.

Appendix 2: Filmography

Black: 2004, Director: Sanjay Leela Bhansali.Cast: Rani Mukherjee, Amitabh Bachchan [A film about Michelle, a girl with visual, auditory, and communication disabilities, and her remarkable bond with her instructor. Michelle's encounter with her teacher dramatically establishes the reversal of roles after he is admitted to the hospital with Alzheimer's].

15 Park Avenue (2005), Director: Aparna Sen. Cast: Shabana Azmi, Konkona Sen Sharma, Waheeda Rehman, Rahul Bose, Shefali Shah, and Dhritiman Chatterjee. [It is a riveting film on schizophrenia and family relationships that reveals an intriguing correlation between human delusions and reality].

Iqbal: 2005 Shreyas Talpade, Naseeruddin Shah, Shweta Prasad, and Girish Karnad star in the 2005 film directed by Nagesh Kukoonoor. [About a teenage boy with hearing and vision disabilities who realizes his dream of becoming a professional cricket player].

Khamoshi ("Silence"): 1996, Director: Sanjay Leela Bhansali, Cast: Seema Biswas, Nana Patekar, Manisha Koirala, Salman Khan, Helen. [The story of a hearing- and speech-impaired couple and their musically brilliant daughter's struggles to communicate with her parents].

Koi Mil Gaya ("I Found Someone") is a 2003 film directed by Rakesh Roshan and starring Hrithik Roshan, Preity Zinta, Rekha, and Rajat Bedi. [The film tells the story of a youngster with intellectual disabilities empowered by an alien named Jadoo.]

Koshish (Effort) is 1972, directed by Gulzar, starring Sanjeev Kumar and Jaya Bhaduri [a tale of a husband and couple with hearing and speaking impairments].

Main Aisa Hi Hoon (I Am Just Like That) was in 2005, directed by Harry Baweja, starring Ajay Devgan, Esha Deol, Sushmita Sen, and Rucha Vaidya. [Tells the story of a father with autism and his young daughter].

Sparsh (The Touch): This 1984 film was directed by Sai Paranjape and starred Naseeruddin Shah and Shabana Azmi. [The film centres on the visually impaired principal of a school for students with visual disability who seeks dignity rather than sympathy for the disabled].

Yugant (End of an Era): [This 1995 film was written and directed by Aparna Sen, starring Anjan Dutt and Roopa Ganguly].

Works Cited

Bérubé, M. (2005). Disability and narrative. *PMLA, 120*(2), 568–576.

Cachia, A. (2015). The (narrative) prosthesis re-fitted finding new support for embodied and imagined differences in contemporary art. *Journal of Literary and Cultural Disability Studies, 9*(3), 247–264.

Carlson, L. (2010). *The faces of intellectual disability: Philosophical reflections.* Indiana UP.

Corrigan, P.W., & Kleinlein, P. (2005). The impact of mental illness stigma. In P. W. Corrigan (Ed.), *On the stigma of mental illness: Practical strategies for research and social change.* American Psychological Association. 10.1037.10887–001

Couser, G. T. (2005). Disability, life narrative, and representation. *PMLA, 120*(2), 602–606.

Davis, L. J. (1995). *Enforcing normalcy: Disability, deafness and the body.* Verso.

Fraser, B. (2018). *Cognitive disability aesthetics: Visual culture, disability representations, and the (In) visibility of cognitive difference.* University of Toronto Press.

Funk, T. (2012). The prosthetic aesthetic: An art of anxious extensions. In *Mid-America college art association conference* 2012. Digital Publications. Retrieved January 4, 2020, from http://digitalcommons.wayne.edu/macaa2012scholarship/1Web

Goffman, E. (1963). *Stigma: Notes on the management of spoiled identity.* Simon and Schuster.

Kittay, E. F., & Carlson, L. (Eds). (2010). *Cognitive disability and its challenge to moral philosophy.* Wiley-Blackwell.

Mitchell, D. T., & Snyder, S. L. (2000). *Narrative prosthesis: Disability and the dependencies of discourse.* The U of Michigan P.

Chapter 13
Changing Social Perspectives on Disability in Hindi Films *Dosti* and *Barfi*

Aahuti D. Dhandhukia

Abstract Literature explores human experience and embeds human values. Literature also reflects contemporary social problems and challenges. Disabled people have lived a life of discrimination, isolation, marginalization, and full of suffering and anguish. In India, disability is popularly viewed as 'past sinfulness' and 'karmic misfortune'. People's perception towards disability is formed by the way disabled people are represented in literature and films, and hence, in Indian context, studying disability depiction in Hindi films becomes crucial as it is a powerful tool to shape collective conscious of the society for understanding, acceptance, and inclusion of disabled people. This paper considers two India's National FilmFare Award winning Hindi films, Dosti (Directed by Satyen Bose, performance by Sushil Kumar Somaya, Sudhirkumar Sawant. Rajshri Production, 1964) and Barfi (Directed by Anurag Basu, performance by Ranbeer Kapoor, Priyanka Chopra. UTV Motion Pictures, 2012), each with two disabled characters with different types of disabilities. Ramu, a poor but brilliant school student in *Dosti* who meets an accident and loses a leg, becomes crippled and homeless who meets Mohan who has acquired blindness. *Barfi* concerns with congenital disability: Murphy Jonson, called Barfi, is a deaf-mute but playful and vibrant young man who takes care of and subsequently marries autistic girl Jilmil Chatterjee. While Dosti stereotypes disability as personal tragedy, the biggest hurdle to 'overcome' and establish the image of 'Supercrip', and projects disabled people as an object of pity, sympathy, help, and charity, *Barfi* is more progressive and realistic in its treatment of disability and addresses a range of issues: sign as language, parental neglect and shelter homes for intellectually disabled, financial crisis, social victimization and indulging in crime, the notion of agency, interdependence, empathy, and care. While exploring the dynamic and complex relationship between disabled persons, these films relate to exclusionary practices and the scope of social inclusion of disabled people.

A. D. Dhandhukia (✉)
Government Engineering College, Gujarat Technological University, Bhavnagar, Gujarat, India
e-mail: aahuti.dhandhukiya@gujgov.edu.in

Research Scholar (Ph.D), Department of English, Maharaja Krishnakumarsinhji Bhavnagar University, Bhavnagar, Gujarat, India

R. Uniyal and F. Rizvi (eds.), *Understanding Disability*,
https://doi.org/10.1007/978-981-99-4925-0_13

Keywords Disability · Congenital and acquired disability · Stereotype · Social exclusion · Inclusive · Society

Introduction

Literature explores human experiences and embeds human values. Literature is also a social creation which reflects contemporary social problems and challenges. Disabled people have lived a life of discrimination, isolation, and marginalization since ages. The recently emerged academic discipline of disability studies aims to develop insight to understand disabled persons as human beings. This paper addresses the need to integrate disabled people into the mainstream to create an inclusive society. It is further significant as, declared in *Disability and Millennium Development Goals*, 2011, that without inclusion of people with disabilities, Millennium Development Goals cannot be realized for post-2015 Development Framework (United Nations 2011, Dept. of Economics and Social Affairs. 3).

People's perception towards disability is formed by the way disabled people are represented in literature and films, and hence, in Indian context, studying disability depiction in Bollywood Hindi films becomes crucial as a powerful tool to shape the collective conscious of the society for understanding, acceptance, and inclusion of the disabled people. This paper considers two India's National FilmFare Award winning Hindi films Dosti (1964) and Barfi (2012), each with two disabled characters with different types of disability, and analyses in the light of disability representation, suffering and self-conception, complex human relationship and care, along with exclusionary social practices and social inclusion of the disabled people.

Literature, Film, and Society

"Literature is a social institution, a social creation. Literature represents life in larger measure" (Wellek & Warren, 1956). Society and literature share a reciprocal relationship as society influences literature and literature shapes social consciousness. The disciplines of sociology and literature are interdependent as sociology studies society and gets its subject matter from different sources including literature, while literature as a social product reflects human nature, relationship, and human society. The close connection between society and literature has been deliberated by different critics like Plato, Aristotle, Dryden, Mathew Arnold, Raymond Williams, and so on. H.A. Taine, the father of sociological approach in literature in *History of English Literature* (1886), has propounded the famous theory of race, milieu, and moment: race refers to temperament and disposition of people, milieu means totality of physical, political, social environment, and moment shows the spirit of particular period. Films, along with the purpose of entertainment, also address social causes and relate to social concerns. As authorial intention operates, the society reflected in literature and films can be realistic, authentic, romantic, sarcastic, or utopian. Being a socio-cultural construct, disability is viewed as a social problem and films depicting disability can unfold issues pertaining to the nature of disability, apathetic attitude, human relationship, social exclusion, marginalization, and changing social perspectives to disability.

Social Exclusionary Practices Towards Disability

Referent terms like 'impairment', 'handicap', 'cripple', 'disablement', 'physically challenged', 'differently-abled', 'special' reveal society's ambiguous attitudes towards disabled people. These different terms refer to 'inability', 'lacking in', and 'burden' or bring under glorified light with 'positive burden'.

Disability can be defined as physical, mental, intellectual, sensory impairment. The World Health Organization explains disability as "impairments, activity limitations and participation restrictions." (WHO par. 13.2) UN's Convention on Rights of Persons with Disabilities (2008) recognizes disability as:

> Disability is an evolving concept and that disability results from the interaction between persons with impairments and attitudinal and environmental barriers that hinders their full and effective participation in society on an equal basis with others. (Article 1)

Baynton rightly observes: "Disability is everywhere in history but conspicuously absent in the histories we write." (ed. Davis ch 2:30). *Past and Present Perceptions Towards Disability: A Historical Perspective* by Chomba Munyi reveals that socio-cultural perspectives towards the disabled have continued to vary and change since ages. Plato had considered the disabled child as a burden to the formation of ideal state and therefore they should be thrown into "some mysterious unknown places" (qtd in Munyi para 3). It is also pointed out that disabled in some cultures were completely rejected, whereas in some cultures, they were outcaste or treated as economic liabilities. Disabled people, in different societies and cultures, have remained "deviant than the inmate in the society" (Lippman 1972, 89) According to Munyi's study, history shows that ignorance, neglect, superstition, and fear are social factors that have caused isolation of disabled people in the society (Munyi 2012, para 15). Widespread social exclusion of the disabled people is also recorded as:

> Disability culture is the difference between being alone, isolated and individuated with a physical, cognitive, emotional or sensory difference. Our society invites discrimination and reinforces isolation. (Kuppers 2011, 109)

Stigma theory as propounded by eminent Sociologist Goffman (1963) theorizes stigmatizing as the process of creating the 'otherness' because stigma becomes the attribute in non-conformity with the social stereotype, and hence, person bearing such attribute is considered as stigmatized. According to Goffman, physical disability constitutes first category of stigma construction (14).

According to *Status of Disability in India* (Kundu, 2000), the ambivalent attitude and treatment to the intellectually disabled as mentally retarded have prevailed since ancient civilization. During Middle Ages, they were considered 'God's innocent children' and they were given care at home or monasteries. Contrastingly, they were also considered as possessed by evil spirit and subjected to which-craft and shame to the family. During the age of industrialization when individuality became the centre and one's functionality and productivity became salient characteristics of personhood, intellectually disabled were perceived as 'social problem' and they were prescribed to institutional care. Advanced medical science and psychology have proposed a classification system and different manifestations of intellectual disability are acknowledged as neurodiversity.

Indian Perspective on Disability

India's census of 2011 states that disabled people are 2.1% of the total population, but World Bank report, 2009, estimates its proportion between 5 and 8%. In India disability being a socio-cultural construct, different factors like geography, polity, employment opportunities, caste and customs, environment, health care, and accessibility to aids and technology tremendously affect the lives and well-being of disabled people. The Honourable Prime Minister of India, Narendra Modi, has attempted to alleviate the attitude towards disabled by attributing the term 'Divyang' (divine embodiment) to them. While it appears the term "Divyang" which alleviates disability experience, ironically, this term also implies that the experience of disability is essentially rooted in one's body.

In India, popular conception and perception of disability are formed under tremendous religious influence. It is quite customary in Indian culture to relate disability to past sinfulness, Karmic misfortune, or divine justice. (Worldbank 2007, ch.2 23) Disability is seen as a punishment given to the person for sins committed either in this life or previous birth.

Indian scriptures provide both negative and positive examples of disabled persons. Dhritarashtra in *Mahabharata* stands for the symbol of 'blind justice', whereas Manthara in *Ramayana* is associated with the stigma of conspiracy and inflicts pain and suffering on others. As against this, Indian scriptures also provide magnanimous examples of Apala and Ashtavakra who with their 'deformed' body stand for spiritual enlightenment. Sage Ashtavakra stands for the glorious epitome of 'disability as opportunity' (Upadhyaya 2018, 59). Ashtavakra's disability is the outcome of his father sage Uddalak's curse. However, Ashtavakra transcends his disability by attaining the highest level of spiritual knowledge as philosophized in *Ashtavakra Geeta.*

Under the influence of different sects' and saints' preaching, Indian people have shown the attitude of 'service to God' in feeding, sheltering, and taking care of the poor, lowly, downtrodden, and the disabled. Under religious-cultural influence, disability in India is largely seen as "culture of charity and welfare" along with "pity, segregation, discrimination and stigmatization" (qtd. in Sukhramani and Verma 2013, ed. Lutz111).

Disability and Social Model

As against the Medical Model that regards disability as 'personal tragedy' and 'life-long dependency', social model of disability that emerged in Britain during the 1970s argues that one is impaired by body and disabled by society. Unaccommodating and inaccessible structure of the society, as well as apathetic attitude makes the impaired person disabled in social environment. Thus, social model shifts the onus of responsibility from an individual to the society and advocates for structural, environmental, and attitudinal barrier removal. However, in Third World country like India with massive population and a crunch of resources, implementing British social model everywhere cannot be feasible (Karah 2019, 21:10). While quoting Lal's study, Sukhramani and Verma state that five phases that indicate society's treatment towards both physically and intellectually disabled from medieval to the present are: extermination, ridicule, asylum, education, occupational adequacy, and with diverge socio-cultural context, these five phases co-exist in the treatment and attitude towards the disabled (112).

Disability activism and social model played significant role in establishing disability studies as an academic discipline with the publication of *Disability Studies: Enabling Humanities* (2002). The Modern Language Association of America has acknowledged disability as the transformative category for humanities. "Disability figures in cultural representation as an absolute state of otherness; opposed to what is standard and normal." (Snyder et al. 2002, 2) Social model has also led to the formation of Disability Laws worldwide. UN had declared the year 1981 as "International Year for the Disabled Persons." UN's Conventions on the Rights of Persons with Disabilities (2008) was very progressive and influential in creating an inclusive society. India's Constitutional provisions for underprivileged and marginalized section of the society apply to disabled people as well. Articles 14, 41, 45, and 46 provide special care regarding employment and education and protect them against injustice and exploitation. India's enactment of "Rights of Persons with Disabilities Act, 2016" is effective legislation for inclusivity and equal participation of disabled people in all the spheres of life.

Disability in Literature and Film

Disability studies in literature provide fresh approaches to literary analysis. Studying disabled characters in literature is crucial because disabled characters are studied as "complex characters living everyday life in distinct ways and not as easy metaphors, tragic victims or medical case study" (Hall 2016, 2). It considers social meaning, symbols, and stigmas attached to the disabled identity (Siebers 2008, 3). It is not through the narratives on law, sociology, economics, or medicine but through literature and film that people learn more about disability. Garland-Thomson, while discussing how disability operates in literary texts, finds the gap between disability experience and its literary representation. The literary portrayal confirms to the social stereotype (Garland-Thomson 1997, 11). Films are significant source for literary, social, and cultural studies. Bollywood Hindi films have raised concern for myriad social problems and represented the lives of the marginalized, the oppressed, and the excluded in different films. Conventional Hindi films like *Bhigi Raat*, Khandaan, *Chiraag*, *Aarzoo*, etc. have depicted disability as tragic flaw, misfortune, or a device to add sensationionalism and melodrama. *Sholey* has exposed the audience to disability with a shocking jerk. However, very few films like *Koshish*, *Sparsha, Sadma, Black, Gujharish, Hichki,* etc. explore disability experience and social perspectives to disability.

This paper undertakes the films Dosti (1964) and Barfi (2012) which are significant to study disability representation and society's exclusionary practices and changing social perspectives to disability experience. Both these films have bagged Film-Fare Awards and hence become landmarks in cinematic representation of disability. These films are also noteworthy as each one portrays two disabled characters with different types of disabilities and hence provides ample scope for disability studies to explore different dynamics of relationship between the disabled characters and the complexity of their relationship with the 'able-bodied' society. Further, while *Dosti* depicts characters with physical disability, the film *Barfi* explores a complex angle by portraying one male character with physical disability and another female character with intellectual disability. Film *Barfi* released in 2012 is set in the 1970s, and thus, the film conceptualizes disability from the eyes of 2012 looking back at contemporary social concepts of disability during 1970s.

Dosti (1964)

National FilmFare Award winning film Dosti (1964), directed by Satyen Bose and produced by Rajshri Productions, as its title suggests, celebrates the universal value of friendship and love between two disabled boys, Ramnath Gupta (Ramu) (played by Shushil Kumar Samaya) and Mohan (played by Sudhir Kumar Sawant). The title of the film does not indicate the film's preoccupation with disability. At the time when Indian audience might not have been accustomed or comfortable with visibility of disability on screen, considering contemporary audience sentiment, the film stayed away from portraying congenital disability and both the characters acquire disability accidentally out of very poor conditions of living. Ramu is a poor but brilliant school student who meets a road accident and loses a leg and becomes cripple, orphan, and homeless who happens to meet Mohan who, all of a sudden, one day acquired blindness at his home in a remote village. His sister Meena has joined service as nurse in the city. The heavy thunderstorm and flood leave Mohan homeless and desolate, and he finds himself with no other option but begging to feed himself. Acquired disability shows fluid nature of disability, that anyone at any time may acquire disability out of accident, disaster, disease, war, or terrorist attack. Though acquired disability blurs the boundary between ability and disability, for the person, it demands intensive adaptation to people, changed situation, and way of life. *While Mohan shows calm resignation to his destiny, Ramu shows resistance to begging.* Ramu's disability is projected as a symbol of the biggest hurdle which one needs to 'overcome' to achieve and to succeed in life and to establish the self as *Supercrip* is the worth of living a disabled life. Ramu proves his mother's words true: "जितनीबड़ी बाधा होगी उसे पार करने में इतना ही बड़ा गौरव है।" ("Bigger the hurdle, greater is the pride to overcome it" my trans.).

This film perpetuates the stereotypes of disability and associates it with poverty, orphanhood, homelessness, wandering life, slum dwelling, and begging. The characters themselves view their disability as personal tragedy, misfortune and they feel self-pity and self-contempt. Ignorance, apathy, and prejudice of the society towards disability cause social exclusion, discrimination, and marginalization of the disabled characters. Ramu is insulted for being a cripple on asking for any kind of job from a rich man. Ramu is attacked by a gang of ruffians and plotted against with false allegations of theft. After acquiring disability and on Mohan's encouragement, Ramu resumes his study at school, but the students not only laugh and mock at Ramu but also falsely blame him for stealing a book. The film depicts a society where the disabled are more vulnerable to victimization and exploitation in their interaction with the society.

The film demonstrates that disabled people with visible disability such as blindness are subjected to 'starring' at public places. When blind Mohan is calling for help to cross the road, the able-bodied passers-by star at him but ignore his calls for help. Ironically, it is crippled Ramu who offers his assistance, and crippled Ramu leading blind Mohan becomes hallmark throughout the film.

Based on empathy, both of them share a deep bond of friendship, care, love and they foster the notion of interdependence of mankind. Severely ill and bed-ridden Manjula can perceive the similarity in her condition and that of Ramu and Mohan. This also illustrates the commonality in the experience of illness and disability. The social stigma of disability operates through family too and elder sister Meena is publicly reluctant to recognize blind Mohan as her brother. However, later on, she and Ashok both overcome their reluctance and prejudice and make provision for eye treatment for Mohan.

The film also juxtaposes the ridicule of the disabled with understanding, acceptance, assistance, empathy, and compassion for them. As against the exclusionary practice of the society as a whole, the inclusive mindset of several people is appreciable through characters like Mausi, the small girl Manjula, teacher Sharma Sir, and the Principal of the school. The film appropriately portrays the School Principal assisting Ramu to lead him to take a seat at his office. He emerges as an exemplary teacher for a disabled student with his dialogue and behaviour: "गुरुजन और गार्जियन में फर्क ही क्या है।"("Is there any difference between a teacher and a guardian?" my trans.; 04:12).

There are many heart-moving scenes and dialogues in the film. The lines of the songs like " एक इंसान हूं मैं तुम्हारी तरह" ("I am a human being just like you" my trans.; 04:54) leave the message that the disabled and their pain and suffering are inseparable part of humanity. It is the collective responsibility of the society that disabled people can live with human dignity and equality.

Barfi (2012)

While *Dosti* remains anonymous for its time and place as it is the saga of universality of love and friendship, another National FilmFare Award winning film *Barfi,* directed by Anurag Basu, presents double perspectives of time as released in 2012, it goes back to depicting the society of Darjeeling and Kolkata of 1970s. The protagonist Murphy Johnson, called Barfi (played by Ranbeer Kapoor), is a congenitally deaf-mute boy who meets, relates with, marries, and accepts the responsibility of the autistic girl Jhilmil Chaterjee (played by Priyanka Chopra). The film, in a straightforward way, portrays congenital disability echoing society's changing perspectives and readiness to being exposed to disability. The title of the film itself becomes significant one as deaf-mate boy pronounces his own name perceived by other as Barfi and the film recognizes Murphy's language with its own dignified meaning. The film does not melodramatise sign language, nor does use it only as visual optics, but sign language becomes Barfi's 'own language' and in a way the film endorses deafness as a linguistic minority rather than disability (Lane 1995, 179). Like the film *Dosti,* Barfi's character is not portrayed with self-pity, but he is a young, charming, playful, and agile boy who engages in playing mischief with people and being chased by the police. Barfi's romantic indulgence with Shruti (played by Ileana D'Cruz) unfolds the complexity of relationship between disabled and non-disabled persons. Although Shruti is about to marry Ranjeet, her fascination for Barfi raises several questions and seems to be lacking in reality. Shruti's mother reveals society's misconception about sustainability, compatibility, and shame of marriage between a disabled boy and an able-bodied girl—"तुम इशारों में बात कर लोगी, दुनियातुम्हें इशारे करेगी|" ("Though you will communicate (with him) through sign language, people will mock at you." my trans.; 42:30). However, Shruti experiences 'fullness' and 'wholeness' of apparently 'imperfect' Barfi's love which is juxtaposed with the half-heartedness of her marital relationship with her husband: "हम पूरे थे हमारा प्यार अधूरा था, बर्फी अधूरा था पर उसकाप्यार पूरा था।" ('we were perfect but our love was imperfect, Barfi, though was imperfect, perfect was his love." my trans.; 01:53:15).

The film also brings out the dynamics of relationship between the deaf-mute boy and the autistic girl Jhilmil Chaterjee. Barfi rescues Jhilmil from kidnappers and provides her not only a stay at his home but also offers his assistance to her to carry out her daily routine. Thus, this relationship originates from a kind of dramatization that brings both the characters together and this relationship develops out of '*access intimacy*'. Jhilmil becomes more reliant on Barfi and he assumes all necessary responsibility for Jhilmil's smooth living. As the end of the film informs, both of them had also get married.

The film also reveals society's perceptions towards deafness and autism and the interface between one's impairment and the barriers in the social environment. In India, unemployment is a burning problem for the youth and it becomes a die-hard reality faced by millions of disabled youth which leads to their further exploitation and victimization. The film does not mention anything about Barfi's education, but Barfi faces financial crisis following his father's death. Having no suitable occupation, Barfi plays mischief and also has to plan the kidnapping of Jhilmil to demand ransom money from her rich father. The film also makes the poignant commentary that as deaf persons cannot defend themselves well, they are easily victimized and plotted for crime and violence. In the absence of evidence, police arrests Barfi for Jhilmil's murder. However, on due clarification, police officer hands over Barfi to Shruti's care.

Autism is a lifelong developmental disability that affects how a person communicates, perceives the world, and relates to other people. Furthermore, there is also a close relationship between autism and mental retardation. (Ghaziuddin, 2000). Even professional awareness about autism started growing from 1980s onwards. The film reflects not only societal but parental ignorance, disgust, and discrimination against the children with intellectual disability. How ironical it is that Jhilmil's mother feels 'shame' for her child, and Jhilmil is brought up either by her grandfather or at a shelter home where she is taken care of with patience and love.

The scene of the film where Jhilmil lies in the bed with ill and hospitalized Barfi to die together with him celebrates empathy, love, care, and interdependence of a disabled couple. Where family fails to take care, it is a physically disabled person who takes lifelong care of a severely intellectually disabled.

The concept of Narrative Prosthesis by Snyder and Mitchell propounds that disability in literature and film is used as 'device' to bring out the good moral character of main 'normal' characters. However here, the whole film is narrated by Shruti Sengupta and it is she who brings out all good characteristics of Barfi and Jhilmil and compares society's incompleteness with wholeness of their humanity. Plotting Shruti's character suggests that the film needed one 'normal' narrative voice to tell us the story of deaf-mute Barfi and autistic Jhilmil.

Conclusion

Despite Disability Laws and accessibility provisions, society still perceives disability as a social problem. The history of disabled people is a history of isolation, discrimination, exploitation, exclusion, and marginalization. Literary disability studies concern with the meaning of social perspectives, stereotypes, and stigma attached to disability. Cinema is a powerful medium to shape society's consciousness and awaken and educate the society for social equality and justice. Films are effective sources to trace social exclusion and tools to raise social awareness and responsibility towards disability issues and challenges. *Dosti* and *Barfi* both address different dimensions of social exclusion as well as attitude to social acceptance and inclusion of disabled people. It becomes noteworthy that while *Dosti* perpetuates social stereotypes of disability and disabled characters experience self-pity and self-contempt for their 'disabled' condition and are in want of social assistance, Barfi portrays realistic representation of disability as a 'different condition' and both disabled characters with their mutual interdependence build their own self-complete world. The fact that the narrator of the film Shruti realizes 'incompleteness' of able-bodied society as against the 'fullness and wholeness' of relationship between Barfi and Jhilmil brings out valuable interpretation for disability studies as it questions the popular notion of 'Normal' and normalizes disability as a 'different condition of living'. We need more of such disability-oriented films for understanding, acceptance, and integration of disabled people for an inclusive society.

References

Barfi. (2012). *Directed by Anurag Basu, performance by Ranbeer Kapoor, Priyanka Chopra*. UTV Motion Pictures.

Convention on the Rghts of Persons with Disabilities. (2008). United Nations, Department of economic and social affairs. https://www.un.org/development/desa/disabilities/convention-on-the-rights-of-persons-with-disabilities.html

Dosti. (1964). *Directed by Satyen Bose, performance by Sushil Kumar Somaya, Sudhirkumar Sawant*. Rajshri Production.

Dosti. (2008). *Guardian Aur Gurujan Me Koi Fark Nahi*. YouTube. Retrieved from September 30, 2020, from https://www.youtube.com/watch?v=02w6-PIi8pA&feature=youtu.be

Dosti. (2014). *All songs*. You Tube. Retrieved from September, 30, 2020, from https://www.youtube.com/watch?v=Bl4VJ3ZJ4jY&feature=youtu.be

Douglas, B. C. (2013). Disability and the justification of inequality in American history. In L. J. Davis (Eds.), *Diability studies reader* (4th ed., pp. 17–33). Routledge.

Garland-Thomson, R. (1997). *Extra-ordinary bodies: Figuring physical disability in American culture and literature*. Columbia U P.

Ghaziuddin, M. (2000). Autism in mental retardation. *Current Opinion in Psychiatry, 13*(5), 481–484.

Goffman, E. (1963). *Stigma: Notes on the management of spoilt identity*. Penguine Books.

Hall, A. (2016). *Literature and disability*. Routeledge.

Karah, H. I. (2019). Social model of disability: Part-1. In *Disability studies: An introduction, created by Indian Institute of Technology, Madras, Week 1, Lec.3, National Programme for Technology Enhanced Learning*. Retrieved from September, 30, 2020, from https://nptel.ac.in/courses/109/106/109106168

Kundu, C. (2000). *The status of disability in India 2000*. Rehabilitation Council of India.

Kuppers, P. (2011). *Disability cilture and comminity performance: Find a strange and twisted shape*. Palgrave Macmillan.

Lane, H. (1995). Constructions of deafness. *Disability and Society, 10*(2), 171–189. https://doi.org/10.1080/09687599550023633

Lippman, L. (1972). *The UNESCO braille courier*.

Munyi, C. (2012). Past and present perceptions towards disability: A historical perspective. *Disability Studies Quarterly, 32*(2), 1–9.

Siebers, T. (2008). *Disability theory*. U of Michigan P

Snyder, S. L., et al. (2002). Introduction: Integrating disability into teaching and scholarship. In S. L. Snyder, et al. (Eds.), *Disability studies: Enabling humanities* (pp. 1–12). The Modern Language Association of America.

Sukhramani, N., & Verma, S. (2013). Disability as diversity: The Indian perception. In R. Lutz (Ed.), *Disability and respect: Problem of perception in the global agenda for social work* (pp. 109–122). Friere Verlag.

United Nations. (2011). Disability and millennium development goals: A review of the MDG process and strategies for inclusion of disability issues in millennium development goal efforts. United Nations, Department of Economic and Social Affairs. www.un.org/disabilities/documents/review_of_disability_and_the_mdgs.pdf

Upadhyaya, J. (2018). Beyond the body: The pure awareness. In M. K. Arora & R. M. Bairagi (Eds.), *Narratives on disabled: Literature and cinema* (pp. 69–85). Unistar Books.

Wellek, R. (1956). *Theory of literature*. Harcourt Brace and World.

World Health Organization. (2018). *Health topics > disabilities*. World Health Organization. Reterived from December 28, 2018, from www.who.int/topics/disabilities/en/

WorldBank. (2007). *People with disabilities in India: From commitments to outcomes*. WorldBank, Human Development Unit. Reterieved from August 10, 2019, from web.worldbank.org/archive/website01291/WEB/IMAGES/DISABILI.PDF

Chapter 14
The Societal Gaze and Stigma: A Study of Mahesh Dattani's *Tara*

Megha Negi

Abstract People with disability are the most overlooked group of society. Stigmatization and marginalization go hand in hand contributing towards the social exclusion of people with special needs. It leads to social, political, and economic exclusion of people. Marginalizing people is more of a social perception and conjectures, and it exists because of prejudices. People with any form of physical impairment are denied social benefits by the self-proclaimed propagators of society, the group which creates binary and defines normal and consider people with especial needs as abnormal. Society creates boundaries of normalcy and able bodies and fails to accept the diverse sets of capabilities treating them as unimportant and insignificant. Keywords: Disabilty, Marginalisation, Gender disparity, Social stigma, Assertion.

Keywords Disabilty · Marginalisation · Gender disparity · Social stigma · Assertion

People with disability are the most overlooked group of society. Stigmatization and marginalization go hand in hand contributing towards the social exclusion of people with special needs. It leads to social, political, and economic exclusion of people. Marginalizing people is more of a social perception and conjectures, and it exists because of prejudices. People with any form of physical impairment are denied social benefits by the self-proclaimed propagators of society, the group which creates binary and defines normal and consider people with especial needs as abnormal. Society creates boundaries of normalcy and able bodies and fails to accept the diverse sets of capabilities treating them as unimportant and insignificant.

Gender disparity and disability together cause an extreme type of marginalization. Garland-Thomson (2001) claims that women with disabilities are the doubly oppressed for being women (the subordinate gender) in male-dominated society and being inferior in society dominated by the able-bodied. Disability with other contributing factors caused multiple forms of harassment, and this paradox is known

M. Negi (✉)
Department of English, Lucknow Christian Degree College, Lucknow, Uttar Pradesh, India
e-mail: mnegi9@gmail.com

R. Uniyal and F. Rizvi (eds.), *Understanding Disability*,
https://doi.org/10.1007/978-981-99-4925-0_14

as "Double Jeopardy". Gender discrimination and disability if they come together are double jeopardy, as women often struggle to lead a dignified life in society. Women face various forms of repercussions as violence, abuse, injustice, exclusion from social life and also leading a low quality of life.

In India, differently abled women are perceived as a burden upon a family as compared to differently abled men. Male child is provided with education, training, and care to be able to survive in a competitive world, whereas women with disabled bodies are categorized as helpless and dependent. Susan Wendell in her essay "Toward a Feminist Theory of Disability" argues that there should be more disability theories which should be feminist, because more than half of disabled people are women and ~ 16% of women are disabled (Fine & Asch, 1988) and because feminist thinkers have raised the most radical issues about cultural attitudes to the body. Several disability theories endeavour towards the concerns of women with disabilities into feminism and feminist perspectives into the disability rights movement. Michelle Fine and Adrienne Asch and the contributors to their 1988 volume, Women and Disabilities, have made a major contribution to our understanding of the complex interactions of gender and disability.

A society represents its culture which is reflected through rituals, customs, sign and symbols, mythology, religion. Various beliefs and attitudes collectively play a major role in marginalizing women with special needs and care. These attitudes are almost universally pejorative, especially towards women. They hold that women with disabilities are pitiful and that disability itself is abnormal. Women being considered as "the other" becomes more vulnerable being physically or mentally handicapped. A disabled girl child is hidden from society; she is considered as liable for disparagement to the family (Rousso, 2003). While discussing disability among women, an important aspect which haunts them is the notion of stereotype related to asexuality. Among repressive stereotypes, the most common one includes the prerogative that they are not fit or accepted for romantic relationship, not suitable for marriages and unfit to be mothers. This gendered stereotyping has resulted in an impact on their nurture, education, living standards, and employment. The irony and hypocrisy of the society are revealed where most of the differently abled (physical and mental) women are victims of sexual abuse and violence. Domestic, maltreatment, and exploitation by the caretaker family or friends are common.

Mahesh Dattani is a leading and serious contemporary playwright in English. Born on 7 August 1958, he is known as a director, actor, and writer. In 1986, he produced his first play "Where There's a Will". There are several other plays written by him like *Tara, Night Queen, Final Solutions, Dance like a Man*, and many more. His plays deal with the social, gender, and contemporary issues. His plays and writings focus on actual life problems and are compared to dramatists Ibsen and Shaw for his inclination towards the theme of women's issues and bringing them in forefront through his play's. He presented the struggle of women in a patriarchal society living with gender bias and prejudices.

Women and girls with disability endure highest discrimination in regard to the access to education. Helen Meekosha presented her thoughts regarding the disparity as "It is because of this gendered experience of disability; we see a pattern of difference between men and women" (Meekosha, 2004). International organizations like UNESCO and World Blind Union have revealed literacy rate of disabled women which is one per cent as compared to men which is three per cent globally (Rousso, 2003). Parents or society refrain from providing required education to differently abled girl children because of the employment and also on the physical appearance which is supposed by them as an imperative factor for a woman.

As literature is the true reflection of our society, it portrays the reality of people treating disability as imperfectness. They assume that the usage of resources upon special people is a waste of resources, as they are incapable and dependable. This has caused existential crisis among especially abled people as they are not able find a space of their own, a community, and world which accepts them without stereotypes and stigmas. Existential confrontation occurs because they are withdrawn from social inclusion. Role of individuals in a society is a kind of affirmation how they perceives themself in a given situation; in absence of such interaction and behaviour, disabled people feel disillusionment and despair.

The implications of literary work critiqued the conditions of especially abled women of the contemporary society. Ideology of concerned writers is expressed through their fictional and non-fictional writings by raising the issues which are confined within the domestic walls. It expressed vociferously literary genre to highlight the negligence towards disability and disparity towards disabled people taking the form of a social evil. With their instrumental works, they advocated steered change in society and among public opinions. Literature is considered as the torch bearers for the depiction of some of the serious social issues.

Performing arts or theatre is the best medium to enlighten audience and society regarding the pertaining social evils. It leaves a prolong effect upon its audiences as theatre effects all the senses of audiences and they utilize their intelligence to understand the implied meaning of the drama to visualize the problem. Theatre helps in making the invisible issues visible which are neglected or suppressed by society. People get intellectually and emotionally involved with the drama. Theatre is the ancient medium to convey ideas among masses, still it is an important discipline in literature. Literature and drama brought the sensitive topic about the struggle of especially abled people in society which is always perspicacious and excludes them by tagging them as abnormal. Mahesh Dattani's *Tara* is one of his renowned plays which highlights the gender discrimination in Indian society. It is a two-act play which puts in the picture a tale of Siamese twins (conjoined), a boy and a girl (Chandan and Tara) born in a Gujrati family. Chandan and Tara were conjoined twins with three legs only. The play depicts the cultural preference of a conventional family as Chandan was given the undue advantage of being a male child. In the surgical operation, it was revealed that the twins were born with three legs and the blood supply to the third leg was from the girl child (Tara). The maternal grandfather of the children and the mother (Bharti) of the twins with Dr. Thakkar decided to give the third leg to the male baby's body so as to complete the child. The unfair and unethical operation made Tara a crippled but could not provide a healthy body to either of them. Destiny had dire plans as Chandan, the male child who was favoured by the patrilocal thinking but was not favoured by science. The bottoms fell out in front of nature as science could not conquer the nature as Chandan was blessed with the leg only for 2 days. His body rejected the leg and it was amputated. It was a piece of dead flesh for Chandan which could have provided a new identity to Tara, but she became a mute victim of the unethical working of the society.

The play is a strong reflection of a patriarchal society with male domination in a family. The role of grandfather of Chandan and Tara is biased towards Chandan, he even donates all his properties and wealth to him. This simple narrative highlights the subordinate role of women in Indian society where even in the developed modern world, the cultural traditions and the caste system don't allow a female to lead a normal life. It also lays emphasis upon the issue of a child being marginalized because of disability. It raises the issue that a female with disabled body is supposed to be dependent, incomplete, vulnerable, and incompetent bodies. Femininity and race are the performance of disability. Dattani's used representation of physical disability as a metaphorical device to question society which isolates women. Society neglects the idea that men and women are two faces of same coin; one's existence is void without the absence of other. It also talks about disability as means of marginalization. The disabled people have been marginalized as a result of their proliferation and the fundamental questions of difference from a more universal perspective. The play goes in flashback where Chandan is reminiscing his childhood days with Tara while penning down his autobiography. He has settled in London with the guilt after the death of his sister and knowing the truth about their immoral surgery. He was disheartened as Tara could not survive after knowing the truth from her mother. The play portrays the camaraderie between the sibling in the lines "we celebrated one life in one womb till we were forced out-separated." (Tara, 3) Chandan even believes that Tara will be more successful as a business woman.

The play focused upon the deep-rooted gender discrimination which gives the glimpse of the famous prose "Judith Shakespeare" by Virginia Woolf. Judith Shakespeare is a fictional sister of Shakespeare created by Woolf to address the disparity created by the structure of the society. Even though being equally talented, she becomes the victim of atrocities because of her physiological difference from her brother. Woolf explains "I think, is a woman in Shakespeare's day had Shakespeare's genius, But I agree with the deceased bishop, if such he was, it is unthinkable that any woman should have had Shakespeare's genius." (2015) In a sarcastic way she explains a woman can never enjoy her life with parity to men. Tara experienced the same psychological and existential dilemma like the fictional character Judith Shakespeare, being a girl child, her life was controlled through patriarchy. She was dissuaded from success and equality because she was a woman. Simone de Beauvoir in her text the Second Sex says, "One is not born, rather becomes a woman" and the play has scenes where Tara felt the disparity when their father wishes only Chandan to visit his office and not Tara. Though they both have prosthetic leg but only Tara was made conscious about the impairment of her body. Bharti in her conversation with Chandan asserts "that this planet will accept you but not her." (20) It is not just the story of the protagonist of the play, but it is the story of every girl child born in Indian urban or rural family.

The character of Bharati is the most discussed one as it questioned the role of mother in taking such biased decision regarding the fate of her children. Her character was caged in shackles of patriarchy. Her life and her decisions were controlled by her father and her husband. It is relevant in a sarcastic assertion by Tara "that the men of the house were deciding whether they go for hunting, while the women looked after the cave." (Tara, 6) this statement clearly depicts the sexual depiction of labour. Men are stereotyped for accommodating works related to step outside home, whereas women were confined within the four walls. Women are suppressed in a way that a mother has no prerogative in taking correct decision for children in her womb. Unintentionally, Bharti becomes the enemy of her own child Tara. Throughout the play, she is depicted as a loving and caring mother, extra thoughtful towards Tara, but as the story unfolds, it is revealed that it is only her guilt which she is covering through her care and love. The way she tries to overprotect her daughter and how she literally pleads to Roopa to be friends with Tara, the way she argues for Tara to her husband can be seen more as an act of self-love to escape the ghost of her own mistakes rather than a sign of motherly love and care.

Tara, the central character of the play, is shown dead in the beginning of the play and her brother presents her character in retrospect. Tara is a confident young girl full of aspirations without any social stigmas and sense of inferiority due to her prosthetic leg. She very confidently displays it to her friends that it is of best quality made of wood from Jaipur. Society should accept especially abled people with open heart hegemonic masculinity which tends to avoid physical display of power. When Roopa (their neighbour) teases Chandan and Tara for deformity of having prosthetic leg, Tara adamantly gives her befitting reply that she does not own sympathies for others that nobody has ever bothered to offer her. She is more intelligent than Chandan, but her father was more concerned about Chandan's career than Tara's. Tara is a loving daughter and sister; she is emotionally attached to her mother. Her faith is shattered when the truth is unveiled regarding the unfair operation. Tara had the attributes of her name. She was bright, full of light and can easily outshine her brother Chandan if provided her equal opportunities. She was an innocent soul; her dreams were crushed under the burden of evils of society.

Chandan as a young boy was introvert. He was more into writing rather than making new friends unlike Tara. Though he is less social but has the ability in understanding people. Chandan is emotional towards Tara who knows her sister in and out. His feelings are revealed in his solitude while thinking about his childhood and Tara. Having a prosthetic leg, there was some sense of shame which reflected through Chandan's hatred for hospitals and his general aversion for claustrophobic spaces which constantly reminds him of an institutionalized structure that gives visibility to his disability. After the death of his sister, Chandan went to London to escape from the guilt because of unfair treatment towards Tara. But he could not escape from the psychological and existential conflicts of his mind. He was unaware about the nefarious acts of his family who were desperate to separate the twins. Chandan was disheartened to know the truth about the surgical operation a decision taken by their family. Apart from physical separation the twins also experienced the mental trauma. In many instances Tara was denied equal rights and became a victim of gender disparity when their father, patel only considered the higher education of Chandan. Chandan's anxiety is visible through the dialogue: "I don't want to go to college alone, without Tara." (45)

"Selections from Stigma" an article by Erving Goffman talks about generalization and social stigma where a society establishes the means of categorizing persons and consciously creates an environment where a disabled person constantly reminded about the impairment as the cause as the social exclusion. Roopa is one such character in the play with a lot of prejudices. She wants Tara to stay away from Prema and Nalini for their lack of English education. Though she is of the same age of Tara and Chandan but she is cunning and rude, she accuses Tara's mother of madness despite all the love Bharati showers upon her. During her argument, she ridicules Tara as the "one legged thing" and declares her friendship as an act of beneficence. She even gets into body shaming at a very emotional moment in the play. The hypocrisy of the society towards the disabled is what Roopa signifies. Bharti persuades Roopa for often visits to their house so that she can provide a company to Tara. In the play, Roopa resonates with a group of people from society that possess power, they are the dominant group, they are blessed with abled bodies and easily make stereotypes and make boundaries for abled and especially abled bodies.

Tara is a play which strongly questions the structure of society, which is patriarchal since ages. It also raises issue of disability among men and women and how they are continuously observed by individuals. The play has often usage of the term freaks for the sibling. The term is usually related to something unusual, differing from the normal. But it arises the next question that who raises the parameters to define what is normal and what is abnormal. It's the common tendency of human being to bifurcate everything between contrasting but mutual categories like virtue and vice; black and white; etc. One is privileged over other on the basis of what it lacks. The major reason for this autonomy of dictating other lies only because of physiological difference. This bifurcation has created dominant category being at the centre while marginalizing the minority section at the periphery. This binary is visible between patriarchal ideologies controlling the patriarchal one. Same is applicable to the larger section of abled body stigmatizing and excluding the especially abled people. Such beliefs had reverberations about victimizing disabled people at different levels and to captivate them within the socially constructed model. Lerita M. Coleman states about the stigma and dilemma related to it as:

> the sense of being stigmatized or having a stigma is inextricably tied to social context. Of equal importance are the norms in that context that determine which are desirable and undesirable attributes. Moving from one social or cultural context to another can change both the definitions and the consequences of stigma. Stigma often results in a special kind of downward mobility. Part of the power of stigmatization lies in the realization that people who are stigmatized or acquire a stigma lose their place in the social hierarchy. Consequently, most people want to ensure that they are counted in the non-stigmatized "majority." This, of course, leads to more stigmatization. (Coleman, 2006)

Mahesh Dattani's Tara is an emotional play, agitating serious issues which are often suppressed because of shame and exclusion. The play written with Indian context very well portrays the unsympathetic society. The physiological changes between the man and woman have sprouted atrocities towards women belonging to every group. The play is a story about two siblings both having prosthetic leg, ready to fight against the prejudices and stigmas, but Tara being a girl becomes the victim of this social system, which controls the minds and actions of the people. Tara a beautiful soul becomes the victim of the misogynistic society. The society refrains to accept her for her sexualities and disabilities.

Mahesh Dattani ushered social content in his writings to modify conventional society amid modernity. Using literary manoeuvres, he made his writings a weapon to end disparities towards people for a social challenge. The plurality of literature reflected various traditions, customs and history. Realizing the need to normalize disability, his literary works made an attempt to confront with the conventional people with a zeal to reform people of their society. Dattani's works contributed as revolutionary literature endeavoured in bringing a transition and transformation of a society with rising of literature from all regions of the country. Voicing for an egalitarian society, Tara as a play also explored disability not as an isolated category of difference but as one that is inevitably interlinked to differences based on gender, caste, religion, class, sexuality, and geography.

Though government and non-government organizations provided various programmes to provide equal platform to disabled women; people with any form of disability face various barriers within their home and also in institutional and societal settings. With lack of inclusion, their abilities are neglected without rendering equal opportunities. Inclusive educational programmes had been initiated to increase the literacy ratio among disabled women. Tara as a play reflects the age-old perception of society towards women and differently abled people. It questions some important yet overlooked issues of the society like why people with disability have to confront with their psychic and society for their acceptance? The answer lies in the various barriers which obstruct gifted-people and specifically women from education and progress.

The negative attitude of society is the biggest barrier towards the inclusion of disabled women in social activities. Non-disabled people often experienced negative behaviour, gaze, bullying, exclusion towards the impairment. People from every corner whisper regarding disability as the consequences for sins or punishment. Rohwerder render a common behaviour from folk considering disability as "a punishment for past sins, misfortune or witchcraft." (Rohwerder, 2015) Another attitude of individuals is based on the gender roles, as the theme of the play, girls are expected to be expertise in household works and so they are refrained from education and schooling as compared to boys. Since stigma is inevitable with disability, women with disabilities are seen as a curse leading to their social exclusion. In this light, an imperative aspect for discussion is the change of attitudes of society towards the gifted-people. The ethics of care approach should be inculcated among every human being towards other souls. Defining human beings as a social animal, living in a community each and every individual requires care from other to live. Whether abled or disabled people require each other helping hand in need of hour. It is essential to give a thought towards our behaviour, to consider the importance of sympathy and empathy. Many influential Intelligentsia like Annettte Baier, Nel Noddings, E. K.

Kittay contributed regarding the importance of ethics of care and ethics of justice in the domain of disability theory. They asserted that hitherto theory of ethics was just considered imperative which is related to including marginalized people to render equality and justice. But philosopher Eva Kittay explored and presented the theory of Ethic of Care, which rests upon the individual needs and dependency. As a feminist thinker, she worked towards the status of women with disability. In order to normalize disability, she focused upon dependency which "must be faced from the beginning of any project in egalitarian theory that hopes to include all persons within its scope" (Kittay, 10).

To conclude, this paper highlights an important aspect about women being controlled by patriarchal society. This paper is an empathetical endeavour to explore the role of literature, revolutionary writers, and social thinker towards the marginalized section of disabled women. People with special need and more specifically women are excluded and hidden from society, and they are not provided equal opportunities which cause immense psychological and existential dilemma. Eva Kittay in her article mentions that "dependancy is created among disabled people, not because of the effects of the functional limitations on their capacities for self-care, but because their life is shaped by economic, political and social forces." It is pertinent to end this approach and In order to enhance the moral status of gifted-people, it is vital to normalize the idea of disabled body. Society needs to rethink about their idea of excluding people on the grounds of gender, disability, or any other man-made thresholds. Susan Wendell presents her views that "the disabled are made the 'other' who symbolize failure of control and the threat of pain, dependancy and death." She expects that there is a need to acquire a more humanitarian line of thought to make it a better place where every life matters.

References

Beauvoir, S. D. (1974). *The second sex*. Division of Random House.

Das, B. K. (2008). *Form and meaning in Mahesh Dattani's plays*. Atlantic.

Dattani, M. (2000). *Collected plays*. Penguin Books.

Fine, M., & Asch, A. (Eds.). (1988). *Women with disabilities: Essays in psychology, culture and politics*. Temple University Press.

Kittay, E. (2011). *The ethics of care: Personal, political and global*. Oxford University Press.

Meekosha, H. (2004). *Gender and disability*. http://disability-studies.leeds.ac.uk/

Rousso, H. (2003). *Education for all: A gender and disability perspective*.

Wendell, S. (2006). *Toward a feminist theory of disability: Essays in the disability studies reader*. Routledge.

Woolf, V. (2015). Judith Shakespeare. In S. Z. H. Abidi (Ed.), *The cactus and the rose* (pp. 152–155). Macmillan.

Chapter 15
Disability and Gender Interface in Dattani's *Tara*

Ankur Konar

Abstract In a circular dynamic conceptualization, Mary Lloyd in *Beyond Identity Politics: Feminism, Power and Politics* (2005) negotiates the prevalent trope of biological body in our ideological society: "Challenging the formulation that 'biology is destiny', feminists proposed the alternative view that sex is natural, grounded in biological body, whereas gender is cultural." (133) Functionally, ideology provides a system that wants to hide the prevalent social lack by filling it with an apparent impression of closure.

In a circular dynamic conceptualization, Mary Lloyd in *Beyond Identity Politics: Feminism, Power and Politics* (2005) negotiates the prevalent trope of biological body in our ideological society: "Challenging the formulation that 'biology is destiny', feminists proposed the alternative view that sex is natural, grounded in biological body, whereas gender is cultural." (133) Functionally, ideology provides a system that wants to hide the prevalent social lack by filling it with an apparent impression of closure. Mahesh Dattani's drama *Tara* (1995), as this article will try to show by using the parameters of disability studies, is the most unified and concentrated expression of biological discrimination in our society that is basically guided by some parochial ideologies. The text, basically dealt with the allotropic state of human biology, projects how the consciousness of human biology ultimately leads to the formation of individual human psychology in his/her own concomitant 'ideological space' (Steele 89) through the baffling variety of prevalent social attitudes. Vis-a-vis the new compelling emergence of different debates over disability studies, what is striking to point out, is the dominance of the engaging relationship between biology and culture. Such critical engagement, as Simi Linton in her oft-cited book titled *Claiming Disability: Knowledge and Identity* (1998) observes, is obviously accentuated to several "social and political circumstances" (4). As the paradigms of disability cannot be formulated in an isolated critical juncture, disability studies, being heavily interdisciplinary and transdisciplinary in nature, will make a literary

A. Konar (✉)
Sir Rashbehari Ghosh Mahavidyalaya, University of Burdwan, Bardhaman, West Bengal, India
e-mail: ankrknr@gmail.com

R. Uniyal and F. Rizvi (eds.), *Understanding Disability*,
https://doi.org/10.1007/978-981-99-4925-0_15

investigation of Dattani's *Tara* by formulating an interconnected link with other parameters like gender, sex, and patriarchy. This article is an attempt to engage with those valuable 'social and political circumstances' when the critical issues related to disability and gender interface each other in the Indian context.

Through a reconfiguration of the prevalent social ideology, Professor G. J. V. Prasad in his article titled "Terrifying Tara" (2007) reads the play as a product of "injustices done in the name of construction of gender identities – this hierarchisation and demarcation of roles as much harm to men as to women" (Multani 141). In fact, the text does dramatize the pedagogic principle of social structures and interrogatory stance of ideological strictures regarding physical disability. The reference to Dr. Umakant Thakkar as having a God-like presence indicates that this supreme master of human biology is an immense controlling force of the play. One should mark how he boasts from his own ideologically airtight situation: "Yes, absolutely, surgery was their only chance of survival. You see they were twins, conjoined from the chest down" (Dattani 331). Biological transplantation is a necessary action for a human body during crisis, and to overcome it, the mechanical conformity of biological science begins. By involving in an ineradicable ideological conspiracy with Tara's mother and Tara's maternal grandfather, Thakkar, the inspirational 'God' and a mathematical liar, has made the biological entity of Tara very critical. By snatching away Tara's leg and giving it to Chandan through the commissioned operation, Dr Thakkar along with Bharati's 'wealthy' father puts Tara in a crisis point of the biological ladder just to be looked at, to be laughed at. Tara's being 'one-legged' proved to be a self-justifying fact of what Linton in the above-mentioned book titled *Claiming Disability: Knowledge and Identity* (1998) promotes for "refusing the medicalization of disability" (2). Interestingly, Thakkar, the assumed master of biology, made no protest at this filthy biological discrimination of society. The ideological grip of the society is so loose that a doctor can easily vote for a male child negating the biological right of the female one. This is obviously a heinous act that ruthlessly promotes a blatant sense of gender discrimination. From his own ideological standpoint, Thakkar can claim the possibility of biological operation, not the possibility of emotional separation; bodily dissociation does not affect the emotional association of Tara and Chandan:

TARA. And me. May be we still are. Like we've always been. Inseparable. The way we started in life. Two lives and one body, in one comfortable womb. Till we are forced out... (Dattani 325)

The obvious outcome of the 'forced out' process is a drastic psychological breakdown of the character concerned. By standing in a different direction, emotional breakdown of Tara or Chandan may be overcome by a strong productive relationship full with fellow-feeling and sympathetic bonding with each other. By making an ideologically fruitful relationship, the ending of the drama invites the readers to go beyond the physical world and to take part in the world of esemplastic imagination offered by Chandan who, being a writer, wants a drastic emotional rapport with Tara through a fulcrum of relationship in a trope of biological and ideological synergy. In the two impeccably researched works on the field of disability studies—Lennard J. Davis' *Bending over Backwards: Disability, Dismodernism and Other Difficult*

Positions (2002) and Alice Hall's *Literature and Disability* (2016), what has been emphasized on is that there should have been a formation of collective bonding among the disabled people so that a growing sense of self-fashioning mode of identity formation could be outreached. Such proposed notion of group activity among disabled people marked by a synergetic mode is prevalent in Dattani's text when the readers are presented the dream world of Tara and Chandan and the unification of their sensibilities.

Even the historical representation of or reference to the 'Patels' for their notorious biologically biased approach of infanticide marks how the intersectional approaches to women and disability interface each other and form the crux of Dattani's drama. Roopa mentions the historical past when innate biology becomes the ideological deciding factor of the brand new discrepancy: "The Patels in the old days were unhappy with getting girl babies – you know dowry and things like that – so they used to drown them in milk." (Dattani 349) Similar to such a biological fatal spin, A. K. Ramanuj, in his short story "In a Lost Love's Turning" (1997), portrays the abandoning of the biologically disabled—the limbless boy by his family right after his birth. As far as the historical representation is concerned in Dattani's drama, Patels, being heavily biologically biased, promote what Linton in *Claiming Disability: Knowledge and Identity* (1998) terms the essentialization of 'devalued' and 'discriminated' forces attached to disability. Allied with the modality of gender discrimination, the Patels cannot resist the growth of an ideological "dowry" system, but can resist the substantial growth of a female body by drowning her into milk. Hence, 'she' becomes the other, the marginalized, and the disabled. Now one must take it for granted what K. Sangari and S. Vaid in their Introduction to *Recasting Women: Essays in Colonial History* (2006) assert that 'historiography', with obviousness, 'acknowledges' that "each aspect of reality is gendered" (2). From cradle to grave, female figures are put under the towering shadow of gendered ideology which is, to use Amy Vidali's phrase, embedded with 'disability metaphor' (51).

The attempt of Chandan to take possession of Roopa's body is a clear case of biological attraction: "He cannot ignore her now. He slowly puts his hand on her shoulder. She freezes. He very awkwardly moves his hand till it is almost on her breast. The music ends." (Dattani 366) Chandan is the victim of an infatuated biological passion through the warped pseudo-sexual violence. Since Chandan wants to sexually 'play' with her body, Roopa accuses him to be an ideological and virtual 'rapist'. On the other hand, Roopa may ideologically pretend to be innocent in the litany of passion, but emotionally she too is interested in that biological game. As rightly pointed out by Tara: "So how does it feel having one tit smaller that the other?" (Dattani 369) Biological aberration betrays Roopa in her projected picture of 'entanglement', in spite of her disclaimer. She may point out the biological disability/abnormality by calling Tara 'one-legged thing', but cannot suppress her own biological 'imbecile' standpoint that needs an immediate ideological correction. As Tara fumes in fury with the smug rhetoric of disability: "I'd sooner be one-eyed, one-armed and one-legged than be an imbecile like you. And imbecile with uneven tits." (Dattani 369) The limitations of biology become crucial to determine the ideological moral standpoint of the characters; for one, the body is a taboo to fulfil the biological desire; for the other, the body is the curse to endure the evils of disabled body. Having a 'natural' biological standpoint, Roopa may smash the colourful flower of friendship and verbally call Tara a 'freak' for the latter's disabled bodily configurations; ironically enough, she pretends to play the role of a mutual friend of Tara at Bharati's bribe to be 'her best friend'. It is very natural that, after a certain time, body-related disability of Tara will definitely become an amusement for Roopa and her other friends that captures the ideological strategy of pseudo-bonhomie and apparent camaraderie. Roopa sticks disturbing posters full with cruel notes and makes a mockery of Tara's physical disability: "We don't want freaks." (Dattani 378) Through her ideological apprehension of biology, she may manufacture the consent of Nalini and Prema by pointing out that Tara "is a real freak of nature", but readers/audiences do not want the 'ugliest girls'. One-legged Tara is always better than dull, insipid, and parochial Roopa; if Tara is biologically a freak, Roopa is ideologically, and if Tara is biologically aberrant, Roopa is psychologically. On an engaging relationship between disability and subsequent responses from society, Roopa acts like an unsocial beast who cannot understand that in our society, 'I' necessarily presupposes a 'we' and that similar ideological (not individual) struggle definitely gives meaning to our social life; otherwise, the recurrence of 'rape' and the consequent horror of 'rape' will be immense.

The conceptualization of the gendered notion of family space is, quite automatically, tantamount to severe ideological discrimination in the domestic field. As Tara and Chandan are biologically different, Tara, though has a smarter approach, will be confined to the domestic boundary and Chandan who is basically homesick and highly inward in nature will have to 'perform' in the public world. Patel always forces Chandan to join his workspace 'to come to the office'; but Chandan is too cold and too shy to respond the invitation; he is trying to be a writer by confining himself within the four walls of the family. When he is seen indulging in the sewing process along with his mother, Patel is equally critical of Bharati and Chandan; involvement in the activities like sewing or knitting by Chandan does not go with the spirit of patriarchal gender construction because he is biologically a male member of the family and should have a concern for what is a male's cup of tea; "iron and saucepans" are always "the eternal flaming racket of the female".[1] Even Bharati always remains "in the kitchen, where else?" (Dattani 334) Patel has a dream of sending Chandan in a foreign academic institution for higher studies; as Patel is more worried about Chandan's career than Tara's, he has already arranged for that through Chandan's Praful uncle. Interestingly, there are no future 'plans' for Tara who is expected to be satisfied within the given, within the supplied, and within the scripted. The argument of Nivedita Menon is critically apt when she observes: "The fact that men and women perform different kinds of work both within the family and outside has little to do with biology and more to do with ideological assumptions" (Bhargava and Acharya 226). Such 'ideological assumptions' posit Tara in the zone of disability in spite of having the potentiality to act in the public sphere. Thus, women, in any patriarchal society, are being disabled through the assigned allocation of the conflicting public/private sphere. Tara who is not timid and who has psychological patterning of impulses has every possibility to be a good businessman as Chandan thinks: "You can take Tara.

She'll make a great business woman." (Dattani 328) In spite of such logic, Tara will not be allowed to cross the domestic space and to take part in public affairs. Domestic space is expected to be Tara's world, and consequently, she should maintain the norm and that patriarchal norm is well scripted in Dattani's text: "The men in the house were deciding on whether they were going to go hunting while the women looked after the cave." (328) Indeed, ironically, she is a 'freak' because she has the courage to mock the traditional ideology of a static society. The strategic interrogation of prevalent ideology and the contemporary ideological fissures decode the objectification of patriarchal proliferation to put the female members in an enclosed space. The patriarchal ideology that has faithfully been based on that biological discrimination through tipsy contentment glamorizes the male who is basically 'higher' and 'abled' and deglamorizes the female who is ontologically 'lower' and 'disabled'. In any patriarchal society that is habituated to promote a model of 'abled'/'disabled' body through gender connotation, a male can easily have the 'higher' professional dream, but a female can dream nothing by strictly remaining in the 'lower' domestic space; ceased professional space and assigned family space should be the world for Tara because the patriarchal ideology measures women to be professionally invalid and disabled; their relevant validity/ability has only been restricted within the domestic level. Thus, patriarchy, by defining the performance space, polishes the dynamic relation between "classes and dominant ideologies" (Sangari and Vaid 5) according to its constructed gendered whims. Patels, as far as the historical reference is concerned in Dattani's text, were ideologically notorious for female infanticide, and the present representation of the Patels is a variation on that notoriety as they will continue to treat Tara as having a disabled identity vis-à-vis performance and profession in the public world. Dattani's text, by presenting the slender representation of the female figures, is a critique of that biological discrimination through ideological rituals, ceremonies, anticipations, and cultural constructs. It is not Tara or Chandan, but the stagnant society that is terribly suffering from the emotional and intellectual paralysis needs an immediate healing from the patriarchal piffle.

Readers can easily assume that the target of the medical journal is Tara's biology—her biological sense and sensibility. Bharati fumes in fury with argumentative standpoint because she fears the ideological investment of the power in print: "I don't want my children being mentioned in any medical journal." (Dattani 326) According to her, Tara's bodily disability should not be universalized by publishing it in a journal but should strictly be hidden by restricting it within the domestic walls of Patel family. In fact, she wants to make a sordid, hidden reality of Tara's case. At this level, biology becomes the ideological fissure and that textuality of disability becomes the essence of Dattani's play. Though Dattani's text is just one step behind from Frances Fukuyama's *The Post-Human/Our Post-Human Future* (2003) that projects the realization of the revolutionary biologists, arguing a proper biological apprehension of human necessity that will resist the growth of posthuman biotechnology, the critics of disability studies like Sim Linton prefer in "refusing the medicalization of disability" (2) as the medical world (represented by Dr. Thakkar and Dr. Kapoor) has the heinous tendency to treat disabled people as essentially damaged. Emphasizing the imaginative recovery, Tara intends that Chandan will write stories about her and those stories will be full of adjectives like 'strong', 'healthy', and 'beautiful', and such positive vibrations from Tara attempt to make a drastic rejection of so-long-projected sense of disability; such organic pulsation of life and corporeal vitality is the ideological dream of Tara to be biologically 'beautiful', spiritedly 'healthy', and sufficiently 'strong'. At this critical juncture, it would be relevant to refer to Sharon Snyder's argument in the essay titled "Infinities of Forms: Disability Figures and Artistic Traditions" which talks of the resignification of disabled bodies: "Disability experiences led to literary achievement, not as mere compensation for physical differences but as necessary re-signification of their bodies in the social register of art." (178) In spite of having extreme physical weakness, Tara can dream of such elevated thoughts. But at certain times, she, through a sudden ideological transformation, no longer wants to exist in reality but tries to take shelter in fantasy because biological disability rouses a tremendous 'embarrassing' (335) strain on her mind; readers who are acquainted with D. H. Lawrence's novels can map Tara's desperate craving for a healing 'release'[2]; the psychological bitterness edged with a disabled body leads to a momentous craving for desperate dissociation from this crude world that can offer no solace but can propagate its own brutalizing indecency. Vis-à-vis such emotional crisis and mental fragility Tara can easily be equated with another sister of American English literature—Laura in the American dramatist Tennessee Williams' *The Glass Menagerie* (1944). Even at many levels, Dattani's text can be read as a variation of *The Glass Menagerie*, not contextually, but thematically. Through the sloppy behaviour of an ideologically perverted society, Tara's biological disfiguration becomes her existential *cul de sac*. She is psychologically strong to resist any weakness related to her disabled body ["I am strong. My mother has made me strong" (Dattani 330)], but the cruel society will repeatedly focus on the visual sense of her biological abnormality. Due to society's ideological adversity to her disabled body, she is ultimately devalued, devastated, and demobilized: "This isn't fair to Tara. She deserves something better. She never got a fair deal. Not even from nature. Neither of us did." (Dattani 330)

Bharati is concerned with her biological strength, having an ideological intention of donating: "Why? What is wrong if ... Why can't she have mine?" (Dattani 343) The constant guilty feeling for any previous misdeed is looming large in her statement. One doubts that whether her showing of excessive love for Tara comes out for real intention! In the aporetic activity, Patel's additional slapping of Bharati in response to the latter's extreme frenzy is a cult biological/physical subjugation, a demonic projection of divisional despair. Is that an evocation of ideological maleness resulting from the assumed biological superiority? In fact, the syncretic representations of different ideological standpoints immensely affect the conjugal relationship of Patel and Bharati in their barbarous world of ego-centric predicament. Taking recourse in Roger Luckhurst's essay "Mixing Memory and Desire: Psychoanalysis, Psychology, and Trauma Theory", Bharati can easily be categorized as a traumatic patient because of her 'retrospective transformation' due to the sense of 'belatedness about responses' (Waugh 501). The text repeatedly throws light on the biological discrimination of human beings through the oppositional and relational grid of difference. Even the biological abnormality of Chandan becomes a subject of instrumentality to be looked at with a touch of a radical alteration of 'fatal attraction':

TARA. Hurt? Embrassed? Not at all. You can say it sort of 'runs' in the family—this leg.

Chandu—show you yours.

Chandu proudly shows his Jaipur legs to her. (Dattani 336)

The immense intention to play with the clay is an interesting game in our hegemonic society. The process of stereotyping is an intrinsic necessity for an ideologically osmotic society. Simi Linton's proposition in *Claiming Disability: Knowledge and Identity* (1998) that the disabled people should have a group identity so that they can have voices of their own as well as spaces of their own sound convincing in the present context of Dattani's text.

The following confessional statement of Patel is a rave revelation of the totem force of biological discrimination in a multitudinal ideological society:

Your grandfather and your mother had a private meeting with Dr. Thakkar. I wasn't asked to come … they would risk giving both legs to the boy … As planned by them, Chandan had two legs – for two days … what a grave mistake they had made. The leg was amputated. A piece of dead flesh which could have – might have – been Tara. (Dattani 378)

The referential and representational dynamics along with the mighty memories of the characters reflected in the above statement unleash the exploration of exploitation. It is shocking that ideological social stratification is prevalent right from the embryonic form of human beings. Superimposed clandestine activities of patriarchal groupings through figures like Bharati and her father bring out the non-egalitarian social structure of a biological discrimination which may be categorized as a dominant issue in the prevailing discourses of disability studies. Dattani's text projects the crystallization of a biological proposition of disability that interfaces gender discrimination during child-rearing. Probably, Tara is a disabled 'performative' dancer due to her mother's humdrum ideological standpoint in the bearing of children.[3] Dattani uses all the 'mainstream ideologies' to subtly hint that the normative structure of our society definitely needs 'freaks' to escape from the insularity of some stagnant ideologies.[4] Truly, regenerative revival is being relocated in the register of reasonable reformation through the language of Chandan: "It's all the same. You. Me. There's no difference." (Dattani 361) This is how the notions of disability and sexuality are strategically constructed by various sociopolitical forces and the attitudinal problems of common men need the politics of changeability to resist the further growth of the "wretched treatment of disabled people over history" (Cassuto 219). The narrated spaces of Dattani's *Tara* through cornucopia of stories discussed above become potential sites where the unpredictable flows and responses of human life vis-à-vis the physical disability of the characters concerned have been inextricably woven together to denote the critical rubrics of art, disability and gender, and their feasible nexus in representing an Indian context.

Notes

1. John Osborne's phrase in his 1956 play *Look Back in Anger*.
2. *Sons and Lovers* (1913).
3. Readers who are acquainted with British literature can easily remember the pathetic episode of great grandmother's amputation in Charles Lamb's celebrated personal essay "Dream Children: A Reverie".
4. Angelie Multani in her article "The Page and the Stage: The Representation of Women in Two Plays by Mahesh Dattani" (2004) rightly observes: "One of Dattani's strategies is clearly to lull readers/audiences into identifying with the characters and milieu of his plays. In order to do this, he openly subscribes to all the mainstream ideologies, at one level, while using the individual characters to subtly undercut those very ideologies." (Panja et al. 246)

Bibliography

Bhargava, R., & Acharya, A. (Eds.). (2008). *Political theory: An introduction*. Pearson Longman.

Cassuto, L. (2010). Disability studies 2.0. *American Literary History, 22*(1), 218–231.

Dattani, M. (2000). *Collected plays*. Penguin.

Davidson, M. (2016). Cripping consensus: Disability studies at the intersection. *American Literary History, 28*(2), 433–453.

Davis, L. J. (2002). *Bending over backwards: Disability, dismodernism & other difficult positions*. New York University Press.

Fukuyama, F. (2003). *The post-human/our post-human future*. Picador.

Hall, A. (2016). *Literature and disability*. Routledge.

Linton, S. (1998). *Claiming disability: Knowledge and identity*. New York University Press.

Lloyd, M. (2005). *Beyond identity politics: Feminism, power and politics*. Sage.

Multani, A. (Ed.). (2007). *Mahesh Dattani's plays: Critical perspectives*. Pencraft International.

Panja, S., et al. (Eds.). (2004). *Signifying the self: Women and literature*. Macmillan.

Ramanuj, A. K. (1997). *The green gardener*. Orient Longman.

Sangari, K., & Vaid, S. (Eds.). (2006). *Recasting women: Essays in colonial history*. Kali for Woman.

Snyder, S. (2002). Infinities of forms: Disability figures and artistic traditions. In S. L. Snyder, B. J. Brueggemann, & R. Garland-Thomson (Eds.), *Disability studies: Enabling the humanities* (pp. 173–196). The Modern Language Association.

Steele, M. (1997). *Theorizing textual subjects: Agency and oppression*. Cambridge University Press.

Vidali, A. (2010). Seeing what we know: Disability and theories of metaphor. *Journal of Literary and Cultural Disability Studies, 4*(1), 33–54.

Waugh, P. (Ed.). (2006). *Literary theory and criticism*. Oxford University Press.

Part III
Dealing with Disability

Chapter 16
People of Determination—Making Achievements, Overcoming Challenges

Pranita Lele

Abstract This paper traces *religious scriptural, historical, mythical conceptualization, and practice of disability with special focus on UAE*. There are a many studies concerning the role of religion, culture, history, and beliefs in sustaining or removing discriminatory practices against persons with disabilities. Drawing on various historical references, resources, and research on disability, this paper looks at the practices which sustain or reject these discriminatory practices. *The Puranas, Garbha Upanishads, Panchatantra, Yoga Sutras of Patanjali, and other religious texts* use stories to comprehend the realities of life and reflect how the attitude towards disability is deeply embedded in cultural order. The meaning of dichotomy between normal and disabled is conveyed through cultural symbols. The paper also looks into the *historical perspective and how the kingdoms of ancient and Medieval India dealt with disability*. It further raises the question that given such cultural and religious contexts, what went wrong? How have we become so insensitive to the condition of the disabled? The humane model that we have forgotten seems to have been adopted by the UAE. The paper makes *in-depth study of the steps taken by His Highness Sheikh Mohammed bin Rashid Al Maktoum, Vice-President and Prime Minister of the UAE and Ruler of Dubai*, who launched a National Strategy for Empowering People with Disabilities. There are *six pillars of national policy and eight tenets of the retreat* which was held in March 2019 in Abu Dhabi, as part of the nationwide efforts to mobilize resources in support of the people of determination. The examination of these practices lends some significant weight and substance to the social model of disability, which construes disability in the context of oppression and the failure of social environments and structures to adjust to the needs and aspirations of people with disabilities. It is essential to know how the perception of 'people with disability' changes to 'People with Determination' when political will is strong. The paper makes a *comparative study between the steps taken for the disabled in India and in the UAE*. Strong will of the government needs to push through legislation that targets cultural and religious practices which are discriminatory as well as undertake effective measures aimed at protecting the 'people of determination'.

P. Lele (✉)
Indian Institute of Chartered Accountants, Dubai Chapter, Dubai, UAE
e-mail: pranitalele@gmail.com

R. Uniyal and F. Rizvi (eds.), *Understanding Disability*,
https://doi.org/10.1007/978-981-99-4925-0_16

Disability Statistics Matter

When we compare disability statistics with other areas of statistics such as labour force, gender, and education, we find disability statistics is highly underdeveloped and unutilized. It is only very recently that governments have begun to recognize the significance and urgency of such statistics for development of better policies and program.

Statistical figures show that almost 16% of the world's population has some form of disability. What needs to be noted is that disability prevalence is higher for developing countries. When converted to absolute figures, we have almost 1.3 billion people in the world who are disabled. This is more than one-fifth of the world's population, and it is alarming.

Disability statistics can provide extensive information on the experience of persons with disabilities. Any government policy without valid and reliable data and without any basis of evidence is a very costly exercise and can prove to be a wasteful conjecture and hypothesis. Lack of data and statistics can create major obstacles to planning and implementation of programs for people with disability. Lack of statistics is a major contributor to the invisibility of persons with disabilities.

Not Disabled, Just Differently Abled

People who are physically or mentally 'impaired' are termed as 'disabled'. Unfortunately, our society is built in a manner that does not cater to their needs. We recognized the rights of the backward sections of the society immediately after independence. We recognized the rights of the women, but the rights of the disabled have been recognized only very recently. One of the leading activists and scholars of disability in the Indian context, Anita Ghai, has always argued that the disabled in our society are invisible to the people and this invisibility of the disabled should be removed. Through her writings, she has constantly questioned the society that why people refuse to acknowledge their presence.

It is important to question the term 'disabled'. People's perception of disability all over the world is flawed. There are some common characteristics and traits which are central to the public perception of 'disability'. Disability is understood as a biological given. It is taken for granted that all problems of a disabled person are because of her/his impairment. They are perceived to be always in need of help. Why should the society view disabled people as 'Victims'? Professor Stephen W Hawking's through his marvellous work in the field of astrophysics has proven that despite having motor neuron problems, he did lot let it come in the way of his success. There is a vast potential of people with disabilities that needs to be unlocked. We will face more problems with disability in the years to come as the ageing population rises. It is a well-known fact that as people age, they face chronic health problems. They find it difficult to walk and have many mental health disorders.

To cope with the physical disability, societies develop their characteristic patterns depending on the way disability is understood and their resources then identified. Social construction and understanding of disability are influenced to a great extent by our social institutions. Narratives in history and in various sacred books have shaped our understanding of disability. Unfortunately, some of these narratives have worked like obstacles in the upliftment of the people with disability. Instead of improving the quality of their life, they have acted as great obstacles.

Ancient India and Disability—Constructing Disabilities Through Narratives of Sacred Texts and Mythologies

Our religious texts narrate stories that reflect the attitude of the society towards disability. These narratives are deeply embedded in our cultural order. We have various cultural symbols that show us the dichotomy between normal and disabled. We must look into the ancient India's perspective of disability.

Inclusive education can be traced back to the Vedic Era. Veda means 'to know'. Vedic education is thought to be almost 5000 years old. Out of the four Vedas, Rig Veda has the earliest recorded system of education. We can trace various practices of learning in Rig Veda. During this period, there was a system of Gurukuls. Students left their homes and stayed with their "guru" or teacher. They would learn by tenets, doctrines, and precepts and would also gain knowledge through actual practical studies and debates. In this ancient Vedic system of education, all children were taught together. During this period, we do not find any references for special schools catering to learning difficulties or any other forms of disabilities. The teacher did not distinguish between the students. They were not categorized as normal, gifted, talented, or physically or intellectually disabled. Students were taught according to their abilities. Those who were not good in academic learning had options to learn other occupations. Thus, they would get an opportunity to be usefully employed. Educated were not considered higher up in the hierarchy as skilled labourers were given equal importance in society.

We can find a precursor of genetics in Garbha Upanishad which was written way back in 187 BC. It explains how foetal development can be affected right at the time of conception. This Upanishad has explained mental disability. Parent's mental state at the time of conception has a very important role to play in the development of the child. The yoga sutra of Maharishi Patanjali is the most authentic and useful exposition that enhances the 'life you are'. The essential philosophy and technique of yoga have been given in 196 maxims. Patanjali has recommended Yoga Therapy for the disabled persons. He has given us a clear picture of what constitutes the mind, its functions, and its limitations. Yoga Sutras of Patanjali are excellent in controlling the mind and the body. Through the writings of Patanjali, we get to know about five states of mind—Mudha (the dull), Kshipta (distracted), Vikshipta (partially distracted), Ekagrata (concentration and focus), and Niruddha (controlled). Mudha, Kshipta, or

Vikshipta describes the state of mind which does not function properly. In Hinduism, disability has been incorporated into God himself! Several examples can be found in classical Hindu texts. One of the Dasavataram refers to Vishnu's appearance as a dwarf (Vaman Avtar). In the Jataka tales, the Buddha appears as a gifted dwarf. Dhritarashtra, the mighty king of the Kuru Kingdom, was born blind. Ashtavakra, the revered sage, is the Indian archetype of disability. He had multiple disabilities. The name "Ashtavakra" means one with eight different types of deformities in his body. This story is referred to in many ancient texts, including the Mahabharata. Ashtavakra says that instead of focusing on physical disability and deformities, one should focus on the soul. The conversation between Janaka and Ashtavakra, pertaining to the deformity of the body, is an eye-opener. Ancient Hindu scriptures like Manu Smriti which is considered as the ancient charter of social conduct encouraged people to take care of the less fortunate. Bhagavad Gita exhorted people to take care of the needy. Dharmashastra called upon the society to look after the weak and disabled without expectation of any returns. King Dhritarashtra was blind, but blindness was not an obstacle on his taking the topmost authority. It should be pointed out that during the Mahabharata period, the kings were expected to provide livelihood and sustenance to the war disabled and their dependents Surdas the blind bard of devotion has given the best description of childhood way back in the sixteenth century. His unparalleled description of Krishna as a lovable child is given in a folk language, known as Brajbhasa. The description is so beautiful and endearing that even today we see Krishna in every child.

Kingdoms of Ancient and Medieval India and Their Dealings with Disability

Our constitution has given a very clear direction towards dealing with disability. We have a progressive constitution and able judiciary. But still all the directives mentioned in the constitution are not implemented.

The care and compassion for the disabled can be traced back in our history. Kings in Medieval India gainfully employed people with hearing and/or speech impairment. Secrecy of confidential government documents had to be maintained while making copies of it. This work of copying was done by people who had hearing or speech defects. In order to ensure that the conversations and discussions within the palace are not leaked out, the royals preferred to keep hearing and speech impaired people as their attendants. Certain occupations were reserved for the blind. For example, the visually impaired would make flower garlands for domestic and religious purposes. Many visually impaired worked as music teachers and would sing or play musical instruments in the temples.

Chandra Gupta Maurya is credited with the setting up of the first (nearly) pan-Indian empire. He contributed a lot to improve the condition of the disabled. There are historical evidences regarding the workshops established by him for the vocational rehabilitation of people with physical impairments. Nazi Germany followed the policy of discouraging reproduction by persons having genetic defects or having inheritable undesirable traits. This was called Eugenics. They also promoted the horrific Lebensborn policy to increase the birth rate of 'racially sound' babies. Those deemed unfit and disabled were the first victims of the Nazi regime. Such policies were opposed to what India had been following since time immemorial.

In the fourth and fifth C BC, Kautilya, the renowned political economist of the Maurya period and author of Arthashastra laid out clear-cut directives to the state to give maintenance to the disabled and helpless people in the society. He awarded work on priority to women who were widowed, single, crippled, and abandoned. This was to make them self-reliant and economically independent. Verbal and behavioural abuse of persons with disabilities was banned and not tolerated. He recognized their right to property and employment. Emperor Ashoka who was the son of Bindusara and the grandson of Chandragupta is known as 'precocious pioneer of humanitarian values'. His edicts record that the king constructed hospitals along all the highways and built many asylums. Dwarfs were given a special status in the Gupta dynasty, and the coins had figure of the dwarf standing beside the throne of the emperor.

The West has newly discovered the term "inclusive education". But in India, we have the legacy of inclusive education since times immemorial.

According to a legend that goes back to around first century B.C, there was a kingdom named 'Mahilaropya' which had a king named 'Amarshakti'. The king had three sons. Unfortunately, all of them were unintelligent and dim-witted. The king was very worried about the future of his kingdom. He needed someone who could teach his sons. After a nation wide search he found Pandit Vishnusarman who assured to train his sons by developing specific tools and techniques. Vishnusarman developed a special strategy for educating the princes by using a collection of animal fables. Through these fables, the princes learnt about values honoured universally. They also learnt about matters related to diplomacy and administration. The efforts of Vishnusarman resulted in a famous book known as "The Panchatantra" which can be termed as a book on special education. Panchatantra weaves the threads of knowledge, entertainment, analysis, wisdom, creativity, and logical thinking. Panchatantra has been translated in several foreign languages too. The stories have found their way in distant lands of Iran, Iraq, and Syria. Panchatantra translations are greatly enjoyed and have great popularity in Arabic narrative literature.

Given such cultural and religious contexts, what went wrong with our dealings with disability? 'Or was it not 'regular and sustained communication' that 'becomes ingrained in the psyche of the 'common man'. From where do people learn to stigmatize the mentally ill and the handicapped? From where does such insensitivity originate? Today in India, terms such as 'handicap', 'crippled', 'blind', and 'deaf' are used as insults. Any deviation from the 'perfect body' is considered as abnormality and distortion. The victim status of the disabled person is increased by our societal conception. Destiny is seen as the culprit, and disabled people are seen as victims. A concept much broader than corporate social responsibility was given to us thousands of years back in the lines—**“Lokah samasta sukhino Bhavantu”** (**लोकाःसमस्ताःसुखिनोभवन्तु**)—maximum welfare of maximum people.

In India, differently abled were never identified as a separate group, nor were they segregated on this count. Destitute, widows, aged, diseased, and disabled people were put together in our constitution.

Perspective of the Arab World on Disability

Islamic philosophy and culture has a positive approach towards the disadvantaged and the needy individuals. The Qur’an and the Hadith have specifically asked the society to care for disabled people and support them in all possible ways.

The Arabs narrate a lot of stories and anecdotes which are replete with compassion towards the disabled. There is an anecdote that tells about a blind boy who found it difficult to reach the mosque for his daily prayers. The father of the boy was very distressed, and he decided to contact Omar Ibn Al-Khattab, the third Muslim leader. Omar Ibn Al-Khattab was a generous and benevolent person, and he built a house near the mosque for the blind boy. It is a well-known fact in the Arab World that the Umayyad caliph, Al WalidIbnAbd al Malik took several steps like building a special care home and a hospital for intellectually disabled. He did not just stop at building homes and hospitals but he also assigned caregivers for the disabled. So it was not just theoretically but such noble practices were actually implemented in the Arabic societies.

It is interesting to look at the UAE model for the special needs and disabled category. It is essential to know how the perception of ‘people with disability’ changes to ‘People with Determination’ when political will is strong. UAE model can be an eye-opener for many other nations as it reveals how strong will of the government can push through legislation that targets cultural and religious practices which are discriminatory. The government has taken initiatives that build a compassionate, civilized, and humane society, where everyone gets appreciation and respect they deserve and they get the opportunity to reach their full potential, in whichever field they choose.

‘The Determined Ones’—UAE and People of Determination

The United Arab Emirates has painstakingly and earnestly tried to take care of the needs of persons with disabilities right from the time of its foundation on 2 December 1971. It considers the disabled as an integral part of society. They have the same rights as other non-disabled members of society. The UAE refers to people with special needs or disabilities as ‘people of determination’ in recognition of their achievements in different fields.

National Policy for Empowering People with Special Needs

As part of its efforts to bring a comprehensive community development, the UAE Government launched a national policy for empowering special needs people. Under the National Policy for Empowering People with Special Needs, they will be referred to as 'people of determination' to recognize their achievements in different fields. As explained on the Abu Dhabi portal, the law defines a person with special needs as someone suffering from a temporary or permanent, full or partial deficiency or infirmity in his physical, sensory, mental, communication, educational, or psychological abilities to an extent that limits his possibility of performing the ordinary requirements as people without special needs.

The policy aims to create an inclusive society for them and their families, through services and facilities that accommodate their needs.

The UAE Government calls the people with special needs or disabilities as the determined ones. It is such an empowering word to be used for such people. The government has assigned service officers for the determined people who act as facilitators of services. All the government institutions have these officials. A national policy has been made under which an advisory council has been set up to give proper directions for helping the people of determination. Advisory council is a representative body which has eminent members of the society and also several local and federal government members.

The Six Pillars of the National Policy

The government of UAE has a clear-cut national policy for the people of determination which is based on six vital pillars which tries to restore the dignity of the people with disabilities.

1. ***Health and rehabilitation***: Global health practitioners and researchers have always stressed on the importance of providing proper health care and rehabilitation programmes for the people with disability. The government of UAE ensures high-quality health care, as well as rehabilitation programmes for the people of determination. The government spends a huge amount on conducting researches about several hereditary and rare diseases that cause disabilities. Medical examinations are done during pregnancy and postdelivery to check and prevent any disability. The government considers it important that early detection of such cases be done and proper help be provided to such people. Rehabilitating such people gives them required independence and facilitates normalization post accidents, injuries or due to any congenital problems.
2. ***Education***: The government of UAE provides special educators and specialists who are responsible for developing learning materials for people of determination. The government believes in a system that is integrative and does not leave behind these people of determination. High-quality vocational courses

have been developed for such students. The government monitors the school curricula to check if it is adapted where necessary to help the students of determination. Supportive technologies have been developed which assists in training the students.

3. ***Vocational rehabilitation and employment***: The government has created a huge database of people of determination who are seeking employment. After getting them trained vocationally, the government gives them support in finding jobs in government and private institutions.
4. ***Outreach***: In order to meet the needs of the people of determination, UAE has upgraded several old buildings. The schools, healthcare facilities, hotels, mosques, parks and recreational areas, shopping malls, etc., have unified criteria for buildings. Their focus is to take care of the needs of the people of determination. The builders have to be in full compliance of the rules and have to ensure that buildings are easily accessible to people of all the abilities. Buildings are regularly audited to bring about the required changes.
5. ***Social protection and family empowerment***: People with disabilities are always at a greater risk of facing abuse and violence from the society. The government of UAE ensures that the people with special needs are protected and various laws in the country are in accordance with the Convention on the Rights of Persons with Disabilities. A hotline is set up to receive any complaints from the people with special needs.
6. ***Public life, culture, and sports***: It is necessary to integrate the people of determination in the society and make them participate in various cultural, sports, and social activities. The government encourages their participation in various competitions and awareness programmes.

The People of Determination Retreat

The people of determination retreat was held in March 2019, as part of the nationwide efforts to mobilize resources in support of the people of determination (people with special needs). Several Sheikhs, ministers, national figures, people of determination, and social specialists participated in the retreat sessions where 31 initiatives and programmes were approved to support the future of this segment of society and ensure their integration across various sectors.

Eight Tenets of the Retreat

The retreat outlined eight tenets to empower people of determination and facilitate their needs at all levels. They are:

1. ***SPORTS***—The retreat underlined the importance of unleashing the talent of the people of determination across all types of sports while ensuring their active participation in all local and international sports events.

   Special Olympics held in Abu Dhabi in 2019 reflects the trust placed by the entire world in the UAE, being a forward-thinking and multicultural centre of tolerance, faith, and inclusion as well as a favoured destination for sportsmen and creative people.

2. ***QUALITY OF LIFE***—The retreat called for ensuring the empowerment and protection of the people of determination and enabling them to attend key national activities among VIPs, approving an initiative to co-ordinate with a university to endorse a training programme for sign language translators.

   Dubai Municipality is a key player in the drive to improve the quality of life of 'people of determination'. It offers guides in Braille language in all public parks and customer service centres. They are exempted from entry fees in public parks and have specialized physical fitness equipment, in addition to free wheelchairs. Children of determination are offered specialized games in public parks.

   The municipality has also dedicated specially designed counters for 'people of determination' in its service centres and specialized pathways on beaches. Trained staff have been stationed in parks and service centres to communicate using sign language if required. Dedicated car parking and complimentary wheelchairs are also available in Dubai Municipality facilities.

3. ***EDUCATION AND LABOUR***—Various initiatives were taken by the government to bring people of determination in the mainstream education. Special educators developed programmes which involved students of special needs right from kindergarten to the university level. **UAE Disability Act (Federal Law No. 29/2006)** was passed in November 2006, and the government took various initiatives to endorse this act. Some of the commendable initiatives are mentioned as follows:

   Way back in the year 2008, the Ministry of Community Development launched an initiative under the slogan '**School of All**'. It was an initiative to include disabled children in education. It was adopted by the Ministry of Education and was aimed for developing general inclusive education practices. It was a step towards the social integration of the disabled and their involvement in the development process.

   In the year 2008, a slogan was raised in the UAE which gained massive popularity. It was '**Our Life is in Our Integration**'. Under this slogan, a project was launched which was known as '**The National Project for Inclusion of People with Special Needs**', and the project aimed at creating an environment for people of determination to gain access to the educational system. Cutting-edge technology is made available to make life easier for them. Such projects are a step towards building a humane society.

   In the year 2013, another massive project was launched by HH Sheikh Hamdan bin Mohammed bin Rashid Al Maktoum, Crown Prince of Dubai. This exemplary project was known as '**My community... a city for everyone**'; it aimed at engaging the people of determination in a fruitful way in their surroundings.

Social cohesion is considered to be of utmost importance in Dubai. In support of this initiative, Knowledge and Human Development Authority—KHDA launched the **Dubai Inclusive Education Policy Framework**. This framework promotes highly inclusive ethos for students of determination (disabled or people with special needs). Mainstream classrooms adapt their strategies, curriculums, testing, and teaching methods to identify and remove the barriers that restrict achievements of all learners. The framework is applied across Dubai and covers the complete education sector. It begins from early childhood services to primary, secondary, and higher education providers. The regulatory authorities and governing bodies in Dubai have been empowered to closely monitor progress of the students and to check its compliance.

The work does not end just by devising this framework. The government works towards making this inclusion a reality. Several **support centres have been set up by the Ministry of Education** which closely evaluate the progress of people of determination before and after integration in schools.

Several national institutes in the field of disability have been set up throughout the UAE. They are engaged with the people of determination. Such institutes are given annual grants and rewards. Professional training is given to the educators who work in the field of special education.

Financial support is given to low-income families who have children with disabilities. This financial help is given by the Community Development Authority (CDA). Up to AED 50,000 (approximately 11 lakh 15 thousand rupees) is given as **tuition assistance in cash** per year to low-income families.

The outcome of such initiatives is laudable. Dozens of disabled people continue their education, many of whom have graduated from higher education and some received their Ph.D.s. Discrimination, abuse, negligence, or exploitation against any person with special needs is not tolerated in this country.

UAE has initiated a **legislation supporting** small and medium enterprises (**SMEs**). Under this legislation, SMEs are given finance through banks and their licences are issued easily. They are exempted from government fees also. The government gives all this support so that the people of determination can be absorbed in this sector.

4. ***INTERNATIONAL REPRESENTATION***—The government ensures that the people of determination can effectively and fully participate in public life on an equal basis with others. They are adequately represented at international conferences and gatherings.
5. ***HEALTH***—The health tenet focuses on giving quality healthcare system to the people of determination. A medical card is issued to them through Emirates Health Services which gives them free medical services. A national diagnosis centre has been set up which provides quality medical services in the field of early detection for autism, developmental delays, problems in speech, etc.

   Dubai Health Authority (DHA) has done tremendous work and has set an international benchmark in specialized intervention programmes. They offer physiotherapy, rehabilitation services, and motor skill therapy for the people of determination.

Zayed Higher Organization for People of Determination (ZHO) is renowned for its assessment of mental, psychological, and social health of people of determination.

6. ***MEDIA***—The retreat recognized the right of persons with disabilities to enjoy access to television programmes, films, theatre, and other cultural activities, in accessible formats. Media institutions were asked to hire sign language translators. It was important to ensure the media presence of the people of determination.
7. ***SERVICE***—The retreat reiterated the rights of the people of determination to decide and outline their future. Youth councils were set up which were led by the people of determination. It recognized the importance of the freedom for the people of determination to make their own choices. **An electronic interactive forum known as people of determination platform** was launched. It identifies and promotes assistive technology to adaptive and rehabilitative technology.

We can see electronic participation by people of determination on various government platforms—for example, the Ministry of Finance (MOF) website provides customized features for people of determination. There are various features like the use of 'speech to read', 'front size adjustment', and 'colour variation' which helps in active participation by the people of determination. They can easily share their views and give a feedback wherever needed.

The retreat also promoted building of houses for Emirati people of determination. Financial grants were approved for such residential constructions.

Sign language is not only a means of communication for the hearing impaired, but it is also a part of their identity. It is important to develop and standardize the signs used by them. UAE has always promoted an inclusive and cohesive society, and therefore in 2018, it launched the first '**Emirati sign language dictionary**'. In terms of the dictionary's wider dissemination, it is also available online. Sign language dictionary is not only for the hearing impaired, but it can be used by everyone for making our societies more inclusive. Preparing this dictionary was a mammoth task as it has 5000 words. These words are not only for people with hearing difficulties, but the dictionary is also important for training sign language translators.

Another massive initiative launched by His Highness Sheikh Hamdan bin Mohammed bin Rashid Al Maktoum, Crown Prince of Dubai and Chairman of the Executive Council of Dubai was known as "My Community… A City for Everyone". This initiative had the dream to transform Dubai into a disability-friendly city by 2020. This dream has become a reality. To make Dubai a more inclusive place, HH Sheikh Ahmed created the Dubai team for travel and tourism. This team engages with the people of determination to understand their requirements when travelling.

The Arabic word Sanad means "to support". The Community Development Authority (CDA) has issued the **Sanad Smart Card** for people with disabilities. The benevolent rulers of UAE have provided this free of charge not only to the Emiratis but also to the expatriates. On showing Sanad card, these people are exempted from public transportation fees, vehicle registration, and Salik fees which is a name given to the electronic toll road system in Dubai. The card offers 50% discount on select services and products that people of determination need like wheelchair and Marhaba service at the airport and discounts on medical, dental, and legal services. The Sanad Card also acts as a tool to build a database for people with disabilities in the Emirate of Dubai.

RTA has assigned dedicated parking spaces for the people of determination. Anyone else using these spaces will get a huge fine of AED 1000.

The taxis in Dubai are thoughtfully fitted with special lifts for the wheelchairs. They have artificial respiratory systems inside the taxis. They also have a wheelchair on board and seats for the companions.

The Arabic word NOL means fare or transport cost. People of determination have been issued personalized **NOL cards**. They can travel free in Dubai Metro and public buses in Dubai using their blue personalized NOL cards.

Metro stations in Dubai have been made disabled friendly.

- For the visually impaired, there are tactile floor paths which are marked with little bumps and ridges. When the cane of a visually impaired person touches these patterned tiles, they get various types of information and these tiles serve as a navigation guide.
- Accessibility of metro for hearing impaired isn't taken lightly. They use their sight to gather information in public places. Metro stations are fitted with CCTV from where they get required information.
- For the visually impaired persons, there are constant audio notifications.
- There are specialized escalators at the metro which are fitted with side hand rests for the convenience of the people with disabilities.
- Parking spaces for people of determination are reserved near the station's entrances, and it is wide enough to enable sufficient access for wheelchair users.
- Automatic doors are perfect in assisting the people of determination through with no physical effort used to open them. Dubai metro stations have such doors with correct dimensions to suit wheelchair access and to ease the entry and exit process.
- Dubai metro has thoughtfully provided designated space for a wheelchair in each carriage which are located close to the door.

The public buses of Dubai are also designed keeping in mind the needs of the people of determination. Marine transport stations and water buses have been designed to be user friendly for them. Suitable spaces have been provided for wheelchairs on Dubai Ferry.

8. ***CULTURE***—It is important to ensure an environment where the disabled persons can present their creative, artistic, and intellectual capacities. The retreat called for creating such an environment where people of determination can participate in all cultural events organized in the country.

Special Olympics World Game

In March 2019, UAE held Special Olympics World Game at Abu Dhabi. Athletes with intellectual disabilities participated in this event. UAE has always actively campaigned against ending discrimination against people with intellectual disabilities. Abu Dhabi welcomed athletes from every culture and every part of the world. Everyone experienced respect and inclusion for people of all abilities.

Caring for People of Determination During COVID-19

The safety and well-being of the people of determination were of paramount importance during the pandemic. Various initiatives were taken to ensure their safety.

The 'rest assured' initiative helped parents and family members to detect if children were getting psychologically affected by the pandemic and if therapeutic intervention was needed. The initiative tried to raise the psychological resilience of parents. A comprehensive home-schooling guide was prepared for students with intellectual disabilities and autism.

The Welfare and Rehabilitation Department for People of Determination issued instructions explaining the situation of pandemic and the need to stay at home. Instructions were given to the parents regarding how to organize the daily schedule of the child with studies, play time, story time, and sleep time so as not to stress him or her. The situation of the pandemic was explained to the child in a very simplified way.

The disability rights movement in India has a rich history, but the current scenario needs a lot of attention. There is much to be done to redefine the concept of disability through government policies and through public education. The societies see people in one dimension and forget that he/she is a human being with multiple facets. A person with a disability is first and foremost a human being who has needs, talents, heartache, and loss, just like everyone else and we need to respect that.

Bibliography

Alana, O., & Shakespeare, T. (2011). *Introduction.* World report on disability. WHO, p. 21. https://www.who.int/disabilities/world_report/2011/report.pdf

Balasundaram, P. (2005). *Journey towards inclusive education in India. Education in ancient India.* 09 July 2005, p. 1, https://style.mla.org/works-cited-a-quick-guide-book/

Factsheet: main messages and recommendations. World report on disability: Fact sheet. World Health Organization. 13 December 2011, https://www.who.int/disabilities/world_report/2011/factsheet.pdf

Fremlin, P. (2016). *Rethinking disability in India, disability and society* (Vol. 31). Taylor and Francis Online. September 2016. https://doi.org/10.1080/09687599.2016.1221665

Ghai, A. (2006). *Understanding disability, (dis)embodied form: Issues of disabled women* (p. 39). Har-Anand Publications.

Government of UAE. (2020a). *People of determination (special needs)*. About the UAE. 05 May 2020, https://u.ae/en/information-and-services/social-affairs/special-needs

Government of UAE. (2020b). *The National Policy for empowering people of determination*. About the UAE. 16 January 2020, https://u.ae/en/about-the-uae/strategies-initiatives-and-awards/federal-governments-strategies-and-plans/the-national-policy-for-empowering-people-with-special-needs

Government of UAE, MOCD. (2020). *Issuing a new card for the people of determination, smart services*. 17 February 2020, https://www.mocd.gov.ae/en/services/issuing-new-card-for-people-of-determination.aspx

Hemlata. (2013). Inclusive education in ancient India, concepts and practices in inclusive education. *MIER Journal of Educational Studies, Trends & Practices, 3*, 197–198. https://pdfs.semanticscholar.org/ee1e/7ee7a5d212113dfec86c3dc256020f8003d2.pdf

Kulkarni, S. (2013). *Panchatantra—Its journey across the globe. Panchatantra—An example of using narratives in teaching in ancient Indian education*. Institutional Repository of the University of Tampere, pp. 201–203. https://trepo.tuni.fi/bitstream/handle/10024/101337/panchatantra.pdf?sequence=1

The People of Determination Retreat. (2020). *Information and services*. July 2020, https://government.ae/en/information-and-services/social-affairs/special-needs

The struggles of the disabled, patterns of social inequality and exclusion (2016). NCERT, pp. 106–107. http://ncert.nic.in/ncerts/l/lesy105.pdf

Chapter 17
Disability and Institutional Failure: A Study of *Good Kings, Bad Kings* by Susan Nussbaum

Sumit Garg and Kumar Sushil

Abstract Disability is a problematic term which is deliberated as an experience that hampers the participation of persons with disabilities in different areas of life. Disability has covered a long journey from being considered as a result of the sins of previous births under religious/moral model during the ancient times to being an individual medical problem under the Medical Model after industrial revolution to being a social construct under the social model of disability recently in the later part of twentieth century. Earlier, an individual with disabilities used to be cared for in informal institutions like family or the village community. But after the industrial revolution, certain formal institutions like workhouses and asylums were established especially for persons with disabilities so that their non-disabled relatives could work freely and participate for longer hours in the production process. These formal institutions are still in function to facilitate persons with disabilities as at times informal institutions like families, village communities, etc., cannot cater to their specific needs. The present paper is an attempt to explore the role played by formal institutions in the lives of persons with disabilities in particular and disability in general through the novel *Good Kings, Bad Kings.*

Disability is a problematic term which is deliberated as an experience that hampers the participation of persons with disabilities in different areas of life. Disability has covered a long journey from being considered as a result of the sins of previous births under religious/moral model during the ancient times to being an individual medical problem under the Medical Model after industrial revolution to being a social construct under the social model of disability recently in the later part of twentieth century. Earlier, an individual with disabilities used to be cared for in informal institutions like family or the village community. But after the industrial revolution,

S. Garg (✉)
University College, Ghudda, Bathinda, Punjab, India
e-mail: sumitgarg23@pbi.ac.in

K. Sushil
Guru Kashi Department of Languages, Punjabi University Guru Kashi Campus, Damdama Sahib, Talwandi Sabo, India

R. Uniyal and F. Rizvi (eds.), *Understanding Disability*,
https://doi.org/10.1007/978-981-99-4925-0_17

certain formal institutions like workhouses and asylums were established especially for persons with disabilities so that their non-disabled relatives could work freely and participate for longer hours in the production process. Later on, such institution acquired even more importance as persons with disabilities were considered to be the responsibility of society and state rather of an individual or family. These formal institutions are still in function to facilitate persons with disabilities as at times informal institutions like families, village communities, etc., cannot cater to their specific needs. But it seems that these formal institutions, established specially for persons with disabilities, are unable to fulfil their role properly. The reasons for the same may be related to either the state or individuals running such institutions or internal or external. The present paper is an attempt to explore the role played by formal institutions in the lives of persons with disabilities in particular and disability in general through the novel *Good Kings, Bad kings*. Obviously, any literary piece has nothing to do with the curing of a person with physical or mental disability in the literal sense of the term, but it provides vitality to fight with the disability psychologically. Being propeople, literature provides multiple perspectives to understand disability which generally are relegated into the background in the age of data.

For persons with disabilities, certain institutions have been established to provide them with facilities for their easy survival. Institutions, in general, are "integrated system[s] of rules that structure social interactions" (Hodgson 3). According to Cambridge Dictionary, an institution is "an organisation that exists to serve a public purpose such as education or support for people who need help." Jack Knight, a political scientist, in his book *Institutions and Social Conflict*, describes institutions as entailing "a set of rules that structure social interactions…" (3). By and large, institutions have either been defined in terms of its members, in terms of specific activities or behaviour patterns or in terms of value systems. Generally, the term institution is applied to both informal and formal institutions. Informal institutions include bahaviour patterns, customs, social norms, or tradition that shape bahaviour which are usually unwritten. Formal institutions, on the other hand, are created generally by government. These institutions are based on certain laws, rules and regulations, and the written constitution which are enforced by official authorities. Formal institutions are the central concern for political rule-making and enforcement of such rules. Failure of such institutions may result in loss of careers, tarnishing the image of government and damaging the public trust. Institutional failures are being looked at from different perspectives. From the perspective of neo-classical economics, it is defined as "private and government sector failure" (Pitelis 17). From the perspective of sustainability, it is defined as an "inability to conserve resources" (Acheson 119). From the perspective of innovation approach, Woolthuis et al. divide institutional failure into "hard institutional failure" and "soft institutional failure" (611). Hard intuitional failure is failure in the framework of regulation and the legal system, and soft institutional failure, on the other hand, is failure in social institutions such as political culture and social values. From these perspectives, it can be said that institutions may reflect asymmetries in power. With the passage of time, even the institutions which are functioning well can begin to fail. Overall, one thing can be said with certainty that "institutional dysfunctionalities have become increasingly common in important social, political, and economics arenas" (Parkash and Potoski 1). These anomalies are also getting reflected in the institution established for persons with disabilities which, in the present paper, will be understood and analysed through the novel *Good Kings, Bad Kings* by Susan Nassbaum.

Disability, as such, does not carry a single meaning as it is contested, multidimensional, and complex and "should be understood in terms of a continuum" (Shakespeare 5). It also elicits varied responses which makes it difficult to define disability across various cultures as "the category itself is a western construct that emerged in particular historical circumstances in Europe" (Whyte and Ingstad 7). Moreover, disability "depends on the hybrid socio-cultural contexts in which it is placed" (Grech 772). Mehrotra in her work *Disability, Gender and State Policy: Exploring Margins* asserts that it is very "difficult to draw a common definition examining disability" (25). Thus, it can be understood as a fusion because "Disability refers to those *personal, cognitive, physical, and behavioral* conditions that have been identified as significantly limiting an individual's ability to function effectively in normal societal situations: family, neighborhood, school, and workplace" (Osgood, xviii). Americans with Disabilities Act describes a person with disability as the one "who has a physical or mental impairment that substantially limits one or more major life activity..." (Brennan 1). As per the Gazette of India (2016), "[P]erson with disability means a person with long term physical, mental, intellectual or sensory impairment which, in interaction with barriers, hinders his full and effective participation in society equally with others" (3). Oliver identifies in his book *The Politics of Disablement* various arguments concerning "how disability should be defined" though "the meaning of disability is distorted" (xii) while trying to gain any "universal acceptance" (2).

Generally, the term impairment is confused with disability, but these are different. The problem of immovability of legs confronted by a person with physical disability is impairment, but non-availability of the facility of ramps leads to making him disabled. Vic Finkelstein's parable supports the above argument in which a village was made suitable for persons using wheelchairs by designing it in such a way to provide comfortable life to persons using wheelchairs. In this village, non-disabled persons walked upright and kept on either hitting their heads in walls which are of size suitable for wheelchair users or bending their backs to survive which created pain in their backbone. Here persons using wheelchairs were not considered different rather persons with non-disabled bodies were termed as 'able-bodied disabled' (Shakespeare 13). Thus, it is social measure rather than the body of an individual that complicates the situation and disability takes a shift from being a mere biological phenomenon to a social construct due to the non-availability of facilities for disabled individuals which also becomes the reason for their exclusion from society. It leads to the strengthening of the idea that persons with disabilities were and are "minorities within minorities, and are therefore without the numbers, access to resources or allies to collectively assert their needs and identities" (Yeo 524).

A lot of works have been written on the themes of disability in order to have psychological, emotional, and therapeutic effects on readers. Herman Melville's *Moby Dick* (1851) is a memorable tale of would be revenge sought by one-legged Captain Ahab against the whale. Earlier the whale severed his leg, and he went back in order to take revenge. Though disability is presented as somewhat equivalent to being mysterious, yet the tale is inspiring. Katherine Dunn's *Geek Love* (1989) is about Binewski family, who used specific chemical so that their offspring must be born with various disabilities so that they can continue their family business, i.e., working in a circus. It changes our notion of being 'normal' and freakish; the ugly and the beautiful; the obscene and the holy. Elizabeth McCracken's *The Giant's House* (1996) is about James Carlson Sweatt who grows over eight feet tall. His height both is and is not a disability constitutes the basic plot. The inner life of Sweatt, his physical issues, and his emotional bond with librarian Peggy holds the novel as the most inspiring one. Stephen Kuusisto's *Planet of the Blind* (1998) is a memoir regarding coming to terms with near blindness. It is about growing up blind in a family who refuse to acknowledge the blindness or make any allowances for it. Terry Galloway's *Mean Little Deaf Queer* (2006) is a memoir portraying herself both as oppressor and oppressed. At nine, everybody's voice disappeared as she became deaf due to antibiotic given to her mother during pregnancy. The work describes her mental breakdowns, her strange identity, and living in a mute world surrounded by characters which cannot be forgotten. Emily Rapp's *The Still Point of the Turning World* (2013) is also a memoir which deals with the loss of her son due to Tay-Sachs disease. It delves deep into the art of parenting. Susan Nussbaum's novel *Good Kings, Bad Kings* (2013) is about young persons with disabilities who are kept in an institute called Illinois Learning and Life Center (ILLC). They are disabled and are treated badly. This is seen as representing state failure in terms of fulfilling the obligation of providing safe and secure atmosphere to persons with disabilities.

Susan Nussbaum is a Chicago-based novelist, playwright, and disability rights activist. She was pursuing her career as an actor at twenty-four, the prime of her life, when she was hit by a car while going for her acting class. She started using a wheelchair since then with her arms in partial use, and all she could do was to read books or watch movies. She decided to be a writer and a disability rights activist. Nussbaum founded the first group for girls with disabilities called 'the Empowered Fe Fes.' She was also named among *Utne Reader*'s 2008 list of 50 visionaries who are changing the world for her disability rights work. Winner of PEN/Bellwether prize for Socially Engaged Fiction, *Good Kings, Bad Kings* (2013) is her first novel which deals with a group of teenagers with disabilities in an institute called Illinois Learning and Life Center (ILLC) specially set up for such kids. The novel focuses upon a segment of society which is often ignored in life as well as in literature. Besides, it also defies our interpretation of being disabled and explores divergent perspectives about people with disabilities and their experiences as residents of an institution especially established for them. Barbara Kingsolver, an American novelist and poet, while reviewing *Good Kings, Bad Kings* considered it "a ferociously honest, funny, completely unstoppable trip through an institutionally corrupt home for disable teenagers" ("Susan Nussbaum").

In the novel *Good Kings, Bad Kings*, the world inside Illinois Learning and Life Skills Center (ILLC) can be identified with the world outside where all sorts of emotions like love, hate, friendship, politics, etc., occur. But ILLC is an epitome of the institutional failure as well as the failure of the government as it does not cater to the needs of persons with disabilities. Here teenagers are estranged and yearning for independence. ILLC, as presented in the novel, is a state-run nursing facility for adolescent youth. Persons with disabilities are put in such institutions either for their cure or for seeking companionship. According to social model of disability, "disabled people are "disabled" by the society they live in and by the impact of society's structures and attitudes" (Purtell 26). It was based on the premise that disability is socially created and can be dispensed with, in a way, by building an environment more accessible to persons with impairment. Moreover, establishing separate structures for persons with disabilities is a recent phenomenon, the roots of which can be traced with the advent of capitalism.

This segregation of persons with disabilities from the rest as per Victor Berel Finkelstein's "general social theory of disability" has "the historical origins…" which can be traced through historical materialism or by understanding the material conception of history (58). Goodley argues, "[H]istorical materialist accounts of disablism offer indispensable insights into [the] exploitative workings of capitalism" (8). Finkelstein's theory is in consonance with historical materialism and its three stages of historical development where phase I, being an agrarian or precapitalistic society, did not refrain the disabled person from engaging in the process of production, either fully or partially. Considered as unfortunate individually, they could contribute towards society's economic progress. Phase II, being a capitalistic society, excludes the disabled people from the process of production. This change affected the disabled people negatively as they were segregated and disability as a separate social category emerged because "[t]he operation of the labour market in the nineteenth century effectively depressed handicapped people of all kinds to the bottom of the market" (Morris 9). Disable people were even considered as an educational and social liability which resulted in the opening of asylums, workhouses, colonies, and special schools for them. As a result, they were not considered to be the part of mainstream social life. Phase III, being socialistic, will help disabled people in getting liberation from the prejudices of society, and they will be able to work with their non-disabled counterparts harmoniously. This leads to the idea of segregating persons with disabilities from the rest of society and setting up formal institutions like ILLC as mentioned in the novel for persons with disabilities.

Such formal institutions set up for persons with disability like ILLC in the novel have failed miserably in reaching at the desired goal because the real intention was not to favour the underprivileged rather profit earning which is the basic trait of capitalism. Nussbaum writes

The characters in my book are dealing with a place that's not one of the worst, but abuse and neglect are rampant nonetheless. Some of them are sucked under by the riptide of repression, some of them bob to the surface against all odds, and maybe one or two find a way to fly away. (11)

The basic purpose of institutes is to provide solace to persons with disabilities, but these are actually working in a reverse order to torment them further as in the novel ILLC comprises "disabled kids that struggling parents and the state don't know what to do with" (10–11). That is why it can be considered as an "old wolf but in a lamb outfit" (11). Moreover, in the novel, ILLC is compared to a jail as "instead of locking up old people they lock up young people" (7).

Joanne Madsen, one of the characters in *Good Kings, Bad Kings,* is hit by a bus and given a desk job at ILLC "generously to apologize for hitting" (19). From the society's point of view, she got the job in ILLC to "overc[o]me [her] disability and [to] bec[o]me a contributing member of society" (10). On the personal level, she was in need of "human interaction" (9). She presents the most apt point regarding much needed consciousness raising details in the most humourous way:

It's well known in crip circles that the best place for a crip to get a job is a place that's swarming with other crips. So [she] applied, emphasizing [her] computer skills, which are pretty good, and how important it is for disabled youth to see disabled adults in the workplace. Places like this love the idea of role models. (20)

This is ironic in the sense that one is contrived to one's place and indicates towards the idea that "the world, Earth, is not a hospitable place for crips" (19). This endorses the idea that persons with disability become a fringe group and find space in institutions like asylums, workhouses, prisons, etc. Further, they have to endure the moral stigma on the twin level. In such institutions, they are sequestered from non-disabled people because of their impairment, but they feel disabled because of lack of facilities in the institute. Their marginalization also resulted in non-disabled body being considered as a norm in the society. Besides, they are doubly marginalized: first, on the grounds of their disability and second, on the basis of not being able to take care of themselves financially as "[t]here are poor people and then there are poor disable people" (8). To simplify, actually a person with disability is not a problem instead the social and economic determinants which promote ableism are problematic. In primitive and agrarian societies, people with disabilities were not excluded from society as Lennard Davis, a disability theorist from America points out "Disability was not an operative category before the eighteenth century…" (50). Due to the onset of capitalism, a non-disabled body was required for the production of things and for the profit of capitalists. Apart from being one of the main reasons for the surge of disability, it "also perpetuates" disability. (Costello)

The novel indicates that the basic infrastructure, the need of persons with disabilities, is not being made available to them in institutes especially set up to help them. Moreover, these institutes do not have any intent to provide such resources as the kids with both physical as well as mental disabilities "should have power chairs so that they could go around on their own" but most of the kids "have manual chairs" which is "against the rules" and unofficial (11). Mia, a young girl in the novel, is provided with a manual chair, and she "has to wait for a staff person or one of the kids who can walk to notice her so she can get a push" (12). She should have been provided with the resources in order to overcome impairment, but due to the lack of such resources, her impairment has been converted into disability as Lennard Davis states, "[D]isability must be socially constructed; there must be an analysis of what it means to have or lack certain functions, appearance and so on" (50). Earlier disability was thought to be an individual deformity or misfortune, but in present times, with the introduction of 'social model of disability,' it is thought to be the outcome of the social environment. Besides, this non-availability of resources in the novel indicates a sort of failure of the basic idea of a society where the actual focus should be on arranging the resources for persons with disabilities, according to Marx, "from each according to his ability, to each according to his need" (Critique 531). Presence of middle man in institutions who opt for corrupt practices also needs a mention as they control things and make these resources scarce for marginalized groups like people with disabilities which is another outcome of capitalism.

With the presence of separate institutions in society for persons with disabilities like ILLC in the novel, the whole idea of inclusive society gets defeated which was, as Siebers says, to "...bring disability out of the shadow of the ideology of ability, to increase awareness about disability, and to illuminate its kinds, values, and realities" (279). The focus, thus, must be to sabotage the ideology of ability in order to "claim disability as a positive identity" (Linton i) which may improve the life of persons with disability. Hence, disability emerges as a social category getting precedence over biological which is regulated by society in general and material conditions of society in particular. Here non-disabled body becomes a temporary identity because all other identities such as caste, gender, and class will be consolidated into some sort of disability identity. Discrimination on the basis of gender, colour, caste, creed, etc., had existed in the society since inception, and this discrimination was justified historically on the grounds of representing the marginalized as disabled as Mitchell and Snyder state, "[S]tigmatized social positions founded upon gender, class, nationality, and race have often relied upon disability to visually underscore the evaluation of marginal communities" (21). Able-bodiedness has always been preferred which relegates disability to an inferior position. As a corollary, persons with disabilities are ostracized resulting in their institutionalization to provide them solace and better opportunities. The whole thing, actually, is ironic as the institutions like ILLC in the novel are playing the role of segregating persons with disabilities from the society by enlarge.

Yessenia Lopez, another character in the novel, refers to ILLC in the beginning of the novel as the "Illinois Learning something something" (1). It indicates her first impression of the institute meant for the rehabilitation of the persons with disabilities like her. While introducing herself she further says:

Before they stuck my butt in this place I went to Herbert Hoover High School in Chicago, Illinois. I went there on account of I am physically challenged, and they send the people which have challenges to Hoover. They send people with physical challenges, but also retarded challenges, people been in accidents like brain accidents, or they're blind or what have you. I do not know why they send us all to the same place but that's the way it's always been and that's the way it looks like it will always be because I am in tenth grade and I been in cripple this or cripple that my whole sweet succulent Puerto Rican life. (2)

It shows that the institute in which she is sent is actually not a great place to live as she is upset with the room in which she is sitting as it "smells like a urinal toilet..." (1). It indicates towards the failure on the part of the institution in particular and the state in general.

The novel *Good Kings, Bad Kings* projects grim picture of institutes which, on the surface seem to be running as a non-profit organization but in reality, are yearning for profits. In the novel, the character of Michelle Volkmann brings out such hypocrisies. She "recruits" residents for the ILLC for 'Whitney-Palm' on incentive basis. The Whitney-Palm is a company which specially deals with such things. Through her character, the working of "the system" is shown in the worst manner (80). Michelle constantly uses the phrase "lifestyle alternatives" without even knowing the meaning of the term in the real sense (38). She moves from place to place in order to fill up many institutions which Whitney-Palm runs. The novel portrays the predicament of people as it seems that the government is in favour of privatization which is causing havoc in their lives in terms of quality of life as well as providing them with the facilities which are mandatory for any state as "places like ILLC were state-run, but the state made a mess of it…" (25). ILLC, in the novel, is handed over to a private company Whitney-Palm and Michelle works for it. The government has disowned ILLC to the private hands as Whitney-Palm "unlike the state, knows how to run a business…" (25). The sole motto of this business run by Whitney-Palms in ILLC is to earn more and more profit even at cost of human values. It indicates the neoliberal regime which came up in 1990s where the government institutions are sold, favouring big business houses. It also reflects the unholy nexus between state and corporate houses. Even Michelle is trained as well as paid to bring new persons with disability in the institute. She does not even know what she is doing as she is brainwashed and put under this notion that she is "getting people off the streets and into warm beds with three meals a day and medical care" (25–26).

Persons with disabilities are not chosen to be put in ILLC for genuine reasons or for their problems rather they are considered business proposals which "can be really profitable" (30). They are just objects rather than human beings as when Michelle meets Cheri Smith, one of the potential residents for ILLC in the novel, she is not at all interested in pronouncing her name the way Cheri wants. Instead she thought "Okay, whatever" (27). She along with her company considered persons with disabilities as commodities who will get her "$300" (25). Even when Cheri was narrating an incident which happened with her a night before when she was kicked out of her house by her parents, Michelle did not trust her and remarked, "The thing about this job is people will tell you anything" (29). Still she kept on "exaggerating a little about having her own room" (30) to "[f]ind[] a potential patient" and earn money which she had "already [been] spending… in [her] head" (30). It indicates the loss of human values, which is one of the outcomes of capitalism. The focus is on earning more and more money. Towards the end of the novel, Michelle changes the most. She is transformed from a naïve employee to an alert person who could see criminals as they actually are. For the major part of the novel, her haughtiness truly matches the profit monger institutes, but gradually, with her exposure to corruption and inhumanity makes her more sensitive. She penned down a conversation during a board meeting called in the emergency where "The PR guy says, 'How many deaths are reasonable? Is there a number?' Mr. Anderson says, However many of them have died. That's the number." (119) For them, persons with disabilities are mere products which are to be kept and in the process may get damaged. Michelle even imagines handing over the copy of details "to some reporter" (120). It shows, sooner or later, humans value human values but the sole purpose of big corporate houses like

Whitney-Palm as indicated in the novel remains profit making which resulted in the failure of institutes such as ILLC.

Disability was, earlier, considered an individual rather than a social problem. Parents of kids with disabilities do not want their kids to be with them as they considered themselves to be "the final authorities on how difficult it is raise these children at home" (261). Even when the residents start calling the media and there arises a situation that the rebellion of the residents may result in shutting down ILLC towards the end of the novel, an "emergency board meeting at ILLC" (258) was called up where Tim, one of the board members says, "The last thing [parents] want is the prospect of ILLC and other residential institutions being closed down" (261). It points towards the attitude of society in general and such institutes in particular towards persons with disabilities.

There is another character Teddy Dobbs in the novel who is so frustrated with the existing system of ILLC that he "got a plan to run away" (37). But he wants to be cautious regarding his escape as he does not want to "end up in a place even worse than this place" (37). Even the allowance which he is getting per month from his father has to come through Mrs. Phoebe, which is reduced to thirty dollars per month as persons at ILLC "keep the rest" (37) which again points at the prevalence of corrupt practices even in such institutions. Persons even get a chance to smoke as "nobody's gonna look in and bother" (39). It shows that ILLC in the novel is rotten and in bad shape. Another problem which points towards the failure of the institution is that there have been many thefts. Louie, another resident, stole money from Teddy Dobbs which he has been saving out of his monthly allowance. To make things even worst, there is nobody who would listen to the pleadings of Teddy as he states: "It don't do no good to complain" as nobody can "prove it they did" (39). Ideally, it is thought that the person who has been admitted to ILLC will be able to get all the amenities which are required that includes, most importantly, the freedom to move as per his/her own will within the institute, but Teddy is "not allowed to loiter…" (40). Moreover, the teens and kids with the disabilities are threatened which "ain't fair" (40).

Mia, another resident of ILLC, has got cerebral palsy. She cannot move without an electric chair, but "she only has a crappy manual one" which shows the lack of infrastructure in the institute or probably the lack of intent to provide that infrastructure because the government is paying the money to look after the persons with disabilities in ILLC (42). Once, even a manual chair was not available and "they made her lie in her bed all day" and when she got the manual chair, "one of the footrest [was] broken and the seat is too big and too wide" and she kept on falling out of it and "they strap her into it…" (42). Mia is in the institution since she was eleven having "scars on her arms", and Teddy is sure that these were "from cigarettes" (43). This shows the amount of atrocities and inhuman treatment the residents of ILLC in the novel have to undergo. Another aspect which should be emphasized behind the establishment of institutions such as ILLC is to foster the feeling of inclusion so that persons with disabilities, like all human beings, despite being different should feel the way every human being should feel. But in ILLC, such kids and teens are made to feel "retarded" in spite of considering the fact that they have "got a different way of learning stuff" (43).

Ultimately, the residents of ILLC turn into activists and heroes as they have to fight for themselves. They constitute the marginalized lot of the society for whom the society has established institutions like ILLC. They have to raise voice against all the atrocities as the amenities are not provided to them. As Yessenia says, "If this is what it means to be award of the state, you can have your award. I don't want it." (214) Yessenia, after that, leads a metamorphic revolution by holding up a handwritten sign "THIS PLACE ABUSE[S] AND KILL CHILDREN" (249), though she is aware that she might get into "real trouble" (250). The act of bravery of standing against oppression has been termed as "circus" by the authorities (251). It shows that the authorities are highly insensitive and non-serious regarding the problems faced by residents of ILLC. Rather than relying on any outside help, they team up and bring the change. It seems to be a kind of self-realization. But one thing is certain such institutes cannot run without the support of state.

Conclusion

Towards the end, it can be said that institutions have many facets and cannot be seen in isolation as these are the parts of larger discourse. These institutions exist everywhere as Susan Nussbaum writes, "Being trapped in one kind of institution or another is the fate of many of us..." (10). On the basis of the novel *Good Kings, Bad Kings*, it can be said that as far as disability or the care of the persons with disabilities is concerned, the institutions like ILLC have failed miserably. There are various reasons which can be ascribed to it. The first and foremost point which comes out is the privatization of the institutes which has resulted in corrupt practices in such institutes as in the novel. Secondly, privatization is one of the manifestations of capitalism which reflects the ill-will of the government for not providing proper space to the persons with disabilities actually. It also shows the unholy nexus of big corporate houses like Whitney-Palm in the novel with the state. Due to privatization, state eschews from its role in providing equal opportunities to marginalized groups such as persons with disabilities, thereby replacing itself with corporate houses which only care for their own profit and treat human beings as just objects which are to be used for making more and more profit. Thirdly, even the very presence of institutions like ILLC in the novel indicates towards the manifestation of capitalism through which persons with disabilities are segregated from the rest of the society. Even if it is believed that the presence of such institutes to be the necessary evil in the present scenario, these institutions do not dispense with discrimination against persons with disabilities. Fourthly, persons with disabilities in the novel are considered to be mere numbers or data and not more than that. There is no value of an individual with disability as a person. The only purpose is to increase the number of such persons which could lead to financial gain from government or from some other sources. The whole framework has taken a more political form rather than being sticking to the individual needs of a person as Susan Nussbaum, on being crippled herself says, "It wasn't personal. It was political." (20) Every problem has a solution. The first and foremost thing which can be done is to recognize the worth of human capital. Persons with disabilities should be kept at their homes along with other members to make them feel like any other human being. Rather than providing financial aid to the institutes like ILLC in the novel, the same can be given to families of persons with disabilities for their care. Besides, some suitable work opportunities for each person with disability can be generated to make her/him feel to be the productive member of society. In specific cases, where families cannot perform the required duties, special institutes like ILLC in the novel can play a significant role, but these should, rather than being private, be public institutions where profit motive should be dispensed with. Moreover, these institutes should be made accessible for family members so that they can spend time with their own family member with impairments and also have a look at others. The visit of the family members should also be mandatory as per their convenience so that they should also feel a sort of responsibility towards their disabled family member in particular and towards persons with disabilities in society in general.

Bibliography

Acheson, J. M. (2006). Institutional failure in resource management. *Annual Review of Anthropology, 35*, 117–134. http://doi.org/10.1146/annurev.anthro.35.081705.123238

Brennan, J. (2013). *The ADA national network disability law handbook.* Southwest ADA Center. www.adata.org/sites/adata.org/files/files/DisabilityLawHandbook_2013-rev-2015.pdf. Costello, C. (2017). How capitalism contributes to ableism. *The Mighty.* www.themighty.com/2017/10/how-capitalism-contributes-to-ableism. Accessed on December 4, 2019.

Davis, L. J. (2002). *Bending over backwards: Disability, dismodernism, and other difficult positions* (pp. 50–52). New York University Press.

Dunn, K. (2002). *Geek love: A novel.* Vintage.

Finkelstein, V. (1981). Disability and the helper/helped relationship: An historical view. In A. Brechin, P. Liddiard, & J. Swain (Eds.), *Handicap in a social world* (pp. 58–64). Hodder and Stoughton.

Galloway, T. (2010). *Mean little deaf queer: A memoir.* Beacon Press.

Goodley, D. (2014). *Dis/ability studies: Theorising disablism and ableism.* Routledge.

Grech, S. (2009). Disability, poverty and development: Critical reflections on the majority world debate. *Disability and Society, 24*(6), 771–784. http://doi.org/10.1080/09687590903160266. Accessed August 5, 2020.

Hodgson, G. M. (2006). What are institutions? *Journal of Economic Issues, 40*(1), 1–25. http://doi.org/10.1080/00213624.2006.11506879

Knight, J. (1992). *Institutions and social conflict.* Cambridge University Press.

Kuusisto, S. (1999). *Planet of the blind.* Faber and Faber.

Linton, S. (1998). *Claiming disability: Knowledge and identity.* New York University Press.

Marx, K. (1978). Critique of the Gotha program. In R. C. Tucker (Ed.), *The Marx-Engels reader* (pp. 525–541). Norton and Company.

McCracken, E. (2019). *The giant's house.* Vintage.

Mehrotra, N. (2013). *Disability, gender and state policy: Exploring margins.* Rawat Publications.

Melville, H. (2011). *Moby Dick.* Sterling.

Mitchell, D., & Snyder, S. (2000). *Narrative prosthesis: Disability and the dependencies of discourse*. University of Michigan Press.

Morris, P. (1969). *Put away*. Routledge and Kegan Paul.

Nussbaum, S. (2013). *Good kings bad kings*. Algonquin Books.

Oliver, M. (1990). *The politics of disablement*. Palgrave Macmilan.

Osgood, R. L. (2008). *The history of special education: A struggle for equality in American public schools*. Praeger.

Pitelis, C. (1992). Towards a neo-classical theory of institutional failure. *Journal of Economic Studies, 19*(1), 14–29. http://doi.org/10.1108/01443589210015926/full/html

Prakash, A., & Potoski, M. (2015). Dysfunctional institutions? Towards a new agenda in governance studies. Wiley Online Library, pp. 1–3. https://doi.org/10.1111/rego.12113

Purtell, R. (2013). Music and the social model of disability. In J. Q. Williams & J. Kingsley (Eds.), *Music and the social model: An occupational therapist's approach to music with people labelled as having learning disabilities* (pp. 26–32).

Rapp, E. (2014). *The still point of the turning world*. Penguin Books.

Shakespeare, T. (2018). *Disability: The basics*. Routledge.

Siebers, T. A. (2013). Disability and the theory of complex embodiment—For identity politics in a new register. In L. J. Davis (Ed.), *The disability studies reader* (4th ed., pp. 278–297). Routledge.

"Susan Nussbaum." *Susan Nussbaum*, www.susannussbaum.com. Accessed on January 14, 2020.

The Gazette of India. Ministry of Law and Justice, 28 December 2016, http://disabilityaffairs.gov.in/upload/uploadfiles/files/RPWD%20ACT%202016.pdf. Accessed August 24, 2019.

Whyte, S. R., & Ingstad, B. (1995). Disability and culture: An overview. In B. Ingstad & S. R. Whyte (Eds.), *Disability and culture* (pp. 3–32). University of California Press.

Woolthuis, R. K., Lankhuizen, M., & Gilsing, V. (2005). A system failure framework for innovation policy design. *Technovation, 25*, 609–619.

Yeo, R. (2015). Disabled asylum seekers?...They don't really exist: The marginalisation of disabled asylum seekers in the UK and why it matters. *Disability and the Global South, 2*(1), 523–550. https://disabilityglobalsouth.files.wordpress.com/2012/06/dgs-02-01-07.pdf. Accessed September 11, 2020.

Chapter 18
Education and Labour Market for Persons with Disabilities in India

Nicky Naincy and Anuraj Singh

Abstract 'Disability' and its related perceptions require a critical reconstruction not only in terms of modelling the known variables from medical theories or social constructs, but from economic and behavioural perspectives as well. The mental health community has taken serious notice of the realities and experiences of disabled people. However, the perceptions are not limited to individual domain when the interpretative task involves practical economic investigation. The periphery of social and psychology-based models requires inputs from behavioural economics to understand and analyse the different variables operating in labour market for disabled people. This article attempts to bring out those nuances.

Keywords Disability · Labour market · Discrimination · Human capital · India

Introduction

Census 2011 enumerated that 2.21% of the Indian population are under the composite category of 'disabled' people. Disability has been reported to be the highest in the age group of 10–19 years, and increment is more observed in urban area as compared to rural one (Census, 2011). Statistical figures depict the numbers of 'differently abled' persons (the connotation indicates a marked departure from the word 'disabled' from its medical and individual definition to the more social one) on the basis of sectorial and social categories. However, the data collecting agencies argue for the need to have a robust database for disabled people in India. Information regarding their socio-economic and socio-demographic variables is not sufficient to develop an inclusive policy for them. It requires information about their functional status

N. Naincy (✉)
Department of Applied Science and Humanities, Institute of Engineering and Technology, Lucknow, Uttar Pradesh, India
e-mail: nzhces@gmail.com

A. Singh
Banasthali University, Tonk, India
e-mail: anurajsingh@banasthali.in

R. Uniyal and F. Rizvi (eds.), *Understanding Disability*,
https://doi.org/10.1007/978-981-99-4925-0_18

and mapping of different stages of disability inflicted on them with their existing scenario in education and labour market. Since two individuals with the same type of impairment may have different difficulties, different interventions are required at different levels of disability (GoI, 2019).

Theoretically arguing, the Medical Model or more precisely the individual model of disability remained the most prevalent one to define and conceptualize the condition of disabled people in India and other societies of the world. However, recent researches have placed the question about the location of disability, that is whether it is the manifestation of individual only or emanating within the society and its other components. This has led to the emergence of social models of disability. The attitude and behaviour towards the disabled people in society and in labour market cannot be analysed in mutually exclusive manner, that is, on the sole basis of medical impairment. It requires an understanding and moderation from different domains of the theoretical thread. Linkage between labour market and education remains discriminatory for the disabled people and is one of those existing threads which remained largely unexplored. The much-discussed human capital approach is based on the premise that development of lifelong skills has larger benefits as compared to investment in physical assets only. The lifelong skills include investment in health and education. Nevertheless, human capital theory is lamented on the grounds that it formally excludes the relevance of disadvantaged section (person with disability) and its conflict while explaining the intricacies of labour market discrimination. In contrast to this, recently it has been argued that human capability approach advocates correspondence between well-being or quality of lives of individual and society through an inclusive educational process and thereby can have intrinsic as well as instrumental roles to play for disabled or other disadvantaged sections of the society. Therefore, it requires theoretical and empirical investigation of discrimination in labour market for disabled people to find out which particular construct has to be taken while formulating the inclusive policies for them. It signifies towards a perspective from behavioural economics rather than resorting to any exclusive theory. The first step begins with the identification of those instruments of discrimination operating in education and labour market for disabled people along with the conceptualization of disability (structural versus functional). This article is an attempt in this direction for identifying and analysing the discrimination for disabled people within the linkage of education and labour market, specifically in Indian context.

Labour Market Linkages and Economics of Education

There is a positive correlation between education and labour market outcomes (Edgerton et al. 2012; Hauser et al., 2000; Mincer, 1958, 1974; Pascarella and Terenzini, 2005; Stiglitz et al. 2009; Tansel, 2004). Ionescu and Cuza (2012) have discussed the various labour market outcomes which have been affected by education. Different aspects of education can influence the labour market outcomes such as schooling, education attained, investment in higher and professional education, etc. Many studies showed that education can influence the various labour market outcomes in the form of earnings, employment, unemployment, worker productivity, nature of work, hours worked, and fringe benefits. The more educated a person, higher will be her/his earning capability (Edgerton et al., 2012; Soloman & Fagano, 1997). The literature argues in favour of established linkages between education attained and labour market outcomes. But there is lack of evidence in the literature where people with same level of education have the same labour market outcome. There are many justifications for the heterogeneity in individual occupational outcomes (Levine, 1976). The important one is human capital theory developed by Becker. This theory is a landmark in explaining the differences in labour market outcomes based on education, experience, and innate ability of an individual. According to Becker, an individual's decision to invest in additional level of education is influenced by his/her expected future earnings and judgement of one's innate ability. If an individual's expectations of future earnings and judgement of innate ability are low, he/she will not invest in additional education. In this regard, Becker argues that investment differential culminates into differential labour outcomes (Becker, 1971). It is further corroborated empirically by Arrow that different outcomes in labour market with the same level of human capital accrue to varied investment rates (Arrow, 1971).

Disability and Discrimination: Education and Labour Market

Persons with disabilities (henceforth PWDs) hold a significant share of labour pool of country's industrial needs given the proper utilization of its untapped human resource potential. International Labour Organisation (ILO) has pointed out the fact that PWDs can fulfil the requirement of human resource for industrial production (Shenoy, 2011). For the inclusive development of any country and to further sustain it, this potential requires to be addressed. Another dimension added by Metts in his study pertains to the developmental parameters of disabled people in developing countries. Through the study, he found that three-fourth of world's disabled people including children reside in developing countries along with high rates of poverty among them as compared to general population (Metts, 2000).

Education and skills act as crucial determinants in labour market participation and outcomes for PWDs. Investment in human capital raises productivity potential in labour market which determines the earning differentials among individuals. Teh same holds valid for explaining the earning differential between an able-bodied individual and a disabled person given the equal market conditions. Kidd and Sloane in their study explained that investment in human capital can majorly explain differentials in earnings and employment of PWDs and able-bodied persons (Kidd et al., 2000). The lack of access to education, particularly higher education, will adversely affect the employment prospects of individuals. This is more applicable for PWDs whose access to higher education has been constrained by the non-inclusive nature of Indian higher education system. Inability to access higher education would act as impediments for the PWDs in recruitment and career advancement. It would also result in substantial earnings differentials between the disabled and non-disabled which would widen the income inequality between the two groups.

The education sector for children with disabilities (CWDs) has a non-universal and stratified structure. Studies conducted by WHO and World Bank and some other individual studies have pointed out that CWDs do not progress well beyond primary level of education and thus become dependent upon beneficiary-related social security schemes run by the government. This has repercussions for their labour market participation and incentivization (Singal, 2010; WHO & World Bank, 2011). This further impacts the skilling and reskilling potential of CWDs.

Employment ratios for the PWDs are significantly low on average than for persons without disabilities. A study by WHO and World Bank (2011) estimated that employment rates for disabled men and women are 53% and 20%, respectively, as compared to 65% for men and 35% for women without disabilities, although rates vary significantly across countries. Individual, societal, and institutional factors make education and workplace inaccessible for PWDs. While PWDs experience discrimination and disadvantage in accessing education and employment, a sizeable section of the PWDs who have the requisite human capital capabilities also faces disadvantage in employment and earnings. Even when the PWDs are employed, they are largely confined to entry level positions (American Indian Foundation, 2014) and their earnings are substantially lower than persons without disability (Baldwin & Johnson, 1994; DeLeire, 2000; Hollenbeck & Kimmel, 2008).

PWDs in India and Labour Market

ILO pointed out that having decent work conditions and employment opportunities have been challenging task for PWDs in India (Shenoy, 2011). PWDs have lower employment rates than the general population across regional and gender parameters. As per the World Bank report of employment rates for the PWDs, it reported a decline from 42.7% in 1991 to 37.6% in 2002. On the other hand, the same has been reported to only 1.1 per cent for the general population, that is, 58.6–57.5% (World Bank, 2007). Government of India in its report estimated that a meagre 0.5% of total PWDs in India are employed in industries. In case of private sector and multinational companies, the percentage becomes much lower to 0.2 and 0.05%, respectively. It is reported that for all types of disabilities 73.6% are out of labour force (GoI, 2007–08, Shenoy, 2011). Apart from this general representation of PWDs in labour market of India, the spatial variation exists across the rural and urban areas of the country. The other factors include gender, type of disability, and education levels of PWDs. Studies conducted by World Bank indicated towards the variation in employment rates among PWDs while considering geographical, demographic, and socio-economic factors.

Mitra and Sambamoorthi in their study found that females with disabilities are less employed than their male counterparts (Mitra & Sambamoorthi, 2006).

Moreover, within the category of different kind of disabilities, the rate of employment varies considerably. For example, people having speech and locomotor disabilities have a better employability ratio than the other categories of disability like mental impairment (World Bank, 2007). In India, employment opportunities for PWDs were largely confined to the public sector due to the three per cent reservation mandated by the Right of Person with Disabilities Act 2016 (known as PWD Act). However, the private sector in India has mostly remained apprehensive towards hiring PWDs. In recent past, few export houses have opened up avenues for PWDs and to explore their potential. Technological innovation in developing different aids to disabilities has helped PWDs to enter into the labour market of private sector. For example, initially they started employing people with orthopaedic and hearing impairment for limited tasks. Later with the technological aids, the avenues of private sector employment also opened up to persons with visual impairment. Although, a major reason behind this inclusion is the corporate social responsibility (CSR) agenda. The benefits of employing PWDs under the CSR include social image enhancement and goodwill from customer and employee. Moreover, companies also enjoy higher level of loyalty, strong performance, and lower rates of attrition (American Indian Foundation, 2014).

Discrimination in the Labour Market for PWDs: Emerging Concerns

This heterogeneity is more pronounced among PWDs which is more or less similar across the globe. Composition of labour market is heterogeneous in itself whereby outcomes are determined by different sets of variables and not only dependent upon skills and education. PWDs on the other hand experience variation in labour market along with the pre-existing heterogeneity emanated through discriminatory practices. As Arrow argues in his study that organizations or employers not only analyse the pecuniary costs for employing PWDs as employees but non-pecuniary aspects are also taken into the considerations by them (Arrow, 1971). This may promote further heterogeneity in labour market outcomes for PWDs in the long run. Expediency of human capital framework does not fit seemingly while discussing the kind of discrimination PWDs suffer in the labour market.

In standard economic theory, the rationale behind discrimination is built on the premise of differences in productivity among individuals. However, in the market, an individual's personal characteristics which are not explicitly related to productivity are also taken into account. These characteristics may include race, gender, ethnic background, caste, or disability depending on the context and space. Arrow (1971) argued that discrimination can be of market or non-market types. Non-market discrimination may include deliberate racial alienation at the point of entering school, prejudiced notion towards a particular segment such as PWDs or discriminatory treatment against children belonging to a particular race or gender by the society. Discrimination may also be made in the upbringing of children in the provision of social services such as education, health, and nutrition. Such discrimination generally affects the quantity and the quality of schooling and the paths to their future occupation, training, and earnings (Tilak, 1980). On the other hand, market-based discrimination is mainly concerned with productivity of workers in the labour market, which might be based on non-market factors. It occurs at the time of entry into the labour market in terms of differences in employment and earnings.

There are various theories of discrimination put forward by different scholars. According to Becker (1971), employers' taste for discrimination results in discrimination. Becker argued that there is a marked differentiation in employers "and employees" perspective while exercising any kind of discrimination and it depends on the nature of output (Becker, 1971). On the other hand, Thurow (1968), Kain (1969), Bergmann (1971) and Freeman et al. (1973) consider that discrimination does not arise out of employers' taste for discrimination, but it is the power of the dominant group that makes discrimination possible. Baran (1966) argues that differences in bargaining strength of the unions are responsible for discrimination.

The demand aspect has gained more attention in economic theories of discrimination in labour market. The supply side of market bases their assumption on "controlled-for" productivity differences or of equal productivity (Cain, 1984). The theoretical challenge remains here is to explain how workers who are intrinsically equal in productivity receive unequal outcomes ignoring other conditions like physical disability. While there are some studies on the labour market discrimination by gender, caste, race, and ethnicity, literature on discrimination against PWDs is quite limited, particularly in India.

Productivity and earnings of PWDs in labour market are affected by their access to basic services like health, transportation, and information. This may account for variability in the productive pattern of a non-disabled person and a PWD. Baldwin and Johnson argue for two types of discrimination, that is, one originating out of unequal earnings and another out of unequal employment opportunities (Baldwin & Johnson, 1994). They further pointed out that earning discrimination for PWDs varies with the type of disability they have. For them, barriers to employment is a more concerning issue than the discrimination in earnings. Further studies conducted by Beegle and Stock corroborate the findings of earlier studies regarding labour market outcomes of PWDs as compared to their non-disabled counterparts (Beegle & Stock, 2003). Empirical studies conducted by Johnson and Lambrinos used social security survey data from the USA to find out discrimination of wage between handicapped men and women, thus adding a gender dimension to the pre-existing differential. Women with disabilities have gender-related discrimination along with the former. However, the wage differential between disabled women and non-disabled women does not account much for the difference in employment rate of both the categories. This further implies that employment opportunities of disabled women are attributed more to other variables than wage differential as a major variable. Social prejudices may play an important role in determining employment opportunities for disabled women, specifically in case of countries like India.

Determinants of Labour Market Outcomes for PWDs in India

Participation in education and employment by PWDs is marked by factors characterized as determinants of education and labour market outcomes. As discussed in literature, in addition to education, training, and experiences (Becker, 1993), labour market outcomes for PWDs are also determined by factors such as accessibility to the workplace (including transportation), access to assistive technology, and job modification. Social and demographic factors play an important role while explaining the variations in employability among PWDs. For example, Mitra and Sambamoorthi in their empirical study find out that rural-urban divide, gender, and geographical locations impact the employability ratios. Women with disabilities are less likely to get employment as compared to men with disabilities. Also the rate of employment in urban areas is higher for PWDs. They bring out in their study that types of disability have an important impact upon PWDs employability pattern. Wide variations were observed across states with Lakshadweep reporting the lowest employment rate of 18.4% of persons with disabilities while Sikkim reporting 46.8% (Mitra & Sambamoorthi, 2006).

There are various factors that determine education and labour market outcomes for PWDs. Education acts as a key determinant of labour market outcome for any individual, and this is more so for PWDs. Educational outcomes for the PWDs are determined by number of years of quality schooling (primary, secondary, and higher), type of schooling (public vs. private), cost of schooling, family income, parental education, and returns to investment on education. In addition to these, factors such as type and age of disability, social attitude, accessibility of school infrastructure, and availability of assistive teaching–learning materials also impact the educational attainment of PWDs.

Indian education system has witnessed many of the structural bottlenecks in terms of educational status of children, viz. caste, gender, poverty, etc. These existing structural factors when combined with the factor of disability of children, the problem gets more aggravated and complex. PWDs have to face structural and the problem of disabilities as well. These factors make PWDs more vulnerable to marginalization in the society and also inhibit their socio-economic development. As earlier noted and also corroborated by the reports of World Bank based on National Sample Survey data from India, children with disabilities are at higher risk of not attending the schools and also more prone to drop out. Educational attainment of these children is much lower than the abled children and lower than the national average of literacy rates. These children are marginalized from social processes with higher intensity than the children belonging to scheduled caste and scheduled tribes (SC and ST). This has culminated in long-term poverty and lower chances of employment to children with disabilities (Singal, 2010; World Bank, 2007).

Data regarding enrolment of children with disabilities in primary education in India do not present a good picture. This is despite of the fact that India has enacted the right to education act for free and compulsory education in 2009 for all children aged between 6 and 14 years. However, the United Nations in its report published in 2015 stated that 34% of children with disabilities in India are out of the stream of elementary education. Further the type of disability has impact on their enrolment percentage. For example, children having specific learning disabilities or intellectual disabilities have more chances to remain out of school as compared to other impairments. Therefore, screening of children's disabilities and their proper addressal at school level are required to bring these children under the ambit of right to education act and to ensure their further inclusion into the mainstream education system.

Apart from the quantity and quality of schooling, the other factor that determines education and labour market outcomes for the PWDs is the nature of education institutions, i.e. inclusive education vs. special education. It may be argued that the nature of education institutions and government policies are such that education opportunities for children with disabilities are highly stratified and non-inclusive. Although regarding inclusion in schools, the emphasis has been put forward for collective and comprehensive inclusion of disabled children with the general community for equal footing on all fronts, which may further incapacitate them with high self-esteem and confidence (MHRD, 1968). However, some of the literature have pointed out the challenges and contradictions while executing this kind of vision in Indian context. For instance, the Kothari Commission has this observation that many of the handicapped children did not find it comfortable to be placed with ordinary children; therefore, special schools are much suited for them (Education Commission, 1966). On the other hand, some of the studies have different observations because of disabled children being withdrawn from special schools because of higher fee and high operational cost (Singal, 2010). This brings to light the existence of a dual education system for children with disabilities.

The underlying concept of inclusive education encompasses the value and belief system of society other than the economic and human capital investment. The learning opportunity for children with disabilities requires community approach rather than individualistic one. Marginalization of children with disabilities from mainstream general education system may prove detrimental to their holistic growth and thereby impacting their long-term efficiency to enter and perform better in labour market. If one takes a closer look at the public education system, there seems to be a lack of clear understanding about inclusive education or special educational needs. The special schools for long have isolated children with disabilities from mainstream social processes, hampering the development of their social skills which are crucial determinants for positive labour market outcomes.

The mainstream educational institutions have many structural deficiencies in providing proper facilitation to PWDs in India (Narasimhan, 2012).

In India, the private sector appears to have greater reluctance in providing equal opportunities for PWDs in comparison with the public sector since the latter has to comply with reservation quotas stipulated by the PWD Act. Currently, private sector initiatives in promoting equal opportunities for PWDs are limited. Private sector has inhibitions regarding the facilitation arrangements and procedures for hiring and maintaining the disabled persons to their workplace as it may escalate their cost (Shenoy, 2011). Furthermore, companies who are willing to hire disabled employees receive little help from organizations working in the disability sector in making their infrastructure disabled friendly or conducting sensitization workshops.

Many employers are sceptical about the potential and abilities of PWDs which prevent them from hiring these persons into the workforce. Industries become specific about the roles performed by PWDs in the job market in terms of skills and adjustment to work conditions. The adaptation of PWDs to their work environment may take time as a result of which they become unstable in the job market (Shenoy, 2011). The time lag between adjustment to workplace and productivity of PWDs becomes higher which eventually results in their drop out from the labour market.

Concluding Remarks

Linkage of education with labour market is well established in economics. Whether it is human capital model or human capability approach or any other social model, it is mostly argued that education acts as a screening device for people in labour market. The point which remains for argument is how to facilitate those skills and capabilities among disabled people or any other disadvantaged section of the society. For this, the social and functional construction of disability is required along with the identification of operating variables for labour market discrimination. Prevailing discrimination for the disabled people in labour market has added a major variable for critically reconstructing and reshaping the theoretical and empirical models of disability. However, this remains to be noted that discrimination in the labour market against PWDs is less explored, specifically in case of countries like India, whereby social and physical prejudices are more pronounced when it comes to the PWDs' employability in labour market. The labour market outcome is effected through the larger set of variables which further include perspectives from employers' and employees' interaction. One of the major propositions put forth by employers about individuals with disabilities is their less productivity than equally qualified individuals without disabilities. Secondly, it will be more costly to hire individuals with disabilities because accommodations or other investments may be necessary to achieve the same level of productivity as people without disabilities. Similar arguments are moulded within the periphery of human capital approach, which uses educational degrees as screening device in labour market. The recent discourse on disabled people has transformed the connotation of 'disability-friendly' into the 'disability-inclusive' domain, which requires the consideration of not only social but economic and behavioural factors of employability in public and private sector as well. Theoretical reflection requires realities and practical experiences of disabled people in labour market that can acquaint themselves with the existing models of disability.

Bibliography

American India Foundation. (2014). *Best practices in the employment of persons with disability in the private sector: An employer survey*. A study by American India Foundation, New Delhi. http://aif.org/wp-content/uploads/2015/03/DisabilityManual_3-2015.pdf, retrieved on 15/10/16

Arrow, K. J. (1971). *Some models of racial discrimination in the labor market*. No. RM-6253-RC. RAND CORP SANTA MONICA CA.

Baldwin, M., & Johnson, W. G. (1994). Labor market discrimination against men with disabilities. *Journal of Human Resources*, 1–19.

Baldwin, M. L., & Johnson, W. G. (2000). Labor market discrimination against men with disabilities in the year of the ADA. *Southern Economic Journal*, 548–566.

Baran, P. A. (1966). *Monopoly capital*. NYU Press.

Becker, G. (1971). *The economics of discrimination*. University of Chicago Press.

Becker, G. S. (1993). *Human capital: A theoretical and empirical analysis, with special reference to education* (3rd ed.). National Bureau of Economic Research.

Beegle, K., & Stock, W. A. (2003). The labor market effects of disability discrimination laws. *Journal of Human Resources, 38*(4), 806–859.

Bergmann, B. R. (1971). The effect on white incomes of discrimination in employment. *Journal of Political Economy, 79*(2), 294–313.

Cain, G. C. (1984). The economic analysis of labour market discrimination. *Focus, 7*(2).

Census of India. (2011). http://censusindia.gov.in/2011, retrieved on 17/10/16

DeLeire, T. (2000). The wage and employment effects of the Americans with disabilities act. *Journal of Human Resources, 35*(4), 693–715.

Edgerton, J. D., Roberts, L. W., & von Below, S. (2012). Education and quality of life. In *Handbook of social indicators and quality of life research* (pp. 265–296). Springer.

Education Commission. (1966). *Education and national development*. Ministry of Education, New Delhi.

Freeman, R. B., et al. (1973). Changes in the labor market for black Americans, 1948–72. *Brookings Papers on Economic Activity, 1973*(1), 67–131.

Government of India. (2019). *Annual report 2018–19*. Ministry of Social Justice and Empowerment, Department of Empowerment of Persons with Disabilities (Divyangjan).

GoI (2007–08). *Annual report of labour & employment*. Ministry of labour and employment, Government of India.

Hauser, R. M., et al. (2000). Occupational status, education, and social mobility in the meritocracy. *Meritocracy and Economic Inequality, 5*(13), 179–229.

Hollenbeck, K., & Kimmel, J. (2008). Differences in the returns to education for males by disability status and age of disability onset. *Southern Economic Journal*, 707–724.

Ionescu, A. M., & Cuza, A. I. (2012). How does education affect labour market outcomes. *Review of Applied Socio-Economic Research, 4*(2), 130–144.

Johnson, W. G., & Lambrinos, J. (1985). Wage discrimination against handicapped men and women. *Journal of Human Resources*, 264–277.

Kain, J. F. (1969). *Race and poverty: The economics of discrimination*. Prentice Hall.

Kidd, M. P., Sloane, P. J., & Ferko, I. (2000). Disability and the labour market: An analysis of British males. *Journal of Health Economics, 19*(6), 961–981.

Levine, M. (1976). The academic achievement test: Its historical context and social functions. *American Psychologist, 31*(3), 228.

Metts, R. L. (2000). *Disability issues, trends, and recommendations for the World Bank (full text and annexes)*. Washington, World Bank.
Mincer, J. (1958). Investment in human capital and personal income distribution. *Journal of Political Economy, 66*(4), 281–302.
Mincer, J. (1974). *Schooling, experience, and earnings*. Human Behavior & Social Institutions No. 2.
Ministry of Human Resource Development (MHRD). (1968). *National policy on education 1968*. Government of India, New Delhi.
Mitra, S., & Sambamoorthi, U. (2006). Employment of persons with disabilities: Evidence from the National Sample Survey. *Economic and Political Weekly*, 199–203.
Narasimhan. (2012). Enabling access for persons with disabilities to higher education and workplace: Role of ICT and assistive technologies. https://cis-india.org/accessibility/technology-for-accessibility
O'Keefe, P. B. (2007). *People with disabilities in India: From commitments to outcomes*. No. 41585. The World Bank.
Pascarella, E. T., & Terenzini, P. T. (2005). *How college affects students: A third decade of research* (Vol. 2). Jossey-Bass, An Imprint of Wiley.
PWD (Equal Opportunities, Protection of Rights and Full Participation) Act. (1995). http://www.disabilityaffairs.gov.in/upload/uploadfiles/files/PWD_Act.pdf, retrieved on 20/10/16.
Saha, L. J. (Ed.). (1997). *International encyclopedia of the sociology of education* (Vol. 8). Pergamon Press.
Shenoy, M. (2011). Persons with disability and the India labour market: Challenges and opportunities. *ILO, 13*(1).
Singal, N. (2006). Inclusive education in India: International concept, national interpretation. *International Journal of Disability, Development and Education, 53*(3), 351–369.
Singal, N. (2010). *Education of children with disabilities in India. Background paper prepared for the Education for All Global Monitoring Report*. http://unesdoc.unesco.org/images/0018/001866/186611e.pdf (retrieved on 17/10/16)
Soloman, L. C., & Fagano, C. L. (1997) Benefits of education. In L. J. Saha (Ed.). *International encyclopaedia of the sociology of education* (pp. 819–829). New York: Pergamon.
Stein, M. A. (2000). Labor markets, rationality, and workers with disabilities. *Berkeley Journal of Employment and Labor Law, 21*, 314.
Stiglitz, J., et al. (2009). *The measurement of economic performance and social progress revisited. Reflections and overview*. Commission on the Measurement of Economic Performance and Social Progress, Paris.
Tansel, A. (2004). Public-private employment choice, wage differentials, and gender in Turkey. *Economic Development and Cultural Change, 53*(2), 453–477.
Thurow, L. C. (1968). *Poverty and discrimination*. Washington DC: Brookings.
Tilak, J. B. G. (1980). Education and labour market discrimination. *Indian Journal of Industrial Relations, 16*(1), 95–114.
World Bank. (2007). *Development and next generation*. World Bank, Washington.
World Health Organization. (2011). *World report on disability 2011*. World Health Organization.

Chapter 19
Honk Honk: Women, You Drive Crazy!

Radhika Bali

Abstract Despite all the progress our nation is leading towards and the policies about gender equality our government is making on papers, gender stereotypes still continue to exist, and patriarchy still is a reality. Gender stereotyping is about the essentialist characteristics, attributes, and roles, which are ascribed to a particular individual or community, thereby making their very existence limited and disabled. In this paper, I am concerned about the disability which women are inflicted upon, in our misogynist and patriarchal society, when they decide to put themselves behind the steering wheel. Whether women are behind the steering wheel on roads, or behind the purdah (veil) in their houses, discrimination and the treatment they get in accordance with their gender expectations ultimately render them disabled.

Keywords Gender stereotype · Disability · Feminine · Patriarchy · Misogyny · Sexist

Before entering the analysis, I should clarify that disability has its broad range and understanding. I may not be talking about any physical, or mental, or any other obvious form of disability here, but I am taking up an equally important aspect of it. Or should I say, the aspect that I shall be discussing here includes both physical, mental, and various other forms of disabilities if only one is sensitive towards the subtleness.

Before entering the analysis, I should clarify that disability has its broad range and understanding. I may not be talking about any physical, or mental, or any other obvious form of disability here, but I am taking up an equally important aspect of it. Or should I say, the aspect that I shall be discussing here includes both physical, mental, and various other forms of disabilities if only one is sensitive towards the subtleness.

Our society, very conveniently, is bifurcated into 'masculine' and 'feminine'. From personal habits to social conducts, hairstyles to attire, from domestic life to professional work, name anything, this unjust binary system is pervasive everywhere.

R. Bali (✉)
Department of English and Cultural Studies, Panjab University, Chandigarh, India

R. Uniyal and F. Rizvi (eds.), *Understanding Disability*,
https://doi.org/10.1007/978-981-99-4925-0_19

How many times have you seen a lady of your house changing the bulbs when the previous one fuses, or fixing the plumbing system with all the tools? Or, how many times have you seen the man of your house carving out the perfect round chapatis, or taking care of all the flowers in your garden? The former occupations are considered macho, while the latter are essential to women. Crisscrossing of professions is generally frowned upon. *Dance Like A Man* by Mahesh Dhattani is one such example where the characters struggle to live up to their gender expectations. The play revolves around the couple, Jairaj and Ratna, both Bharatnatyam dancers, and maps their arduous journeys they face in the due course of the dancing career.

Amritlal Parekh is Jairaj's autocratic father who opposes their dancing and becomes the perfect epitome of patriarchal subjugation in the play. Jairaj's dancing career gets his father's wrath because the very notion of dancing is opposed to that of 'maleness' and deemed perfect for females (it is considered perfect for females because dance has its long history of *Kotha* culture, where women would dance in front of men to lure them into their charms). The very title "Dance Like A Man" is suggestive that Dattani has explored the issues of male stereotyping and the identity crises Jairaj undergoes. Jairaj's passion is condemned, gender is questioned, and his identity is stigmatized.

Sex dictates or necessitates our sociocultural meanings and experiences. Gender performativity which Judith Butler has talked about suggests that how the acts of gender and its performances are constructed, but taken to be as the core reality. In her essay *Performative Acts and Gender Constitution: An Essay in Phenomenology and Feminist Theory,* she says,

> Gender reality is performative which means, quite simply, that it is real only to the extent that it is performed. This implicit and popular theory of acts and gestures as expressive of gender suggests that gender itself is something prior to the various acts, postures, and gestures by which it is dramatized and known; indeed, gender appears to the popular imagination as a substantial core which might well be understood as the spiritual or psychological correlate of biological sex. (527–528)

The problems arise when we demarcate the gender roles based on its sex. Judith butler has fortified this claim in the same essay, as distinguishing between sex and gender,

> ...if gender attributes and acts, the various ways in which a body shows or produces its cultural signification are performative, then there is no pre-existing identity by which an act or attribute might be measured; there would be no true or false, real or distorted acts of gender, and the postulation of a true gender identity would be revealed as a regulatory fiction. That gender reality is created through sustained social performances which means that the very notions of an essential sex, a true or abiding masculinity or femininity, are also constituted as part of the strategy by which the performative aspect of gender is concealed. (528)

The widely accepted view among the general public is that men and women fundamentally differ, and that a distinct set of fixed traits characterize masculinity and femininity. As Erwin Straus in his *Phenomenological Psychology* has stated, "the remarkable difference in the manner of throwing of the two sexes" (157). A man will always throw a ball by making use of his whole body, moving all of his limbs, making use of his lateral space around, as if he is the very ball which is to be thrown. A woman, on the other hand, does not often make much use of her (limited) lateral space available to her. She would not move her body much, except for the arm which is involved in throwing. This remarkable difference is however not because females have this innate femaleness in them, but because their comportments and movements are being supervised from an early age.

> Genders, then, can be neither true nor false, neither real nor apparent. And yet, one is compelled to live in a world in which genders constitute univocal signifiers, in which gender is stabilized, polarized, rendered discrete, and intractable. In effect, gender is made to comply with a model of truth and falsity which not only contradicts its own performative fluidity, but serves a social policy of gender regulation and control. Performing one's gender wrong initiates a set of punishments both obvious and indirect, and performing it well provides the reassurance that there is an essentialism of gender identity after all. That this reassurance is so easily displaced by anxiety, that culture so readily punishes or marginalizes those who fail to perform the illusion of gender essentialism should be sign enough that on some level there is social knowledge that the truth or falsity of gender is only socially compelled and in no sense ontologically necessitated. (Butler 528)

Gender stereotype is a serious issue. But it is even grave, when meted out to women. There are official stats that show that gender stereotyping poses a significant challenge to the lives of women. For instance, the attribute of fertility—it is considered to be the women's duty to bear children (boys preferably), even if there lie issues of incapacity within men. But the fingers would be pointed out at women for their entire life, while the fertility problems of men would be swept slyly under the carpet. Unfortunately, the very notion of fertility is considered to be feminine. Something which is quite natural to women only.

I remember the days when I had learned driving recently, and did not have much confidence on roads; making a U-turn on a two-lane road used to be a task for me. I had to think twice before making my move. Not that I did not have the courage to do so, or did not know how to do it, but people have zero patience when they have to wait even for five seconds in their lives. The very first time when I took a U-turn, I got stuck diagonally on the middle of the road, because nobody would give me my way. The lane was not that wide, so I had to reverse a bit in order to form the full turn. But! those five seconds of my life, full of honking as I caused the movement to stop, and full of aggressive remarks, *apne ghar ke verandah mei chala* (Drive in your house's veranda).

Daring To Drive by Manal Al-Sharif is a memoir of the author's hostile experiences in the man's kingdom. In an oppressive environment of Saudi Arabia, Manal and her family has to deal with the ruthless laws of the country as Manal has violated them by driving a car publically. (In Saudi Arabia, driving vehicles by women of the country is considered *haram.*) The law also forbids women from leaving the house without a close male relative. It refuses to give identity cards to women and practices female genital mutilation as a norm.

> Even a woman in labour will not be admitted into a hospital without her guardian or at least a mahram (provide meaning). Police cannot enter a home during a robbery, and firefighters are

> forbidden from entering a home during a fire or medical emergency if a woman is inside but does not have a mahram present. It is not a stretch to say that death is preferable to violating the strict code of guardianship and mahrams. (7)

Manal has painted the horrific picture of her home and school life, suffering repression and suppression of all sorts in her book. As driving was forbidden for women, women relied solely on men for their 'movement'. (Ironically, Saudi men call women "queens" and say queens don't drive at all.) In May 2011, Manal al-Sharif appeared in a black *abaya* behind the steering wheel of a car and recorded herself driving fearlessly. The video later went viral on the Internet, which has caused her troubles thereafter. She told her audience in Arabic that her kingdom was home to many educated women, but none with driver's licenses. Her goal is to demonstrate to Saudi society that while she is a woman, she is equally competent to sit behind the wheel of a car.

> As I opened my door and stepped inside, I did not hate men in their cars who had seen fit to harass me. I hated the rules that caged me inside my compound, that kept women tethered to the whim of our guardians, and that kept us shut inside our homes more effectively than any lock. (208)

In reality, "Nothing, absolutely nothing" (209), in the official traffic codes of Saudi Arabia indicated such oppressive and illegal ban on women's driving. This whole idea of suppressive measures rested on the religious fatwa—Women "would destroy Saudi society" (213) and "destroy Saudi family life" (213). Women driving "would lead to corruption and moral decay" (213). There is a journalist called Maysa, whose father died in front of her eyes because he fell ill and no other man was at home, and Maysa couldn't drive him to the hospital.

Eternal notions of innate feminine are making women disabled at every juncture. Once and for all, driving (and almost everything) is considered to be a man's thing. It involves technology, rationality, and holding on to your senses. It involves the art of analysing and handling of the stressful situations and being quick with the reflexes. In short, it involves everything that our patriarchal and misogynistic society does not expect out of women. Nevertheless, women drive, and they drive crazy. Firstly, because seductiveness is what is attributed as their natural essence, in the patriarchal society, that needs to bring sexual drives in men, and secondly, as the famous proverb goes, "women can't drive".

Driving is a neutral phenomenon as dancing is, cooking is, carpentry is, photography is, and every single thing that exists in this world is. But we, compelled by our prejudiced notions of making societal constructs and morals, oblige to the wicked ways of such hierarchies. Hierarchy that has vested in men its prime importance at everything, and that has made women, as De Beauvoir would say, the "other". De Beauvoir has argued in great lengths that there exists no such thing called feminine essence or femaleness. It is our misogynistic society that reduces the stature of women to nothing but their reproductive function, thereby casting them as somebody that men require in order to fulfil their sexual desires. They have been made into these fragile things, which must be picked up and coaxed into movement, a thing which needs to be looked at, and acted upon. Furthermore, there have been many evolutionary theories in the Neuroscience of sex differences, which have suggested that the size of the brain of women is relatively smaller than that of men and which is why they lack the competence in them. However, scientists have proved various sexual dimorphisms of the brain, but they do not think sex had any impact on how the human brain performs everyday tasks. As Beauvoir once said, "Every human existence is defined by its situation; the particular existence of the female person is no less defined by the historical, cultural, social, and economic limits of her situation."

Driving a vehicle has its connotations much beyond simply just being able to plying on roads. Having a hold of a steering wheel in your hand is more like having the hold of your life in your hands, which is a virtue women are generally deprived of. Being able to drive means that you are mobile and not just sticking inside the four walls of your house. You have the agency to take your vehicle (self) in whatever direction you want to. You are not dependent on somebody to take you to places, you have your own identity and will. But this scenario is a bizarre and far-fetched phenomenon in the case of women. It's mostly the husband, father or brother who is driving the vehicle, and the lives of those around them.

Women driving on roads would often attract heads towards them, sometimes in rebuke, sometimes in lewd remark, and other times in different ways of misconduct. First of all, there are fewer women drivers because their families they come from do not allow them to drive, and secondly those few who are comparatively privileged fall in the trap of ongoing road oppression, due to which most of them lose their self-confidence to drive alone. Women are made to live in contradictions from the very start. Even if they are told that they could achieve anything as men could, yet their every action is watched and judged. They are made conscious about their bodies and its various ways. From a young age, they acquire timidity, which obviously fortifies with age. Women are not as open with their bodies as men. Women are told not to laugh loud and freely in public as good girls laugh decently, not to sit with wide open legs and cross when men are around, to watch out for their gait, thereby having a minimum spatiality around them from which they are not supposed to move beyond. Iris Marion Young observes some points put forth by Straus, in her *Throwing Like a Girl*,

> …between the way boys and girls throw is that girls do not bring their whole bodies into the motion as much as the boys. They do not reach back, twist, move backward, step, and lean forward. Rather, the girls tend to remain relatively immobile except for their arms, and even the arm is not extended as far as it could be. (142)

Women in the sexist society are both physically and mentally handicapped. They hegemonically complicit themselves to the sexism, as they are made to. Due to this lack of confidence, they live their bodies as a burden that needs to be tagged along, dragged, and protected at the same time. Thus, there is no relation between being a female and not being able to ace at driving as men. Lack of practice in using their bodies, performing tasks, driving for that matter, and not being able to move out of the house for most of the time is why women are not being able to drive as men under the skies of misogyny oppression. If given the proper environment without any prejudice and discrimination, women could prove to be the more careful drivers than men.

Lady Driver edited by Jayawati Shrivastava is a book forecasting twelve real-life stories of various women who decided to get the command of steering wheel in their hands. In the short story "Mother and Daughter, Co-travellers Off the Beaten Track" by Deepti Priya Mehrotra, there is a mother-daughter duo who take up driving as a profession. This story is based on a true event that smashes the patriarchy and misogyny in their faces. The duo get themselves enrolled in Azad Foundation, whose motto is to have "women on wheels". Azad as the name suggests is constantly freeing women from the chains of tortures they are bound to. It is empowering all those women who have suffered the extremity of tortures in their lives. Both Savitri (mother) and Poonam (daughter) learnt driving there and got themselves hired as professional chauffeurs. Savitri's husband Dayaram was himself scared of driving, so he never learnt. He was very supportive and said to Savitri, "It's your choice, the important thing is that you should be happy. If you want to learn something, go ahead and learn! If you wish to take up a job, do so" (30). Hailing Beauvoir once again, an individual is always the product of its situation, indeed is correct. Because Savitri and Poonam came from a family where the man did not pose any hurdle, so things turned out to be pretty well for them. Savitri's childhood was spent in Rae Bareli. She had two sisters and three brothers. She spent her childhood in poverty and could not go to school. As the tradition continued, she was soon married off into a village close by. When the situations were not favourable for her, she could not achieve anything. But now, as Savitri said, "New windows of life and living have opened for me now. And more importantly, I hope I've opened some doors for other girls" (30). Dayaram not knowing the driving himself subverts the idea that driving is essentially a macho thing to do. Gender stereotypes are being questioned here. Dayaram is the one who cultivates flowers and vegetables, while the women of his house are driving fearlessly. This spirit of openness and understanding within families, and society at large, is the need of all times.

Several women who drive today with full confidence, without paying any heed to what people say around them, must have faced all sorts of humiliations and tortures at some point of time indeed. Yet another non-fiction tale "The First Woman Auto Driver in the Pink City" by Anita Mathur, from the same anthology, is a real-life story of Hemlata who also joined Azad Foundation and learnt driving. She is recognized as the first woman to drive an auto in Jaipur. But her fate was as similar as every other woman.

> Hemlata created a bit of sensation at the auto-stand when she first started to go there. The male drivers had never seen a young woman doing what was 'their' task and parking her auto alongside theirs. Some of them were curious, but most were suspicious and many scoffed at her. Some tried to prevent her from parking or blocked the space so she could not get her auto in there, and others insulted her. (39)

The proverb "women can't drive" does not originate either from their anatomy or physiology and certainly not from their innate femaleness. Rather it originates from the situations where upbringing of women is conditioned and institutionalized by the fundamental sexist oppression. The growth of women in the sexist world is physically and mentally inhibited, and their very existence is objectified. Women have been treated without any dignity, solely as an object of sexual desire. The society in which we live encourages toxic masculinity. At every juncture, women have been looking for affirmation in the eyes of their men. Because they are subjected to the whims and choices of their men, women have the greater tendency to underestimate their bodily capacities. They become the hysterical puppets in the hands of their men and start abhorring the experiences of their own bodies.

There is no harmony between the environment present inside of women and outside of them. They are often made to live as a contradictory identity. Their very existence becomes a paradox. No matter how much their gut wants it, how well sure they are of themselves, there are outer societal constructs which are ever readily present to condition their selves. It is like when you marinate chicken by putting various ingredients of your choice, so once it is cooked you get all the flavours you had put in it. I could use innumerable examples right now; anything that has wings. This lack of harmony within women is the reason they cannot perform as men. This is the reason why they get complicit in holding back on their own kinetics.

"Empress of Her Heart" by Sunita Thakur tells the story Rabbunisha, who is a thoughtful girl. She does not question herself, but the system which delimits them.

Why do all religions make laws and regulations only for women?

So many men make life hell for their wives and children, and women just bear this silently because this is what their religion teaches them. (46)

Rabbunisha is fearless because she learnt one great lesson in her life from *Jagori Rural Charitable Trust*.

> Today you can leave this neighbourhood, but how do you know you will not face the same situation elsewhere? Stay, face the situation, and fight for justice. Remember, if you move, and someone else comes in, they'll target them. So take the only route that you must take when fighting for justice—fight with grit and determination. (49)

In a study in 2014, it was discovered that suicide is responsible for the 71% violent deaths in women due to the gender discrimination they are subjected to go through. Around the globe, women are undervalued and neglected everywhere—by the government officials, communities, and even within their own families. Stats show that sexism impacts mental health and misogyny kills. Women's rights are violated everywhere, from their personal life to the public domain. The list of the violations against women's human rights is the longest. It includes violence against them in the form of bride burning, child abuse, child marriage, domestic violence, female foeticide, eve teasing, infanticide, sexual harassment at the workplace, and much more. They are often deprived of their personal liberty and bound by rules which are made by the self-proclaimed superior males. But what do you think is wrong with the world? From the wide range of global crisis that we feel in today's world—whether it is about the contemporary issues in Syria, or Kashmir, or in any part of the world, and even the crisis that our world has gone through before, like the World Wars, to the crisis at personal level, one thing that remains constant and underlies at every situation is the 'need to control others'. Psychoanalytic studies show that the oppression of women stems largely from men's inherent psychology to subjugate women; the intense desire for power and control over them. This very same need, throughout history, has driven men to try to conquer and subjugate groups or nations which they felt were inferior to them. The supreme feeling that they could oppress weaker classes or groups anywhere drives them to dominate and oppress women as well. Since men feel the urge to gain as much power they can and have their control all over, they steal away the freedom and control from women. They deny women the right to make decisions so that they can decide for them. They leave women unable to direct their own lives whether behind the *purdah* or behind the steering wheels, so that they can direct their lives for them.

In a patriarchal society, women have often suffered in silence. They remain silent because of the fear of being labelled as a fallen/bad/characterless woman, the names are in variety. They do not speak up, or try to separate themselves from the abusive treatment they are subjected to, because they fear that status of an outcast which their society will subject them to. This is the reason why they refrain from discussing or accessing remedies, and because they keep silent, their trauma is not properly addressed and the abuse perpetuates. When a woman gets married, the only piece of advice she gets from her own parents is to compromise in every situation whatsoever. She should be rather educated enough to maintain her self-respect, and confidence, and run away from the husband's house if need be. Societal change or cure could only be developed when the very sources of the oppressive thoughts towards women, that reside in one's subconscious, are uprooted. Before anything else, toxic masculine psyche needs to be understood, addressed, and destroyed. Looking at women through the lenses of inferiority needs to be corrected.

What is happening in the recent 2020 Hathras gang rape and murder case of a 19-year-old Dalit girl, who is allegedly raped by four upper caste Thakurs? The girl died after struggling for her life for two weeks. The family of the victim has claimed that the funeral took place without their consent, when the police forcefully locked them all inside, and petrol was used in fire in order to cremate her body. This incident has shaken the senses worldwide. But now the scenario has taken altogether a different turn, and a political discourse has emerged out to be. It has always been quite convenient in our society to dodge the actual problems. Now the narrative has become blaming and defaming the government. Bhakts allege that the whole incident has been framed as a rape case in order to defame the Yogi government. They say issues of casteism are being dragged deliberately to advantage the vote banks of the opponents. They deny of any rape done to her. The battle that needs to be against female oppression and violence has digressed its course from the actual problems to the vicious election game. But before everything else and amid everything else, life of a girl has been lost. This is not a first incident of its own kind, but zillions of lives have been lost till date due to the whole sole misogynistic oppression and violence. But there has been a ritual to dodge from the actual problems. This pattern of oppression is profoundly integrated into society, thus creating and sustaining patriarchy each day. Had there been some rule of honking, when every time a crime is done against women, the whole world would have gone sick, each individual, due to the noise pollution by now.

Bibliography

Al-Sharif, M. (2017). *Daring to drive*. Simon & Schuster Uk Ltd.

Butler, J. (1988). Performative acts and gender constitution: An essay in phenomenology and feminist theory. *Theater Journal, 40*(4), 519–531. JSTOR, https://www.jstor.org/stable/3207893

De Beauvoir, S. (2010). *The second sex* (C. Borde & S. Malovany, Trans.). Vintage Books.

Dhattani, M. (2006). *Dance like a man: A stage play in two acts*. Penguin.

Garland-Thomson, R. (2011). Integrating disability, transforming feminist theory. In K. Q. Hall (Ed.), *Feminist disability studies* (pp. 13–47). Indiana UP.

Mathur, A. (2017a). The first woman auto driver in the pink city. In J. Shrivastava (Ed.), *Lady driver*. Zubaan Publishers.

Mehrotra, D. P. (2017). Mother and daughter, co-travellers off the beaten track. In J. Shrivastava (Ed.), *Lady driver.* Zubaan Publishers.

Strauss, E. W. (1966). *Phenomenological psychology*. Garland Publishers.

Thakur, S. (2017b). Empress of her heart. In J. Shrivastava (Ed.), *Lady driver*. Zubaan Publishers.

Young, I. M. (1980). Throwing like a girl: A phenomenology of feminine body comportment motility and spatiality. *Human Studies* (3), 137–156.

Chapter 20
Contesting Representation, Writing Self: A Critical Study of Disabled Life Narratives in *A Bumblebee's Balcony* and *One Little Finger*

S. Gokul

"Disabled people have been spoken about, and spoken for, but rarely listened to." (Sherry M)

Life narratives are first-person testimonies. They record certain events that narrate the writer's life. While some life narratives are inspirational, others convey an awareness message. John Beverley comments that testimonies are an assertion of the individual subject which may suggest individual growth or transformation in connection to a group or class's situation marked by oppression, struggle, and marginalization (Beverley 103). Questions that emerge about life narratives: Who writes for whom and what is conveyed through the life writings? Earlier, it is considered that disabled used to write to earn sympathy, but now there has been a shift in writing and understanding of the disabled self. Now, disabled life writings deal with stigmatization, preconceptions, and attitudes of the society towards the disabled. This happened when the shift from the Medical Model to the social model of disability took place. The understanding that emerged is that one is disabled not because of his/her impairment but because of society's mindset that stereotypes and marginalizes the impaired individuals. This paper focuses on questions of how representations of disability differ from the self and urban-rural representations of the disabled. At the same time, rural and urban representations are viewed in terms of their depiction in India and the way it differs from the west, in terms of accommodating and accepting the disabled. Exploring these questions, the paper shows why writing about the self is important through the study of two disabled life narratives, *A Bumblebee's Balcony* and *One Little Finger*.

The term 'autobiography' is of Greek origin; *autos* denote 'self', *bios*, 'life' and *graphe*, 'writing'. Taken together the words, *self-life writing* indicates what

S. Gokul (✉)
The English and Foreign Languages University, Hyderabad, India
e-mail: gokulloyola13@gmail.com

R. Uniyal and F. Rizvi (eds.), *Understanding Disability*,
https://doi.org/10.1007/978-981-99-4925-0_20

an autobiography is (Smith1). The autobiography is seen as a democratic, inclusive, and accessible literary genre to give voice to disabled people. Their voices have been heard in the public space in the USA only after the Americans with Disabilities Act (1990). By the end of last century, the West had numerous life narratives of the disabled. However, in the Indian context, till date there are only a few life narratives, such as Firdaus Kanga's *Trying to Grow* (1991), L. Subramani's *Lights Out* (2014), Ved Mehta's *Face to Face* (1957), *Vedi* (1982), *The Ledge between the Streams* (1984), *Sound-Shadows of the New World* (1986), *The Stolen Light* (1989), *Up at Oxford* (1993), and *All for Love* (2001). On the other hand, it took a century for disabled Indian women's voices to be heard in the form of life narratives. Disabled Indian women's life narratives were published only after the 2000s. Life narratives are a valuable and liberal medium of representation for the experience of disability because they involve self-representation. Life narratives can be seen as 'counter-discourses' (Couser, 1997), helping the self to project his/her own identity. They also problematize images of the disabled created through fictional projections of the third-person narratives. They are also valued for their talkback nature against the dominant understandings and ideas of the disabled as deficit. In disabled life narratives, disability is a complex social, political, and embodied condition, portrayed as the author's legitimate experience. G Thomas Couser comments that disabled life narratives are stereotyped as 'inspirational' by the 'able' society. The essential nature of disabled life narratives is self-consciously political and challenges the conventional perception of disability.

Life narratives can be considered to be an outcome of various experiences and give shape to them. In this sense, narrative and the self are considered to be one. Self is broadly understood as unfolding reflective awareness of being in the world, including a sense of one's past and future. The unity of narrative and self is grounded in the assumption that individuals are given meaning through experienced life events. This promotes narratives as an essential tool in the struggle of bringing experiences with mindful awareness. At any point in time, our sense of individuality, including ourselves, is an outcome of our subjective association with the world. The third-person representations are seen as fictional rather than factual. The first-person representation through disabled life narratives can be considered more authentic because people writing about disability in third person might not have experienced the pain, sufferings, and trauma of the disabled. Their writing would be based on experience of interacting with disabled people. In the first-person narrative, the 'self' finds a proper representation thereby giving a more authentic impression.

"Identity is the sameness of a person at all times or in all circumstances; individuality or continuity of personality; personal or individual existence" (Winslow 45). Life narrative can serve as a powerful and effective tool for constructing identity and to express unheard voices and views. Socially marginalized groups such as women, tribal people, and the disabled can use life narrative as a medium to share their experiences, especially their traumas. Life narrative is a channel of communication between the marginalized and the society to establish their voice and identity in the world.

Disabled life narratives cannot be seen simply as autobiographies. An autobiography is "the writing of one's history; the story of one's life written by oneself" (Winslow 16). The author writes and interprets his own life experiences, unlike in a biography where someone else writes about him/her. In fictional autobiographies such as Charles Dickens' *David Copperfield*, the author writes the story as a first-person narrative to bring the readers close to his real-life experiences. Michelle Obama's *Becoming* (2018) is an autobiography where she records her voice and experiences as the first lady of the USA and her role as the mother of her kids. Disabled life narratives are significantly different from autobiographies. They do not merely reflect the identity of an individual or an individual story of victory. Rather, disabled life narratives are seen as the voice and representation of the whole disabled community. For instance, Preeti Monga's *The Other Senses* narrates her experience of visual impairment in her childhood days, abuses faced in marriage, and how hardships in life mould her destiny in life as an aerobic trainer, public speaker, and director of a company. This becomes a representation and identity of not just herself, but the voice of the visually impaired community by and large as can be vividly observed in her narrative.

According to Couser, autobiography deserves a prominent place in disability studies by the same logic that has made it essential to other areas of study. As the first-person narratives, autobiographies mirror the life of the writer. Disabled people are much spoken about, but they are hardly listened to and hence the first-person life narratives of the disabled are important for an analysis and understanding of disability in the society. Only they can express the pain, suffering, and trauma that life events caused in them. The third person who is just a mere spectator or listener can't express the feelings of the disabled at any point. Therefore, autobiography occupies the first place in the study of disability. It is also to be noted that literature from the margins has a different cultural context when it is read. It raises question about whose life is counted and why these stories are worthy of narrating. Marginalized first-person writings are considered to be the voice of the oppressed. People with impairment should write their own stories because every impairment has its own limitations, and therefore, the needs of impairment or life of all disabled cannot be treated in the same manner. A ramp is a need for a wheelchair user but not for the hearing impaired. The writings of the disabled are products involving one sense devoid of others, and they cannot be treated as homogenous representations of entire disabled community.

This study aims to read life narratives of Sundari Sivasubbbu and Malini Chib, both of whom have cerebral palsy. Malini is born in Kolkata, and she had a family that could relocate to London for her treatment. On the other hand, Sundari is born in a small village in Tamil Nadu where she is treated for orthopaedic problems, due to ignorance about cerebral palsy. Malini completed her education in London and Mumbai, whereas Sundari is educated in Chennai. These two people are born in different locations with different levels of awareness about cerebral palsy. When Malini is born, cerebral palsy is treated as mental retardation in India and Sundari is being educated in SPASTN when she is nine years old. These are two people with the same impairment but two different ways of living. These two books illustrate how impairment is also affected by economic status.

A Bumblebee's Balcony: Celebrating Life with Cerebral Palsy is the life narrative of Sundari Sivasubbu who was born with cerebral palsy, a neuro-skeletal and muscular condition that limits most physical activities and poses several challenges in day-to-day living. It included problems with vision, hearing, balancing, co-ordination, muscle power, and motor skills. Sundari holds the position of a communication specialist with the corporate social responsibility division of HCL. Earlier, she worked in a multinational bank and as a subeditor in *The New Indian Express*. Published in 2019, *A Bumblebee's Balcony Celebrating life with Cerebral Palsy* speaks of the internal conflict between the mind and body where, "the mind is organized, independent, ambitious and self-motivated and the body was dependent, needed a lot of help, was chaotic, wobbly, weak and powerless" (Sivasubbu xv-xvi). This book has thirty-four chapters along with a prologue and an epilogue. It narrates Sundari's life as a girl born with cerebral palsy in a small town called Srivaikuntam in Tamil Nadu. It describes how she suffered during her childhood days due to ignorance about cerebral palsy at that time and how her life changed when she moved to the city of Madras. The book ends with the epilogue describing her visit to the same village where once she was seen as an object of pity but today is as a person with self-esteem and identity.

Malini Chib's *One Little Finger* is the story of Malini's quest for independence, identity, and passion to live a meaningful life despite a lifelong disability. This book is divided into four parts which narrate the events from her birth to getting employed. Malini is seen as a symbol of hope today. She was once declared a vegetable by doctors, but today she is a pioneer for people with cerebral palsy in India. Malini Chib has cerebral palsy, a neurological condition similar to an adult stroke, which makes body movement and speech extremely difficult. Malini is a senior events manager at Oxford Bookstore, Mumbai. She is the founder and co-chairperson of Abled Disabled All People Together (ADAPT). She holds international master's degrees in Women's Studies, Library Sciences and Information Management. She is the author of *One Little Finger* (2011) that narrates the story of her struggle against adversities, prejudices, stigmas, and stereotypes of society and her will to succeed in search of her identity.

Self-representations Versus Societal Representations

Religion is often seen as a problem in the life of the disabled as disability is widely represented as symbolic of a moral or spiritual condition rather than a lived reality. Ruth Cameron Webb's *Journey into Personhood* that records her life account as someone with cerebral palsy narrates that she is told, "Ruth, you have the special mission from the lord, The Great Spirit. . . you are asked to reflect God's glory in your disabled body..." (180). Thus, in this Christian view, birth with impairment is a result of your sins or it gives you the special status of being close to God. It does not normalize disability but gives it the colour of being special.

Marriage, especially for girls, is an important aspect of Indian society. In *A Bumblebee's Balcony*, the author narrates how a girl with disability is viewed by society. Both education and marriage are seen as futile for her, and disability is seen as an ancestral sin. The following lines from the book illustrate these views:

Ayyopaavam! She is a girl! She is a mere girl child, that too a disabled child! Why do you both fuss about her so much? Anyway, she'll not be able to do anything. You both are moving to the city to educate your disabled girl? Ridiculous! You can always put her in-home for such children. Poor girl! Must be a sign of some evil ancestor that she's born this way! How will she get married? Only God can bring a solution to her life. (Sivasubbu 229)

The lines mentioned above are representative of disability in Indian society as experienced by Sundari. She is looked down upon as an object of pity and as a burden described to her parents as 'fit for nothing.' She is a young girl stuck in an impaired society, but she rises above her condition to prove that she has some reason for being born, to spread her wings and fly. While society sees her as impaired, Sundari in her life narrative sees herself as a bumblebee, as indicated in the title of the book. Sundari comments in the preface that as a human bumblebee she fights thousands of battles in her daily life to prove that assumptions, norms, and standards are wrong. In the eyes of society, she is just an object without a future, her life destined to end in the suffering of impairment. On the contrary, she considers herself as a bumblebee that flips its wings 500 times to raise high from the ground. She is a bumblebee who faces slurs to fly high in an impaired society.

Malini was born after 40 hours of labour pain, and the doctors were sceptical about her chances of survival. They thought she would not survive or if she did would remain in a "vegetable" state for the rest of her life (Chib 5). This notion was nullified with proper treatment and rehabilitation. The current status of her life today proves the medical statements about her to be wrong and based on ignorance: "It was a mistake should have carried out a caesarean; let's see if she survives... I'm not sure if she survives, at the most 72 hours" (Chib 3). These above words are uttered by the doctor at her birth. If her parents had stopped with the words of doctors, her existence would have been precarious. However, they started searching for a way out with hope and they found that cerebral palsy could be treated: "Every doctor my parents met in India told them that I could be a vegetable and nothing could be done for me" (Chib 5). This statement suggests that the doctors in India were not aware of cerebral palsy or the medical infrastructure required for its treatment. It also hints at a miraculous struggle for survival that proved the medical assumptions wrong.

Malini was taken to London for her education and treatment. In a more advanced society where she was treated on par with others and she had the freedom to do things on her own in an accommodating and accessible environment. Here it is evident that having economic resources can result in a different experience of disability. She was born in an economically well-off family which could afford her treatment in London. This opens up the argument of Eastern and Western representations of the disabled. In India, she points out that she faced remarks like, "I think these people should be locked up' but today she claims that 'we are seen everywhere…if the public spaces are accessible, you can see us everywhere" (Chib 193).

Urban and Rural, East and West in Representations of Disability

Apart from the representation of self and society, *A Bumblebee's Balcony* is also unique in bringing out the differences in rural and urban life of the disabled. Sundari was born in a small village in south of Tamil Nadu. She suffered for nine years because she didn't know that she had a problem in her brain and she was given treatment for her legs. When she came to Madras, she started experiencing a new life. In the urban region, people had little knowledge of disability and they started seeing activities of the disabled with awe. Sometimes little knowledge can be of great danger and keeps the life of the disabled in a bad condition.

The rural Indian lifestyle is different from that of the urban. The joint family system that survives in rural India and to some extent in urban India can be a boon and a bane. Families provide assistance and support to the disabled, but most of the times they and their parents are always discriminated against in public spaces for having a disabled child at home: "Except that someone or the other reminded us every day that I was 'disabled.' That I had a major flaw in my existence. That I was the manifestation of an ancestral sin. As a rule, my disability was the only thing visible to many people in the village" (Sivasubbu 43). When Sundari entered home after school, relatives sometimes mocked at her unsteady steps:

"Somebody must have committed a grave crime in the past in the family. Hence, the girl was born this way..." (Sivasubbu, 47).

In rural India, the parent of a disabled child is always criticized for bringing up a disabled child in their house. Disabled people are always considered to be worthless, and whenever they are made to feel included in the familial space, it is considered as a futile action: "Why should the girl try to walk and fall like this unnecessarily? She knows that she can never walk. She should be put in a home for such children. Why spend for school? The government also gives schemes for such cripple children" (Sivasubbu 48).

In the chapter "The Alien that Wheeled on the Earth," about the life of the disabled in the urban and the mindset of urban people towards disability and the disabled, the title implies the mindset of urban people in assessing the disabled. They see the disabled as an object of wonder that will never exist in the universe. Little understanding of the disabled and disability is always a problem. One day, when Sundari was waiting for the lift, her junior asked her, "How do you bathe," she replied ironically that she had a cream imported from a laboratory aboard which kept her fragrant even after years of not bathing. During her tenth-grade examinations, the external invigilator commented to the other person, "she can understand what we speak and she answered every question very well (220)". When she was about to deliver a talk in an auditorium, one of the guests asked "are you feeling normal HERE?" she replied "you can find the answer for this after my speech" (222). She also states that urban people see her existence as a matter of wonder and make her feel awkward by continuously staring at her. People just wonder how the disabled exist and how they perform activities at par with able-bodied individuals. They feel as if the disabled are super beings on earth living with them and forget to make the world normal for them by removing the barriers. The difference in attitudes in urban and rural areas can be understood in Sundari's life narrative.

In *One Little Finger*, the difference in rural and urban attitudes towards the disabled is presented through the difference between the West and India. The greater understanding and accommodation of disability she experiences in London warm her heart, and she draws comparisons with the lack of infrastructure in India: "London was the place where I had blossomed, where I acquired stability with excellent management for the first time since my birth. I had learned to read, do well intellectually and began to walk. People here loved and accepted me for what I was" (Chib 15). When Malini moved back to India, she has to face difficulties in mobility, education, and medical facilities. This is the reason why she hated being in India. Every Indian cannot afford a life in London. She was so lucky to get access to such a society. For that reason, she hated the experience of being in India.

"The paramedical staff treated me as if I did not have ears or could not understand. To them, I was a non-thinking person who needed fixing and fitting into the mould of being normal. I hated the whole experience" (Chib 16).

Finding an inclusive school had become difficult for Malini in Bombay. She faced loneliness without school or friends of her age. Even her brother studied at an elite school, but she had no place to go: "Inclusive education was a concept which had not yet developed and my mother did not even consider asking this elite school to admit me (Chib 28)".

The following lines illustrate an instance of how Indian society reacts to the disabled person. This incident takes place in her college where the lift is inaccessible and she faces the attitude of people who just witness things rather than coming forward and helping her: "Oh no, why is this lift so damn small and why do these chauvinist bastards persist on staring rather than helping?' Elsa used swear words freely and I quite liked to hear them, as it would somehow release all the venom in me" (Chib 64).

Malini records her experience of holidays in Goa where the road was filled with potholes and people just stared at her wheelchair and friends in a swimsuit:

"In Goa we came across the potholes of Baga Beach and the stares of the locals. Either they were gaping at my wheelchair or Susan's body" (Chib 162).

The dominant view is that Western society is more disabled friendly and is inclusive. Certain experiences of Malini show that being independent is not allowed for the disabled by Western societies. They are always expected to have a caregiver, as being by themselves would suggest neglect. In the mind of every person with disability is the desire to do things independently, at least, in a known space. Malini faced discrimination when she was alone in public spaces of London as people would ask why she was left alone but no one thought of her as independent in her habituated space.

During her admission for masters in gender studies, the institute denied her hostel accommodation in the campus and asked her to look for care homes outside. She also comments that the West was more expensive for the disabled to meet their needs:

"You can't stay in the hall alone due to fire hazard and your disability', everywhere I went I suffered acute discrimination" (Chib 136).

"It upset me a great deal and immediately i went and told Gregg. This was the downside of how disabled people were treated here; everything had to be special and costly" (Malini 136). She often encountered unpleasant reactions to her being alone in a public space:

"Once as i entered the lift, i said 'six please'. Looking very alarmed, the lady quizzed, 'Are you alone? where's your helper?" (Chib 140).

"I am going to go call the management. I know what these people are like, they don't know their minds', she repeated. 'Someone must be with her. She can't be on her own. I have worked with these mental people. It can be very dangerous', the girl said as she got up. One of the UCL security guards with his radiophone came with the girl" (Chib 142).

When Malini narrates these events to her friend Gregg, he explains Western society thus: "Society here is so used to seeing disabled people being accompanied by their ty. Where a society thinks that you have to be with your helper around the clock on the other you who was unaccompanied and needed help' analyzed Gregg" (Chib 143).

So, the above extracts from the life of Malini show how the disabled can't be independent in the West. It reflects a conflict between the psyche of the self and the society where society thinks that disabled can't be alone and independent. On the other hand, the disabled thinks that he/she should carry out things like others independently. The implication is that the disabled are not nurtured to become independent in supporting spaces either.

Writing Self

Disabled people have to write their own stories to counteract the misinterpretations of the society. Mitchell and Synder in *The Body and Physical Difference* write that the autobiographical narrator provides the subjectivity that evolves out of experiencing disability as a physical, cognitive, and social phenomenon (9). As discussed earlier, it's only Sundari who can tell her experience of being affected by cerebral palsy in Indian rural and urban societies, and only Malini can share her experience of being born in India and brought up in London, where she distinguishes the West and East in terms of accommodation and acceptance. This is because its Sundari and Malini who have experienced the trauma, pain, and sufferings and made their way to success. Disabled life narratives are not fairy tales which can be enjoyed by the readers. Rather, they point out sociocultural flaws which keep an impaired as disabled in the society. Sundari's life in rural and urban is two extremes, as also is Malini's in India and London. Finally, both find their path to success, crossing hurdles that can be narrated only by them. Disabled life narratives present a more intimate and direct link to readers as first-person narratives and are more factual and less imaginative than third-person narratives.

The first-person narratives of Sundari Sivasubbu and Malini Chib are about the life of people living with cerebral palsy in India. Their stories are not just individual accounts and may be seen as the voices of people with cerebral palsy in India. Their lives show the realities of two different times. Malini is born in 1966 when there was little awareness in India about cerebral palsy. Sundari was born in a village where the medical facilities couldn't help in arresting the death of her brain cells due to lack of oxygen. These books also expose how economic power influences the life of the disabled as well. Malini's parents were rich enough to take her to London for a better life, but in Sundari's case, it took nine years for her parents to understand what she was undergoing. The exposure which they got in life was ultimately different in terms of education, medical treatment, and rehabilitation.

Disabled life narratives are not written by great people for fame. Common people face discrimination and stigmatization in the society due to their impairment but manage to rise facing all ordeals of life and tell their own life stories which serve as a guiding light to many disabled individuals. These life narratives don't glorify life, rather, they point out pitfalls of the society. Narratives of the blind, orthopaedic, or paraplegic are not the voices of individuals but the voice of a community. As Garland Thomson writes, "it is a story of despair, catastrophe loss, excess, suffering and relentless cure seeking" (Thomson 114). Only the impaired self can write about his/her pain, hopes of recovery, struggles of surviving, and quest for recovery. They self-project their own factual experiences which cannot be produced by fictional writers.

Conclusion

Third-person representations often look upon the disabled with pity or as super human beings and cannot address the real concerns of the disabled. The disabled therefore seek to claim their identity by telling their own stories—"to define ourselves, name ourselves, speak for ourselves, instead of being defined and spoken for by others" (Lorde 43).

Mitchell and Synder's *The Body and Physical Difference* points out that life narratives have given space for the disabled as individuals and disability as a social phenomenon (12). This paper examines the self-representation of the disabled which breaks the stereotypical notions of society about them. It also shows how urban and rural societies present different experiences for the disabled as also Western and Indian societies. Self-narratives thus are seen as more nuanced and much more important than other forms of literature in being closer to the reality of lived experience of disability. Disabled life narratives serve as a tool for the disabled to express their views. In being both factual and more intimate, they are more authentic and not just inspirational or sympathetic texts.

Bibliography

Beverley, J. (1992). The margin at the centre; On testimonia. In *De/colonizing the subject; The politics of gender in women autobiography* (pp. 91–114). University of Minnesota Press.
Chib, M. (2011). *One little finger*. Sage Publications.
Couser, T. (1997). *Recovering bodies; illness, disability and life writing*. University of Wisconsin Press.
Garland-Thomson, R. (2007). Shape structures story; fresh and feisty stories of disability. *Narrative, 15*(1), 113–123.
Lorde, A. (1980). *Cancer journals*. Aunt Lute Books.
Mitchell, D. T., & Snyder, S. L. (1997). Introduction—Disability studies and the double bind of representation. In *The body and physical difference* (pp. 1–31). University of Michigan Press.
Sherry, M. (2005). Reading me/ me reading disability. *Prose Studies, 27*(1 and 2), 163175.
Sivasubbu, S. (2019). *A Bumblebee's balcony celebrating life with cerebral palsy*. Notion Press.
Smith, S., & Watson, J. (2010). *Reading autobiography*. University of Minnesota Press.
Webb, R. C. (1994). *A journey into personhood*. University of Iowa Press.
Winslow, D. J. (1995). *Life writing*. University of Hawaii Press.

Chapter 21
Shaping the Disability Discourse: From Theoretical Groundwork to Lived Experiences

Amrita Sharma

Abstract 'Disability studies,' as an emerging field of discourse, has shaped itself as a discipline across the later decades of the twentieth century through a range of contributions by theorists, disability rights activists, and writers. The long-associated stigma with a 'disability' in any form is gradually gaining wider attention with a growing demand for equal rights for persons with disabilities in the society. This paper aims at analysing the literary factors that have and continue to play a crucial role in shaping this disability discourse. While a few theoretical concepts and studies remain foundational in laying the groundwork for future scholarship within the disability studies, a number of literary narratives emerging out of a direct lived experience of disability also remain significant. The paper thus attempts to highlight this theoretical groundwork and lived experience that play a role in shaping the disability discourse.

Keywords Disability · Lived experiences · Literary discourse · Narratives · Theory

As the reaction to prolonged marginalization and oppression has often led to the creation of a 'new' discourse that refutes the identity politics, 'disability' remains one of the crucial constructs that has emerged as a significant subject of study. With a long history of discrimination and oppression relating to persons with disabilities, an effort to deconstruct the disability stigma has led to the creation of anew discipline. Formally established by the Modern Language Association as a 'division of study' in 2005, 'disability studies' remains particularly sensitive to the concept of 'disability as a social construct' and its perception among the masses. Having evolved as a distinct discipline within the literary and academic circles, the subject remains a crucial combination of contributions made by both the persons with disabilities having a 'first-person experience' as well as theorists or writers presenting a 'third-person' account of it.

A. Sharma (✉)
Department of English, Sri Venkateswara College, University of Delhi, Delhi, India

R. Uniyal and F. Rizvi (eds.), *Understanding Disability*,
https://doi.org/10.1007/978-981-99-4925-0_21

While the discourse relating to the rights of persons with disabilities has recently emerged in the late twentieth century, it significantly draws upon the works of theorists like Erving Goffman and Michel Foucault as well as disability rights activists and their real-life encounters. The literary and cultural narratives emerging as a part of this discourse also remain a composite of the theoretical concepts as well as the activism surrounding social injustice. With persons with disabilities actively coming forth with narratives drawing upon their own personal experiences, an interrelated dynamics operates between the larger intellectual framework that included disability as a part of the overall social discourse and the lived experience narratives. The paper presents an analysis of a few key theoretical ideas that have emerged central to the discipline, followed by examples of select literary narratives that draw upon the first-hand experiences of the authors. Though distinct in their approach, both the former and the latter collectively contribute to the discipline.

Many sociological studies on the discrimination with people suffering any form of 'difference' from the mainstream also included an analysis of the condition of persons with disabilities. A key text in this regard remains the sociological treatise titled *Stigma: Notes on the Management of Spoiled Identity* written by Erving Goffman. Goffman, often regarded by many as the most influential sociologist of the twentieth century, remains one of the earliest social psychologists dealing with the condition of 'disability' as a 'stigma' whose works remain significantly influential for providing a theoretical framework. In *Stigma*, Goffman points:

> The stigmatized individual is asked to act so as to imply neither that his burden is heavy nor that bearing it has made him different from us; at the same time he must keep himself at that remove from us which assures our painlessly being able to confirm this belief about him. Put differently, he is advised to reciprocate naturally with an acceptance of himself and us, an acceptance of him that we have not quite extended to him in the first place. A PHANTOM ACCEPTANCE is thus allowed to provide the base for a PHANTOM NORMALCY. (Goffman)

While theorizing on 'stigma' as a larger concept, Goffman's work remains notable for articulating a clearly distant theoretical record of a sociological study that also finds relevance in understanding disability as a social stigma. As a disabled individual is often forced to associate with a community of other disabled persons, Goffman's theory helps in understanding the notion of ambivalence that a stigmatized individual may experience when going through such forced associations. The form and extent of disability and its interplay with everyday experiences of an individual thus become secondary to the psychological trauma experienced as a result of such social stigmatization.

Goffman also includes an example of a lived experience of disability in his text to highlight the "stigma" associated with it. He provides the example of a 'newly blind girl' who is taken to the Chicago Lighthouse as soon as she leaves the hospital. He describes her nauseating experience as she is suddenly exposed to a world of "destructive segregation" where only the blind people ate, met, sang, and worked together. As the social service agency takes pride in reassuring the girl of a safe world, Goffman explains the horrifying trauma experienced by the girl of being forced into a community of blind people. Thus, the lived experience of a 'stigma' exponentially grows with segregation and forced associations.

However, while Goffman used descriptions of lived experiences of disability to elaborate on the stigmatization and social devaluation of marginal identities, his work provided a larger intellectual groundwork that was not specifically devoted to the study of disability and its lived experience. Though still significant today within the disability discourse, Goffman's work also faced criticism by disability theorists in particular. Susan Wendell, herself having a lived experience of disability, remains a notable theorist on the subject, and her critique of Goffman found in her work titled *The Rejected Body* also brings forth a contrast between the first- and third-person perspectives on the subject:

> Goffman repeatedly fails to appreciate the possibility that having at least some disabilities may be, like membership in some other groups that are stigmatized, as good as or better than 'normality.' He discusses valuing one's difference only as a coping strategy of the stigmatized, without calling into question the objectivity or permanence of the values that regard them as less than 'normal.' On the contrary, he rates valuing one's difference and identifying closely with those who share it rather low, even as a coping strategy: The first set of sympathetic others is of course those who share his stigma. Knowing from their own experience what it is like to have this particular stigma, some of them can provide the individual with instruction in the tricks of the trade and with a circle of lament to which he can withdraw for moral support and for the comfort of feeling at home, at ease, accepted as a person who really is like any other normal person. (Wendell)

Thus, disability studies activists have gradually moved from a generalized marginal identity towards the study of a disability specific experience that takes into account the social and cultural parameters that emerge out of a disabled identity.

One of the key theoretical concepts that has provided a firm grounding to the perspectives about disability is the distinction between the medical and the social model of disability. While the former treated disability purely as a medical condition within an individual, the social model has radically challenged this former notion. The social model presents disability as an outcome of social factors rather than an individual's condition. Simi Linton, in her work titled *Claiming Disability*, emphasizes the need for "refusing the medicalization of disability" (2) and providing a composite identity to all people having varied lived experiences of disability and the "social and political circumstances that have forged us as a group" (Linton 4).

As the social model provides a starting point for advocating a change in the social and cultural factors, the intellectual framework surrounding disability has further been enriched by scholars who have attempted to deconstruct the disability stigma through diverse approaches. Lennard J. Davis, one of the leading theorists in this field, in his article "Constructing Normalcy: The Bell Curve, the Novel, and the Invention of the Disabled Body in the Nineteenth Century" provides a ground for exploring the idea of the 'normal' in the society and its relating impact on the perception of 'disability' at large. He presents a clear idea of the prevalence of this state of 'normalcy' in the opening lines as he writes:

> We live in a world of norms. Each of us endeavors to be normal or else deliberately tries to avoid that state. We consider what the average person does, thinks, earns, or consumes. We

> rank our intelligence, our cholesterol level, our weight, height, sex drive, bodily dimensions along some conceptual line from subnormal to above-average. We consume a minimum daily balance of vitamins and nutrients based on what an average human should consume. Our children are ranked in school and tested to determine where they fi t into a normal curve of learning, of intelligence. Doctors measure and weigh them to see if they are above or below average on the height and weight curves. There is probably no area of contemporary life in which some idea of a norm, mean, or average has not been calculated. (1)

This idea, Davis states, remains crucial to the understanding of the idea of 'disability' in order to scrutinize the problem at its root. The argument remains significant and provides a wide ground for reflection. It is important to read Davis's work and his arguments on the idea of disability being inherently related to the idea of a 'norm' or a standard that is regarded as normal by the society. Also, pointing to the introduction of a wide range of lexicon relating to this at varying points of history, Davis makes it evident as to how the society has been moulded by a tendency to compare everything to a standard value.

Similarly, Tom Shakespeare in his work "The Social Model of Disability" also does not restrict his analysis to just the "social" approach but rather advocates for an understanding of disability as one that needs varying levels of study "ranging from the medical to the socio-political" (Shakespeare 204). Extending upon the idea of the interaction of a disabled body with the cultural factors, David Mitchell and Sharon Snyder, in their work *Cultural Locations of Disability*, proposed a "cultural model" to understand disability. On the other hand, Tobin Siebers, in his 2008 book titled Disability Theory, presents the idea of "complex embodiment" that defines disability in relation to both the body and the environment and looks at disability as an epistemology that does not attempt to conform to any other law except that body needs to be valued as what it was and willingly accepts any form that it takes or becomes. According to Siebers, disability discourse must provide a ground that brings up both the negative and positive aspects of disability and work as a medium that speaks for and about persons with disabilities.

While a range of scholarship regarding the Disability Theory has emerged within and outside academia, disability activism has also contributed significantly in this regard. A notable example of the latter may be found in a human services-based approach called the Social Role Valorization Theory or often noted as the SRV theory. The theory relates to a "dynamic set of ideas" that have laid the foundation of the Keystone Human Services that primarily work in the area of disability. Operating on an intellectual framework of "valued social roles" in the society, the theory remains a significant example from contemporary disability activism. Explaining SRV, Joe Osburn, in "An Overview of Social Role Valorization Theory" writes:

> Social Role Valorization (SRV) is the name given to a concept for transacting human relationships and human service, formulated in 1983 by Wolf Wolfensberger, PhD, as the successor to his earlier formulation of the principle of normalization (Lemay, 1995; Wolfensberger, 1972). His most recent (1995) definition of SRV is: "The application of what science can tell us about the enablement, establishment, enhancement, maintenance, and/or defense of valued social roles for people". (Wolfensberger, 1995a) (7)

Though moving from a broader to a specifically disability-oriented approach in its initial years, the disability studies in the contemporary times again continues to draw in from larger social theories like SRV that include disability as one of their key elements.

While the research on the theoretical groundwork analyses the social dynamics that lead to the marginalization of the disabled community, a range of narratives of lived experiences of disability also contribute to the disability discourse at large. A significant number of authors having a first-hand experience of disability have contributed through various non-fictional and literary narratives and diverse cultural platforms like digital media and life blogs. The following section highlights a few of such narratives and their significance.

A key example of a contemporary expression of lived experiences of disability is the collection titled *Disability Visibility: First-Person Stories from the 21st Century*, edited by Alice Wong published recently in 2020. Appearing amidst the COVID pandemic crisis, the work contains thirty-seven essays by authors having a lived experience of disability, compiled by another disabled writer and activist. With a powerful dedication that calls out to all persons with disabilities, Wong's collection remains notable on many grounds. Brenna Swift, in the review of this collection, notes:

> Wong's highly anticipated collection celebrates the lives of disabled people while making a powerful political statement about the need for disability justice, representation, and an end to violence in all forms. By foregrounding the stories of disabled people of color, it rejects the whiteness of rights-based disability discourses and builds the intersectional strength of the disability justice movement. In the book's introduction, Wong shares that her goal in making disability visible is not to inspire those without disabilities or offer up the lives of multiple marginalized disabled writers for analysis. Rather, the collection is a statement of community, love, and solidarity for disabled people. (2)

With contributions by diverse authors with a wide range of physical and mental disabilities, this contemporary collection of lived experiences significantly contributes towards the strengthening of a disability discourse that continues to thrive against a lack of greater recognition and acceptance.

A dynamic collection of narratives relating to disability and healthcare systems also find expression in the three editions of *The Social Medicine Reader*. With contributions from lived experiences that survey the socio-medical challenges, the compilation contains essays providing insights into the real-life conditions and the human psyche. "On Being a Cripple" by Nancy Mairs, also appearing as a part of the third edition of this collection, presents a moving and powerful example of a lived experience of disability. Mairs, suffering from multiple sclerosis, writes of her own perception of a disabled identity. Her introductory paragraph distinctly encapsulates the potency of a personal narrative:

> The other day I was thinking of writing an essay on being a cripple. I was thinking hard in one of the stalls of the women's room in my office building, as I was shoving my shirt into my jeans and tugging up my zipper. Preoccupied, I flushed, picked up my book bag, took my cane down from the hook, and unlatched the door. So many movements unbalanced me, and as I pulled the door open I fell over backward, landing fully clothed on the toilet seat with

> my legs splayed in front of me: the old beetle-on-its-back routine. Saturday afternoon, the building deserted, I was free to laugh aloud as I wriggled back to my feet, my voice bouncing off the yellowish tiles from all directions. Had anyone been there with me, I'd have been still and faint and hot with chagrin. I decided that it was high time to write the essay. (1)

The acceptance of a disabled identity and its challenges by such lived experience narratives serves to empower the notion of a so-called normal existence and attempts to positively shape the disability discourse. A similarly powerful example of a lived experience narrative of autism may be found in Temple Grandin's *Thinking in Pictures* where she humorously points:

> In an ideal world the scientist should find a method to prevent the most severe forms of autism but allow the milder forms to survive. After all, the really social people did not invent the first stone spear. It was probably invented by an Aspie who chipped away at rocks while the other people socialized around the campfire. Without autism traits we might still be living in caves. (7)

Thus, presenting a positively driven account of coping with severe medical impairments, many examples of personal accounts of living with disabilities have provided dynamic perspectives to the disability discourse. Attempting to deconstruct the stigma associated with disability through their own real-life examples, such narratives make significant contributions to the discipline of disability studies.

Many examples of disability narratives also find expression across varying genres of literature. While characters with various forms of disabilities have been a part of literary narratives since the classical ages, giving a central place to characters with disabilities and bringing forth the fictionalized first-person narratives of lived experiences of disability remains a rather recent phenomenon. Some of the examples that stand out for their unique treatment of disability as their central context have gained widespread recognition. The 2003 novel titled *The Curious Incident of the Dog in the Night-time* by Mark Haddon won the Whitbread Prize and the Commonwealth Writer's Prize and remains one such text that includes a first-person narrative of a 15-year--old boy with behavioural difficulties. Presenting a narrative that perceives the world in a different way, the novel's treatment of disability remains exemplary for its emphasis on a unique lived experience.

Apart from non-fictional and fictional narratives, a few other examples of literary texts that portray the lived experiences of disability may also be found in theatre and poetry. An important example from the former is the collection titled *Beyond Victims and Villains: Contemporary Plays by Disabled Playwrights* edited by Victoria Ann Lewis. Lewis, who is the founding figure behind the Mark Taper Forum's Other Voices Project, has been actively involved in disability rights activism and founded the "Other Voices Project" to create a professional space for playwrights with disabilities. Also, poetic works like Ginsberg's "Kaddish" and Gwendolyn Brooks' "sick man looks at flowers" also delve upon the subject of disability in different forms.

As the interrelations between disability and its social understanding by both the ablest and the disabled community remain complex and unclear at times, theorizing disability in its complete manifestation remains difficult. While even within the disabled community, persons with varied disabilities may experience significantly different challenges, and the theoretical framework may at times appear less flexible in adapting to individualistic concerns. However, at the same time, the diversity of the lived experiences of disability both contributes to its practical understanding as well as problematizes a completely uniform definition.

Thus, as 'disability' remains a human phenomenon that pervades across all cultures and creeds, it remains significant to shape a discourse that gives a voice and space to persons with all forms of disabilities. While the theoretical groundwork to disability studies may have contributions by diverse scholars, an integration of the lived experiences to the intellectual models and literary narratives holds potential for a greater outreach. While no marginal discourse can truly serve the purpose of empowering the disempowered without a constant strife towards the mainstreaming of the subject, disability studies, with contributions from both within and outside disabled community, have witnessed a substantial growth in its scholarship in the past few decades. With a socially rooted theoretical groundwork and culturally interwoven lived experiences, the literary discourse surrounding disability thus continues to evolve. While opening new perspectives and possibilities within literary scholarship and creating awareness of basic human rights, the disability discourse holds tremendous potential for future research and advancement.

Bibliography

Albrecht, G. L. (Ed.). (2005). *Encyclopedia of disability* (Vol. 5). Sage.

Barnes, C., & Mercer, G. (2010). *Exploring disability.* Polity Press.

Burch, S., & Longmore, P. K. (Eds.). (2009). *Encyclopedia of American disability history* (Vol. 3).

Burch, S., & Rembis, M. (2014). *Disability histories.* University of Illinois Press.

Campbell, F. K. (2009). *Contours of ableism: The production of disability and abledness.* Palgrave Macmillan.

Davis, L. J. (Ed.). (1997). *The disability studies reader.* Routledge.

Goffman, E. (1986). *Stigma: Notes on the management of spoiled identity.* Simon & Schuster Inc.

Grandin, T. (2009). *Thinking in pictures.* Bloomsbury Publishing.

Johnstone, D. (2001). *An introduction to disability studies.* David Fulton Publishers.

Linton, S. (1998). *Claiming disability: Knowledge and identity.* New York University Press.

Mairs, N. (2019). On being a cripple. In *The social medicine reader* (Vol. II, 3rd ed.). Duke University Press.

Mitchell, D., & Snyder, S. (2006). *Cultural locations of disability.* University of Chicago Press.

Osburn, J. (1998). An overview of social role valorization theory. *The International Social Role Valorization Journal/La revue internationale de la Valorisation des roles, sociaux, 3*(1), 7–12.

Shakespeare, T. (2006). The social model of disability. In L. J. Davis (Ed.), *The disability studies reader* (pp. 197–204). Routledge.

Siebers, T. (2008). *Disability theory.* The University of Michigan Press.

Wendell, S. (1996). Disability as difference. In *The rejected body.* Routledge.

Wong, A. (Ed.). (2020). *Disability visibility: First-person stories from the 21st century.* E-book, Vintage Books.

The manufacturer's authorised representative in the EU is Springer Nature Customer Service Centre GmbH, Europaplatz 3, 69115 Heidelberg, Germany. If you have any concerns regarding our products, please contact ProductSafety@springernature.com

Printed and bound by CPI Group (UK) Ltd, Croydon, CR0 4YY
30/09/2026
02225319-0006